Reform as Process

Reform as Process

Implementing Change in Public Bureaucracies

Martin J. Williams

Columbia University Press

New York

Columbia University Press
Publishers Since 1893
New York   Chichester, West Sussex
cup.columbia.edu

Library of Congress Cataloging-in-Publication Data
Names: Williams, Martin J. author
Title: Reform as process : implementing change in public bureaucracies /
Martin J. Williams.
Description: New York : Columbia University Press, 2025. |
Includes bibliographical references and index.
Identifiers: LCCN 2025025843 | ISBN 9780231215763 hardback |
ISBN 9780231215770 trade paperback | ISBN 9780231560962 epub |
ISBN 9780231565028 PDF
Subjects: LCSH: Civil service reform—Africa, Sub-Saharan |
Civil service reform—Africa, Sub-Saharan—Case studies
Classification: LCC JQ1876.Z1 W55 2025
LC record available at https://lccn.loc.gov/2025025843

Cover design: Kuukuwa Manful

GPSR Authorized Representative: Easy Access System Europe,
Mustamäe tee 50, 10621 Tallinn, Estonia, gpsr.requests@easproject.com

THIS BOOK *is dedicated to public servants around the world who go to work every day and try to make their institutions serve the public a little bit better, not because they expect recognition or reward but because it's the right thing to do. And because it matters.*

And to my mum, who taught me to be curious and to ask hard questions.

Contents

Acknowledgments

This book has been over a decade in the making, and I owe thanks to so many people that writing this section feels like an almost impossible task. I have done my best, but to anyone I've missed, please forgive me and know that I am grateful.

I am thankful for the scores of individuals who gave their time to be interviewed. Some had known me for years, and others had never met me before, yet all generously shared their experiences, insights, and questions in the hope that others could benefit from it. Some are named in the pages that follow, while many others were interviewed anonymously. Though interviewees naturally had different perspectives and opinions—many times, even of the same event—I hope that each sees something of their experience reflected in this book, as well as my deep respect for them and their work.

I am also grateful to the authors of the hundreds of government and NGO reports, academic books and articles, student theses and dissertations, and media stories on which this book has also relied. In discussing this book project with people around the world, I often heard some version of the sentiment, "There is so little written about civil service reform." While I agree that it hasn't been studied enough, given its importance, it isn't true that little has been written about it. Rather, it's that many people do not pay attention to what already exists, bother to look for it, or give it the credit and analytical attention it deserves. This occurs in the context of huge global inequalities in access to resources and conversations among researchers and of the frequent discounting of practitioners' knowledge and insights by scholars. In this book, I have sought to highlight and build upon the incredible work already done by these writers, particularly those who are from and/or working in the countries and governments that they write about.

In addition to those that are referenced in the main text and appendix, I have also created an online-only supplementary appendix that lists additional sources that I consulted but did not specifically reference to give them due recognition and so other researchers can find and consult them. I hope this book makes clear the ways it exists not in isolation but in relation to existing conversations, that it makes at least a small contribution to connecting and advancing conversations, and that future writers will also be able to build upon it.

I am also thankful to many, many people for helpful conversations and feedback on the content and writing of this book. First and foremost among these are my writing support group buddies, Nana Akua Anyidoho and Peace Medie, and Angie Bautista-Chavez. Thank you for sharing the suffering! A very partial list of people who read drafts, had helpful discussions with me, or gave other inputs includes Joe Abah, Tina Akonnor, Yuen Yuen Ang, Leonardo Arriola, Joseph Ayee, Tony Bertelli, Jurgen Blum, Christian Breunig, Simukai Chigudu, Ranil Dissanayake, Patrick Dunleavy, James Dzansi, Javier Fuenzalida, Bob Gibbons, Matthew Grimes, Zahid Hasnain, Aung Hein, Alisha Holland, Dan Honig, Emily Jones, Allan Kasapa, Bob Keohane, Igor Kolesnikov, Clare Leaver, David Lewis, Akshay Mangla, Aaron Maniam, Erin McDonnell, Calum Miller, Sylvester Obong'o, Frank Ohemeng, Tunji Olaopa, George Owusu, Andrew Pettigrew, Alison Post, Woody Powell, Karthik Ramanna, Imran Rasul, Dan Rogger, Stuart Russell, Folashadé Soulé-Kohndou, Chris Stone, Henry Telli, Guillermo Toral, Lars Tummers, Jamie Walsh, Joachim Wehner, Jennifer Widner, and Ngaire Woods, as well as participants in workshops or seminars at Oxford, Stanford-CASBS, Bergen, the LSE, UC Berkeley, IPEA, FGV, Cambridge, EUI, UT-Austin, the World Bank, IGC, MPSA, APSA, and the University of Michigan. I know there are many others I've missed on this list, and to them, I ask forgiveness and express my gratitude.

Thank you to the many colleagues, too numerous to name, with whom I've had the honor of working over the years in Ghana's Ministry of Trade and Industry, National Development Planning Commission, Office of the Head of Local Government Service, Ministry of Finance and Economic Planning, Management Services Department, Civil Service Training Centre, Ghana Health Service, Public Services Commission, Office of the Head of Civil Service, and other MDAs. You've been immense sources of inspiration, learning, and laughter. I am grateful to three successive Heads of Civil Service—Woeli Kemevor, Nana Agyekum-Dwamena, and Evans Aggrey-Darko—who have not only supported research but also strived to put the creation and use of evidence at the heart of how the Civil Service operates. I am especially thankful to Nana Agyekum-Dwamena for asking the question that launched this book and trusting me to learn something useful to share.

This book's research was facilitated by a number of institutions and individuals. These include Ghana's Office of the Head of Civil Service, Ghana's Public Records and Archives Administration Department, Zambia's Ministry of National Development Planning, the International Growth Centre Ghana and Zambia country offices, as well as Tayo Aduloju, Ofovwe Aig-Imoukhuede, Alpha Ousmane Aw, Tonye Cole, Binta Zahra Diop, Baye Elimane Gueye, Tom Hart, Marja Hinfelaar, Mark Miller, Abraham Rugo Muriu, Aïda Ndiaye, Chioma Njoku, Kachi Nwachukwu, Anand Rajaram, Oulimata Sarr, and Twivwe Siwale, and many others (including some I have already thanked above) who helped make connections or supported in other ways.

This book would not have been possible without exceptional research assistance from Liah Yecalo-Tecle, Allan Kasapa, Bashar Hobbi, Oshmita Ray, Aisha Jore Ali, and Morgan Dacosta. It was a joy working with each of you, and I can't thank you enough for your dedication, patience, and excellent work. Thank you also to the brilliant Sarah McAra, who coauthored the teaching case on which chapter 8 is partly based (and which is available free online for educators and practitioners—see chapter 8 for details), and to Kim Fuggle, Armando Zozaya, Ingrid Locatelli, Miriam Mendes, and the rest of the Blavatnik School research, finance, and human resources teams.

Funding for this research came from the University of Oxford, People in Government Lab (which was funded, in turn, by the BRAVA Foundation, Lemann Foundation, República.org, and the Humanize Institute), UKRI Global Challenges Research Fund, International Growth Centre, Stanford-CASBS, and University of Michigan.

At Columbia University Press, I am fortunate to have been able to work with two excellent editors, Eric Schwartz and Alyssa Napier. Thank you for your time, guidance, and feedback throughout this process.

This book was deeply shaped by the two institutions at which I did the vast majority of this work. The first is the Blavatnik School of Government at the University of Oxford, where I was an associate professor in public management from 2016 to 2024 and remain associate faculty. At the Blavatnik School, I was fortunate to be immersed in a unique academic environment where the quality of research is defined primarily not by the prestige of the journal in which it was published but also by its usefulness to people working in government and its positive impact on the world. Without this intellectual community, I doubt I would have had the courage to take on such an ambitious and almost impossibly difficult project. Just like in government, building and maintaining this culture is an ongoing process that depends on the small moments and decisions that people make every day, from the bottom of the organization to the top. I am grateful to everyone at the school who has contributed to this culture and who supported and encouraged me with this project.

The second institution is the Center for Advanced Study in the Behavioral Sciences (CASBS) at Stanford University, where I was a Fellow from 2022 to 2023 and have participated in the Summer Institute on Organizations and their Effectiveness community since 2019. CASBS provided the perfect physical, intellectual, and social environment for writing the bulk of this book, and it encouraged and sharpened my interdisciplinary instincts in a way that nowhere else could. Thank you to the entire CASBS team and, particularly, to Woody Powell and Bob Gibbons for their support and guidance. Finally, thank you to the wonderful members of the 2022–2023 Fellows cohort for all the dish walks, lunchtime discussions, and camaraderie.

I am also grateful to the many people who have welcomed me in my new institutional home, the University of Michigan—a model of excellence in service of the public.

Thank you to all the friends around the world who have kept me sane and smiling. You know who you are.

And to Kuukuwa, for her love, patience, and laughter through it all, and for always reminding me why it matters.

Reform as Process

PART I

Setting the Scene

I

The Puzzle of Reform

Congratulations! You've just been appointed an advisor to the head of the civil service. Your job is to recommend how to improve the effectiveness of dozens of government ministries and departments. These organizations, in turn, are responsible for delivering public services, developing policies, building infrastructure, implementing regulations, and nearly everything else the economy and society depend on. But your civil service is widely perceived—by civil servants, politicians, and ordinary people alike—as ineffective, even dysfunctional. Budgets are tight, and there are major political and legal constraints on your ability to hire or fire personnel. How would you advise the head of civil service to go about designing and implementing reforms to improve the performance of the civil service?

This question represents one of the most pressing practical problems facing governments around the world. It also poses an intellectual challenge of the first order. Ultimately, civil service reforms aim to change the day-to-day behavior and routines of the huge number of people who collectively make its decisions, enforce its rules, and deliver its services. But government is not a machine with simple levers that produce predictable responses when pulled. It is a complex system of interdependent organizations and teams inhabited by a diverse range of people, each with their own interests, preferences, experiences, and biases. The wrecks of failed reforms that litter the junkyard of public administration history can testify to the difficulty of transforming bureaucracies. What can this history of reform efforts teach us about the prospects for systemic reform to improve the inner workings of government?

This book aims to answer these questions by documenting and analyzing how six countries in Africa have repeatedly sought to reform their civil services over the past three decades. These countries have been global hotbeds of experimentation in public administration reform, collectively undertaking over one hundred performance-oriented reforms during this period. The types of problems they have sought to solve and the solutions they've attempted to adopt and implement will be familiar to reformers around the world. Sometimes these reforms have been driven by public servants, and at other times they've been driven by donors or politicians—or often combinations of two or three of these. They have been influenced by global trends as well as homegrown ideas. So public managers and researchers from around the world have much to learn from the history and patterns of reform in these six countries.

I use a rich range of primary data and secondary literature to document and analyze the content, process, implementation, outcomes, and politics of each of these reform efforts. I then use this comprehensive portrait of reform efforts to identify repeated patterns in design, implementation, and outcomes that recur across many reforms, across all six countries, and across time. Of course, every reform effort and context is unique to some extent, and when we look at each reform in isolation, there are many potential explanations for why events unfolded as they did. But if we don't look historically and comparatively across efforts and across contexts, we risk missing the forest for the trees. Beyond these particularities and idiosyncrasies, are there repeated patterns we can identify and learn from?

I argue that there are two features that characterize the vast majority of large-scale reform efforts and that help to explain the persistently disappointing results of these reforms. First, most reforms focused mainly on changing formal structures, rules, and processes. This took different shapes across different reforms, but the common thread is an emphasis on creating formal processes that would compel or incentivize bureaucrats to behave differently. Second, reforms were typically conceived of and executed as discrete, one-off, often time-bound interventions. This means that reforms often ended up as projects with their own predefined work plans, acronyms, timetables, budget lines, and implementation teams. In other cases, they took the shape of new laws or structures on paper that, in practice, were implemented halfheartedly (if at all) or had purchase for a year or two before fading away. Together, these constitute reforms' two main *mechanisms of failure*. I demonstrate how and why this approach was largely ineffective at changing the complex system of organizations, rules, and perceptions that constitute government bureaucracy, and how and why it undermined reforms' potential to change the way that bureaucrats think about and carry out their everyday work.

At the same time, the history of reforms is much more than a story of failure—most reforms did achieve something, even if they fell short of their lofty goals. While reforms tended to make more changes on paper than in practice, some reforms did have positive and meaningful impacts on the actual day-to-day work practices of civil servants. When they did so, it was usually through two linked *mechanisms of success*: creating opportunities for civil servants to discuss performance and how to improve it, and building energy and momentum to do so. These mechanisms of success worked not because they forced unwilling bureaucrats to improve their performance, but rather because they helped create an environment where bureaucrats who wanted their teams and organizations to work better were able to find ways to make this happen. Though these mechanisms of success often coexisted with mechanisms of failure within the same reform effort, they usually took a backseat role in the dominant reform approach.

If this is the diagnosis that explains the track record of past reform efforts, what is the prescription for how future reformers should approach their work differently? What can we learn from this history to help us better advise a head of civil service or other prospective reform leader on how they should go about improving performance across a whole bureaucratic system?

I argue that, instead of treating reform as a one-off change to formal processes, reformers should approach it as *catalyzing an ongoing process of continuous improvement in actual practices*. This alternative approach reframes the goal of reform as the improvement of day-to-day bureaucratic behaviors, both in terms of adherence to formal processes as well as the undertaking of the many tasks that are important for performance but can't be fully codified on paper. It reconceptualizes how to implement reform as a process of collective learning-by-doing that must be open-ended in order to get people to make these behavior changes. And it casts the task of reform leadership in a different light as a matter of enabling and supporting decentralized change at numerous points throughout the bureaucratic system rather than trying to legislate it or force it from above. This approach of *reform as process* aims to minimize the mechanisms of failure and maximize the mechanisms of success that have characterized past reform efforts, and to serve as a viable alternative for the many reformers and researchers who are seeking a different—and hopefully better—way to make changes in public bureaucracies.

Of course, there are many practical and political challenges to approaching reform as a process. The book discusses these obstacles and how to navigate them, based in large part on evidence from reform leaders who have experimented with these ideas and whose thoughts and efforts have helped inspire this book. Even so, it is definitely not easy, perhaps not even always achievable. But in most cases it represents a more promising approach—grounded in evidence, theory, and illustrative examples—to a challenge that has confounded generations of reformers and researchers alike and that represents one of the main barriers to improving performance in government organizations around Africa and worldwide.

The question I posed earlier—how you should advise a senior leader to go about designing and implementing reforms—isn't just a hypothetical scenario. In 2014, I sat in the office of Ghana's newly appointed Head of Civil Service, Nana Agyekum-Dwamena, who said: "I've got five years, and I want to change the way this place works. But I want to do it in an evidence-based way." What, he asked, did academics have to say about how to approach this? Agyekum-Dwamena brought nearly thirty years of experience in Ghana's Civil Service to tackling this challenge, but as a scholar, I felt uncomfortably limited in my ability to con-tribute either a broad and rigorous view of the evidence or a straightforward set of theoretical insights on designing and implementing system-level bureaucratic reforms. Given the complexity and context-dependence of such reforms, I wasn't even sure what an answer to this question would look like.

This book represents my effort to grapple with this challenge—to be able to offer stronger evidence and more useful conceptual frameworks to the numer-ous smart, dedicated, and experienced civil servants searching for insight to help them improve the effectiveness of their institutions. Doing so throws up an inter-esting set of puzzles and opportunities for researchers. This process has involved collecting and analyzing a great deal of new data, as well as learning from and synthesizing the immense amount of research already conducted on these issues by academics and practitioners from Africa and around the world.[1] I have tried to do this in a way that amplifies and complements this existing work on reform design and implementation and connects it to the rapidly growing adjacent liter-atures on bureaucratic performance, state capacity, organizational change, long-term development, and complex systems. While I think the book makes some novel theoretical and empirical contributions, it also reports on and builds on a great deal of insight from other researchers, and I have done my best to highlight these intellectual lineages and debts throughout the book.

I have also sought to draw as much as possible on the experience of practi-tioners themselves, not just as data points but also as deep theoretical insights. To the extent this book succeeds at its goals, it is largely because the generosity of numerous civil servants has enabled me to benefit from their ideas and bring their experiences into conversation with one another across countries and across time. Many of them are also frustrated with the shortcomings of past reform efforts and have long been actively thinking about and experimenting with alternatives. Their perspectives on these issues are naturally diverse and often contradict one another, and of course, the responsibility for the book's analysis and synthe-sis of this vast range of ideas and evidence rests with me. Nevertheless, I hope that they—and other readers who have tried to make change in government bureaucracies or large organizations anywhere—see some of their experiences reflected in what I have written, together with a deep respect for their work.

Most of all, I hope that this book can help revitalize and recenter the study of large-scale bureaucratic reforms in social science research and policy thinking. Recent years have seen a general shift away from asking "big questions" toward focusing on more narrowly formulated research questions and interventions that are easier to implement and evaluate. But academics and practitioners alike need ways to bring evidence and theory to bear on complex challenges and questions that require systemic reforms, even if these are rarely amenable to clean, closed-ended, provably correct solutions. To paraphrase the political scientist Henry Farrell, studies of such questions are impossibly big and likely to be wrong (or, at least, not fully right) but nonetheless help us understand something important a little bit better.[2]

This book is written in that spirit. It asks a question of first-order importance for both research and practice: How should bureaucratic leaders design and implement systemic reforms? It attempts to answer this question by grounding itself in solid conceptual foundations, systematically collecting a vast amount of data, analyzing it carefully, and using these empirical findings to build a better understanding of why systemic reforms often fail and how they might be approached more successfully. But the answers it generates are not simple, closed-ended, provably correct solutions because that is not the nature of the research question—or of the task facing reformers. So this book is not intended to be the final word on studying and implementing bureaucratic reforms. Rather, its more modest goals are to help advance the state of empirical evidence and substantive insight on civil service reforms, to contribute some new theoretical ideas and methodological tools, and to encourage more researchers and reformers to grapple with the big, systemic challenges—and opportunities—facing government bureaucracies around the world.

THE CHALLENGES OF RESEARCHING SYSTEMIC REFORMS

That effective government bureaucracies are essential to prosperous economies, fair and open politics, and healthy societies is one of the few issues on which there is near-unanimity among academics and practitioners from across the ideological spectrum. This point has been demonstrated by hundreds if not thousands of academic studies—not to mention the lived experience of anyone who's ever worked in or depended on a government bureaucracy. If you've picked up this book and made it this far, I take it that you don't need to be convinced that effective bureaucracies that implement policies well and deliver services efficiently are generally a good thing and that taking steps to improve their performance is important.

When we think about the kind of evidence we'd want to help us do this, both academics and practitioners tend to ask questions like, "What is the effect of this intervention or reform on performance?" or, "What interventions or reforms should I adopt to improve performance?" There are many versions of this question, but they are all variations on the same underlying question of what lever needs to be pulled to improve performance. For example, reformers or researchers might investigate the effects of adopting a new performance management policy that aims to link measured performance to some type of rewards or sanctions. (Indeed, this book will show that such policies are among the most common reforms governments adopt to try to improve performance.) Or they might seek to understand whether certain structural variables outside the immediate control of the country's civil service—income levels, colonial or administrative legacies, political competition, and so on—help determine the effectiveness of the civil service.

These are questions of causal inference, and modern social science is increasingly dominated by methods that try to answer them in precise and rigorous ways, from quantitative randomized control trials or natural experiments to qualitative process tracing. There's a great deal of excellent research on bureaucracies and service delivery in this vein, and it has helped shed more light not just on the effects of incentive schemes on various dimensions of bureaucratic performance but also on selection, monitoring, motivation, funding, management, and politics.[3] I've also contributed to some of this research alongside various coauthors, including through a long-term collaboration with Ghana's Civil Service that has included surveys, qualitative studies, and a randomized control trial—all of which also stemmed from the 2014 conversation with Agyekum-Dwamena that I referred to above.[4]

Despite the importance of these approaches, I want to argue that if we want to adopt an evidence-based approach to learning about reforming civil services at the *system* level, we need to be able to temporarily set aside our causal inference mindsets—or at least augment them with other forms of evidence and insight. There are two main reasons for this.

First, the systemic, multifaceted nature of large-scale reforms and bureaucratic performance makes it incredibly difficult to apply causal inference methods at the level of rigor that researchers and evaluators have come to expect. While causal inference approaches vary greatly in their methods, they share a set of minimum requirements: interventions or policies that are narrow and precisely specified enough to be coded as binary or categorical treatment variable(s); exogenous variation in the application of the reform across units of analysis in a way that creates a clean counterfactual or "control" group; and good measures of bureaucratic performance across all (or at least most) dimensions that might be affected by this policy. But system-level civil service reforms nearly always bundle together numerous policies and processes that include both "hard" and "soft" elements and apply them to the whole of the system (i.e., to all units of analysis) simultaneously. Additionally, bureaucratic performance is notoriously difficult to measure in a consistent and comprehensive way, especially across ministries and agencies with very different functions and with multiple competing goals and tasks that have different levels of measurability and often require collaboration across various teams and stakeholders.[5] And that's without going into questions of whether the reform cases being studied are representative of the contexts to which we want to apply the evidence. It's not impossible to meet these requirements for applying causal inference methods to large-scale reforms—and researchers should try to do so where possible—but it's definitely easier to do so for microlevel interventions, small-scale pilots, and isolated behavioral nudges. Thus, the emphasis on obtaining causally identified answers to narrow, closed-ended questions has come to dominate research on changing bureaucracies.

Second, when we ask how to make bureaucracies more effective, every interesting answer is endogenous to the system we are trying to study. To be more precise, the prevailing emphasis on identifying exogenous variation in the explanatory variable of interest pushes researchers to only study variables over which current policymakers have no control—this is the definition of exogenous—and thus inadvertently avoid studying the very processes and situations that reformers might actually be able to change. An extreme example of this is studies that examine how macrohistorical or geographic factors have influenced present-day governance quality.[6] It might be true that these deep and unchangeable variables explain much of the cross-country variation in various measures of government performance. But it's often not a very useful insight for a present-day head of civil service, except, perhaps, in a very abstract sense. Even studies in which researchers collaborate with governments to run field experiments that test a specific policy in a real-world setting are not immune from distortion. While such trials or pilots can generate evidence that is valid and useful in that context, the same features of the setting that often make a rigorous field experiment possible—leaders' interest in generating and using evidence, involvement of a skilled researcher, performance data availability, careful experimental control, an intervention that is self-contained enough to be delivered to some units but not others—also mark out most such settings as atypical of bureaucratic contexts more widely. Of course, both macrohistorical research and randomized control trials (and many causal inference questions and methods in between) can provide important pieces of the puzzle of understanding bureaucratic performance and improvement. My point is not that we should do fewer of them but rather that limiting our research to factors or reforms for which we can obtain exogenous variation risks also limiting the types of reforms we study and the contexts in which we study them. If we want to generate empirical evidence and theoretical insight on complex, systemic bureaucratic reforms, we need to be able to ask and answer research questions about reforms that have been endogenously adopted and driven.

THIS BOOK'S APPROACH

Everything about this book has been profoundly shaped by these intellectual challenges. How can research on systemic reforms be as empirically grounded and as systematic as possible once we let go of the prescriptive strictures of causal inference—especially when the focus of our investigations is on these inherently endogenous reforms? What does generalizable knowledge look like when the adoption, implementation, and effects of reforms are subject to high-dimensional complementarities and contextual contingencies? How can we avoid the trap of throwing our hands up in the air and saying that it's all very complex, it all depends, and that no, we couldn't possibly use simple, straightforward language to offer a few actionable insights? And what would it look like to build a theory on implementing systemic reforms that is parsimonious but not oversimplified, profound but still actionable?

First, the guiding *question* of this book—How should bureaucratic leaders approach the task of systemic reform?—is a deliberately unusual one for an academic manuscript. A more orthodox approach would be to formulate a closed-ended research question ("Does X cause Y?") that can be answered by deductive testing of a theory-driven, falsifiable hypothesis about the impact of one (exogenous) variable on another variable. Alternatively, when researchers do ask open-ended questions, they often ask variations of the question, "What factors cause Y?"[7] My guiding question contains elements of both approaches while also insisting on seeking answers that are both actionable, practical, and generalizable enough to communicate to nonacademics—all in a setting where I've argued that conclusively establishing causal relationships between reform adoption and bureaucratic performance is nearly impossible. This research question is, therefore, an especially challenging one to tackle, but it is (in my view) the most important question, so I maintain it as my guiding star and aim to find answers that are both grounded in evidence and useful for decisionmakers—incomplete and imperfect as these answers may be.

Second, the nature of an *answer* to such a question must consist not of a definitive one-size-fits-all solution but rather an insight into the theoretical *mechanisms* through which reforms succeed or fail that can be applied across a range of settings. Researchers and practitioners alike often desire unambiguous, causal answers: reform X causes outcome Y; adopt this reform, and it will improve performance. I've argued that for both practical and conceptual reasons, such evidence is near-impossible to generate for systemic civil service reforms. Even if it could be generated, different governments are facing different challenges at different moments with different existing structures and different reform histories; it should be obvious that there can't be a one-size-fits-all answer to this question that holds across all contexts.

Instead, useful and generalizable knowledge about systemic reforms has to consist of a set of midrange theoretical insights about different parts of the reform process, mental models that reformers can absorb, remix, and apply to the unique demands, constraints, and opportunities of their own particular contexts. In other words, learning from evidence about reform isn't like following a blueprint that tells you exactly what to do. Instead, it's like compiling a toolbox and learning what each tool does and doesn't do so that you can use these tools to solve your own challenges in your own context. In this book, then, I use empirical evidence to identify and explore what I refer to as *mechanisms of success* and *mechanisms of failure*, patterns that repeat themselves across contexts and that often coexist within a given reform effort. Learning about these mechanisms is analogous to learning how the tools in the toolbox work and is the kind of answer that this book aims to provide.

Third, the *scope* of the empirical analysis on which my arguments are based is broad rather than deep. Instead of trying to deeply understand the effects of a small number of cases of reform in great depth or conduct a deep history of reform in any one country, I study every identifiable effort at system-level, performance-oriented civil service reform in six different African countries over the last thirty years. This includes everything from high-profile reform efforts that have already been well-researched to little-known reforms that were announced but never got off the ground and quickly faded into obscurity. (I'll give more details about definitions and scope in a moment.) This approach gives me a relatively large sample of reforms to study and eases concerns about inadvertently picking unrepresentative cases based on existing perceptions of success or failure or on which cases have the most information available about them. Even more importantly, studying many reform efforts across multiple countries makes it possible to start to distinguish broader trends and patterns that occur across many cases, whereas focusing on a single reform or single country often lends itself to identifying a wide and often overdetermined range of idiosyncratic failures that seemed to cause success or failure in that particular case. In my conversations, I have often heard the failure of a reform attributed to factors like a lack of political will, poor implementation, or a country's perceived work culture. And so reformers often think that a particular reform might have succeeded if only they had tried a bit harder or gotten a bit more lucky, or, alternatively, that their country is just uniquely unsuited to reform. But when we zoom out, we often see *repeated patterns* of similar efforts leading to similar results time and time again, often in quite different contexts. These repeated patterns can then be linked to the type of theoretical mechanisms of success and failure that provide generalizable insight to reformers. Studying a broad scope of reform episodes across several countries thus helps us move from idiosyncratic explanations to generalizable patterns.

The six countries I study are Ghana, Kenya, Nigeria, South Africa, Senegal, and Zambia. My temporal scope is roughly the three decades leading up to 2019, during which improving performance became a central and explicit goal for bureaucracies worldwide, but my starting year for each country varies between 1986 (Senegal) and 1999 (Nigeria), depending on the timing of key political transitions or reform waves. The countries are all democracies (at least, during the periods I study) and have undergone numerous reform efforts, but they span across western, eastern, and southern Africa and are diverse in terms of their size, wealth, and historical legacies. All inherited administrative structures and traditions from their colonial past but from different countries and with different characters, and these had each evolved and changed in different ways prior to the time period I study. While not randomly selected or fully representative of the continent or the world, as a sample, they strike a balance between comparability and contextual variation. It is important to emphasize that the aim of the book is not to make cross-country inferences about how exogenous characteristics affect reform experiences: the fundamental unit of analysis for the book is the reform effort, not the country, and reform cases differ as much within as across countries. By design, countries that have not been democracies for the majority of the past three decades are out of the scope of the book, as the dynamics of civil service reform are considerably different. This book, therefore, aims to speak mainly to reformers and scholars in countries with democratic, pluralistic political systems. While I do not gather systematic empirical data on reforms in any countries outside Africa, I do frequently draw on examples and evidence from all over the world—including high-income countries—to motivate my analysis and consider the extent to which the patterns and mechanisms I describe are generalizable.

Within each country, I study system-level, performance-oriented reforms to the core civil service. By core civil service, I mean the central government ministries, departments, and agencies responsible for developing, implementing, and overseeing policy. I focus mostly on bureaucrats, administrators, and technical experts in offices in the capital or other large cities rather than on "frontline" employees like nurses, teachers, or local government officials dispersed around the country in public-facing service delivery roles.[8] By reforms, I mean strategic and intentional structural or managerial changes to the internal administration of civil service organizations, whether de jure or de facto, aimed at improving bureaucratic performance. By performance, I mean the extent to which a government bureaucracy effectively delivers on its goals and objectives at the level of individuals, organizations, and the civil service as a whole.[9] My focus is not on whether civil services are adopting optimal policies but on how well they are delivering on the policies they have adopted. And by systemic, I mean reforms that apply not just to a single agency or sector but to the whole civil service.[10]

My scope thus includes a wide range of reforms, from staff salaries and career structures to individual-level incentives and performance management, organizational performance and management, processes for monitoring and improving service delivery, and more. At the same time, it excludes reforms that take place within a single organization or sector, reforms that are exclusively customer-facing or that affect frontline workers only, reforms that are exclusively oriented around budgeting and fiscal issues, decentralization or other local government reforms, and anticorruption interventions. Of course, these kinds of reforms all potentially affect performance, as do many other factors besides reforms, such as politics, leadership, economic conditions, and so on. These are all important and worth studying—and have been researched extensively—but fall outside the scope of this book.

I collect data on each reform effort from a range of sources, both primary and secondary. I try to document the *content* of what changes the reform aimed to make; the *process* of how it was designed and implemented; the actual *implementation* of the changes it envisioned; the *outcomes* of the reform in terms of changing the everyday behavior of civil servants and improving overall bureaucratic performance (to the extent these are possible to gauge, given the challenges of measurement and causal attribution); and the *politics* surrounding the reform effort, both the "high politics" of parties and elections as well as the "low politics" of workplace relationships and vested interests. To do this, I draw on nearly one thousand systematically collected academic studies and government documents, fifty-one interviews with elite civil servants who were personally involved in designing and implementing these reforms across all six countries, thirty-three interviews with rank-and-file civil servants who were affected by these reforms (in Ghana and Zambia), and in Ghana, archival records from the Office of the Head of Civil Service and Public Records and Archives Department. Table 1.1 summarizes these data sources. The amount and reliability of data I am able to gather, of course, varies dramatically across different reform efforts, and my own data collection and analysis are subject to many of the challenges of measurement and inference I highlighted above. I therefore calibrate the strength of my claims depending on the strength of the underlying evidence, particularly with respect to judgments about the impacts of reforms on bureaucratic behavior and outcomes. But by synthesizing and triangulating across these sources, it is possible to present a rich and fairly comprehensive picture of the design and implementation of dozens of reform efforts across thirty years and six countries.

Applying these criteria, I identified a total of 131 reform efforts across the six countries during this time period. When I began research for this book, I had originally planned to code the characteristics of these reforms to undertake quantitative or configurational analysis of how reform content and process were associated with implementation and outcomes, possibly moderated by political context. However, the process of compiling data and beginning to analyze it convinced me that such an analysis would be oversimplified and imply false precision at best, and be misleading and biased at worst. To some extent, this was due to

TABLE 1.1 Countries and data sources

	Ghana	Zambia	Kenya	Nigeria	Senegal	South Africa
Government, donor, and media documents	✓	✓	✓	✓	✓	✓
Existing academic literature	✓	✓	✓	✓	✓	✓
Interviews with elite reformers	✓	✓	✓	✓	✓	✓
Interviews with rank-and-file civil servants	✓	✓				
Government archives	✓					

Source: Author.

challenges of measurement—limited data availability, contradictory accounts, and the inherent ambiguity of many bureaucratic and political processes meant that it was often challenging to capture basic features like the end date of each reform with a single number, let alone its implementation process or outcomes. Even more fundamentally, reform episodes couldn't be analyzed as independent cases because the boundaries between reform cases were blurred: each reform built (in part) on what had come before and linked (in part) to other reforms that were ongoing simultaneously. Sometimes these influences reflected positive path dependence and efforts to maintain continuity and complementarity across reforms. Other times, the perceived failings of a preceding reform led its successors to try to do the opposite, or simultaneous reforms worked at cross-purposes because they were led by rival institutions. This means that even something as simple as counting reforms is difficult—the 131 figure I cited above is indicative, but different approaches to drawing case boundaries could lead to the number being far higher or lower. Trying to analyze these reform efforts as independent cases would be invalid, even without attributing causality to the observed relationships.

Rather than treating these methodological challenges as "bugs" to be worked around, I decided to treat them as inherent "features" of the phenomenon and processes of systemic civil service reform. So instead of relying on assigning codes to these episodes as discrete cases, I used my data to compile a narrative history of reform in each of the six countries, which presents a rich description of the reforms, their contexts, and their interconnections. These narrative histories serve to collate and harmonize messy data sources and diverse reforms into a format that is fairly consistent across reforms and countries while still permitting enough flexibility of exposition to capture complexities and nuances that formal coding would obscure. They then serve as the basis for producing descriptive generalizations about what governments are trying to do and how they are trying to do it, as well as abductive analysis of mechanisms of failure and success.

OUTLINE AND MAIN ARGUMENT

This book is, in some ways, two books in one. The first book is a narrative history of systemic, performance-oriented civil service reforms in each of the six countries. The second book is a thematically organized analysis of the track record of these reforms and what we learn from them, which draws on the narrative histories as data. However, the first book, containing the country-by-country narrative histories as well as further details of data and methods, is located at the end in an extensive appendix. The thematic analysis thus comprises the main text of the book, and the contours of my arguments closely follow its structure.

Chapter 2 lays out a theoretical framework and empirical evidence for conceptualizing performance. Consistent with my abductive approach, this chapter focuses on building strong conceptual foundations as a starting point for empirical analysis rather than on developing hypotheses to be tested. The chapter begins by introducing the book's key theoretical building block: the idea that performance in organizations requires some actions that are *verifiable* (formal) and others that are *nonverifiable* (informal).[11] Formal actions are those that can be precisely specified ex ante and measured ex post; they are the kind of actions that can be easily described in a manual of standard operating procedures or measured on an annual performance appraisal. Informal actions, however, encompass all the other crucial actions that workers must undertake to carry out their jobs effectively but are too unpredictable, too complex, or too unmeasurable to be fully codified. I illustrate these theoretical distinctions with empirical evidence that these unformalizable aspects of performance are pervasive in public sector organizations, whether one looks at the level of organizational outputs, individual behaviors, or management processes. Thinking of public sector performance in this way helps us gain clarity about the core challenge of systemic bureaucratic reform: How can a reform leader (like a head of civil service) design and implement reforms to strengthen the performance of both formal and informal actions by thousands of bureaucrats across different organizations working on different tasks, in different teams, under different managers?

Part II of the book (chapters 3–6) is the empirical core, examining the track record of these six countries' reform efforts over the past three decades. It documents how governments have approached reform, how successful they have been, and what have been the main mechanisms of failure and success of these reforms.

Chapter 3 presents the key descriptive themes that characterize the history of civil service reforms across the six study countries. Chapter 3 begins by presenting a single reform case (Zambia's Public Service Capacity Building Program, 2000–2005) to give a tangible example of the kind of reform episodes this book studies—although these are very diverse and there is no single "typical" reform. The chapter then builds on this illustrative case by using the full range of data collected on reform histories to answer a basic set of descriptive questions:

1.   How frequent have reform efforts been?
2.   What has been the content of these reforms—the structures, processes, and practices they have tried to introduce?
3.   How successful have reforms been?

In brief, my answers to these questions are:

1. Reform efforts were very frequent and often overlapping within each country. On average, in each country, a new reform effort was launched every 1.3 years, and there were 3.8 reforms simultaneously active.

2. Reform episodes mostly tried to achieve similar outcomes in terms of improved performance and did so mainly by repackaging and recombining a few different types of reforms (such as individual-level performance management, salary and career reform, and organizational capacity-focused interventions) into new bundles, meaning that countries often tried to implement the same types of reforms over and over again.

3. There were no examples of reforms that fully met all their goals, and most reforms fell far short of their (often overambitious) goals. But few were total failures. Most did achieve some of their aims—although more in terms of making changes on paper than in practice and not always through the mechanisms intended by the reform's designers.

Finally, the chapter examines what factors drove the design and timing of reform efforts, considering three sets of potential factors: the incentives and processes of key stakeholder agencies, in particular, international donor organizations and various agencies within governments; political cycles and time horizons; and the persistence, diffusion, and recurrence of ideas across and within countries. Much existing literature focuses on the roles of donors and politics, suggesting that reforms fail because they are externally imposed and not "owned" because governments are only pretending to reform in order to satisfy external donors and lenders or because African governments are forced to adopt and imitate models from the Global North rather than developing homegrown solutions.[12] I find some evidence consistent with each of these explanations, but also many cases in which reform implementation fell short despite a genuine desire within governments to improve performance and genuine belief among reformers that the proposed solutions were appropriate. Donors and political economy are thus both important parts of the story and often initiated or intruded on reform efforts, but they weren't the whole story, and the reformers I interviewed frequently pointed out ways that they themselves had major influence over reforms that, from the outside, appeared to be driven solely by external donors or political imperatives. Instead, reforms were usually shaped to a significant degree by reformers' own understandings or performance and reform, which were, in turn, shaped in path-dependent ways by their own idiosyncratic experiences, their institutional socialization, and by international trends and thinking. In sum, mental models, ideas, and inspiration mattered. This offers some hope for researchers (like me) who hope that evidence and insight on such reforms might not just be of academic interest but also practical use.

Chapter 4 documents the first of the two main mechanisms of reform failure. It shows that most reforms tended to focus heavily on creating or changing *formal structures and processes* to try to force bureaucrats to perform better by using rules, carrots, and sticks. To illustrate this, the chapter focuses on one of the most common types of reforms introduced across countries: individual-level performance management policies, which aim to systematically link individual bureaucrats' performance to rewards and sanctions. There were thirty-four total efforts to introduce individual-level performance-linked incentives in these six countries over three decades. But despite careful design and widespread acceptance of the aims of these reforms, there were zero instances in which differentiated rewards and sanctions were actually delivered sustainably and systematically to civil servants. Only two delivered differentiated incentives at all—both of which ceased doing so within a few years—but neither delivered sanctions for poor performance. The neglect of the importance of unformalizable bureaucratic behaviors undermined both the implementation and impact of these policies. This pattern also emerged with respect to other common types of reforms, such as performance improvement funds, salary structure changes, and organizational performance reviews. These also tended to focus primarily on formal behaviors and formal rules and processes for changing them, and this pattern helped explain why they so consistently fell short of their goals.

Chapter 5 then examines the second main mechanism of reform failure: reforms were usually conceived of as discrete, one-off, often time-bound interventions. The chapter shows how this *projectization* of reform distorted the expectations, content, implementation, leadership, and politics of reform efforts in ways that undermined their ultimate goal of improving performance. Projectization thus explains a wide range of observed features and patterns of reform, from the overselling of reforms' potential benefits to its tendency toward top-down leadership styles, its focus on formalizable outputs and targets, and its frequent lack of political sustainability. While often politically and bureaucratically convenient, the projectization of reform was thus a second common mechanism through which well-intentioned reforms failed to live up to the expectations set for them.

Chapter 6 turns to investigating reforms' two main mechanisms of success: creating opportunities to discuss performance and how to improve it and creating energy and momentum for change. Opportunities for discussion gave civil servants who cared about performance the chance to find one another, empowered them to identify and enact potential improvements, and spread the message that performance mattered. For example, annual staff appraisal systems never succeeded in systematically changing behavior through carrots and sticks but sometimes spurred workers to have conversations with their bosses for the first time about what they were responsible for and how they were doing. Energy and momentum helped to shift civil servants' expectations of one another from a negative equilibrium of low effort and low performance to a more positive pattern of extra effort and good performance being recognized and reciprocated. These mechanisms of success were driven largely by nonverifiable behavior changes: meaningful discussions can't be forced, workers can't be directly incentivized to care, and it's hard to drive innovation or problem-solving through predefined targets. While the means through which these mechanisms operated often involved formal structures and processes to some extent, they could also be easily crowded out by governments' efforts to use these formal systems for accountability and incentivization purposes. But when reforms were able to induce widespread and meaningful improvements in performance, one or both of these mechanisms usually played a leading role.

The four chapters of part II thus paint a rich portrait of the big-picture patterns of reforms and of the repeated mechanisms of failure and success that emerge when we analyze them collectively. While this book's main empirical analysis focuses on six countries in Africa, each of the chapters in part II also presents suggestive evidence that these patterns and mechanisms are also present in many other countries and other regions, including in high-income countries. Of course, these mechanisms manifest to different degrees, in different ways, and in different combinations across different reform efforts. But while each reform effort and context is unique in some ways, recognizing broader patterns can help us step back from these idiosyncrasies and realize that there is both a need and scope to rethink how we approach systemic reform more generally.

So if part II of the book focused on the "diagnosis" of the ways that reforms have failed and succeeded, part III (chapters 7–9) revolves around the "prescription." How can we conceptualize what an alternative approach to reform might look like and assess both its potential and the challenges it would face?

Chapter 7 draws together the empirical analysis of the previous chapters with the theoretical framework on organizational performance from chapter 2 to develop a theory of reform as *catalyzing an ongoing process of continuous improvement in actual practices*. This theory of reform as process reframes the goal of reform, focusing attention directly on changing the day-to-day work practices of rank-and-file civil servants and their managers rather than implicitly assuming that changes in behavior come from changes in formal rules. It reframes how reforms should be implemented, conceiving of change as an ongoing process of many locally driven changes rather than a master plan rolled out through a one-off project or intervention. And it casts the role of senior leaders in a different light, seeing their task not as driving or forcing reforms from the top down but rather as catalyzing, enabling, and inspiring decentralized local change efforts by thousands of staff and teams spread throughout the whole civil service.

Chapter 8 then examines what reform as a process can look like in practice by conducting a focused case study of reforms led by Nana Agyekum-Dwamena during his time as Head of Ghana's Civil Service. His decades of experience with projectized reforms had convinced him that when he took charge, he wanted to focus not on introducing new policies or new structures but on improving the implementation of existing ones; on changing the management practices that guide ordinary bureaucrats' behavior and routines on a day-to-day basis; and on transforming the mindsets and culture of civil servants across the various ministries and departments that comprise the Civil Service. This chapter documents these reform efforts as well as their successes and limitations. I was privileged to be conducting research in collaboration with Ghana's Civil Service throughout this time period, alongside several coauthors, at Agyekum-Dwamena's request, so I witnessed many of these discussions and reforms as they unfolded. Not all of Ghana's problems were solved, and not all efforts at change were successful. But many were, and overall, the evidence paints a picture of a Civil Service that has made gradual yet meaningful improvements in a wide range of areas—all while diverging, in many respects, from the formula that guided previous reform efforts in Ghana and elsewhere. The chapter closes by discussing how Agyekum-Dwamena navigated the political and institutional challenges that arose in approaching reform as a process.

Chapter 8 also distills this alternative approach into a set of three simple rules of thumb that reformers everywhere can apply to their own contexts:

1. Focus first on what can be done within existing formal rules and processes; think of changing formal rules and processes as a last resort rather than a first step.
2. Approach change as a process of collective learning-by-doing rather than as rolling out a predesigned blueprint. The priority should not be to make the perfect plan but instead to start changing actual practices—even small or apparently minor ones—as early as possible.
3. Decentralize the leadership of reform as much as possible. The role of a leader is to encourage and support dispersed improvement by other actors across the system rather than to drive it by themself.

Of course, exactly what actions these rules of thumb imply will be different in different times and places and for actors in different roles. They are general principles rather than rigid guidelines: Changes to formal rules are sometimes important, some types of changes ought to be rolled out as discrete projects, and top-down leadership is occasionally necessary. But both theory and the evidence of how and why reforms have persistently fallen short of expectations suggest that reform leaders—whether operating at the level of whole systems, single organizations, or even just their own teams—would generally be better served by using these rules of thumb to guide their thoughts and actions.

Chapter 9 concludes the book by exploring the nuances and scope of these findings and recommendations. To do so, it discusses how the dynamics of reform might differ along four dimensions: the *purpose* of the reform, in terms of whether it is aiming to change mostly verifiable or mostly nonverifiable practices; the *context* of the reform, in particular the degree to which compliance with formal rules is enforced and expected; who the *people* driving the reform are, both in terms of their seniority and position and whether they are internal or external to the bureaucracy; and the *politics* surrounding the reform, especially the time horizon of the reformer(s) and the degree to which external actors impose pressures or constraints on the bureaucracy. The chapter suggests that these factors determine the extent to which this book's analysis and advice is likely to hold for other countries, other change efforts, and other types of organizations. While there are reasons to think that this book's diagnoses and prescriptions are widely applicable, the determination of how relevant they are to any particular situation ultimately rests with you, the reader, and your knowledge of your own context and goals.

You've likely noticed by now that the book does not have dedicated chapters on two issues that are often discussed in the context of civil service reform in Africa and elsewhere: the role of international donor institutions and the politics of reform. This is because I made a deliberate decision to focus not on the external forces that constrain or influence reform leaders within country governments but on reformers' agency and room for maneuver within these constraints. To be sure, donors are important stakeholders and funders in many (but far from all) of the reforms I study, so I do discuss their roles and influence extensively—but always as members of the supporting cast, not as the leading actors. With respect to politics, I treat it the same way that public servants typically experience it: neither as an afterthought to technical discussions nor as entirely deterministic of reform opportunities but rather as inextricably bound up with the technical and organizational aspects of reform. Each of the core chapters, therefore, integrates analysis of how political considerations have shaped the past track record of reforms and must also be navigated by any alternative approach while still fore-grounding the agency of reformers in doing so.[13]

Finally, it's important to emphasize that this book has many allies, cousins, and forebears in its effort to rethink how we conceptualize behavior, performance, and change in organizations in general and public bureaucracies in particular. In the realm of academic research, scholars from diverse fields and perspectives have written about bottom-up approaches to reform, relational contracts theories of management practices, backward mapping in policy implementation, continuous improvement, process-oriented methods for studying organizational change, problem-solving and muddling as change strategies, the importance of organizational cultures and bureaucratic autonomy, transformational leadership and system leadership, the building of pockets of bureaucratic effectiveness, polycentric governance, agile government, and problem-driven iterative adaptation and other complexity science-inspired ways of thinking—to name just a few of the areas of existing literature that this book connects with, draws inspiration from, and seeks to build on.[14] I'll discuss these theories as they arise over the course of the book, especially in chapter 7. And of course, reformers around the world have been grappling with these ideas for far longer than academics have been writing about them.

So in analyzing how past reform efforts have fallen short and what a better approach might look like, I don't mean to imply that no one else has ever recognized any of these challenges before or tried to experiment with solutions. Still less do I want to suggest that overcoming these challenges is easy. On the contrary, systemic bureaucratic reform is complex and difficult, both conceptually and practically, and most past reforms were themselves the product of smart, dedicated people trying their best to piece together something that they thought would work. I don't pretend that this book has all the answers, but I hope that reading it helps you feel at least a little better prepared than I was the next time a head of civil service—or a minister, mayor, CEO, manager, or other leader—calls you into their office and says, "I want to change the way this place works, how would you recommend I go about it?"

2

Theory and Evidence on Organizational Performance

What do civil service bureaucracies do? And what does it mean to do it well?

The last chapter argued for the importance of studying large-scale, systemic reforms by asking whether and how they actually affect the everyday behaviors of rank-and-file individuals and their managers. This chapter builds answers to these two questions from the bottom up, focusing on understanding performance and behavior at the levels of individuals, teams, and organizations. In so doing, it weaves together a conceptual framework that serves as a foundation for the book's subsequent investigation of how system-level reforms do or do not translate into improved performance at the micro- and meso-levels.

The first section of the chapter focuses on defining bureaucratic performance and building a simple but powerful theoretical framework for thinking about it. I approach this not by asking what we want civil services to look like in terms of macrolevel characteristics or structures but by asking what performance looks like in terms of everyday individual behaviors and organizational processes. Some of these behaviors can be formalized with tools like key performance indicators and standard operating procedures, but other important behaviors are too difficult to specify or measure to be effectively formalized. In the language of organizational economics, the former are verifiable (formal) behaviors, and the latter are non-verifiable (informal). The core challenge of organizational performance—and of performance-oriented civil service reforms—is thus how to get employees to undertake both types of behaviors.

After setting out this conceptual framework, I then present three empirical "stylized facts"—midrange empirical patterns that broadly hold true across a range of contexts—about performance in bureaucracies at the organizational and individual levels. First, most of the tasks that government bureaucracies are responsible for are not fully verifiable in that they either can't be perfectly specified in advance or perfectly measured after the fact. Second, most organizational management processes are also not fully verifiable, meaning that they require individuals to undertake informal as well as formal actions. Third, there are large variations in organizational performance even among organizations in the same context operating under the same set of formal rules and external constraints—due, in part, to the challenges of getting people in the organization to undertake both the formal and informal parts of these processes. Taken together, this evidence paints a picture of public service organizations in which the nonverifiable, unformalizable aspects of performance are pervasive.

The role of this chapter is to provide a simple, evidence-grounded, micro- and meso-level foundation from which to undertake the abductive analysis of system-level reforms that is the empirical core of the book. Rather than setting out hypotheses to be tested against subsequent empirical evidence, it provides a starting point for analysis and a framework for interpreting it. So while this chapter doesn't posit any answers to this book's motivating question—how a head of civil service should approach performance-oriented reform—it does give us a structured way to think about what bureaucratic change efforts must achieve to improve performance and why that is so challenging. With that in mind, let's begin by defining what we mean by performance.

DEFINING PERFORMANCE

Throughout this book, I use the term *performance* to refer to the extent to which an individual or organization delivers on its goals and objectives. In economic terms, this means maximizing internal efficiency subject to externally given goals, policies, and constraints. In administrative terms, it means implementing policies and processes as they are intended to be implemented. Used this way, performance can refer to a property of individual behavior or to an emergent collective property of the cumulation of linked individual behaviors within teams or organizations. It can also apply to the undertaking of specific actions or tasks, the execution of organizational processes, or the production of final outputs or outcomes by an organization (or even a set of organizations).

This definition is simple, intuitive, and flexible, but that inevitably comes at the price of abstracting away from a great deal of complexity. Agreeing on a precise definition of public sector performance is hard because government organizations always have multiple goals that sometimes conflict with one another (e.g., service delivery, transparency, cost-effectiveness, impartiality, democratic accountability), and different observers disagree about how to weigh these in measuring performance. Most of these goals are heavily influenced by factors external to the bureaucracy—political, social, economic, environmental—and so the more comprehensively we attempt to conceptualize performance in terms of the outcomes citizens care about, the less control the bureaucracy itself has over their achievement. Measuring public sector performance is also hard because many (perhaps most) public sector outputs are nonpriced (i.e., they are not market goods), and their quality and/or quantity often cannot be characterized precisely and objectively. These conceptual and definitional challenges are the subject of dozens, if not hundreds, of books and articles on public sector performance.[1]

While these nuances and definitional debates are important, I opt for a simple and limited definition of performance as the implementation of defined policies and processes for three reasons. First, the reforms I study in this book differed in their own definitions of performance, often without grappling with these complexities or specifying how they balance these different goals. So my definition must be flexible enough to capture what these varied reforms were aiming at. Second, I do not attempt to construct my own formal performance measures for civil services or reform success, relying instead on the diverse measures and perceptions of civil services themselves, interviewees, external evaluators, and academics. Third, the idea of the civil service as primarily charged with implementing politically defined goals and objectives corresponds closely to the legal role of the civil service as the executive arm of the government and, thus, to the main objective of a reformer like the head of civil service. So while I do engage with some of these complexities in later chapters and the appendix with respect to evaluating the success or failure of reforms and in discussing strategies for reform, I deal with these conceptual and practical difficulties as they arise rather than trying to impose a rigid conceptual schema on them in the abstract.

The task and institutional context of civil services also affects how we conceptualize bureaucratic performance. The majority of civil servants are not workers standing alone at fixed assembly lines performing repetitive tasks to create standardized widgets under the direction of a single boss. They work on many tasks at the same time, often collaboratively in teams or cross-organization networks. The tasks themselves are often not repetitive or well-defined, requiring bureaucrats to use their discretion or initiative to figure out what needs to be done. The quality or value of what has been produced is often hard to measure, and attributing good or bad outcomes to individual bureaucrats or organizations is difficult. And far from answering to a single boss, most bureaucrats must simultaneously balance multiple managers and institutional imperatives, each of which is embedded in numerous layers of hierarchy. So the performance of individual bureaucrats is a complex thing to define and understand. Is there a simple way we can think about whether and how well bureaucrats do what they're supposed to do on a day-to-day basis that incorporates these nuances but still gives us a clear vision of what good performance looks like?

VERIFIABILITY

All bureaucratic operations ultimately consist of individuals (agents) taking actions at the behest of their manager or organization (principal) in pursuit of organizational goals. Some of these actions are written down in regulations or standard operating procedures, some are delegated by managers, and others rely on individuals themselves taking some initiative. Performance—in the sense I defined above—consists of getting individuals to reliably take the actions they're supposed to take in order to achieve organizational goals.[2]

The challenge with getting public servants to do what they're supposed to is that it's not always clear in advance what the right action to take in a given situation will be, nor is it always clear after the fact what an individual actually did. If everything bureaucrats needed to do could be specified in the standard operating procedures and everything bureaucrats actually did was perfectly observable by their managers, then getting them to perform would be easy: Just fire anyone who doesn't do what they are supposed to. But anyone who's worked in an organization knows that it's not that simple. Regulations and organizational handbooks might be a good starting point for defining what workers are supposed to do, but there are always lots of unforeseen situations or little details that can't be written down—not to mention situations when the written rules specify a course of action that conflicts with the organization's goals. And whether public servants are working in remote forests or in open-plan offices in ministry headquarters, most of the time, managers can't or don't watch their every action. And even if they were, they might struggle to measure exactly what it was that the official did, particularly in jobs where most work is cognitive and team-based rather than physical and individualized. So writing and following rules is only one part of what is required to achieve good performance.

Let's make this intuition a bit more precise, using the concept of *verifiability* from organizational economics.[3] An action is verifiable if a third party (e.g., a court, tribunal, auditor) can objectively determine if the agent took the correct action in a given situation on behalf of the principal. Actions are only verifiable if two things are both true: (1) the correct course of action to take in the situation can be specified ex ante, and (2) what the agent actually did can be measured ex post. Of course, in reality, these two properties can hold to a greater or lesser extent, so verifiability is a spectrum rather than a dichotomy. But for convenience, I will generally refer to actions as either verifiable or nonverifiable. Or, in less technical language, as formal or informal, formalizable or unformalizable.

This matters because if an action is verifiable, then organizations can compel it to be performed with formal rules or contracts associated with rewards or sanctions. Think of your own employment contract: It probably includes a specified list of duties that you can be fired for not performing—even if you work in a highly unionized or regulated sector, as is often true of public sector workers. But this list probably consists of a few bullet points or paragraphs that leave lots of ambiguity about what this looks like in practice, and there's probably also some vague language around "and other such tasks as may be required" but with no clear way to define what might reasonably be asked of you. Your contract or job description might also say that the quality of your work should be "of a high standard" or something similar, but it's impossible to precisely specify or measure that in all circumstances in an objective way. If you were sanctioned for one of these fuzzier parts of your job description, you would probably be able to appeal to an administrative tribunal or sue in an employment court, and your employer would have a hard time proving their case. So it is much easier for organizations to compel compliance with the highly verifiable parts of your job than the less verifiable parts.

But these hard-to-formalize actions are often crucial for performance at both the individual and organizational levels. This is particularly true in environments like the civil service, where the quality of outputs is hard to measure, individuals have to collaborate across stakeholder networks on complex and often unpredictable tasks, and individuals often have to innovate or use their discretion—their own judgment of a situation or their common sense about what is the right thing to do—to navigate day-to-day challenges. Doing only the formal, verifiable parts of a job is akin to following the letter of the law, whereas achieving the spirit of the law—the course of action that will lead to achieving organizational objectives—often requires supplementing these with informal actions that can't be fully specified beforehand or perfectly measured after the fact. These informal aspects of work are so important that refusing to perform them by "working to rule"—when workers perform only the specific actions listed in their contracts or job descriptions but do none of the extra or unspecified tasks that actually make everything work—can even be used as a form of industrial protest because it is so disruptive to overall organizational functioning.

Let's again draw on the language of organizational economics to make this intuition more precise and distinguish between three stylized levels of performance. Doing exactly what a rule or contract says—nothing less, nothing more— is called *perfunctory performance*. Complying not only with formal rules but also supplementing them with informal practices that give meaning and fulfillment to them is called *consummate performance*. When actors neither comply with formal procedures nor undertake supporting informal practices, we can characterize this as a state of *nonperformance*. Getting to consummate performance is thus the core goal—and core challenge—of improving organizational performance. Table 2.1 summarizes these definitions.

The verifiable/nonverifiable distinction is similar in many respects to some other terms that are widely used in public administration and development. For example, James Q. Wilson famously categorized public agencies by how "visible" their outputs and outcomes are, and he wrote about how managing agencies with highly visible tasks was different from those with less visible ones.[4] Similarly, Lant Pritchett and Michael Woolcock and Matt Andrews and colleagues have categorized public services according to, among other factors, whether they require agents to exercise discretion or are nondiscretionary.[5] And terms like *hard* and *soft*, *tangible* and *intangible*, and so on are widely used by scholars and practitioners alike to capture similar distinctions. These concepts aren't all identical, and I think there are some analytical advantages to thinking in terms of verifiability. But these terms do aim to capture similar distinctions and are more alike than different.

The next section fleshes out these ideas with examples and evidence. Before proceeding to this, however, an important clarification: the term *informal* is sometimes used among public administrators as a euphemism for "corrupt," "illegal," or "improper," but this is not at all the sense in which I use it in this book. I use *informal* simply as a synonym for nonverifiable: not fully specifiable by law but also not necessarily contravening any laws. Understood in this way, the vast majority

TABLE 2.1 Three stylized levels of performance

	Nonperformance	Perfunctory performance	Consummate performance
Formal practices defined and executed?	No	Yes	Yes
Supporting informal practices undertaken?	No	No	Yes

Source: Author.

of informal practices are completely legal, and many informal actions and processes are necessary for carrying out even the most basic organizational functions. Almost everything an individual civil servant or an organization as a whole does has both formal and informal components, albeit to varying degrees. These formal and informal elements are both important, both take effort and coordination, and undertaking both together is a crucial goal for organizational management.

MOST ORGANIZATIONAL TASKS ARE AT LEAST PARTIALLY NONVERIFIABLE

The idea that much of what bureaucracies and bureaucrats do is hard to specify and measure has a long intellectual tradition, from the observation that many public servants do work that can't be easily monitored to theories of differential observability of agency outputs and outcomes, the consequences of delivering nonpriced goods and services, and the openness to interpretation of organizational goals.[6] While much of this literature has assumed that these characteristics vary at the level of organizations—some ministries do things that are easily measurable, others less so—another strand focuses on variation in measurability across different tasks or outputs within an organization. In economics, theories of multitasking explore how management tools like incentives can cause bureaucrats to focus their effort on more measurable tasks rather than less measurable ones,[7] and public administration scholars have examined whether and how strict targets for one bureaucratic activity can distort public servants' efforts on that task or divert it from other ones.[8] So there's a scholarly consensus that difficulty in clearly specifying and measuring bureaucratic action is a salient factor of public management—but does this refer to a small part of what government does or to the majority of it?

One effort to quantify this was undertaken by Imran Rasul, Daniel Rogger, and myself as part of a research collaboration with Ghana's Office of the Head of the Civil Service (OHCS) that stemmed from Agyekum-Dwamena's request for assistance in building an evidence base to help inform OHCS's reform efforts.[9] In 2015, members of our research team worked with staff from OHCS and Ghana's Management Services Department to collect, digitize, and hand-code characteristics of every task or output listed on the annual workplans and reports of each ministry and department in Ghana's core civil service. These tasks included work on physical infrastructure projects (e.g., "construction of secondary data centre at Kumasi," "identify bungalows and initiate procurement process"), public-facing activities and awareness-raising (e.g., "talk shows in four rural district markets in the region on the GIPC act held," "sensitize printers and suppliers on the procurement law and packaging"), internal administrative tasks (e.g., "preparation of 2014 annual report," "conduct second phase of housing audit"), as well as tasks related to policy development, training, financial management, permitting and regulation, and other categories.[10] Altogether, we examined 3,620 tasks from thirty government organizations.

For each task, we coded: (1) ex ante clarity, or the extent to which "the task can be defined in such a way as to create little uncertainty about what is required to complete the task;" and (2) ex post clarity, or the extent to which "a report of the actual action undertaken leaves little uncertainty about whether the task was effectively completed." These correspond closely to the characteristics of pre-specifiability and measurability that together comprise the concept of verifiability. These two variables were coded on a scale from 1 to 5, with 5 meaning "no ambiguity" and 1 meaning "undefined or so vague it is impossible to assess what completion would mean."[11] Coders had relatively little information on which to base their coding—usually just a phrase or sentence in a reporting table—although this is also the exact same information used by organizational management and by OHCS to monitor performance, so it presents a fairly realistic way to quantify the verifiability of tasks.

The results of our coding are reproduced in figure 2.1. Just 22.7 percent of tasks were judged by the coders to be perfectly clear ex ante (score of 5), and 19.1 percent were judged to be perfectly clear ex post. Only 11.2 percent of tasks were coded as completely unambiguous in each category—that is, perfectly verifiable. At the same time, very few tasks were completely unverifiable. The vast majority of tasks were partially clear on both measures. Based on this measure, then, almost 90 percent of what civil service bureaucracies do is at least partially nonverifiable—and organizational managers thus have to find ways to guide, monitor, and encourage both completion of formalizable and unformalizable tasks or task components.

ORGANIZATIONAL PROCESSES AND INDIVIDUAL PERFORMANCE HAVE NONVERIFIABLE ELEMENTS

The formal versus informal distinction can also help us understand the organizational management processes that direct, coordinate, and monitor individuals and teams as they work to achieve these tasks and outputs. In 2013, I conducted interviews with sixty civil servants across forty ministries, departments, and agencies in Ghana's public service about how a common set of fifteen different organizational

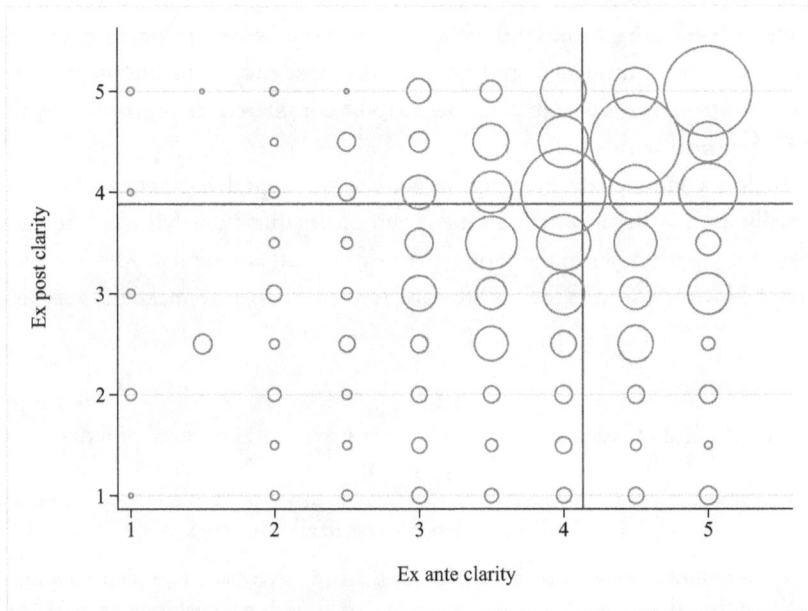

FIGURE 2.1 Task Clarity, Ex Ante and Ex Post

Notes: Circle size is proportional to the number of tasks that fall within each bin of width 0.5. Lines indicate mean values for each measure of task clarity. Reproduced with permission from Imran Rasul, Daniel Rogger, and Martin J. Williams, "Management, Organizational Performance, and Task Clarity: Evidence from Ghana's Civil Service," *Journal of Public Administration Research and Theory* 31, no. 2 (2021): 259–77.

processes worked in their organization.[12] Our conversations focused on how these processes were actually executed in practice—not just what they were supposed to look like on paper. For some of these processes, the formal aspects were actually defined at the system level rather than the organizational level, so in principle, the process should have looked the same in every organization.

What I observed in practice was a huge variation in de facto management processes across organizations. This variation corresponded naturally to the three categories of performance I defined above: nonperformance, perfunctory performance, and consummate performance. To illustrate this, let's first examine a process that was meant to be the same in every organization: annual staff appraisals.[13] In each organization, this was supposed to involve completion of the same appraisal template by each officer, as well as the same annual cycle of defining targets and responsibilities in conjunction with the officer's supervisor at the start of each year, assessing performance at the end of the year, and feeding the performance assessment into decisions on training allocation. These assessments were also intended to feed into promotion decisions; while these were made at a central level rather than by the organizations themselves, in practice, organizations had some influence on promotions because they could choose whether and how strongly to recommend officers to be considered for promotion by the central authorities.

Table 2.2 summarizes the range of annual staff appraisal practices that were actually used in organizations. One group of organizations fell into the category of nonperformance: the formal parts of the staff appraisal process were not complied with, nor were there systematic informal efforts to make the appraisal

TABLE 2.2 Variation in formal and informal staff appraisal practices, Ghana 2013

Standardized *de jure* process in all ministries

All officers should sit with their manager at the end of year and complete an annual appraisal (based on a standardized template) to assess performance against pre-defined targets.

Variation in *de facto* practices across ministries

	Nonperformance	Perfunctory performance	Consummate performance
Formal aspects of practice	Appraisals are not conducted annually. Instead, multiple years are filled out at the same time when individual are due for promotion.	Appraisals are always conducted annually.	Appraisals are always conducted annually.
Informal aspects of practice	The appraisal is a self-assessment; actual discussions about officers' performance rarely happen.	Appraisal discussions are not meaningful, and process is viewed as a formality.	Appraisals are used as an opportunity to give meaningful feedback, and are supplemented by discussions in weekly divisional meetings.

Source: Adapted from Martin J. Williams, "From Institutions to Organizations: Management and Informality in Ghana's Bureaucracies," working paper, London School of Economics and Political Science, September 9, 2015.

process function as intended. In these organizations, the appraisal process was often not even carried out annually; rather, individuals tended to complete several years' worth of appraisals retrospectively as they neared the date for their promotion interviews, simply entering a different year on each form. In these organizations, the appraisal itself was regarded as essentially a self-assessment that the supervisor merely signed off on, except in cases of extreme misconduct, with no link to any rewards, consequences, or remedial action. As one interviewee explained, "The appraisals don't improve the system. They're a formality." Another reflected on the disconnect between assessed performance and the allocation of training opportunities, saying, "One director even says he'll send you 'if your face looks nice.'"

Another group of organizations carried out the process perfunctorily. Interviewees reported that appraisal forms were indeed carried out each year, and supervisors and supervisees did sit together to complete a list of targets at the start of the year and assess performance at the end of the year, but the target-setting process was often disconnected from the actual work officers did during the year, and the assessment tended to be equally uninformative. In a similar vein, research on Ghana's performance appraisal system around this period by Justice Nyigmah Bawole and colleagues describes it as "rhetoric rather than an important practice."[14] and Frank Ohemeng and colleagues refer to the process as "much ado about nothing."[15]

A third group of organizations undertook the staff appraisal process with what can be described as consummate performance. These organizations not only carried out the formal appraisal process as designed but also instituted complementary informal measures to make the formal process more meaningful. Supervisors held the standard annual and midyear performance review meetings with each of their staff but also held informal discussions on performance in weekly divisional meetings so that individuals were not only kept aware of their own performance but also how they compared to others in the division. Due to the centrally imposed constraints on pay and promotions, organizations found other ways to recognize and reward good performance: awards nights for top performers as voted by their colleagues, occasional written letters of recognition for exemplary work, opportunities for training, and so on. While accelerated formal promotions were rare, given the rigidity of the system, it was common for these organizations to reward star performers with "informal promotions": appointment to committees, roles as a focal person, and other opportunities that further career development and may also entail some financial benefit. As one interviewee remarked, "This is one of the ministries where you are recognized based on your work, not your rank."

The same pattern was evident with respect to other types of management processes, including those that pertain to the organization as a whole rather than individual managers and officers. For example, each organization was mandated to hold regular management meetings to discuss performance, but the ways this formal mandate was implemented varied wildly. Some ministries didn't even comply with the mandate, holding performance review meetings on an irregular and ad hoc basis only, perhaps four to five times per year. Even when these meetings were held, they were typically not very useful, with one interviewee reporting that such meetings were "more for human management and the condition of the office and that kind of thing than results management. There's very little discussion of what are we supposed to do and where are we."

Other organizations complied perfunctorily, holding regular management meetings (most commonly once a month) at which some matters related to performance were reviewed. But these discussions rarely were communicated to non-management staff or had implications beyond the management meeting; they were merely a formality. These organizations could truthfully say on their annual report that they had held regular performance meetings, but the nonverifiable reality was that such meetings likely contributed little to performance improvement.

Another group of organizations carried out these performance reviews consummately, holding regular management meetings for operational and administrative issues (usually more frequently than monthly) as well as periodic broader reviews. Management staff would typically hold follow-up meetings with their teams to brief them after the management meeting so that staff were aware of what was happening elsewhere in the organization and how it affected their work, and cross-team working groups were formed to tackle issues that arose. For these organizations, the formal process was not only carried out but also prompted and underpinned a wide range of less formal supporting practices that were important for achieving the intended goal of the formal process. These supporting practices were difficult to formally mandate but were nonetheless carried out systematically in the group of organizations that executed this process consummately.

While thinking of management processes and their performance as comprising both formal and informal aspects is broadly useful, some nuances and clarifications are in order. First, not every organization I interviewed fell neatly into one of these categories, and there was some variation across managers within each organization. So these three levels of performance—nonperformance, perfunctory performance, and consummate performance—are not rigid, discrete categories but rather simple heuristics for characterizing the inevitably more complex world of organizational processes and practices. Second, there is a fourth potential category of performance that could exist: organizations that don't have or

TABLE 2.3 Variation in formal and informal organizational performance review practices, Ghana 2013

	Standardized *de jure* process in all ministries		
	All organizations should hold regular (usually monthly) meetings of management-level staff to review performance and coordinate across divisions, as well as quarterly and/or annual reviews with participation from a broader range of staff.		
	Variation in *de facto* practices across ministries		
	Nonperformance	Perfunctory performance	Consummate performance
Formal aspects of practice	Management meetings are held occasionally but sometimes don't happen. Quarterly reviews exist some of its programs, but only the donor-led ones are regular.	Performance review meetings with management staff happen every month, as do annual and/or quarterly all-staff meetings.	Performance review meetings happen monthly or even weekly with management, as well as periodically with different groups of staff, so everyone gets to know about the agency's performance.
Informal aspects of practice	Quarterly and annual reports are seen as a formality undertaken to meet external requirements, not an opportunity to review performance. Management meetings "more for human management and the condition of the office and that kind of thing than results management. There's very little discussion of what are we supposed to do and where are we."	Directors are supposed to brief their officers after management meetings, but this does not always happen. More senior officers would learn about the organization's performance through working with their directors. Agreed actions would be minuted to the officer responsible. "That's if the minutes can be done in good time, sometimes they can take long."	Directors meet regularly with their divisions to update them on discussions from management meetings and to review their own performance, sometimes holding informal briefings immediately after management meetings. Even routine reporting requirements, like quarterly reports, are seen as opportunities to document and improve performance.

Source: Adapted from Williams, "From Institutions to Organizations."

don't carry out the formal aspects of these processes but do systematically employ informal practices to achieve the goals of the process. This is a theoretical possibility, but in practice, I didn't observe this as a deliberate managerial approach in any of the forty ministries, departments, and agencies I studied. To the extent performance-oriented informal practices did exist without being linked to or supported by any formal practices, it was nearly always a matter of individual managers trying to do their best to cope with organizational failings rather than a conscious strategy for good management. Third, with these two management processes, as well as the other types of formal management processes imposed by the reforms I study later in the book, my focus on the execution of formal processes is not meant to imply an assumption that each of these formal processes is optimal or even necessarily positive for performance in the organization as a whole. Rather, I focus on execution or implementation under the much weaker assumption that civil services aim to implement the processes that they define for themselves in meaningful ways and that doing so, in general, will lead to performance improvement (overall, if not necessarily for every single process). In other words, it's likely that some processes defined by any given civil service are likely to be suboptimal or even harmful for performance and, hence, need to be continuously evaluated and improved. In a similar vein, the design of formal processes cannot necessarily be separated from their implementation—a theme we will return to later in the book.

The evidence described above and this book's conceptual starting point is that good organizational performance generally stems from both executing the organization's defined formal processes, at least for the most part, and from simultaneously carrying out complementary informal practices that give meaning to these formal processes. This view of management and performance as comprising both formal and informal components that must complement each other also accords with evidence from other types of organizations around the world.[16] So moving toward consummate performance of organizational processes, as opposed to perfunctory or nonperformance of them, can serve as a simple, parsimonious, and broadly applicable goal for performance improvement efforts.

PERFORMANCE VARIES ACROSS ORGANIZATIONS WITHIN THE SAME CONTEXT

These process-level variations aggregate up into substantial differences across organizations in overall management quality and performance. Academics and practitioners alike sometimes assume that the picture of performance in the public sector is uniformly bad. But a large body of evidence points to a different conclusion: There is actually substantial variation in performance across organizations, teams, and individuals within any given government. This is despite these organizations sharing the same national-level variables that are commonly thought to affect bureaucratic effectiveness—geography, political settlements, administrative structures and legacies, colonial history, societal education and human capital, and so on[17]—and in many cases, operating under the same set of formal civil service laws and regulations.

The interviews I conducted in 2013 across forty Ghanaian ministries, departments, and agencies described in the previous section provide one way to illustrate this point. In addition to recording qualitative information about the management processes being used, I also quantitatively benchmarked the quality and consistency of practice within each organization. Adapting the influential and widely used World Management Survey methodology developed by Nicholas Bloom and John Van Reenen,[18] in each organization, I scored each of the fifteen processes I studied on a scale from 1 to 5, where 1 meant that the organization had essentially no structured or consistent approach to the process, and 5 meant that the organization consistently and thoughtfully implemented both formal and informal aspects of that process. The interviewing and benchmarking procedures incorporated a wide range of methods to avoid bias and ensure comparability across organizations,[19] and the benchmarking criteria were designed to be neutral with respect to the style of management and instead focus on whether for each practice the organization had a process or routine that was consciously designed and was followed in reality.

Figure 2.2 shows the portrait of management processes that emerges from aggregating these scores within each organization, with the black diamonds representing the organization's average score across practices and the grey circles representing the organization's score on each process. (In this figure, all scores have been normalized so that the mean is equal to 0 and the standard deviation is equal to 1.)[20]

The resulting picture was one in which there was substantial variation both across organizations in overall management quality and within each organization across different processes. Some organizations were better managed than others, and some organizations that were managed quite poorly (or well) overall had specific processes that they executed well (or poorly). So the qualitative differences in how organizations implemented each management process aggregated up into broader differences in overall management quality despite these organizations all operating in the same institutional context.

Organizations in the same government also vary in their level of performance. In the research that Imran Rasul, Daniel Rogger, and I conducted in

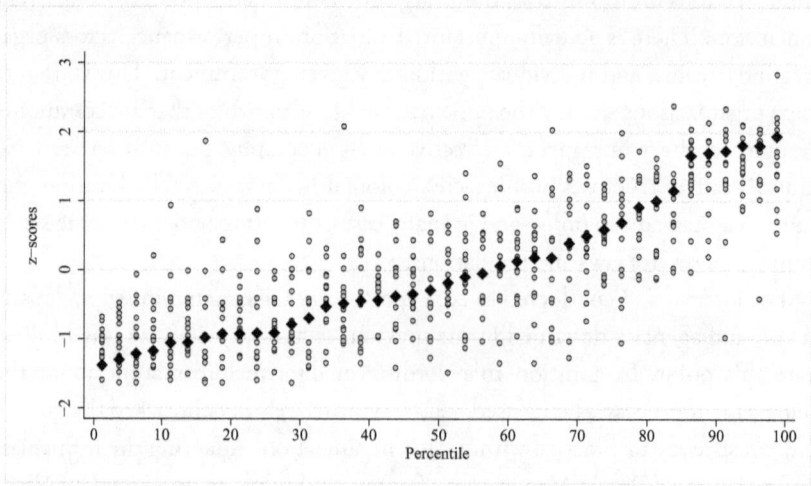

FIGURE 2.2 Variation in Management Quality Across and Within Organizations, Ghana 2013

Notes: Black diamonds represent the overall management quality score for the organization, grey circles represent the score for each of the fifteen management processes individually. All figures are normalized z-scores. Reproduced from Williams, "From Institutions to Organizations."

collaboration with Ghana's OHCS in 2015, we not only coded the ex ante and ex post clarity of each of the 3,620 tasks (as I described earlier in the chapter) but also the degree to which the organization completed each task. We coded completion using the information provided in the organization's own reports, with checks on data quality and accuracy,[21] also using a 1–5 scale where 5 meant "no action was taken towards achieving the target" and a score of 5 meant "the target for the task has been reached or surpassed."[22]

Figure 2.3 shows the average task completion rates for each of the thirty organizations we studied (black diamonds) and each division within them (grey circles). The picture was again one in which there was substantial variation in performance both across organizations and within them.

As part of this research, we also partnered with Ghana's OHCS to conduct a large-scale survey of 2,971 civil servants across forty-five ministries, departments, and agencies. We asked about the de facto management processes these civil servants experienced on a day-to-day basis, using a 1–5 coding methodology similar to what I had used in my earlier interviews and Rasul and Rogger had previously used with Nigeria's Federal Civil Service.[23] Using this quantitative metric based on thousands of interviews, we again found the same pattern: substantial variation in management process quality across organizations, across divisions within

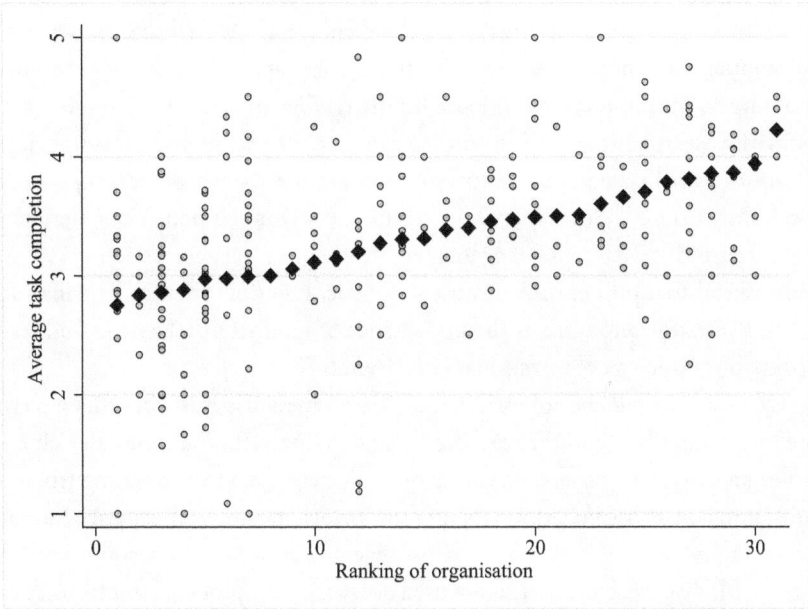

FIGURE 2.3 Variation in Task Completion Across and Within Organizations, Ghana 2015

Notes: Analysis undertaken for Rasul et al., "Management, Organizational Performance, and Task Clarity." Black diamonds represent organization average task completion rates, grey circles represent division average completion rates.

organizations, and across different process types within organizations. This variation in management quality was strongly associated with variation in task completion, even after controlling for a range of other features of organizations, tasks, and personnel. So better or worse organizational performance could be traced back (in part) to better or worse organizational management quality, which could, in turn, be traced back to variation in the execution of both formal and informal aspects of specific management processes.

These studies are far from unique in finding that there is variation in performance among organizations undertaking similar functions in similar contexts. In Ghana, for example, Francis Owusu used survey-based methods to identify high- and low-performing agencies within government and argued that organizational recruitment criteria and remuneration levels were associated with variations in performance.[24] Also in Ghana, Erin McDonnell conducted in-depth qualitative research on four high- and four low-performing teams within the same organization and showed how managers of high-performing teams simultaneously tried to create distinctive performance-oriented cultures while also carving out the autonomy to build and maintain these cultures.[25] More broadly, there is a substantial literature on "islands" of effectiveness and "pockets" of excellence, building on the foundational work of Judith Tendler and Merilee Grindle, which primarily uses qualitative case studies to demonstrate that high-performing organizations exist in the public sectors of states around the world with supposedly weak institutions.[26] Surveying this literature, McDonnell points out that even the patterns of which types of agencies perform better vary across countries—an observation that pushes back against simplistic, function-oriented explanations for this variation and hints at the importance of internal management and leadership in producing organizational effectiveness.[27]

Quantitative evidence of variation in effectiveness also exists in other governments around the world. For example, Daniel Gingerich, Katherine Bersch and colleagues draw on different sources of quantitative data to show that there is substantial cross-organization variation in various measures of capacity (among other variables) in the governments of several Latin American countries.[28] In Russia, Michael Best and colleagues used data on public procurement from 2011–2016 to show that 39 percent of the variation in prices paid for identical items is due to the differential effectiveness of individuals and organizations.[29] In their work in Nigeria's Federal Civil Service, Rasul and Rogger report that infrastructure project completion rates vary from 4 percent to 89 percent across different organizations. In the United States, Patricia Ingraham and colleagues document a wide range of variations in management and performance across federal government agencies.[30] Even among private sector firms, a large empirical literature documents "persistent performance differences" among firms producing identical products in the same market, as Robert Gibbons and Rebecca Henderson summarize and theorize.[31]

Taken together, these studies demonstrate that while forces external to organizations (history, politics, geography, etc.) might encourage or inhibit bureaucratic performance to some degree, they do not fully explain it. This finding is a hopeful one for reform efforts in that it suggests that internal management processes also play an important role in determining organizational performance— and thus that reforms that find a way to succeed in improving management might also be able to improve overall performance.

• • •

This chapter has sought to provide a conceptual and empirical starting point for this book's study of systemic, performance-oriented civil service reforms.

To do so, it zoomed in to the levels of individuals, teams, and organizations and introduced the language of verifiable and nonverifiable—formal and informal—actions and processes to characterize what civil servants do and what it means to do it well. It also provided empirical evidence to illustrate and support this view of work in public organizations.

What this chapter hasn't done is attempt to provide any answers to the question of how governments should design and implement reforms. Rather, the point of this chapter is to better frame the goal of (and key challenge for) performance-oriented reforms to provide a strong foundation for the subsequent parts of the book. The four chapters in part II will thus aim to document and explain the track record of such reforms across the six governments covered in this book. Part III will then turn toward trying to provide an answer, generating a theory of organizational change and system reform that is informed by the evidence from part II and that builds on the foundations laid in this chapter. With this conceptual framework in mind, then, let's proceed to part II.

PART II

Understanding
Patterns of Reform

3

What Does Reform Look Like? Mapping Reform Efforts over Time

This chapter, like the book as a whole, focuses mainly on describing big-picture patterns in reform design and implementation that repeatedly recur across countries and time periods. But before we look at these broader patterns, it might be helpful to delve into the story of a single reform: Zambia's Public Service Capacity Building Program (PSCAP), which began in 2000. PSCAP was neither remarkably successful nor unsuccessful, but it did exemplify several of the most common features of reforms around the continent.

To understand PSCAP, we first need to know a bit about the context in which it was designed. PSCAP was Zambia's second major effort at civil service reform since the country's return to multiparty democracy in 1991. Zambia's first effort—the Public Service Reform Programme (PSRP, 1993–1999)—had been shaped by two linked imperatives for the new government: first, the need to reduce the government wage bill in the context of fiscal retrenchment and structural adjustment; and second, the perception by President Frederick Chiluba's democratically elected administration that the existing civil service was bloated by unqualified patronage hires of former President Kenneth Kaunda under the preceding decades of single-party rule. These two imperatives together shaped the goal of the PSRP to create a "more efficient but smaller public sector."[1] This was to be achieved by two main strands of central government reforms: (1) laying off 25 percent of civil servants but imposing higher education requirements and improving pay and conditions for those who remained and (2) "link[ing] pay and performance in a way that would attract and retain skilled professionals in the civil service."[2]

The PSRP achieved neither of these goals, though it did take some steps in each direction. Many staff were laid off, but fewer than envisioned, and the actual cost savings were minimal. This was due to a combination of resistance from unions, the political pain of imposing mass redundancies, costly retrenchment payouts and lawsuits, and allegations of partisan bias in who was laid off. Even when older workers appointed by the Kaunda administration were fired, there was a widespread perception that (despite many being patronage appointees) these experienced staff actually had more practical know-how than the younger workers with more formal education who replaced them. As one civil servant working during that time explained, "We ended up with people that were qualified, but surprisingly not competent."[3] A new staff appraisal system was created to link performance to pay and promotion, but it was no more than a formality, with no actual rewards or sanctions attached. Other redundancies—both forced and voluntary—were targeted at "nonessential" staff, which resulted in hospitals that had surgeons but no mortuary attendants or staff to clear operating rooms, as well as boarding schools with no cooks. This caused service delivery to "hit a disaster level, especially when it came to the frontline services like health and education."[4]

PSCAP was born of these perceived failings. PSRP had been driven by the assumption that bringing in more qualified staff with better salary structures would improve civil servants' performance, but when this did not materialize, it was argued by some (including many civil servants) that perhaps they lacked the necessary equipment and resources to improve. PSCAP's mantra and core goal were, therefore, to improve individuals' and institutions' "capacity to deliver" (hence the emphasis on *capacity* in its name).[5] PSCAP had a total anticipated cost of US$45 million and was funded by a World Bank project loan of US$28 million, US$16 million from the UK Department for International Development (DFID) and other donors, and US$1 million from the government of Zambia.

The main vehicle for directly trying to increase capacity was a Performance Improvement Fund (PIF), to which service delivery organizations in priority areas could apply to fund discrete, quick-win projects to demonstrate that reforms could yield tangible results. PIF applications were formulated by the organization itself, and this bottom-up process led to several innovative ideas for projects such as mobile hospitals and mobile education labs, including a UN award for a grant addressing the scarcity of medical facilities for deliveries in the country's Copperbelt region. These PIFs were intended to be embedded within the broader organizational strategic plans that began to be developed under the PSRP, serving as a small-scale accelerant and demonstration of success.

But despite these initial successes, PIFs did not catalyze the broader impact they were intended to. Whereas the funds were meant to be targeted toward seven priority service delivery organizations, the World Bank reported that "in the early stages of the project, PIF funds were made widely available to all restructured ministries, regardless of whether they had a direct public service delivery orientation or not."[6] After a refocus on service delivery, an internal review of the PIF found that only fifteen of thirty-eight projects funded under the PIF had "an observable impact on service delivery," indicating "a disconnect between the service delivery and strategic planning basis for PIF funded projects and the projects actually funded."[7] Of the innovations introduced, reportedly only the mobile labs in education were sustained after the end of the project funding. Another study found that the PIF: "has not lived up to expectations. The logic of PIFs and quick wins was not sufficiently embraced by the MDAs [ministries, departments, and agencies]. PIFs were seen as supplementary financing to government allocations. As a consequence, most applications for PIF funding were inappropriate (for example, cars and computers), lacked both innovation and a focus on performance improvement, and were not linked to MDAs strategic plans."[8]

The perception that the PIFs became viewed mainly as a way to purchase equipment gave rise to a joke I heard from several people about PSCAP's acronym: that it stood for "please sir, can I have another Pajero," in reference to the 4×4 vehicle model popular with officials of government agencies (as well as with donor and NGO staff). At the same time, the severe spending restraints in place meant that there were real shortages of equipment within the government. As one former civil servant involved in designing and implementing the reforms explained, ministries would approach the implementing secretariat and say, "We are incapacitated because we don't have a vehicle," so there was actually some service delivery rationale for these purchases—even if there were also distortions of the PIF's intent.[9]

Alongside its organizational performance component, PSCAP also undertook a set of staffing and pay reforms following the PSRP. In reaction to the growing unpopularity of layoffs, PSCAP continued the organizational restructuring and associated retrenchments but reframed this as "rightsizing" rather than downsizing and did increase hiring in some areas, particularly in frontline social service delivery roles. Despite this rhetorical change of tack, staff numbers continued to decrease, with a net reduction of twenty-four thousand staff between 2000 and 2003. Although there were some hiring increases for teachers and nurses, ongoing fiscal challenges with overall payroll figures meant that staff strength was sometimes increased on paper (through notional approval for higher staff numbers), but financial clearance was not given to actually hire people, resulting in positions being left unfilled for many years.

At the same time, PSCAP also reiterated the PSRP's goal of establishing performance-linked incentives for individual civil servants. The government's *2002 Medium-Term Strategy for Enhancing Pay and Conditions of Service* ("the

Valentine report") was unequivocal about this: "The newly articulated pay policy should as much as possible, aim at explicitly linking pay to performance, signaling a major change in the incentive system and in performance expectations. Rewards and penalties are both vital for a well functioning incentive regime. . . . Meaningful performance incentives are a must." [10]

The government aimed to achieve this goal of instituting performance-linked incentives through two channels: the proper implementation of the Annual Performance Appraisal System (APAS) introduced during the latter stages of the PSRP reform for rank-and-file civil servants up to the level of director and the creation of performance contracts for permanent secretaries (bureaucratic heads of ministries).

With respect to APAS, PSCAP did not change the formal design of the system substantively but sought to actually attach incentives—such as differential pay increments, accelerated or delayed promotion, and meaningful sanctions—to the results of officers' APAS appraisals. This effort was not successful. External reviews in both 2005 and 2008 reported that there were no rewards or sanctions attached to the results of the APAS appraisal, with one report stating that "good performance is not rewarded while poor performance goes unpunished" and remarking that many employees do not even go through the appraisal process on an annual basis.[11] These faults are blamed not on the system itself, which is "adequately designed," but on the system's implementation and "low commitment of its users."[12] The second evaluation's overall assessment was that the APAS system "results in little individual or organizational performance improvement," and was devastatingly frank about the situation: "As time has passed the real purpose of the APAS report has become the justification of pay increments and promotions. This has led to the a [sic] view that completion of the form is a necessary evil to which one should devote as little time and thought as possible. The result in many instances is a report replete with inconsistencies, contradictions and very little assessment of performance that bears little relation to a real work plan and virtually none to the organisational and strategic plan."[13]

For more senior bureaucrats (permanent secretaries) who were not subject to the APAS system, PSCAP introduced a system of performance contracts that were intended to establish and measure organizational performance targets and link the renewal of permanent secretaries' contracts to these formal assessments. However, what ended up happening was that permanent secretaries were put onto fixed-term three-year contracts at the end of 2001 (rather than the permanent and pensionable civil servants they had been) but without meaningful setting of targets, assessments, or incentives. Permanent secretaries were willing to accept the temporary contracts because they promised a lucrative three years prior to retirement, and the arrangement was also "user-friendly" to politicians in that it gave them greater discretion and leverage over permanent secretaries.[14] However, permanent secretaries lacked not only annual targets but also basic job descriptions, so in practice, there was no formal linkage between performance and incentives. These problems were easily foreseeable, with a World Bank–funded consultancy reporting in 2002: "It is unclear at this point on what basis performance will be measured. What benchmarks will be used to objectively distinguish between levels of performance, particular[ly] since the MDAs have not completed the strategic planning process [that was also a component of PSCAP] and thus do not have clear performance targets."[15]

Taken together, these major components of the PSCAP reform—the Performance Improvement Fund, "rightsizing" redundancies, pay reform, the institutionalization of the APAS appraisal system, and the creation of performance contracts for permanent secretaries—fell short of the transformative impact on service delivery that they envisioned. The overall sentiment regarding the limited performance impacts of the PSRP and PSCAP reforms is well-captured by a 2008 review of Zambia's linked performance management reforms to date, which found that they resulted in "only marginal impact on the effectiveness and efficiency of the public service and result[ed] in little individual or organizational performance improvement."[16] PSCAP had initially been envisioned as a three-phase, thirteen-year program running from 2000 to 2013. As a result of these perceived shortcomings, however, PSCAP was terminated in 2005 at the end of phase one.

But PSCAP was only one reform among many in Zambia, and Zambia is only one of six countries whose reform histories are examined in this book. Let's step back now and look at the big picture of reform activity across all these countries based on the reform mapping described in chapter 1 and the appendix.

PATTERNS OF REFORM

This section asks and answers three descriptive questions about reforms:

1. How frequent have reform efforts been?
2. What has been the content of reforms (i.e., the structures, processes, or practices they have tried to introduce)?
3. How successful have reforms been?

How Frequent Have Reform Efforts Been?

Here's the simple answer to this question: There have been *a lot* of reform efforts, and they overlap with one another both in timing and substance. That said, defining and counting reforms is surprisingly difficult to do precisely. I'll talk through the evidence underlying this answer and discuss the challenges in quantifying it.

Figure 3.1 presents timelines of reform for each of the six countries. The top row lists the party and president in office during each year, the bottom rows list all the reforms that fit my definition that were underway in each country at each point in time, and the middle row lists what reform era (or eras) the many distinct reforms ongoing at any point in time can best be grouped into. Full country-by-country narratives of these reform histories are contained in the appendix.

In each country, there was almost always a reform underway in each year—usually several. We sometimes assume that civil service reforms are occasional upheavals with long periods of stagnation or that they are only initiated when political conditions are propitious. That might be true of the highest-profile reforms, but taking the approach of mapping out the universe of reforms—including minor, abortive, or little-known reforms—reveals that, in reality, new reform efforts were constantly being initiated in every country.

What's more, these reforms overlapped with one another in several ways, and the boundaries between them were unclear. For example, in Zambia, PSCAP was clearly the main reform ongoing between 2000 and 2005. Some of the pay and salary structure reforms were folded into PSCAP, while others—such as the Valentine report on pay policy and the creation of performance contracts for permanent secretaries—were not formally part of the PSCAP project but were designed and implemented with awareness of PSCAP and an aim to ensure coherence between them. Should they be counted as three different reforms or one? Or should the semi-independent subcomponents of PSCAP, such as the PIF and operationalization of the annual Performance Appraisal System (APAS), be separated from PSCAP as a whole and counted as reforms in their own right? In other words, did Zambia have one reform ongoing between 2000–2005, or three, or more? Should government-led reforms be counted as separate from the donor support projects that helped fund them—and does it matter if they have the same or different names or if the start and end dates align? Just looking at these timelines reveals not only the degree to which different reform efforts overlap with one another temporally (and thus are linked in planning and execution) but also the nonoverlaps of start and end dates (which hint at the less-than-full coherence of these efforts).

(a) Ghana

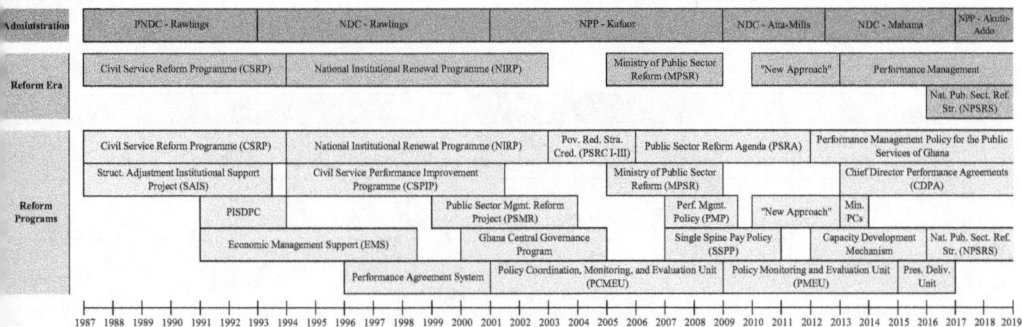

(b) Kenya

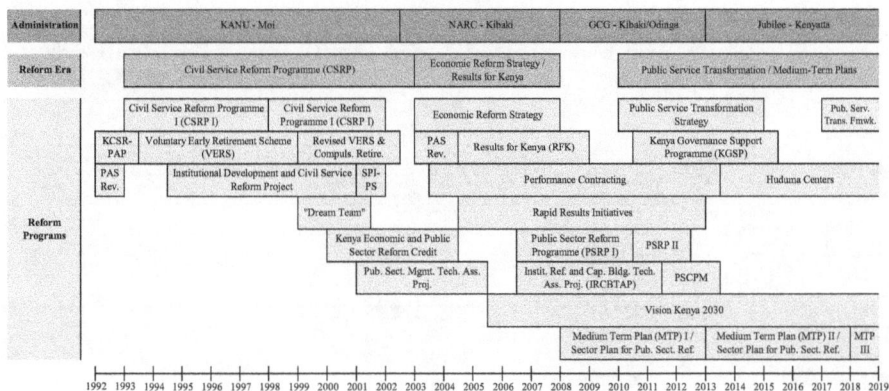

(c) Nigeria

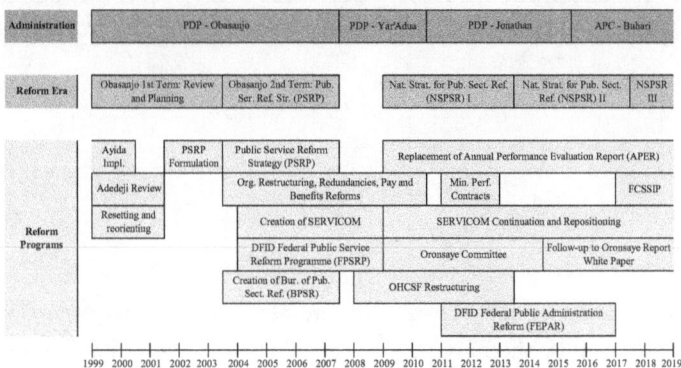

FIGURE 3.1 Timelines of Reform Efforts in Six Countries

Source: Author's synthesis. See appendix for more details and full names of each reform.

(d) Senegal

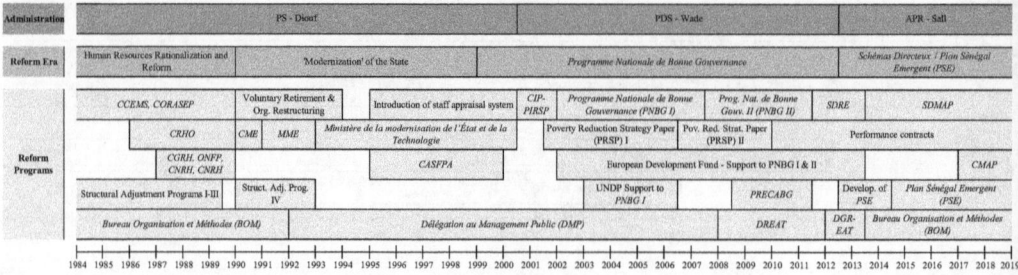

(e) South Africa

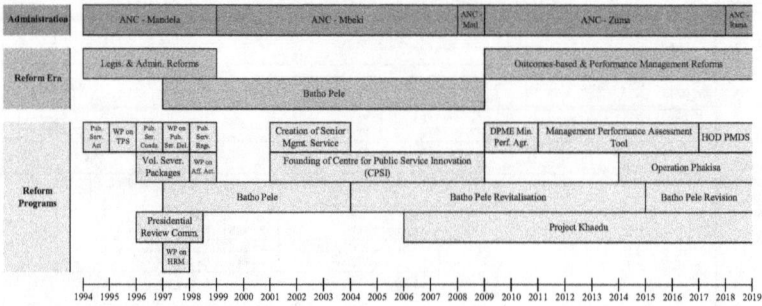

(f) Zambia

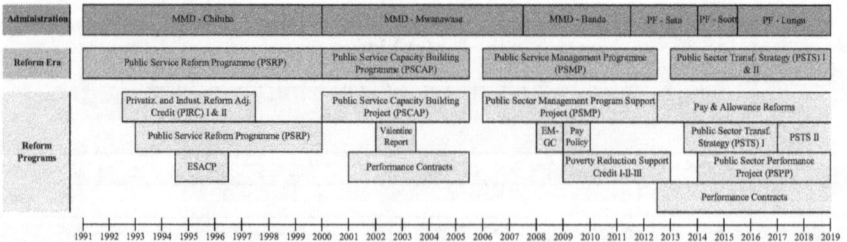

FIGURE 3.1 *(continued)*

The boundaries between reforms are blurry in another way: Each reform was influenced by the reforms that came before it. Take the example of Zambia's PSRP (1993–1999) and PSCAP (2000–2005). In some instances, this path dependence reflected reformers' efforts to build on prior reforms. In Zambia, for example, PSRP designed and introduced the APAS system; PSCAP then tried to make it function as envisioned. But in other instances, reformers did the opposite and deliberately tried *not* to connect their efforts to what had come before in an effort to avoid their perceived failings and being associated with them. Indeed, PSCAP's core approach and rhetoric—focusing on supporting bureaucrats' capacity to deliver—was deliberately chosen in reaction to the widespread perception that PSRP had negatively affected service delivery. Other elements of PSCAP combined both types of path dependence, such as the continuation of PSRP's efforts to rationalize staff numbers and allocation but with the rebranded goal of "rightsizing" rather than "downsizing." Thus, while PSRP and PSCAP are clearly distinct reform efforts in many ways, they are also inextricably linked. So no matter how one decides to aggregate the various reforms ongoing in a country at any given point in time, any analysis of these reforms has to take into account that none of them are actually independent from the others.

There is also the question of where to draw the line in terms of when a reform comes into existence. Is it when it gets an official plan and acronym, when a press conference announcing it is held, when the first internal brainstorming meeting happens, or when a particular idea first crosses someone's mind? And how should we treat reforms that got discussed but, for various reasons, were never formally adopted? For example, one civil servant in Ghana told of an idea to create a senior management service in the mid-2000s that was discussed and researched internally but never saw the light of day due to opposition from the civil service union.[17] Similarly, some types of reform efforts—those that generate news coverage, official documents, and academic studies—are more likely to be recognized as reforms both by researchers as well as public servants themselves and thus may be more likely to appear in the data. These measurement questions are further complicated by the possibility that the same factors that determine whether a reform gets launched might also be related to its success, so from a causal inference perspective, even the existence of a reform case to analyze is endogenous. So the sample of reforms that we have to count and study is almost certainly biased in many ways despite the numerous methodological steps I took to recognize and minimize the extent of this bias (detailed in the appendix).

In compiling reform histories, these dilemmas repeated themselves across each country and each time period, as there were multiple interpretations possible of the definition and measurement criteria I set out in chapter 1. In the end, I opted for a balance between consistency of approach across all six countries and representing reform histories in a way that would be qualitatively recognizable to individuals who worked in each civil service during these reforms. Representing both individual reforms (rectangles in the bottom rows of figure 3.1) and overall reform eras (rectangles in the middle rows) on the timeline also hints at the multiple possible ways of viewing these reforms. All in all, from an analytical perspective, these reform efforts are best regarded as semi-independent cases with blurry boundaries between them, which makes it problematic to attempt precise quantitative coding or analysis of the data.

With those caveats in mind, it's still useful to give some kind of numerical answer to the question of how frequent reforms are. The simplest and most true-to-reality way to do this is to count the number of individual reform efforts (bottom row rectangles) represented on the timeline. Doing so yields a figure of 131 reforms across the 173 country-years captured on the timeline. That equates to a new reform effort being launched in each country once every 1.3 years, on average. In some ways, this actually understates the amount of reforms undertaken since many of these efforts are actually bundles of multiple changes packaged under the same banner—as the next section discusses.

Figure 3.2 shows the distribution of the number of active reforms that were simultaneously ongoing during all country-years in the data—the number ranged from zero up to nine.[18] The modal number of reforms active in any given year across the whole sample was four.

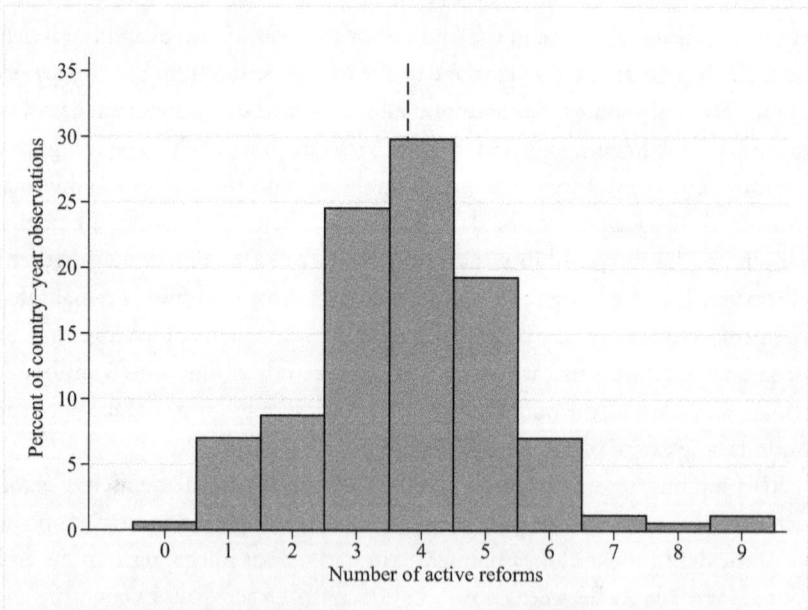

FIGURE 3.2 Number of Active Civil Service Reforms Per Country-Year

Source: Author's calculations.

Choosing different ways of aggregating and linking reforms could give lower (or even higher) answers. But by any measure, civil service reform efforts in these countries were very frequent, with significant (but not perfect) overlap with one another.

What Has Been the Content of These Reform Efforts?

These reform efforts encompassed a wide range of attempted changes to structures, processes, and practices in their respective civil services. But the pattern that emerges most clearly from an analysis of the content of these reforms is that governments frequently tried to implement similar types of reforms over and over again.

To see this, let's begin by looking at the content of the reforms implemented across the four major eras of reform in Zambia, as represented by table 3.1. For each cluster of reforms, I classified if it attempted to introduce each of ten different types of change, split across five different categories.

The first content category, individual-level performance management, captures reforms that tried to link some measure of individual performance to some type of extrinsic reward or sanction. Individual-level performance management reforms fall into two categories: those aimed at rank-and-file civil servants (like Zambia's APAS) and those aimed at senior leadership and managers (like Zambia's performance contracts under PSCAP).

The second category, organizational management or capacity, captures reforms that aimed to use organizational reviews, routines, or resources to improve collective performance at an organizational level. One subcategory of these was performance improvement funds established for specific, demand-driven reform activities—like Zambia's PIF. The other subcategory constitutes a range of non-resource-related performance improvement measures. The only example of these in Zambia was the ministry-level strategic planning system put in place under PSCAP, which aimed to create clear and consistent organization-level work plans that could be cascaded down to inform the individual-level performance management systems. Other examples in other countries included the system of organizational performance reviews and performance improvement plans created in Ghana under its Civil Service Performance Improvement Programme (CSPIP) or the organizational service delivery evaluations undertaken by Nigeria's SERVICOM for service delivery organizations in Nigeria. (For brevity, in the main text of the book, I will often refer to reform episodes without describing them in

TABLE 3.1 Content of civil service reforms in Zambia

	Public Service Reform Prog. (PSRP), 1993–1999	Public Service Capacity Building Project (PSCAP), 2000–2005	Public Service Mgmt. Prog. (PSMP), 2006–2011	Public Service Transf. Prog. (PSTS) I & II, 2013–
Individual performance mgmt.				
Leadership performance agreements		✓		✓
Individual staff appraisal & performance management	✓	✓	✓	✓
Org. mgmt. and capacity				
Org. reviews/ perf. improv. plans/ perf. mgmt.		✓		
Performance improvement funds		✓		
Service delivery-focused reforms				
Client-focused reforms			✓	
Sector-driven reforms				
Salaries and structures				
Staff redundancies & org. restructuring	✓	✓	✓	
Pay regrading/ reform	✓	✓	✓	✓
Other reforms				
Cross-government coordination				✓
Other				

Source: Author's synthesis based on document review and interviews.

full. In such instances, interested readers can refer to the relevant country narrative history in the appendix for more extensive details and evidence.)

The third category, service-delivery-focused reforms, captures two types of systemic reforms that aimed directly at improving service delivery (as opposed to upstream management issues of personnel and operations). The first subcategory, client-focused reforms, is exemplified by Zambia's effort to establish service charters that published information on services available, along with standards and timelines for accessing them, under its Public Service Management Programme (the successor project to PSCAP). Another example is Senegal's Comité d'allègement et de simplification des formalités et procédures administratives (CASPFA, Committee on Alleviating and Simplifying Rules and Administrative Procedures) in the late 1990s, which aimed to simplify procedures for the public to access services (as well as internal administrative processes). The second subcategory, which I dub sector-driven reforms, captures reform efforts that are systemic (in that they are centralized and span multiple sectors simultaneously) but have some inbuilt cross-sector variation in exactly what they aim to do. An example is Ghana's New Approach from 2009–2012, in which the secretary to the cabinet launched a coordinated push to get ministers to come up with sectoral strategies to improve service delivery in a number of priority sectors, particularly related to job creation and food security. As is evident from these examples, this category is relatively more internally diverse than the previous two categories.

The fourth category, reforms to salaries and structures, captures efforts both to downsize or "rightsize" staff numbers (as in Zambia's PSRP and PSCAP) as well as efforts to restructure pay scales and compensation systems (as also happened under PSRP and PSCAP). The former subcategory was often motivated by both fiscal savings and performance improvement, usually with some version of a "smaller but more efficient" logic, and can also include or be driven by organizational consolidation (as in Kenya's effort to reduce the number of government ministries under its Civil Service Reform Programmes and Economic Recovery Strategy in the 1990s and 2000s). The latter category was often driven by a desire to decompress salary scales—i.e., to increase the pay gap between junior and senior civil servants—as a way to indirectly incentivize performance by increasing the pay increments associated with promotion. Such reforms were also often intended to help retain more senior and more skilled staff, or to rationalize compensation by bringing off-salary benefits and allowances into core salary.

As its name indicates, the fifth category of reforms (other reforms) is a residual category for other types of systemic performance-oriented reforms that fit my definition of reform but did not fall into one of the above categories. One set of these is cross-government coordination reforms, which aimed not to improve the performance of organizations in isolation but to better coordinate their activities, particularly around key priorities. Examples of this include Ghana's repeated efforts to establish and reestablish this function with its Policy Coordination, Monitoring, and Evaluation Unit (PCMEU, 2001–2008), Policy Monitoring and Evaluation Unit (PMEU, 2009–2014), and Presidential Delivery Unit (2015–2016). A final residual subcategory captures all other reforms, ranging from Nigerian SERVICOM's creation of a weekly radio "help desk" program for service clients to air complaints and help resolve issues to South Africa's creation of a Center for Public Service Innovation to Senegal's creation of ministry-level specialists and units to coordinate training and personnel management in each organization (*conseillers en ressources humaines et organisation*, or human resource and organization councilors, and *cellules de gestion des ressources humaines*, human resource management units).

It's useful to get a sense of the relative frequency of each type of reform, but attempting to count and aggregate in this way requires many of the same caveats as the reform number calculations above. The boundaries between reforms (and thus the number of efforts) are unclear and subject to interpretation, and content categories and subcategories are each internally diverse and not necessarily mutually exclusive of other categories. While there's no perfect way to do it, the simplest and most transparent way to do so is simply to count the number of reforms or reform clusters that attempt each subcategory of reform, as per the six country-level reform content tables in the appendix.[19] The absolute number of these reform efforts could be counted in various ways, but our main interest here is in the relative frequency of each type, which is less sensitive to different approaches to classifying and aggregating reforms.

With those caveats again in mind, table 3.2 sums up the number of efforts to introduce each subcategory of reform across all six countries. The most frequent are individual performance management reforms (thirty-four instances), followed by salary and organizational structure reforms (thirty) and service delivery-focused reforms (twenty-seven). (Note that the aggregation of these reforms for the purpose of qualitatively representing content focus, taken from the reform content tables in the appendix, is different than the aggregation used for the rough estimate of reform frequency given above, so these figures on reform content aren't directly comparable.)

What's perhaps more interesting, though, is the frequency with which countries repeatedly attempt to implement the same type of reform over and over again. This pattern is most striking for individual-level performance management reforms: across my study period, and subject to the above caveats about counting and aggregation, these were attempted three times in Nigeria, four times in

TABLE 3.2 Content of reforms across countries

Type of Reform	Ghana	Kenya	Nigeria	Senegal	South Africa	Zambia	TOTAL
Individual performance mgmt.							
Leadership performance agreements	4	2	1	1	4	2	14
Individual staff appraisal & performance management	6	4	2	3	1	4	20
Org. mgmt. and capacity							
Org. reviews/ perf. improv. plans/ perf. mgmt.	1	3	3	2	3	1	13
Performance improvement funds	1	0	0	0	0	1	2
Service delivery-focused reforms							
Client-focused reforms	3	3	2	3	2	1	14
Sector-driven reforms	2	2	3	2	4	0	13
Salaries and structures							
Staff redundancies & org. restructuring	2	2	3	5	1	3	16
Pay regrading/ reform	3	2	2	1	2	4	14
Other reforms							
Cross-government coordination	3	2	2	1	1	1	10
Other	0	0	3	5	1	0	9

Source: Author's calculations.

Senegal, five times in South Africa, six times each in Kenya and Zambia, and ten times in Ghana. This pattern also appears with many other types of reforms, too—for example, Ghana attempted to introduce ministerial service charters as part of CSPIP (1994–2001), the Public Sector Reform Agenda (2006–2011), and the National Public Sector Reform Strategy (from 2016). These attempts to implement the same reform repeatedly hint at the less-than-full success of prior efforts to do so.

But while this is the most striking pattern in reform content, it is not the story of every reform. There are also many cases of governments trying to implement a reform once and then dropping it, as well as governments including a particular component in repeated reforms as a way to institutionalize and sustain it. Examples of the latter include the sustained use of Rapid Results Initiatives in Kenya across successive reform waves, Ghana's sustained use of Chief Directors Performance Agreements in the 2010s (in contrast to its failure to do so in the 1990s and 2000s), and Senegal's sustained progress in digitization of service delivery since the 1990s.

These patterns and variations in reform content naturally question how successful these reform efforts have been, to which we now turn.

How Successful Have Reforms Been?

The most striking observation that emerges from examining reforms' record of success is how little apparent variation there is: Not a single reform succeeded at achieving all its goals, but almost all achieved some of them. There is, of course, some variation across reforms in the degree to which each succeeded and in what ways, and I initially expected that this book would be focused on trying to measure and explain this variation. However, the most salient descriptive fact about reforms is not how large the gap between the most and least successful reforms is but how small it appears to be. Indeed, nearly every reform can be viewed both as a partial failure and as a partial success.

This pattern is difficult to show quantitatively because trying to formally code or quantify reform success is even more fraught than the (already heavily caveated) summary figures I presented above about reform frequency and content. Success for civil service reforms can only be judged against expectations, but these expectations might be too high or too low. This means that a very ambitious reform could achieve a lot but look like a failure, whereas a half-hearted reform with easy targets could get closer to achieving them despite changing little. In-depth qualitative research on reform efforts can often give a good (if sometimes contested) sense of both the ambition of the goals of the reform as well as its actual achievements of the reform, but trying to codify this into a dataset that could be summarized or analyzed quantitatively would do too much violence to this messy reality.

Instead of using quantitative summaries, though, we can illustrate that there is surprisingly little variation in achievement of goals by comparing two reforms: one that was perceived as relatively successful but still fell short of its goals, and another that was perceived as relatively unsuccessful but still achieved some improvements. An example of the former is Ghana's adoption of a Performance Improvement Facility (PIF) under the Civil Service Performance Improvement Programme (1994–2001), while an example of the latter is Zambia's adoption of a Performance Improvement Fund (PIF) under PSCAP (2000–2005) that I described above. The design of the interventions in each case was very similar: the creation of a discretionary fund administered by a central reform institution and financed by a donor grant, to which individual ministries could submit proposals for rapid disbursement of small amounts of money to meet the costs of innovative, demand-driven service delivery improvement initiatives, linked to a larger process of strategic organizational planning and performance review.

But whereas Zambia's PSCAP was widely seen as donor-driven, generated jokes about how it paid mostly for cars, and was terminated early by its donor partner, Ghana's CSPIP was almost universally seen as "homegrown" and driven from within the government itself by a charismatic head of civil service.[20] It established a deeply participatory and thorough performance review and improvement planning process that linked closely to the PIF, was generally seen to be generating positive impacts, and its donor partner wanted to extend it for a second phase.[21] Ghana's PIF under CSPIP was carefully administered by a highly motivated team that undertook extensive scrutiny and monitoring of each application and disbursement.[22] Internal records of the first years of Ghana's PIF showed that the disbursement committee not only applied a high quality filter to applications (funding only one of the initial five received) but also sought to remedy these perceived problems by undertaking a set of workshops for ministries to help them improve their conceptualization of and applications for these funds.[23] Ministries took this seriously and reportedly began competing with one another to access the PIF.[24] Nana Agyekum-Dwamena, who served as secretary of the PIF's disbursement committee as a young civil servant during the late 1990s, recalled applications from local governments for containers to put rubbish in as part of sanitation drives and giving the Passport Office funds for a generator so it could work through power outages. While the CSPIP reform was curtailed by changes in political and bureaucratic leadership after 2000, during its years in full swing, it represented something close to an ideal scenario for serious, innovative, government-driven civil service reform.

But Ghana's PIF still fell short of its goals. One review found that "although many organizations duly prepared their performance improvement plans and were rewarded with small grants, in a larger sense little overall improvement in performance resulted."[25] Agyekum-Dwamena also highlighted the mismatch between having funds available to support about ten small projects per year through the PIF and having about seventy organizational performance improvement plans waiting to be implemented at the height of CSPIP.[26] Another officer said that the project's five-year review found that, while the project was delivering its anticipated outputs, it was failing to achieve the outcomes envisioned for the PIF.[27]

At the same time, Zambia's PIF under PSCAP was far from a total failure. The program was heavily criticized for funding mainly asset purchases, but as one of its administrators explained, there were also real needs for computers, cars, and other logistical tools in many cases.[28] It also paid for some innovative projects that won international recognition and were sustained beyond the project's lifespan. And while PSCAP's internal review criticized the PIF because only fifteen of thirty-eight projects funded under the PIF had "an observable impact on service delivery,"[29] one could also take the glass-half-full perspective that the PIF managed to have observable impacts in fifteen different areas of service delivery. Though it fell far short of its expectations, it wasn't as if nothing was achieved by Zambia's PIF.

These two patterns were not restricted to PIFs as a reform category. Rather, they repeated themselves across the other types of reforms I studied: (1) reforms didn't all fail, but they did all fall short of fully achieving their goals; and (2) some reforms were more successful than others, but these distinctions were narrower and more ambiguous than one might expect. These patterns were also consistent across countries—it's simply not the case that reforms were successful in some countries and unsuccessful in others. One veteran of many reform efforts reflected that reforms have been about 60 percent successful,[30] for example, while another commented that "the reforms were not a total failure, but they did not achieve the transformation that was expected."[31] (For those who are interested, the country-by-country reform histories in the appendix give more details on the successes and shortcomings of each reform episode and reform era in each country.)

This pattern of reforms falling short of their goals is not restricted to Africa. Indeed, much of the literature on civil service reform in OECD countries has remarked on similar patterns in these contexts.[32] A classic article titled "Why Civil Service Reforms Fail" by Charles Polidano begins: "Most reforms in government fail. They do not fail because, once implemented, they yield unsatisfactory outcomes. They fail because they never get past the implementation stage at all. They are blocked outright or put into effect only in tokenistic, half-hearted fashion."[33]

I don't mean to imply that the patterns or causes of reform outcomes are the same everywhere. This literature should instead act as a caution to the common tendency outside (and sometimes even inside) African governments to assume that disappointing reform results must be due to specific challenges of administration or politics in Africa. This assumption can lead us to seek out explanations that mainly pertain to the context rather than to the difficulty of changing performance in large bureaucratic systems more generally. I won't attempt to explain here why we observe these patterns, as that is (part of) the job of the next two chapters. But from a purely descriptive standpoint, the story of reform success is clear: Every reform fell short of its goals, but reforms were not all complete failures, and most reforms did achieve something.

DRIVERS OF REFORM

The final question this chapter addresses is: What actors and factors shaped the timing and design of reforms? I consider the evidence for three potential explanations: politics, donors, and ideas.

Politics

One set of theories about what drives civil service reform centers around the role of national political leaders and dynamics. For example, scholars like Mai Hassan have shown how political leaders manipulate the posting of senior bureaucrats for their own political advantage, and Sylvester Obong'o has examined how resistance by politicians to reforms that would reduce their patronage powers—such as redundancies and greater professionalization of hiring and promotion powers— explains much of Kenya's history of failing to implement reforms.[34] Work by Daniel Appiah and Abdul-Gafaru Abdulai and by Frank Kwaku Ohemeng and Felix K. Anebo also highlight the role of electoral cycles that lead to leadership turnover and policy discontinuities as a factor in disrupting the continuity of reforms.[35]

Within my reform data, I found many examples of reforms that were interrupted or otherwise went unimplemented due to these dynamics but also many counterexamples and patterns that are not well explained by these theories. The picture that emerges is one in which these and other political factors play important roles but nonetheless are not fully determinative of the timing, content, and implementation patterns of reforms.

With respect to the idea that politicians might resist fully implementing politically painful reforms, there are, of course, numerous examples of this both in secondary evidence and from my interviews. However, these examples were heavily concentrated within a single category of reforms: those that related to downsizing employee numbers and/or reducing the number of ministries, such as Zambia's PSRP, Kenya's CSRP, or Nigeria's Oronsaye Committee on Rationalizing the Structure of the Federal Government. This makes sense, given that these reforms directly threaten the livelihoods of urban elites and middle classes, some of whom may be political supporters, and threaten to restrict the number of patronage appointments politicians can dole out both at the highest level (e.g., ministers) and at the frontlines (e.g., teachers, drivers, cleaners).

But the reasons why politicians might object to the other categories of reforms, such as the use of organizational performance reviews, one-stop service centers for clients, or policy coordination units, are less obvious. If anything, political leaders generally stand to gain from improvements in service delivery, and there are numerous examples of senior political leaders and their advisors being strong and proactive advocates of these types of reforms. Examples of such full-throated support at the highest political levels for service delivery-oriented civil service reforms include the Economic Reform Strategy and Results for Kenya initiatives from 2003–2007 under President Kibaki, South Africa's Batho Pele initiative from 1997 under President Mandela, and Ghana's Public Sector Reform Agenda from 2006 under President Kufuor. Self-interested political opposition certainly helps explain the failings of some types of reforms but is not a universal explanation for them.

There is also a second category of reforms that sometimes fall victim to opposition from politicians but for which the politics are more nuanced: individual performance-linked incentives. As I discuss in more depth in the next chapter, senior political leaders typically support these systems in the abstract, and there are even examples of presidents choosing to introduce them for their ministers in Nigeria, Senegal, and South Africa. However, the implementation of these systems generates costs both for politicians and managers that often lead to their abandonment or nonimplementation. So while they are also a type of reform for which political considerations turn out to be very relevant, their politics can't be boiled down to a matter of crude support or opposition from politicians.

What of the role of leadership transitions that result in the discontinuation of reforms initiated under the previous leader? There are certainly some examples of reforms that correspond to political cycles in this way: the high-profile Economic Reform Strategy (2003–2007) that started under President Kibaki's administration in Kenya, President Obasanjo's launching of the Public Service Reform Strategy in 2003 shortly after winning a second term in office, President Zuma's adoption of Ministerial Performance Agreements on taking office in 2009, and so on. But there are also many examples of reforms that span changes in political administrations, such as Ghana's Single Spine Pay Policy reform (initiated under President Kufuor, implemented under President Atta-Mills), Kenya's continued use of Rapid Results Initiatives and Performance Contracts (initiated by President Kibaki, continued throughout the Grand Coalition Government with Prime Minister Odinga), or Nigeria's continued effort to reform its Annual Performance Evaluation Report system (spanning the administrations of Presidents Yar'Adua, Jonathan, and Buhari). In other cases, a reform appears to have been discontinued and a new one initiated, but the actual content was maintained. For instance, President Wade's administration in Senegal had developed the Schéma Directeur de la Réforme de l'Etat (SDRE, State Reform Master Plan) in 2011 but lost elections in 2012. Under President Sall, it was relaunched in 2013 as the Schéma Directeur de Modernisation de l'Administration Publique (SDMAP, Public Administration Modernization Master Plan), with verbatim identical components and summary diagram.[36] So while there is some evidence to support the idea that leadership turnover can undermine reform progress, there are also plenty of counterexamples.

The example of Senegal's retaining the content of the SDRE under the SDMAP—despite the SDRE having been designed during the administration of a political opponent—illustrates another important observation about the politics of systemic civil service reforms: Many reforms deal with relatively dry and obscure administrative rules and processes that do not correspond to existing political cleavages and inspire little political mobilization. Mass layoffs are highly politicized, but the finer points of organizational performance reviews or internal structures of service delivery agencies tend to be lost not just on voters but also on most politicians. A large proportion of the existing research on the politics of reform focuses on highly politicized types of reform precisely because they are the most visible and, in some ways, are the most attractive to study, but examining the broader universe of reform initiatives pursued by countries also

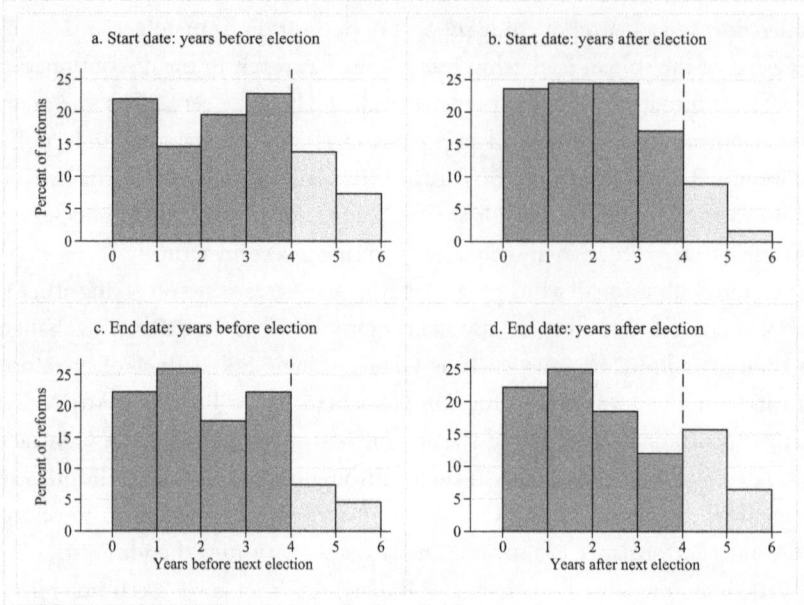

a. Start date: years before election

b. Start date: years after election

c. End date: years before election

d. End date: years after election

Years before next election

Years after next election

FIGURE 3.3 Comparing Reform Cycles to Electoral Cycles

Source: Author's calculations.

reveals many reforms for which political factors were less salient or were focused more on the relatively mundane workplace politics that exist in any large organization anywhere in the world.

Can we detect any general patterns with respect to how reform cycles do (or do not) coincide with electoral cycles? One way to do this is to compare the timing of the start and end of reforms with the dates of elections in each country. Figure 3.3 does this by showing (a) how many years before the next election each reform started; (b) how many years after the last election each reform started; (c) how many years before the next election each reform ended; and (d) how many years after the last election each reform started.[37] This has some methodological challenges and limitations as a test of the impact of political cycles on reforms, but if political cycles are a dominant factor in determining reform cycles, we should see at least some visual evidence of it in these graphs.

There is no obvious pattern of reform timing with respect to elections on any of these graphs. (The lower numbers of reforms after year four of each graph are driven by the fact that most gaps between elections are not that long due to shorter electoral cycles and deaths in office, so those are drawn in a lighter shade.)

Although there are certainly cases of reforms being initiated or terminated due to leadership transitions and political cycles, in the aggregate, we see little evidence that political cycles are the main factor driving reforms.[38]

This is not to say that political factors don't play an important role in driving some aspects of the design and implementation of civil service reforms. They obviously do, and the reform histories in the appendix highlight numerous instances when reforms were driven or undermined by political imperatives— indeed, political factors often impelled reform while simultaneously undercutting its implementation. But political incentives on their own are only part of the explanation for the broader patterns we observe.

Donors

A great deal of research has explored how reforms in Africa (and elsewhere in the Global South) have been driven by the incentives and dynamics of international donor institutions and their interactions with national governments. To highlight just a few examples from this extensive literature: Nicholas van de Walle describes how African governments in the 1980s and 1990s strategically avoided implementing reforms that international financial institutions demanded of them in order to access loans and grants as part of structural adjustment programs;[39] Matt Andrews writes of international donors ignoring local context by naïvely transplanting "best practice" reform models and of developing countries "adopting reforms as signals" in order "to garner short-term support from the international community";[40] Rosina Foli and Frank Kwaku Ohemeng argue that reforms often fail because international bureaucrats in donor institutions do not adequately understand local contexts and operate according to different logics than recipient governments do;[41] Mark Buntaine and colleagues find that donors' institutional reform projects often choose "shallow" targets related to what the reformed institutions should look like rather than targets related to effectiveness or service delivery outcomes because these are more attractive both to donor agencies and country governments;[42] Tunji Olaopa attributes reforms' focus on measurable short-term gains over more meaningful but longer-term behavioral changes to donors' need to "show quick results to convince their domestic constituents";[43] and many studies have examined the role that international institutions play in diffusing norms, ideas, and reform fads around the world.[44]

These dynamics are all evident across the reforms in my data to varying extents. But both from documentary records and from interviews, it is equally clear that the activities and incentives of international donor agencies are only one factor among many in the design, implementation, and outcomes of these reforms.

One way to examine the limitations of donor influence is simply to count how many of the reforms I identified corresponded exactly to projects run by international donors. Of the 131 reforms in all six countries (using the counting methodology described above, with all its caveats), just thirty-one—under a quarter—were identified as projects by a donor organization like the World Bank, UK DFID, or UNDP. Some of these were generic omnibus loans or grants that included a civil service reform component (e.g., Senegal's Structural Adjustment Program IV, 1990–1992), others were donor projects that corresponded directly to a government reform policy in that they had the same or similar name, dates, and content (e.g., Kenya Civil Service Reform Programme II, 1998–2001), and others were standalone donor projects that funded government reform activities but had no directly analogous reform policy or program in government (e.g., DFID's Federal Public Administration Reform project in Nigeria, 2011–2016).

Of the remaining ninety-nine reforms, many—it's impossible to definitively say what fraction—had some financial support or technical assistance from donors. But many did not or only intermittently had it.[45] And while some of these reforms may have been designed in the shadow of donor influence or with an eye toward trying to attract funding or signal a commitment to reform, at the end of the day, these ninety-nine reforms were neither designed nor implemented by donor institutions. Reformers' choices may have been constrained by donor pressure or willingness to provide financial support, but governments were still the ones navigating these constraints and deciding whether and how to invite donor involvement.

Even among reforms that corresponded directly to donor funding projects, governments often exerted more agency than is typically assumed. At one end of this spectrum lie reforms like Ghana's Civil Service Performance Improvement Programme (CSPIP, 1994–2001), which was almost fully funded by UK DFID but was wholly designed and driven by reformers in the Office of the Head of Civil Service (OHCS). Indeed, OHCS had approached DFID after rejecting a new project offer from the World Bank that wanted OHCS to continue the cost-cutting and downsizing focus of the preceding years. This "homegrown" approach to reform within the framework of a donor-financed project was facilitated by a strong head of civil service with a clear reform vision as well as progressive thinking by DFID staff "who bought into our methodology" and gave OHCS a "free hand" to formulate the reform.[46]

At the other end of the spectrum lie reforms like Kenya's Civil Service Reform Programme (CSRP, 1993–1997 and 1998–2001) and Zambia's Public Service

Reform Programme (PSRP, 1993–1999). These reforms were (and mostly still are) widely perceived to have been designed and driven by donors and bore many of the hallmarks of donor-driven reforms: direct correspondence of the reform name to a donor project, majority donor funding of activities, donor pressures for downsizing of staff and regrading of salary scales to increase inequality between the highest- and lowest-paid officers, and the adoption of internationally legiti- mated reform instruments like performance-linked incentives.

But interviews with some of the civil servants who were involved in the design and implementation of these reforms reveal a more nuanced picture. One civil servant who had worked in the Zambian Management Development Division, which was the lead institution within government for the PSRP, emphasized that within his team, there was both a recognized need for and commitment to change and that they insisted on government staff being at the forefront of both design and implementation (despite occasional involvement from consultants).[47] In his view, the donor conditionalities that were in place were a kind of backstop to ensure that the reforms were implemented, but he and his colleagues felt like they owned the reforms.

Similarly, most observers perceived Kenya's CSRP and the Kenya Civil Ser- vice Reform Programme and Action Plan that laid the foundations for the CSRP as donor-driven, and the CSRP itself was a largely donor-funded program.[48] But while fiscal crisis and donor dependence did drive President Moi to take actions (such as compulsory redundancies and reduction of the number of ministries) that were half-heartedly implemented at best, many senior public servants were also concerned about the country's trajectory and saw a need for reform.[49] When asked whether the CSRP was donor-driven, for instance, one former civil servant closely involved in implementing the CSRP replied:

> No, the Civil Service Reform Programme and the Action Plan was actually put together by civil servants. . . . We did have a few people we would share our thoughts with. One of them of course was at that time the Swedish government, there was an officer who would come and meet with us quite regularly. I think it was only that person, because the other times we would then meet maybe after a quarter just for the UN basket[-fund] people to find out how we're progressing and how we're using available funds. But they did not direct where those funds should go.[50]

When I asked another civil servant involved in several reforms in Ghana in the 1990s and 2000s whether they were donor-driven, he first replied, "Reforms are almost always donor-driven," but then proceeded to explain that there was agreement across the board that reforms were needed and that donors didn't bring their own agenda and tell countries to "take it," with the details of reforms instead being a product of mutual discussion."[51]

The idea that African governments exert agency in their negotiations with international donors is a theme of the literature on aid more generally. For example, Folashadé Soulé-Kohndou shows how bureaucrats in Benin find ways to overcome asymmetrical power relations (both with respect to Chinese donors and their own political leaders) in order to improve infrastructure project agreements.[52] Similarly, the contributors in Lindsay Whitfield's edited volume *The Politics of Aid: African Strategies for Dealing with Donors* emphasize the ways that African governments are far more than passive recipients of donor programs and contrast their approach to the donor-centric assumptions of much of the literature.[53]

In his research, Sylvester Obong'o presents yet another argument against centering the role of international donors in the analysis of reform implementation. He points out that Kenya—like many other African countries—launched several reform commissions in the two decades after independence that were endogenously driven and designed specifically for the Kenyan context, with little influence from international donors. However, the implementation record of these reform efforts was no better than for the more donor-influenced CSRP in the structural adjustment era of the 1990s. The poor implementation record of these reforms cannot, therefore, be explained simply by the presence or absence of donors.[54] Similarly, the presence of significant reform implementation issues in OECD countries (as noted above) as well as in countries that relied relatively less on donor funding (e.g., South Africa and Nigeria) suggests that while the dynamics of donor involvement do sometimes play important roles in reforms, they are far from the sole cause of implementation challenges.

One reason why a large share of research on civil service reform in Africa (and the Global South more broadly) focuses on international donors is likely that these reforms are usually more visible and easier to study than reforms where donors play less of a role. Donor institutions produce huge volumes of documents, reports, and project success metrics that are often made publicly available; donor staff are often easier for researchers to access than government officials; and the bureaucratic and cultural logics of donor institutions mean that they are often systematically trying to compare performance and learn lessons across many projects and countries, so they produce the kinds of data and processes that facilitate researchers' efforts. In conducting research for this book, my research assistants and I were able to identify nearly every reform in which donors were heavily involved from our initial review of existing donor project databases and secondary literature. In contrast, we only identified many government-initiated reforms in the course of interviews with civil servants because there was usually much less written documentation on them in the public domain. Studying reform by focusing only on donors or using only donor-produced data would have produced a partial, skewed picture of the reality of reform in each country.

A second possible reason why attention tends to focus on donors' role in driving reforms is that the normative and epistemological frameworks through which many observers view governments in Africa make it easier to attribute agency to international actors who are perceived to be intervening from "outside" the system, rather than to actors who are operating "within" it. Normatively, it is easy for many people (again, especially those based outside Africa) to see donors or NGOs as imperfect but well-intentioned actors altruistically trying to help solve problems, while African politicians or bureaucrats are seen as self-interested principals or agents embedded in a negative equilibrium they can't escape from. Methodologically, assuming that international donors are outside the system they're intervening into makes it possible to treat their interventions as exogenous (in certain cases at least) and thus able to be evaluated using social scientists' causal inference toolkit in a way that would be harder to justify for endogenously designed reforms. This is not to criticize researchers that do focus on the role of international donors—they are important actors, and studying them from various angles is important—but rather to advocate for the importance of also recognizing the agency and crucial role of reformers within government.

Ideas

What else, then, drives the actions of individuals and organizations working within these governments with respect to the design and implementation of civil service reforms? As in any organizational field, there are, of course, many possible factors: public service motivation, prestige, the search for legitimation from other members of their profession, desire to do their job well, and pecuniary self-interest. And all these played important roles to different extents for different people at different moments.

In the remainder of this chapter, though, I want to focus on one set of factors that emerged as especially powerful and pervasive in my interviews: reformers' own ideas, understandings, and mental models about the problems that reforms were trying to address and how they might do so. Civil servants were not just inert, passive actors responding to external pressures. They used their experience, training, and available evidence to come to understandings about what wasn't working in their institutions and why, and they formulated hypotheses and plans about how to fix it. These ideas and mental models thus guided the choices they made about what issues to prioritize, what reform instruments to adopt and try to implement, and how to navigate the external pressures, constraints, and opportunities within which they were working.

I went into this research expecting to hear stories from civil servants about how they were forced by donors or politicians to adopt reforms that they didn't believe in. These complaints did sometimes arise, but they turned out to be relatively infrequent. Instead, interviewees overwhelmingly highlighted the failure to implement reforms as the problem rather than the objectives or content of the reform per se. For instance, one rank-and-file civil servant in Ghana stated, "The objectives of [the] reform were good, but during the implementation of the reform, there is always an issue."[55] Similarly, a former civil servant who was instrumental to many of South Africa's reforms lamented, "The sad part was that [the reform] was all very well on paper, it just never translated into practice."[56] There were, as with public servants everywhere in the world, frequent laments about perceived political barriers to reform success, such as lack of political will or leadership turnover. But most of the reform ideas and directions themselves (with the partial exception of staff cuts or downsizing efforts linked to structural adjustment programs in the 1980s and 1990s) were broadly perceived by most interviewees as positive ones for the civil service—if only they could be implemented.

There were also numerous examples of reform leaders and ordinary civil servants speaking out in favor of reforms that had been adopted in ways that went above and beyond the standard level of support for government policies that public officials are expected to show in routine press conferences or meetings with donors. This was most evident through the direct engagement of reform leaders with academic research. To cite just a few of many examples, Ghana's then-Head of Civil Service, Robert Dodoo, authored a 1997 article in the academic journal *Public Administration and Development* on how the CSPIP reform was taking on the task of setting and measuring performance standards for organizations and institutions.[57] In 2006, Margaret Kobia (then Director of the Kenya Institute of Administration, later Chairperson of the Public Service Commission and Cabinet Secretary for the Ministry of Public Service, Youth and Gender Affairs) and Nura Mohammed presented a paper to the African

Association for Public Administration and Management on Kenya's experience with performance contracting, giving a detailed international history of the idea, how it came to be adopted in Kenya, and the successes and challenges of its implementation, based in part on survey research they had undertaken with Kenyan civil servants.[58] And Geraldine Fraser-Moleketi, South Africa's Minister of Public Service and Administration from 1999–2008, wrote a detailed and thoughtful master's thesis in 2006 documenting and analyzing South Africa's postapartheid reform journey.[59]

A number of interviewees expressed concern about uncritical transplantation of reform ideas from other countries into African contexts without appropriate adaptations. However, most civil servants I interviewed mainly expressed this as a criticism of "us" (i.e., civil servants) rather than "them" (i.e., donors). At the same time, many reformers in government were actively seeking out experience from the reform trajectories of other countries in Africa, elsewhere in the Global South, and in high-income countries. The process of formulating Kenya's dynamic and internally driven Results for Kenya program (2004–2008) included study visits to the UK, Sweden, and Canada, whose Results for Canadians program directly inspired the Results for Kenya name.[60] South Africa's Management Performance Assessment Tool (2011–2016) was inspired by Canada's Management Accountability Framework, which had been encountered during a study visit.[61] And several reforms in Zambia were modeled on or benchmarked against similar reforms in Ghana.[62] This view was expressed neatly by Robertson Nii Akwei Allotey—then acting Chief Director of Ghana's Ministry of Public Sector Reform, subsequently a Commissioner of the Public Service Commission—in a 2008 interview with Princeton University's Innovations for Successful Societies program:

> I would say that the—one cannot be an island, especially Ghana, cannot be an island at all. . . . Citizens' charters, for example, are good for everybody no matter where they are, Singapore, America, etc., because then it puts the responsibility on the organizations to perform, and Ghana has borrowed them, and we are working with that . . . So, it's nice to borrow, but at the same time, you adapt it to suit your circumstances, and that's what we are doing in Ghana here. We are also lucky, because other African countries come to Ghana to learn exactly what we are doing here and try to adapt it to what they have in their various countries. I've been very fortunate to have participated in conferences abroad, and I speak to the issues concerned, and they also are very keen to learn as to what we are doing here. So, it's more of sharing best practices and experiences. We are so welcome to that, because it helps us in a way. [63]

While adaptation of reform ideas to local contexts is always both challenging and important, the global diffusion of reform ideas is driven not just by uncritical mimicry or the imposition of "best practices" by donors as is sometimes assumed but also by a real desire on the part of civil servants to gain inspiration and learn lessons from other countries' experiences. The myriad ways that civil servants processed their experience and training, formulated plans and advocated for them, and consciously and critically sought to learn from other countries' experiences illustrate how important civil servants' own ideas about performance and reform were for the choices they made.

Having said that, I don't mean to suggest that the ideas of key reform actors in government were the sole drivers of reforms. Political incentives and constraints, as well as pressures from international donors, certainly helped shape the trajectory of reforms in each of the six countries I studied. And—at the risk of stating the obvious—civil servants often disagree among themselves about everything from how future reforms should be approached to the origins of past reforms.

But the reasons that I nevertheless emphasize the role of reformers' own ideas and agency are threefold. First, this theme emerged from my interviews far more strongly than would be indicated by much of the existing literature and theory. Second, failing to note this would do a disservice to the thought and dedication that so many public servants in these six countries and around the world have poured into reform efforts over the years. And third, if ideas and mental models do matter—even a little bit—then there is at least some scope for more evidence and new theory to help current and future generations of reformers better understand their institutions and formulate strategies for improving them. This is a hopeful perspective for reformers and researchers alike.

• • •

This chapter has aimed to distill the empirical richness of the detailed narrative histories in the appendix into a number of big-picture descriptive findings and trends. In doing so, it has covered a lot of ground, so let's briefly summarize the four key messages. First, all six countries undertook many reforms, and these reforms overlapped one another, so the picture was not one of occasional spurts of reform but of constant and interrelated reform efforts. Second, many of these reforms entailed repeated efforts to implement the same type of reform. Third, these reforms have universally fallen short of achieving their full expectations, but they were not all failures, and there were many meaningful successes. Fourth, political factors and donor involvement both contributed to shaping the adoption, design, implementation, and outcomes of reform, but so did the ideas, mental models, and agency of reformers within government.

The next two chapters turn to the task of describing two common mechanisms of reform—focusing on formal rules and structures (chapter 4) and approaching reform as a one-off intervention (chapter 5)—and analyzing how they led to the observed patterns of implementation and impact that this chapter has summarized. Both mechanisms were driven in part by structural factors but also in part because they corresponded to mental models of how bureaucracies work and how to improve them that are commonly held by civil servants, politicians, donors, and scholars alike. Understanding these two *mechanisms of failure* is a key part of explaining the track record of past reforms and of beginning to envision an alternative approach.

4

The "What" of Reform

Focusing on the Formal, Neglecting the Informal

I f you want civil servants to perform their duties better, why not reward people who perform well and punish people who perform badly? In the messy and complicated world of government bureaucracies, this intuitive and apparently simple proposition has motivated countless reforms around the world over the past several decades.

Indeed, the introduction of policies that attempted to link individual performance to some type of reward or sanction was the most common type of reform in the six countries studied in this book. There were thirty-four efforts to establish and/or operationalize such systems, both for rank-and-file civil servants as well as for senior-level leaders—just over a quarter of all reforms. These policies have also been popular elsewhere around the world.[1] In the Organisation for Economic Cooperation and Development (OECD) group of high-income countries, for instance, thirty-two of thirty-seven member states had some version of these policies in place for their senior managers as of 2019.[2]

But while individual-level performance-linked incentive policies hold an obvious appeal, among the reform efforts I studied, their track record of implementation was dismal. Of the thirty-four performance-linked incentive reform efforts in these countries, *zero* succeeded in sustainably delivering differentiated rewards and punishments. Only two delivered differentiated financial rewards at all—both of which ceased doing so within a few years—but neither of these delivered sanctions for poor performance. In the majority of such reform efforts, systems quickly converged to an equilibrium where nearly every employee received the same score, and incentives (if they were given at all) were not differentiated according to performance. Indeed, the fact that countries repeatedly tried to introduce such schemes is evidence of the shortcomings of preceding efforts to do so.

Viewed in isolation, the failure of each particular effort might be attributed to failings in implementation, cultural mismatch, a lack of political will, or some other combination of idiosyncratic factors. For instance, a 2008 review of Zambia's Annual Performance Appraisal System (APAS, part of the PSRP and PSCAP reforms discussed in the previous chapter) argued: "Users of APAS rarely blame its limitations on the design of the system itself. More often, the blame is placed on the human factor, which includes lack of management support, inadequate resources and little commitment to its implementation. . . . In summary, the basic problems with the current system are in its implementation and, as explained earlier, the lack of a supporting performance culture."[3]

But viewed together, the results of these thirty-four reform efforts appear not as isolated implementation failures but as a *repeated pattern* of nonimplementation, despite a widespread belief that they would be an important—even necessary— lever for improvement. I argue that this pattern emerged because of an inherent mismatch between the highly formalized rules and processes introduced to administer the incentives and the often unformalizable sets of actions that civil servants must undertake to perform their duties effectively. Faced with this mismatch, one of two things happened. Most frequently, the targets set for individuals were vague and/or obviously incomplete, which made it difficult to objectively rate each individual's performance, and so concerns around fairness and morale meant that almost everyone ended up with the same score—which undermined the whole point of the incentive system. In the instances when reformers insisted on imposing objectively measurable targets on individuals and linking their measured achievement to high-powered incentives, this quickly led to civil servants distorting their efforts to meet targeted goals while ignoring nontargeted ones and/or finding ways to water down their targets. In the face of complaints and resistance from actors inside and outside the bureaucracy, such systems were either abandoned or became much less rigorously implemented. Either way, the differentiated incentives that were meant to act as carrots and sticks to spur better performance always failed to be systematically and sustainably implemented.

This chapter explores how focusing on the formal so often became a mechanism of failure for reforms. To do so, the first two-thirds of the chapter zooms in on individual-level performance-linked incentive reforms in these six countries, as they provide perhaps the clearest illustration of this mechanism. But focusing on the formal as a mechanism of failure wasn't unique to these six countries, nor was it restricted to individual-level performance-linked incentives. The final third of the chapter, therefore, zooms back out to argue that such patterns also exist with performance-linked incentive policies in many other countries around the world as well as with other types of reforms within these six countries.

REPEATED EFFORTS TO INTRODUCE INDIVIDUAL-LEVEL
PERFORMANCE-LINKED INCENTIVES

At the beginning of this book's study period in the 1980s and 1990s, all six countries had legacy staff appraisal systems that essentially consisted of each officer's supervisor filing an administratively oriented and confidential annual report about them. These typically involved no participation, target-setting, or formal assessment of performance against targets. In 1991, for instance, Ghana's then-head of state, Jerry Rawlings, lamented that the "confidential reports on individual performance are just a matter of routine; almost everybody, that is, the hard-working and the lazy, get a good confidential report."[4] Furthermore, the results were often withheld even from the officers themselves. As one Zambian civil servant remarked of these old-fashioned legacy systems, "That Annual Confidential Report was so confidential you wouldn't even know what is in it!"[5] Where they were shared, as in Kenya, the assessments were implemented perfunctorily, with the outcome being conveyed in an impersonal letter that merely conveyed the absence of any adverse findings.[6] There was thus a widely shared perception that making these annual appraisal systems more performance-oriented and linking them to rewards and/or sanctions should be at the top of the reform agenda.

In Ghana, Kenya, Senegal, South Africa, and Zambia, efforts to introduce formal performance assessments and incentives formed crucial parts of the first generation of civil service reforms in the 1980s and 1990s. (Nigeria also began to undertake a similar reform but slightly later.) Staff appraisals were to be participatory, involving joint target-setting between officials and their supervisors at the end of the year combined with formal assessment and feedback at the end of each year. This assessment was intended to be linked to pecuniary incentives like promotion decisions, financial incentives, and/or potential job termination. Broadly inspired by ideas associated with the New Public Management movement and similar efforts around the world, in each country these reforms were first implemented in the context of downsizing and structural reforms that aimed to create smaller but higher-skilled, higher-paid, and hopefully more motivated civil services.

In each country except Nigeria and South Africa, these systems were adopted as part of donor-linked programs, but they also had broad support from governments, which envisioned them as ways to reward performance and improve remuneration. In Ghana, for instance, one internal planning document (undated, but from around 1991) stated, "When it is known by the members of the organization that decisions on promotion, salary increment, training and dismissals shall be fairly made on the basis of performance appraisal results, then the exercise achieves high respectability and serves as a motivator."[7] An internal circular in the same year directed ministries to set aside 10 percent of their personnel budgets for the provision of merit-linked cash and noncash awards.[8] In 1993, minutes of a meeting on the CSRP stated, "It should be made easy to remove non-performers from key positions."[9] Similarly, in Zambia, a 2002 report that laid the groundwork for PSCAP's pay and incentive reforms stated: "The newly articulated pay policy should as much as possible, aim at explicitly linking pay to performance, signalling a major change in the incentive system and in performance expectations. Rewards and penalties are both vital for a well functioning incentive regime. . . . Meaningful performance incentives are a must."[10]

In each country (again, except Nigeria), the new appraisal systems were formally established within a few years. However, the implementation of these systems fell far short of expectations. First, no country established any rewards or punishments for good performance, as the illustrative quotes in table 4.1 highlight. Second, to varying extents across countries, years, and organizations within each country, many civil servants did not even undertake these assessments each year—the formal system was simply not consistently enforced, and the lack of consequences for not doing the appraisal led to either the supervisor or supervisee neglecting to complete the process.[11] Recall, for example, the practice in some ministries in Ghana (described in chapter 2) of officers completing multiple years' worth of appraisal forms with different dates at the same time and getting them signed by their supervisors in order to be eligible for promotion—a practice which was also reported by rank-and-file interviewees in Zambia.

The disappointing results of this first wave of incentive-linked performance appraisal reforms led in each country to repeated efforts over the following decades to reintroduce or effectively operationalize similar systems—except in South Africa, where such efforts were focused more on senior managers than rank-and-file staff (see below). These sometimes modified the formal details of the system—the name of the system, format of the appraisal template, stipulated timing or process for supervisor-supervisee discussion, type of incentives to be offered—and other times were simply announcements of renewed efforts to get officers to actually complete the appraisal process or of the intention to link incentives to measured performance.

Table 4.2 illustrates the number of times such reforms were attempted in each country. Ghana, for instance, launched its first performance-linked appraisal system in 1991. In 1993, the minutes of an internal governmental meeting record the then-head of civil service as stating, "The merit pay system was well designed but it is not working. The government has a lot to gain by solving problems

TABLE 4.1 Illustrative quotes on the failure of individual
performance-linked incentive systems

Ghana

- "I cannot rely on this instrument to tell me anything. . . .Everybody is very very good, but you and I know that when it comes down to productivity, not everybody is excellent."

Kenya

- "[It] was being taken as a routine thing . . . even if your performance was not very good, nothing would happen to you. You would still be getting your salary, you still even get promoted, and so on. So it wasn't really taken very seriously. . . ."

Nigeria

- "APER is not useful, it does not assess anyone."

Senegal

- "We evaluate in a routine, mechanical way. One does the evaluation, gets a rating, and gets promoted. . . . But in reality, we haven't sufficiently integrated the dimension of officers' performance to improve the quality of services."

South Africa

- "I don't think there was a single public manager dismissed from the public service because of poor performance . . . lots of these things were put in with good intentions, they were simply just watered down to an extent that they just became tick box exercises . . . everyone signed the agreement, everyone did the assessment after six months, everyone did the annual assessment, and if you look at the most of those assessments, everyone got their average assessment, so they got their performance [increment] on an annual basis and they were quite happy with that."

Zambia

- "APAS has mainly been used for administrative convenience. . . . I have never seen someone be demoted due to bad performance."

Sources: Quotes in alphabetical order of country: interview, GHA13; interview, KEN2; interview, Tunji Olaopa; interview, Ibrahima Ndiaye; interview, SA5; interview, ZAM17.

TABLE 4.2 Reforms aiming to introduce or operationalize individual performance-linked incentives

	Annual performance appraisals (for rank-and-file staff)	Performance contracts (for senior leadership)
Ghana	• Civil Service Reform Programme, 1987–1993 • Civil Service Performance Improvement Programme, 1994–2001 • Public Sector Reform Agenda & Single Spine Pay Policy, 2006–2011 • Performance Management Policy, 2007–2009 • Performance Management Policy for the Public Services of Ghana, 2012– • National Public Sector Reform Strategy, 2016–	• Performance Agreement System, 1996–2000 • Public Sector Reform Agenda & Single Spine Pay Policy, 2006–2011 • Minister Performance Contracts, 2013 • Chief Director Performance Agreements, 2013– • National Public Sector Reform Strategy, 2016–
Kenya	• Civil Service Reform Programme I & II, 1993–2002 • Economic Recovery Strategy / Results for Kenya, 2003–2007 • Public Service Transformation Strategy, 2010–2014 • Public Service Transformation Framework, 2017–	• Economic Recovery Strategy / Results for Kenya, 2003–2007 • Public Service Transformation Strategy, 2010–2014
Nigeria	• Replacement of APER with AUTOPAS, 2009– • Federal Civil Service Strategy and Implementation Plan, 2017–	• Minister Performance Contracts, 2011–2012
Senegal	• Modernization of the State, 1990–1999 • Programme Nationale de Bonne Gouvernance I & II, 2002–2011 • Reform Master Plans (Schémas Directeux) / Plan Sénégal Emergent, 2011–	• Performance Contracts, 2010–
South Africa	• Legal and administrative reforms (1994–98)	• Senior Management Service and Performance Management and Development System (2001–) • Ministers Performance Agreements (2009–10) • Head of Department Performance Management and Development System Relaunch (2017–)
Zambia	• Public Sector Reform Programme, 1993–1999 • Public service Capacity Building Project, 2000–2005 • Public Service Management Programme, 2006–2011 • Public Service Transformation Programme I & II, 2013–	• Public Service Capacity Building Project, 2000–2005 • Public Service Transformation Programme I & II, 2013–

Source: Author's synthesis.

in this area because it would reduce labour unrest."[12] In 1995, a letter from the Office of the Head of Civil Service to heads of all ministries and departments chastised them:

> By the Circular Ref No. PNDC/SCR/A. 08/15 issued in September 1991, all MDAs were requested to institute a Merit Pay Scheme. Under this scheme, staff of Organisations found to be achievers in their job were to be identified and given awards each year. Thus you were required by the Circular (copy enclosed) to create the necessary conditions for making the scheme effective.

2. A survey of the MDAs has revealed that the scheme is yet to see the light of day in all institutions in the Civil Service.
3. One of the guiding principles of the on-going Civil Service Performance Improvement Programme is the emphasis on performance measurement (output orientation). It is thus reasonable to recognize achievements of officers. It is therefore opportune to get the Scheme under way so that achievers can be rewarded appropriately.[13]

This link did not occur under CSPIP either, and after four further efforts to effectively operationalize or modify this system between 2006 and 2012, the key policy document of Ghana's most recent reform wave (the National Public Sector Reform Strategy) once again listed under its activities: "Introduce a performance-related pay based on a well-designed performance contracting system" and "Develop and institutionalize a non-monetary incentive policy and scheme to motivate and retain high performing public sector workers."[14] In Kenya, Senegal, and Zambia, such policies were included in reform packages covering almost every year from the early 1990s through 2019. Yet, despite these repeated efforts—indeed, as evidenced in part by the need for repeated reform efforts—differentiated rewards and consequences were not consistently linked to individuals' performance in any sustained or systematic way in any of these cases.

These performance management systems for rank-and-file civil servants were paralleled in each country at the level of senior leadership by performance contracts or performance agreements for heads of organizations, other senior managers, and even (in Nigeria and South Africa) ministers. The details of each scheme and the timing with which they were adopted in each country were different—as early as 1997 in Ghana and as late as 2011 in Nigeria—but they shared the same combination of participatorily set performance targets linked to organizational work plans, formal scoring of achievement against these targets, and linking of rewards and/or punishments to these assessments. As with annual appraisal systems, these were often inspired by international experience and sometimes (though far from always) linked to donor projects, and in some countries (e.g., Kenya), they had been piloted with state-owned enterprises prior to their rollout in civil service ministries.

Each of these reform efforts had its own idiosyncratic implementation story (detailed in the appendix), but as with the annual appraisal reforms, they shared a common fate—the failure to sustainably link differentiated rewards and punishments to measured performance. Some of the schemes resulted in perfunctory assessments in which everyone scored well; others managed to give differentiated assessments but were not able to link them to meaningful carrots and sticks, and others collapsed after just a year or two.

I was only able to find evidence of two instances in which significant pecuniary incentives were actually delivered for multiple years. Under Kenya's Performance Contract system for permanent secretaries in the mid-2000s, staff members of the highest-scoring ministry were given a "13th-month" salary bonus for several years.[15] Even this suffered from delays, distortions, and implementation problems, however, and eventually fell from prominence in central government. It was also a group incentive rather than an incentive for individual permanent secretaries, and there were never any explicit consequences for poorly performing individuals or ministries (despite the system's intention for such punishments to exist). In South Africa, the Performance Management and Development System for senior managers reportedly delivered differentiated assessments linked to bonuses in its early years but quickly deteriorated into a situation where "people were just getting our performance increases irrespective of their performance . . . so I didn't think that, you know, overall the performance management system worked very well because there are no consequences for poor performance."[16]

The only other partially successful use of performance contracts was in Ghana during the 2010s. Under the performance contract system that had operated for a few years in the late 1990s, one chief director's contract was reportedly not renewed due to poor performance, but soon after, the entire system was scrapped, and contracts ceased being upheld.[17] A later effort to reintroduce performance agreements for chief directors began implementation in 2013 and was still being conducted annually and delivering differentiated performance scores as of 2019, making it relatively long-lived. But the only incentives attached to these assessments were soft ones like recognition or mainly symbolic rewards despite the intention to link these to explicit rewards and consequences.

Why did these efforts to introduce individual-level performance incentives into civil services keep failing to actually deliver incentives? The answer has to do with their focus on creating an objective and highly formalized system to force change in individual behaviors that are, in large part, informal and unformalizable. To see why, let's first lay out how these systems were supposed to function and then examine how, when, and why they deviated from these intentions.

HOW THEY WERE INTENDED TO WORK

Each of these systems was designed to begin with a target-setting phase at the start of each year. Each individual would meet with their supervisor and agree on a set of targets—tasks, activities, deliverables, outcomes—that they would be responsible for delivering over the course of the year and that were linked to broader goals or deliverables for their team, their organization, and/or the civil service as a whole. In the jargon of management, these targets should be S.M.A.R.T.: specific, measurable, achievable (or attainable, depending on who you ask), relevant (or realistic), and time-bound. Different reforms specified the target-setting process in slightly different ways, but the basic idea was always the same: Establish clear and objectively measurable targets that track the work individuals will be doing during the year and against which their performance can later be measured. As one rank-and-file civil servant in Zambia explained, "That is why we set goals and targets, we need to show if we met the target. We need to prove we shine. . . . It is about time people realized they are being paid for something."[18]

At the end of the year, each worker was to be assessed on their actual performance against their targets, sometimes with interim check-ins or feedback points during the year. The idea was that these assessments would be differentiated. Good performers score well, and bad performers score badly. Since workers' targets were mutually agreed upon with their supervisors and were S.M.A.R.T., these performance assessments were, therefore, intended to represent an unbiased indicator of performance accepted by all parties.

Finally, these performance assessments were meant to be used as the basis for delivering some form of reward and/or punishment to the individual, according to their measured performance. The range of rewards envisioned by these thirty-four reforms included financial incentives like bonuses or piece-rate payments; career benefits like accelerated promotion or contract extensions (for senior leaders who are often appointed on nonpermanent contracts); social

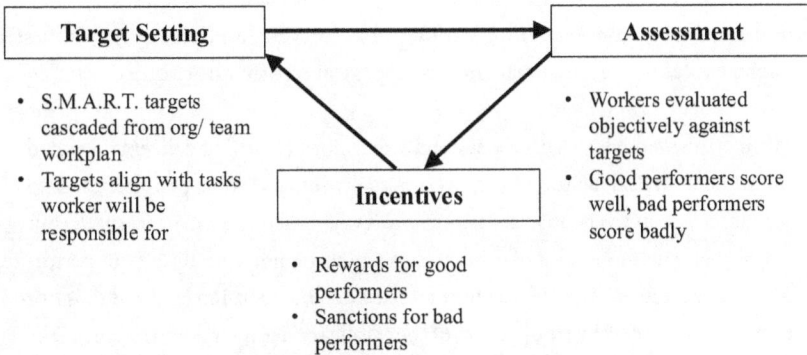

FIGURE 4.1 Intended Structure of Performance-Linked Incentive Systems

Source: Author's synthesis.

recognition like best worker awards or published "league tables"; or sometimes other nonfinancial rewards. For example, a 1991 government circular issued under Ghana's Civil Service Reform Programme suggested "tangible objects, eg. Clock, cloth, wrist-watches, furniture, set of books, radios, scholarship for a child for one year."[19] The range of punishments envisioned was just as broad, up to and including censure, demotion, pay reduction, or dismissal. Though the details and types of rewards and sanctions thus differed, the common thread was that extrinsic incentives to elicit greater effort from bureaucrats through the promise (or threat) of carrots and sticks were the key mechanism through which these annual performance management systems were envisioned to change bureaucratic behavior. Figure 4.1 illustrates this idealized annual performance management cycle.

HOW THEY ACTUALLY WORKED

In reality, however, there were common patterns in the ways that these individual-level performance-linked incentive systems fell short of the aspirations at each stage.

Target-Setting

At the target-setting stage, there was an inconsistency between the ideal of establishing S.M.A.R.T. targets linked to organizational work plans and the reality of how difficult it was to ex ante specify exactly what each individual civil servant should do during the year. The senior public servant and researcher Sylvester Obong'o explained of one performance appraisal reform effort in Kenya:

> What happened with that new system is that not everything deliverable ended up in the appraisal, so the targets were actually set, and some people ended up setting targets on very easy things [to achieve], which are then measured, but you also end up doing a lot of other things which are not actually in your perfor-mance contract.... Ninety percent of what I do and what I'm engaged in is not part of those targets by [the] nature of the public service... it doesn't really make a lot of sense to have these targets at the beginning of the year, which you put two or three, but what you end up doing is not what... you plan to do.[20]

An evaluation of Zambia's performance appraisal reform efforts also high-lighted the inherent unpredictability of much of the work that civil servants do, particularly in the types of policy and oversight roles prevalent in the core civil service: "The best laid work plans can be de-railed when urgent and press-ing work duties displace work plan targets.... Political directives from above, and outside of the scope of the work plan, must be recognized as part of the working culture."[21]

A further issue is the disjuncture between individual effort and team or orga-nizational performance that arises in contexts where team production is preva-lent, like most civil service settings. The scholar Danny Sing describes how this affected South Africa's Performance Management and Development System (PMDS) appraisal system for managers: "Another concern that emerged was the appraisal process may not reflect adequate correlation between individual per-formance and overall organizational performance. It is generally accepted that an outstanding rated performance of an HOD [heads of departments], means, that he/she is leading an organization which performs optimally. However, the PMDS does not provide an instrument to deal with the potential disjuncture between individual performance and organizational performance."[22]

The intended linkage between individual targets and organizational work plans also created problems when the work plans themselves were flawed, incom-plete, or even absent. For example, when performance contracts were first intro-duced in Zambia under PSCAP in the early 2000s, permanent secretaries lacked not only annual work plan targets but also basic job descriptions.[23] A subsequent effort to reintroduce performance contracts in 2015/2016 fixed this by creating clearly delineated schedules of targets each year that were largely extracted from the ministry's work plan, which in turn came from the National Development

Plan.[24] However, since the National Development Plan itself was too ambitious, each permanent secretary's target was unrealistic, and so almost all of them scored poorly on their assessments.[25]

Similarly, for rank-and-file staff, it was often difficult to create individual targets that were both linked to organizational work plans *and* could be used for individual performance measurement since many important and measurable actions or outputs depend on team production and/or complementary inputs from other teams. But, on the one hand, targeting these directly risked the individual being measured as low-performing due to the inaction of others (or vice versa). On the other hand, focusing on more narrow and individualized targets risked ignoring the individual's contributions to team efforts, which in the civil service can seldom be reduced to the sum total of prespecifiable individual tasks.

These technical challenges, combined with workers' understandable desire to avoid poor performance assessments—particularly when these ratings were intended to be linked to rewards or punishments—pushed many workers toward setting targets that were vague, easy, or soft. One South African civil servant explained of senior managers' appraisal targets:

> The way they design it is that it's not something that comes back to them . . . for example, a simple one would be you need to build X number of houses per year, so you receive a budget of X billion rand, you need to build so many houses, the manager was simply right there to oversee the building of houses so whether we build ten when we were supposed to build twenty, I have overseen the building of the houses. I didn't put a target on building 20 houses although I received funding for 20 houses and therefore when you do the assessment, [you can say] " . . . I did oversee it, these are the reports. . . ." So it's the manipulation of the system to a large extent.[26]

These dynamics manifested themselves even in relatively more successful cases, such as Kenya's widely hailed use of performance contracts in the mid-2000s. Some officials perceived that the incentives built into the system pushed organizations over time toward setting easy targets. Others reported that there were "a lot of accusations about soft targets" in centralized ministries with administrative remits, whereas service-delivery-oriented ministries, such as health or agriculture, faced targets that were more tangible and harder to affect.[27] Researcher Abraham Muriu reports that a government-appointed expert review panel in 2010 found that the "setting of targets had not been well coordinated and that the [performance contracting] process was not in tandem with the budget process hence impeding on performance improvement efforts."[28]

This litany of failings in the target-setting process boiled down to one root problem: Important parts of what civil servants do cannot be fully and objectively specified in advance. This might be because some tasks require contextual judgment, because they are hard to anticipate, or because they must respond to changing circumstances or actions of other colleagues and stakeholders. There are, of course, better and worse ways to handle these technical challenges and more and less serious ways to approach the target-setting process. But as long as at least some important aspects of performance are not fully verifiable, the ex-ante setting of formal targets is necessarily incomplete. And as we examine next, this incompleteness of targets—indeed, even the perception of it—undermines the ability to use them to assess performance.

Assessment

The dominant empirical pattern that unfolded at the assessment stage of individual-level performance incentive systems was a lack of differentiation of performance ratings. Most commonly, almost everyone scored highly; less commonly, nearly everyone scored poorly. Either way, there was little differentiation in measured performance. How and why did this happen?

First, the fact that even the most precise targets only specified a fraction of what each individual was responsible for during the year meant that individuals were de facto expected to undertake many actions that were not prespecified but were important for their own performance, their team, and their organization. But since these tasks were not captured in their formal targets, their performance on them could not be rated in the same way as the prespecified tasks. Nor was it possible even to define what percentage of an individual's work comprised prespecified versus unforeseen tasks. Sticking rigidly to considering only prespecified tasks when giving performance ratings would risk undervaluing these unformalizable, nonverifiable tasks and distorting individuals' effort away from them—at the expense of overall performance. As one South African public servant remarked, "In the public service, where what you're actually trying to achieve is much more nebulous and harder to define, it doesn't work very well."[29] Most supervisors (or central rating authorities, in the case of senior leadership performance contracts), therefore, erred on the side of generosity in their assessments.

Second, supervisors seemed to recognize that individuals' performance against their targets often depended on the provision of adequate inputs, on the completion of complementary actions by other people, or on other factors outside the individual's control. The most obvious manifestation of this is related to the provision of the financial resources needed to undertake many activities. Organizational work plans were often underfunded, and even when budgetary provision was made, the promised funds were often not actually released during the year. For example, one expert involved in Zambia's PSRP reform explained that individual targets were usually taken from organizational work plans but since the Ministry of Finance frequently gave ministries budget ceilings of only 65 percent of the cost of these work plans, it was inevitable that many activities would never be completed—how, then, could an individual be blamed for not meeting their targets?[30] In Nigeria, the development practitioner and former senior civil servant Joe Abah explained that a performance contract system for ministers was discontinued one year after it was found that "not one minister met the targets that they had agreed to" and described how ministers objected to the system's premise. "How can we meet these targets when you didn't release all the money for the budget, and we have no control over our staff . . . we can't hire and we can't fire, so how can you hold us accountable to something that we have no control over?"[31] In several contexts, attempts were made to address these issues by creating a section of the evaluation that listed mitigating factors or that released individuals from their obligations if the government did not provide adequate resources, but given the inherent uncertainties of government fiscal management, this tended to further undermine the perceived objectivity of the ratings and thus the ability to give differentiated performance rankings.

Third, while supervisors might have had a good sense of how well each officer was performing against their responsibilities, proving it in an objectively verifiable way was challenging except in cases of serious malfeasance or law-breaking. This wasn't a problem of information per se. Among my interviewees at various levels of seniority, it was widely agreed that everyone within a team basically knew who was a good or bad worker. This makes sense in the context of core civil services. These are people who interact and work together every day, mostly in the same office buildings. They know who has the best technical expertise, who always turns memos around promptly, and who can't be relied upon for important tasks. But compiling the evidence trail needed to justify a poor performance rating or a sanction to a third party was difficult and time-consuming, and in cases where important dimensions of performance couldn't be or weren't prespecified, it could be impossible. Supervisors thus often shied away from giving low scores even to individuals they knew were underperforming. As one senior public servant in Ghana remarked on performance appraisal scores, "Everybody is very very good, but you and I know that when it comes down to productivity, not everybody is excellent."[32]

Efforts to improve the rigor of performance reporting had the perverse effect of reinforcing the incentive (discussed above) for individuals to set targets that were less meaningful but were under their sole control: "We went through a phase where people were trying [to focus targets on results and outcomes] but the Auditor General also started auditing our performance data and expressing concerns about whether our performance data was also reliable and accurate and all that. And that made everyone go back to input and process targets. They were very strong on the SMART principle, they were using that in doing the audits."[33]

Finally, the nondifferentiation of performance ratings was also due, in part, to a misalignment between the systemic benefits and private costs of having differentiated ratings. The costs of giving bad performance ratings fall entirely on the supervisor doing the rating, while many of the benefits of having functioning and differentiated performance ratings are diffuse and system-level. Put yourself in the shoes of a supervisor who is considering giving a subordinate a poor performance rating. It will probably be an unpleasant conversation. They are likely to perceive your rating as unfair, subjective, and potentially biased. They may react not by working harder next year but by becoming demotivated and creating negative dynamics within the team. They might even complain to their union, the media, an opposition party, or even your own bosses that you are persecuting them due to their political allegiance, ethnicity, or as a result of your own wrongdoing—an allegation that would be harmful to you regardless of whether or not it was true.[34] In contrast, the biggest benefit (from a system perspective) of giving them a poor rating would be that the central authorities know not to promote them and other managers know not to offer them transfers into their teams, so you are likely to be stuck with that individual even longer. Supervisors, thus, have little strategic incentive to give bad performance ratings. As one former South African civil servant explained, supervisors "shy away from any form of conflict and just do the tick-box exercise . . . [they think] 'it's not my problem, it's somebody else's problem' and they managed it on that basis and it just goes away, nobody bothered."[35]

Incentives

It's easy to see why having nondifferentiated performance assessments makes it impossible to give differentiated performance incentives. But it's also worth considering why it is hard for bureaucracies to actually give out rewards and punishments even if individuals do have differentiated performance ratings.

Individuals have various options to resist if they feel that they are being punished unfairly or that they also deserve rewards that others are receiving—which is to say always, given the difficulties of perfectly prespecifying targets and then objectively proving performance. As discussed above, they can appeal to public service commissions; file suit in courts; complain to unions, the media, or opposition parties; and take other actions that create costs both for individual managers and for the government as a whole. And the stronger the incentive, the stronger the resistance it will provoke: No one is likely to complain about a nonfinancial recognition award to a "best worker," but if significant money or the continuation of their job is on the line, many workers will claim—rightly or wrongly—that they are being unfairly and subjectively persecuted and take whatever steps they can to resist.

Furthermore, it is common in civil services in Africa and worldwide for individual civil servants to have connections to other powerful figures, both in higher ranks of the bureaucracy and in political offices. These connections represent an additional avenue through which individuals can contest the allocation of incentives. For example, in Ghana, there was reportedly one instance in which the Office of the Head of Civil Service tried to terminate the contract of a chief director who had been assessed as performing poorly, but that individual made a direct appeal to the Office of the President and was able to secure a contract renewal.[36] Similarly, one South African former civil servant explained: "But there's also the political influence, the moment you start taking action against individuals, there's also—because there's links to politicians [of those] who got appointed through the politicians. . . . So those played a role as well, so therefore the moment you initiate a process . . . you end up with political interference to some extent. Or even if it's not political, you still get administrative interference from higher up the chain. So managers then sit back and say 'but why do I need all those stress[es] in life' so you just rather not get involved."[37]

A related challenge for following through on performance-linked incentive schemes arose when the institution or individual that appointed them had different priorities from those that were written in organizational work plans or official performance targets. For example, a minister might have different personal or political objectives than those laid out in a ministry's medium-term plan, especially as ministers come and go or political situations change. This challenge was especially acute for senior civil service leaders, who sit in the middle of the political-administrative interface—not only responsible for carrying out work plans and administrative processes but also expected to be responsive to the political priorities of their ministers. While these two roles are intended to coincide, they can often diverge. When a manager scores poorly on their formal performance metrics but the political leader who appoints them is happy with them (or vice versa), then there is a natural tendency for the preferences of the political leader to win out. Managers know this, which undermines the credibility of the performance contract. As one retired Zambian civil servant reflected, if permanent secretaries' main loyalty is to the authority that appointed them, then how can a performance contract be anything more than symbolic?[38]

Interestingly, interviewees across all contexts reported that it was not impossible or even uncommon for individuals to be fired or disciplined. However, this was generally only for cases of severe or criminal misconduct rather than poor performance. Individual failings in such cases were highly verifiable: Regulations and codes of conduct provide relatively clear and complete ex ante specifications on what to do or not do, and many forms of criminal or financial malfeasance are ex post provable to third parties. Of course, not all instances of misconduct were caught or punished. But the possibility of levying strong sanctions for such infractions in at least some cases stands in contrast with the near-universal inability to do so for reasons of poor performance. As one former South African civil servant commented, "There are no consequences for poor performance . . . it was always difficult to dismiss people on the basis of poor performance. You could do so on misconduct but poor performance it was very difficult, so you just keep them in the system."[39]

In addition to provoking resistance, efforts to attach strong incentives to performance also tended to distort earlier stages of the performance management process by encouraging individuals to set easily achievable targets and increasing the pressure on managers to give positive assessments. For example, with Kenya's performance contracting system in the mid-2000s, once rewards began to be introduced, "people started to look for easy targets where they could score highly and then be rewarded," often by setting targets related to carrying out processes rather than to the ultimate impact of their actions.[40]

Because of all these challenges in delivering differentiated incentives, most such schemes either dropped the incentives completely or delivered them in a largely nondifferentiated fashion. For instance, a consultancy report on Zambia's efforts to operationalize its APAS annual appraisal system during the PSRP and PSCAP reforms described this outcome in devastating fashion: "As time has passed the real purpose of the APAS report has become the justification of pay increments and promotions. This has led to the a [sic] view that completion of the form is a necessary evil to which one should devote as little time and thought as possible. The result in many instances is a report replete with inconsistencies, contradictions and very little assessment of performance that bears little relation to a real work plan and virtually none to the organisational and strategic plan."[41]

Target Setting → **Assessment**

Incentives

Target Setting

Empirical patterns:
- Targets are vague, incomplete, and/or not aligned with actual tasks
- Targets are too easy (or too hard)

Why?
- Tasks can't be precisely specified *ex ante*
- Job descriptions or org. workplans non-existent/unrealistic

Incentives

Empirical patterns :
- Performance-based rewards not given or not differentiated
- Sanctions almost never applied

Why?
- Performance assessments not differentiated
- Perceived subjectivity in assessments

Assessment

Empirical patterns :
- Hard to assess performance objectively
- Almost everyone scores high (or low)

Why?
- Tasks can't be precisely measured *ex post*
- Private costs to managers who give low scores

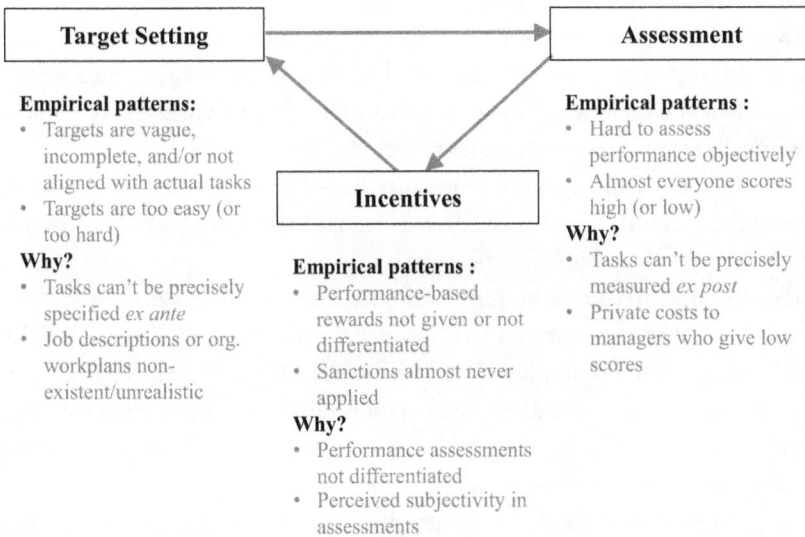

FIGURE 4.2 Actual Operation of Performance-Linked Incentive Systems

Source: Author's synthesis.

Similarly, in South Africa, one public servant remarked, "We got into a phase where you were almost guaranteed a performance bonus. . . . And there wasn't much of a correlation between unit or department performance and performance bonuses. Performance bonuses became a 13th check almost, it was expected."[42] Figure 4.2 summarizes the most common ways in which the actual implementation of these performance management systems diverged from how they were intended to operate.

PERFORMANCE-LINKED INCENTIVES OFTEN FAIL IN HIGH-INCOME COUNTRIES, TOO

In my interviews with civil servants and donors alike, I often encountered a pair of common perceptions about performance-linked incentive reforms. First, that such systems frequently existed and functioned properly in high-performing civil services in rich countries. Second, that their implementation failures in African countries were due to contextual factors like nonindividualistic or nonperformance-oriented cultures, political interference, or low bureaucratic effectiveness. In other words, it was often perceived that these systems were the kinds of things that high-performing civil services did, that doing them was the way to become high-performing, and that failures and challenges were due to historical, social, or political factors specific to Africa.

While a global review of performance-linked incentives is far beyond the scope of this already broad book, even a cursory look at how such systems have tended to operate in high-income contexts challenges these perceptions. (As an aside, the widespread assumption that richer countries always have more effective government bureaucracies than poorer countries is also contentious, but that's an argument for another book.) It also helps illustrate this chapter's main argument—that the root of implementation failure for these systems is their focus on creating formal, objective, and mechanistic links between measured performance and rewards or sanctions.

A good place to start is New Zealand, whose experiments in the late 1980s and early 1990s with public sector performance contracts (along with a host of other New Public Management–style reforms) were often seen as a model and provided much of the initial inspiration for their global spread. For instance, as early as the late 1990s, the scholar Allen Schick famously discussed the global influence of New Zealand's reforms on reform thinking in developing countries.[43] The archived draft minutes of a 1993 meeting of the steering committee of Ghana's Civil Service Reform Programme (CSRP) provide direct evidence of one attempt to import ideas and experience from New Zealand into reform planning in Ghana, with the minute-taker recording that one foreign consultant representing the World Bank at the meeting "said that he could see some similarities between the circumstances facing the New Zealand Civil Service and the Ghana Civil Service" and another stating that "it would be advisable to look at what had been done in the U.K. and New Zealand."[44] Similarly, South Africa's 1997 Presidential Review Commission report discussed having referred to documentation on New Zealand's reform experience that was "particularly relevant to its work."[45] And Zambia's performance contracting system for permanent secretaries in the early 2000s was reportedly based, in part, on a suggestion by an expatriate consultant from New Zealand.[46]

But the actual details of New Zealand's performance contracting system differed in important ways from the image of it that traveled around the world and the performance contract systems that were based on it, at least in these six countries. These details are contained in a number of contemporaneous documents and academic studies, but to better understand the original intent of these systems, I also interviewed Ian Ball, who worked as a civil servant in the Treasury during this period, helping to design and implement these reforms and later worked as a consultant and academic.

First, Ball emphasized that the term *contract* was a "metaphor"—the contracts were never intended to be enforceable. Indeed, as Ball emphasized (and documents confirm), they were almost always called performance "agreements" rather than contracts, although the latter term is sometimes used as a verb (*contracting*). Although many governments around the world took this metaphor literally and tried to create systems that were objective and enforceable, Ball explained why such literal interpretations were misguided:

> We knew we operated in a complex world and nothing was as simple as a fully specified contract anywhere, whether the private sector or the public sector, so we didn't expect to be doing that. . . . The idea that you would have a formulaic relationship between services and remuneration and that alone would be what you meant by chief executive performance is kind of, to me, is very simplistic, is not what we were trying to do. We were trying to create a management system where the whole system—formal and informal—would work with the personnel and financial management elements working in harmony.[47]

Second, while performance contracts in many of the cases I studied were criticized for focusing on intermediate actions rather than final outcomes like service delivery, in New Zealand, "there was a deliberated decision not to seek to use outcomes in order to define the accountability of chief executives and their departments. The reason for this is that the individual chief executive very rarely has sufficient control over outcomes to make accountability effective."[48] Ball explained:

> The other thing that was very much in our minds in thinking about how this would work was that any system works with formal components but also informal components. So for example, in relation to outcomes, you would want the system to be working in such a way that the Chief Executive was concerned not just with the delivery of the pre-specified outputs, but also with whether or not those outputs were adding value in terms of the outcomes that they and the ministers were trying to achieve. . . . We explicitly were regarding outcomes as the ultimate rationale for public actions, but saying you can't contract those or reach agreements for those in the way that you can for outputs, so you would have wanted the Chief Executives also to be contemplating whether the particular set of services was contributing to the outcomes that the agency was seeking to achieve—and other informal components of their performance.[49]

Enforcement challenges also motivated this focus on outputs rather than outcomes, with Ball noting in a 1992 conference presentation that "accountability for outcomes was rarely made to stick."[50] As a 1996 review of reforms by the scholar Allen Schick commissioned by the government of New Zealand emphasized, "The focus on outputs is in contrast to both its previous input-based appropriations and the outcome-oriented system favoured in much of the management reform literature."[51]

Third, the main envisioned driver of improvement from the performance agreements was the discussion and clarity that they would give rise to, rather than the carrots and sticks. As Ball wrote in a 1994 journal article: "The emphasis placed on contracting before a period begins, as distinct from measuring performance after it ends, is another key feature of the reforms. Our emphasis has been heavily on the former . . . a focus on ex ante contracting, rather than ex post performance measurement, has been hugely helpful in clarifying the roles and performance expectations of chief executives, and has provided much better focus to departmental activity."[52]

At the same time, even this emphasis on ex ante specification was observed to sometimes cause managers to approach it as a perfunctory exercise: "The focus on ex ante specification has sometimes led to a checklist mentality which is positive from the perspective of having managers take accountability seriously for tasks they are expected to complete. It is less desirable if it narrows responsibility to simple compliance with what is on the list, and prompts Chief Executives to disregard responsibility for items not specified."[53]

Fourth, the evaluation of performance and delivery of associated incentives was not objective, transparent, or highly differentiated. Rather—and by design—it contained important elements of subjectivity and judgment, was largely confidential, and seems to have led to relatively little actual differentiation in extrinsic rewards. Ball recalls that the actual evaluation of performance by the State Services Commission "was treated as a personnel, in-confidence kind of issue" rather than being done in public and that he and his colleagues "would never have expected you could put that into a formula, that there would be a formula which would say 'this is the relationship between the chief executive's income and the service delivery.'"[54] And even with this subjectivity and nontransparency, there was little differentiation of rewards or punishments for performance—although judging this involves some speculation, as information on it was never made public.

The understanding that I had at the time is that . . . 90 percent of people got the same [rating and remuneration]. That the SSC was very reluctant or unable or unwilling, whichever it was, to differentiate in a way. I suspect it was that they weren't confident in differentiating in a way that they could support and justify.... I know within the Treasury we felt that the State Services Commission was very reluctant to determine that one Chief Executive would get a significant performance component in their remuneration and another would arguably even get a reduction in their remuneration.[55]

Similarly, Schick's 1996 review noted the widespread perception that the State Services Commission "has been reluctant to dismiss weak performers or to use pay differentials to reward strong managers and penalise weak ones.... It is unrealistic to expect SSC to approve large pay differentials in response to differences in chief executive performance.... In practice, pay differentials tend to correlate more with departmental size than with performance."[56]

Thus, New Zealand's system of performance agreements was far less focused on formalizing every aspect of the process and on leveraging carrots and sticks than most of the systems it inspired around the world, including in the six countries covered by this book. This is not to imply that New Zealand's system in the late 1980s or 1990s was perfect or even necessarily effective—again, this is a debate for another book[57]—or that countries should try to imitate it. Rather, my point is that even one of the key global archetypes of individual performance-linked incentive systems in government was far less focused on forcing change through formal incentives than is typically imagined. It was designed this way because of many of the same challenges of target-setting, performance assessment, and incentive delivery that undermined the performance contracting and performance appraisal reforms in the six countries described in this chapter.

Many of the same patterns are present in other high-income countries' governments. For example, in the United States, a 2016 report found that 99.7 percent of US federal civil servants were rated excellent *or above* on their annual staff appraisals.[58] While many interviewees in the six African countries studied in this book attributed the nondifferentiation of performance ratings at least partially to cultural factors, the fact that there is so little differentiation in a context like the United States—often considered to have a highly individualistic culture in which economic incentives are prevalent and widely accepted—ought to cause us to be skeptical that national cultures are the main constraint on such systems' operation. Similarly, a study of local governments in Italy found that performance ratings exhibited very low differentiation both because objectives are hard to define ex ante and differentiated ratings ex post "may ruin the internal climate," with the result that "additional money is often not seen as a recognition for achieving a predefined set of objectives, or more generally for a superior per-formance, but it is taken for granted as additional salary."[59] Indeed, a 2005 report by the OECD found that across its member states: "there is often a gap between the stated existence of a so-called 'performance-related pay scheme' and its con-crete functioning, which may be barely linked to performance. . . . Performance pay is an appealing idea, but the experiences reviewed in this study indicate that its implementation is complex and difficult. . . . Performance measurement in the public sector requires a large element of managerial judgement. The notion of performance itself is complex, owing to the difficulty of finding suitable quanti-tative indicators and because performance objectives often change with govern-ment policy."[60]

It further noted that "highly detailed and inflexible performance criteria and rating frameworks, though they can be reassuring to managers and managed alike, are often detrimental to the smooth running of a PRP [performance-re-lated pay] scheme" and reported the findings of an earlier OECD report that "in most PRP schemes in use in the 1980s, more than 95 percent of managers were rated as 'fully satisfactory or better.'"[61] These findings echo much of the litera-ture on performance management at the organizational (rather than individual) level in OECD countries by scholars such as Beryl Radin and Donald Moynihan, who argue that overly formal and mechanical approaches to managing agencies' performance fit poorly with the complex reality of large bureaucracies in demo-cratic contexts.[62] Of course, this is not to say that performance-linked incentive systems always fail, nor that good performance always goes unrewarded. Indeed, evidence from the Global Survey of Public Servants reveals significant variation both across and within countries in the percentages of public servants who say that their performance matters for pay rises and/or career prospects[63]—although the survey does not explore the extent to which that linkage is due to the type of highly formalized performance-linked incentive systems examined in this chap-ter as opposed to more flexible and discretionary mechanisms.

Taken together, then, the frequent difficulties encountered in successfully operationalizing performance-linked incentives in civil services around the world pose a deep challenge to explanations for the nonimplementation of per-formance-linked incentive reforms that rely on contextual factors unique to African countries or to low- and middle-income countries. Rather, many of the same patterns appear even in high-income countries with very different contexts, resources, and constraints. Instead, this evidence reinforces the interpretation that the nonimplementation of these reforms stems from their overfocus on try-ing to force behavioral changes through formal systems and incentives.

OTHER TYPES OF REFORMS ALSO FOCUSED MAINLY ON
CHANGING FORMAL RULES AND STRUCTURES

The formal focus of reforms was not restricted to performance-linked incentive programs alone. Rather, it was a consistent feature of almost all the reform efforts undertaken in these six countries over the three-decade span I studied.

This is most obviously the case for the category of reforms I term "salaries and structures," which focused on organizational restructuring, staff redundancies, and changes to staff pay scales. Even more than the performance-linked incentive systems, these reforms focused exclusively on changing formal structures and employment contracts with the idea that these would lead to better performance. Indeed, they were often paired with—or viewed as predecessors to—performance-linked incentive reforms. The idea was typically that downsizing would create fiscal space to enable better pay for high performers or that decompressed pay scales would give staff more incentive to perform well in order to be promoted. But the linkage of these changes to measured performance never arrived. For example, Ghana's Single Spine Pay Policy reforms of 2006–2011 envisioned first harmonizing and improving pay to provide the basis for a subsequent reform that would explicitly link performance to pay, but by the time the new pay scales were adopted, the cost had ballooned out of control, years had passed, and there was no appetite for the envisioned incentive reform. Across countries, despite the myriad shortcomings of existing pay scales and organizational structures, formal salary and structure reforms typically yielded no obvious performance improvements and ended up saving far less or costing far more than was anticipated.

Organizational management and capacity reforms sometimes recognized the importance of informal practices for performance, but then tended to revert to a focus on formal structures and processes in how they actually tried to make change. Performance improvement funds in Ghana and Zambia accurately identified the potential for bottom-up improvement based on ideas generated in a decentralized fashion, but the support they then offered to these ideas was in the most formal of currencies within government bureaucracies: budget allocations, with all the spending and reporting requirements they entail. Similarly, most organizational performance review mechanisms focused overwhelmingly on objectively verifiable indicators of performance, whether in terms of activities, outputs, or outcomes. This focus on formalizable processes and measures in organizational performance management systems encountered the same implementation challenges, behavior distortions, and limitations as did their individual-level counterparts described above.

South Africa's Management Performance Assessment Tool (MPAT, which operated from 2011–2016), under which detailed audits of the implementation of a range of management processes were undertaken each year, is, in some ways, the exception that proves the rule. Attuned to the risk of overfocusing on the formal, the designers of the MPAT assessment created a performance rating scale of 1–4 for each process, in which scores of 1–3 represented various degrees of noncompliance or perfunctory compliance with the formalizable aspects of required and recommended organizational management processes. The highest score of 4 was reserved for organizations that demonstrated that the process was not only being followed in the letter of the law but was also being used to improve performance—in other words, for consummate performance.

This effort to encourage such unformalizable behaviors was a promising and unusual part of the MPAT reform. However, it was undermined to an extent by the system's intention to use the resulting scores as accountability tools and metrics for delivering incentives. This required a burdensome process of seeking documentary evidence for all these behaviors—which itself ensures that many unformalizable behaviors will be missed—and also led to distortions. As one civil servant close to the scheme explained,

> People started learning the system and started playing us, because then it became about the rating and the scoring. We did initially introduce competition and give awards out and say who's the best and who's the worst to try to motivate people to make the change, but unfortunately it then became about the score. So we tried to give awards about who's the most improved department, but it became a lot about the scores, not about "am I improving," "are we getting better." . . . Then we started getting a huge amount of pushback from the departments and the [directors-general] and that, saying "why are we focused so much on compliance and we should rather focus on outcomes and all that."[64]

As with the individual-level performance-linked incentive reforms, the focus on assigning formal scores to use as the basis for doling out carrots and sticks undermined the learning potential of the participatory diagnostic process, discouraging line ministries and central management agencies alike from engaging openly and frankly in discussions of performance and how to improve it. The case of the MPAT thus illustrates that even organization-level performance rating systems could trigger backlash when used for accountability purposes: "It didn't go well with the ministers and the departments that were at the bottom. We also went public with the results which put further pressure. And politically it wasn't liked by some, the approach, and that's kind of why it died a quiet death, because maybe we were too transparent and pushed too much."[65] In the same way as with individual-level performance incentives, organization-level performance management systems collapsed when they tried too hard to force changes in behavior through formal incentives and accountability systems.

Within the category of service-delivery-focused reforms, the most common intervention was the creation of new customer-facing units charged with making it easier to access services, such as "one-stop shops" or client service units. In most cases, these were also formal-focused ways to try to solve complex organizational problems by creating a new unit with a new name, new physical infrastructure, separate budget line, and separate staff. And in most cases, these new units showed initial promise but fell into disuse once the donor project that funded their construction ended or the political leaders that launched them moved on. Kenya's Huduma Centers, launched as one-stop decentralized service access points in 2013, are perhaps the most salient exception: Widely viewed as fairly successful (even if still facing some challenges), the main difference between them and other similar reform efforts lay not in their formal design but in the sustained and gradual improvements in services offered, reliability, and performance monitoring and feedback in the centers. Thus, the creation of formal systems, structures, and processes in itself is not bad; indeed, it is often a necessary part of reforms in large bureaucracies. But the creation of these formal systems alone isn't sufficient for them to change people's behavior in the ways they generally aim to.

Once again, this pattern of focusing reform efforts on formal rules, structures, and processes—and the limitations of doing so—appears in reform experience and evidence beyond these six countries. To cite just a few examples: Matt Andrews notes the widespread tendency of donor-supported institutional reforms in developing countries to focus on the form rather than the function of institutions;[66] Kate Bridges and Michael Woolcock observe that 92 percent of indicators of public financial management reform projects in Malawi focus on formal "regulative" processes "targeted at shaping behaviour through the threat of sanction";[67] and Jeffrey Braithwaite comments in his review of health reforms in high-income countries that, "The boxes on the [UK National Health Service] organisation chart have regularly been redrawn to little benefit. Although such reorganisations do produce structural change, they do not greatly alter entrenched cultures, much less downstream clinical outcomes," with similar evidence in Australia and other countries.[68]

In emphasizing the tendency for reforms to focus and rely upon formal changes, I don't want to caricature these reforms or their designers. Many reforms did contain important informal elements, many reformers recognized that formal changes didn't automatically translate into practice, and there were a handful of reforms that consciously focused on achieving unformalizable changes, whether through informal interventions or by leveraging formal processes to support informal changes. I explore these in more detail in chapters 6 and 7 as a way of exploring alternative approaches to reform. But such efforts were usually secondary to the dominant focus-on-the-formal approach, which tended to predominate in the vast majority of reform efforts. Ultimately, the success of a reform depends on the interaction between its formal and informal aspects, which must be deliberately designed to complement and reinforce each other—a goal that requires reformers to think beyond forcing compliance with formal processes as a mechanism for positive change.

• • •

In chapter 3, I argued that reformers' ideas about performance and bureaucratic change—their perceptions, mental models, and understanding of evidence and practice from other contexts—are key determinants of the adoption and design of reforms. The same is true of why so many reforms focus on performance-linked incentives: The conceptual logic is direct and intuitive, and many people think that such systems are widely successful in other contexts.

The evidence in this chapter should lead us to be skeptical not just of claims that performance-linked incentives are necessary to improve performance but also of their viability as a tool for sustained improvement when adopted at scale in civil services. This is certainly true of their track record of implementation in the six countries I study, and similar challenges have been experienced in many high-income countries as well. More broadly, bureaucratic performance is simply too hard to specify and too hard to measure—too nonverifiable—for positive behavior change to be forced by reforms that focus on changing formal rules and processes alone.

This failure to deliver differentiated incentives across these thirty-four reforms ought to be striking not only for reformers but also for researchers. The impacts of performance incentives in government are the subject of an entire cottage industry of studies by academics and policy researchers, making them one of the most intensively researched reforms for improving service delivery around the world. However, in order to isolate the causal impacts of the incentives on performance, these researchers usually study the rollout of incentives in carefully controlled settings: randomized control trials, donor projects, and small-scale pilots in specific sectors. These studies have mixed results in terms of their impacts on service delivery,[69] but this chapter's findings suggest a more fundamental problem for such policies: They seem to be almost impossible to implement and sustain at large scale outside of carefully controlled or limited settings in many (perhaps most) contexts. There have been a handful of economic studies on high-profile implementation failures in scaling pilot performance-linked incentive reforms,[70] but as with qualitative case studies of such reforms, these have often been viewed as examples of isolated and idiosyncratic challenges rather than part of a broader pattern.

While I hope that this chapter has provided new evidence and helpful ways to think about these issues, these insights also reflect the thinking of many thoughtful civil servants and reform designers. To cite just two examples, in his 2014 analysis of the failures of past reform efforts in Nigeria, Tunji Olaopa cited reforms' "Overemphasis on changes in structures and procedures in disregard for the most critical and challenging soft side of culture change that enables shift in business behaviour."[71] Similarly, Joe Abah explained his time as Director-General of Nigeria's Bureau of Public Sector Reforms, "It's actually something we've actually always argued throughout all of the work of performance management while I was at the Bureau . . . performance management, and performance contracting and tying performance to incentives has always failed. In Africa at least it has. People attacked me for it at the time but nobody could show me any evidence of sustainable success from anywhere. So we've always been very aware . . . not to tie [performance] to remuneration, not to tie it to pay, period."[72]

Abah carried on to lament that "this fixation on this use of force rather than meeting of minds continues until this day. And that has been the challenge."[73]

5

The "How" of Reform

Projectization and Its Consequences

T he second main mechanism of failure that recurred across reforms was related to the process through which they were designed and implemented rather than the changes they tried to make. In other words, the mechanisms of reform failure weren't only about the "what" of reform but also about the "how."

How these reforms were designed and implemented was, of course, highly varied. As chapter 3 and the appendix discuss, some reform efforts were driven by high-profile political initiatives with great fanfare and others by bureaucratic processes that almost no one outside the civil service was even aware of. Some were initiated and funded by governments, others by donors, and others by both. Sometimes, they were inspired by reforms conducted in other countries; other times, they were homegrown.

But one common feature across the majority of reforms was that they were designed and implemented as one-off projects. They tended to diagnose a performance problem with the civil service system, propose some kind of intervention into that system, and posit that this intervention would "fix" the problem once and for all. Bureaucratic reform was typically viewed as a discrete and often time-bound action: the passing of a new law, the implementation of a three-year plan, or the creation of some new bureaucratic process. This mental model of reform as a one-off intervention—the *projectization of reform*—constituted the second main mechanism of reform failure.

Projectization shaped reforms in several related ways that made it more difficult for them to spur broad-based improvement. In the design phase, it created incentives to exaggerate the potential benefits of reforms, setting them up to be viewed as failures when they inevitably fell short. It also reinforced the tendency for reforms to focus on making changes on paper to formal structures and processes rather than changing actual behaviors—especially nonverifiable ones. In implementation, viewing reform as a one-off intervention undermined the belief among civil servants that the changes being made were here to stay and, thus, undermined their ability both to improve compliance with existing processes and get bureaucrats to undertake important but nonverifiable actions. Projectization also encouraged reforms to be led top-down and be more closely identified with particular political and bureaucratic leaders, potentially increasing not only the pace of change in the short term but also decreasing broader buy-in and sustainability in the medium and long term. Approaching reforms in a projectized way thus undermined their ability to improve bureaucratic behavior and get closer to consummate performance.

This chapter starts by defining *projectization* as I use it, giving examples of various ways it manifested in civil service reforms in the six countries covered by this book and linking it to existing research on organizational change in these and other contexts. It then explains how the mechanism of projectization shaped five aspects of reforms:

1. The *expectations* or goals of reforms
2. The *content* of reforms—i.e., the changes they aimed to make
3. The *implementation* of these measures
4. The *leadership* style of reforms
5. The *politics* around reforms

If projectization was a mechanism of failure, then these were five submechanisms that comprised it in various combinations. Together, they undermined reforms' ability to generate sustained improvements in civil servants' day-to-day behaviors. The chapter closes by recontextualizing these arguments about projectization in the broader picture of reform and discussing whether and when some degree of projectization might be appropriate. It also begins the transition from trying to understand why so many reforms failed to discussing the ways they succeeded—and how they could be even more successful.

WHAT IS PROJECTIZATION?

As an approach to reform, the core feature of projectization is its one-off nature. Projectized reforms perceive a civil service system that is in an undesirable state;

design and deliver some kind of intervention into that system; and expect that once that intervention has been made, the system will operate in a more desirable state. Projectized approaches to reform reflect the influential model of behavioral change and organizational development proposed by psychologist Kurt Lewin in 1951. Lewin argued that planned change unfolds in three steps: the unfreezing of existing undesirable patterns of behavior, making desired changes to these behaviors, and refreezing these new behaviors into new patterns. In this "episodic" model of change, reform is a discrete intervention into an otherwise stable system.[1]

In the realm of civil service reforms, projectization also often takes on several other features, including the following:

- **The separation of reform activities from core organizational processes.** The process of designing and implementing change is seen as something special, unusual, and exceptional and is carried out separately from the routine, repeated, day-to-day tasks of service delivery and administration. Often (but not always), reform activities have their own acronyms, budget lines, and/or implementing teams. Reform is something that is done *to* the organization's core tasks and processes rather than *as part of* them.

- **A clear distinction between the design phase and implementation phase of reform, often resulting in the predefinition of activities and outputs.** Reform is designed by a distinct and dedicated team of senior leadership, consultants, and/or a specific unit. Staff and stakeholders outside this team may be consulted or "sensitized" about the reforms but only for inputs into this otherwise separate design process. The design phase specifies a set of changes, activities, and outputs that are then to be executed or delivered as part of the subsequent implementation process, often with little scope for flexibility or adaptation.

- **An envisioned end to the reform process.** In some cases, projects have predefined start and end dates (e.g., three-year donor projects or four-year reform plans). In other cases, the reform ends once the envisioned change or output—the passing of a new law, the establishment of a new organizational process, the conducting of a set of trainings or organizational performance reviews—has been completed.

Thus, projectization is an umbrella concept for this set of linked and overlapping features of reform design and implementation that flow from conceiving of reform as a one-off intervention. These were typically present in some combination in most reforms, although not all were always present. Reforms also differed in the extent of their projectization and in the specific ways that projectization manifested in their design and implementation.

Some reforms, such as Zambia's PSCAP (which we discussed in chapter 3), exhibited all these features of projectization. It was implemented by a dedicated project implementation team, was designed by donors and elite Zambian civil servants, then was rolled out across the wider civil service and had its own dedicated budget (funded mostly by donors but also by the government of Zambia) that had to be spent by the project's end date and accounted for against its predefined outputs. The three phases of PSCAP that were envisioned—developing and piloting new systems, rolling out of these systems to the whole civil service, and consolidation—even corresponded roughly to the three steps of Lewin's three-step episodic change model.[2]

On the other end of the spectrum, some reforms exhibited only a few of these features. For example, the basic structure of Kenya's Rapid Results Initiatives (RRI) was designed by a dedicated team, but the content of each individual initiative was codesigned with each specific ministry and aimed at restructuring core operational processes. The direct costs of the RRI and much of the staff time came from the line ministry rather than a project- or reform-specific budget line, and the intended operation of the RRI system in the civil service, in general, was indefinite. At the same time, the RRI system depended on a dedicated team of RRI coaches with its own funding stream, and each individual initiative was a short-term, one-off effort to make a specific change in each ministry. So as a reform, it still had some features of projectization.

Nearly all the reforms studied in this book had some, often most, of the features of projectization. However, measuring and classifying the degree of projectization exhibited by each reform is near impossible. To some extent, this is due to the practical challenges of inconsistent data availability across reforms. More conceptually, though, projectization is best understood not as a rigidly defined list of observable, binary characteristics but as a linked set of mechanisms that manifest differently across different contexts and types of reforms. How these mechanisms were related to the formal features of reform content and process was also highly variable. For example, even a seemingly binary feature like whether a reform has a predefined end date can be differentially reflective of projectization depending on its intent—for example, indicating an intent to stop reform activities in one situation but an intent to transition to a new phase of reform in another. There's also a sample selection problem: Some of the features that make a reform projectized, like an acronym and budget line, also mean that there is more likely to be documentation on it and that individuals are more likely to think of it as a reform, so it is more likely to be included in the reform histories I compile.

Subtle distinctions and challenges like this can be teased out and dealt with qualitatively for many reforms through the type of careful, triangulated description and analysis contained in the reform histories in the appendix and drawn on in these chapters. However, they would be impossible to consistently and precisely code in a quantitative fashion for each and every observed reform without oversimplifying the concept so much that it would lose most of its analytical force and without inadvertently conveying a false sense of precision. In chapters 3 and 4, I used some quantitative measures to summarize certain reform patterns (with many caveats); in this chapter, I'm not even going to attempt to quantify the extent or consequences of projectization. The rest of this chapter, therefore, analyzes these mechanisms of projectization qualitatively—albeit with as much precision as possible and closely grounded both in theory and empirical reform histories.

Let's now examine how the mechanisms of projectization manifested in the design and implementation of reforms in these six countries. I examine the features associated with projectization, how projectization led to reforms taking on those features, and their consequences for reform across five domains and submechanisms: expectations (i.e., goals), content, implementation, leadership, and politics.

HOW PROJECTIZATION SHAPED REFORM EXPECTATIONS

One of the most striking features of nearly all reforms was their extraordinary level of ambition. Reform plan documents almost always followed the same pattern. They began by deploring the existing state of the civil service and detailing its shortcomings, which they blamed on outdated structures, lack of motivation, and poor work culture. Then, they introduced a new reform agenda that promised to solve these problems, usually in a three- to five-year period. For example, an official pamphlet issued by Ghana's Office of the Head of the Civil Service described the Civil Service Performance Improvement Programme (CSPIP, 1994–2001) as intended "to improve efficiency and effectiveness in the delivery of services and outputs through: Institutional Capacity Strengthening in all Ministries, Departments and Agencies, Regional Coordinating Councils and District Assemblies; and Instituting a good governance culture in all aspects of the organisation and management of the Civil Service." It aimed "to do this through promoting performance improvement in individual institutions and by addressing efficiency, productivity, work ethic, service delivery, management and governance problems in the public sector." It then set out eight more specific objectives (with a further four added later) that were each also broadly defined, such as "i. promote the capability of civil service institutions to discharge their functions effectively in a transparent, competent and cost-effective manner thereby contributing positively to accelerated growth and equitable social development."[3]

Even in cases where the reforms' main motivation and content was oriented toward making fiscal savings or changes to salary levels, such as Ghana's Civil Service Reform Programme (1987–1993) and Single Spine Pay Policy (2007–2010), solving performance problems was cited as a major motivation and goal for reform.

There are several reasons why reforms tended to be couched in such ambitious language and expectations. One was the sheer magnitude of the shortcomings and necessary changes that reformers perceived. As Zambia's late Secretary to the Cabinet and Head of Civil Service Roland Msiska explained in an interview, "Anything less than overambitious in this country won't have a dent on our poverty."[4] Another was the difficulty in precisely measuring performance in a rigorous and comprehensive fashion across an entire civil service (as opposed to for a single process, service, or sector), which made it hard to demonstrate tangible improvement against a baseline and thus forced reform designers to resort to stating vague and overly broad goals that would be impossible to achieve. These were, perhaps, also compounded by the "planning fallacy"—the well-known behavioral bias of humans to be overoptimistic about how long tasks will take to achieve.[5]

Another major reason for overambitious goals, however, was the projectization of reform. Projects need to be approved in order to go ahead, and the existence of an approval process encourages reform designers to oversell the potential benefits of reform for the simple reason that the projects that appear most promising are the ones that tend to get approved. Anand Rajaram, former sector manager of public sector and governance work in Africa for the World Bank, explained that both governments and donors demanded ambition in projects:

> [Governments] are saying we have a big problem and if we say we are going to take a small crack at this then it is not inspiring. So part of it is built into the nature of that challenge that you have to excite the imagination by acknowledging the size of the problem in some way and that your effort will try to address it . . . saying we are going to solve the performance problem in four years may sound appropriately blood curdling and exciting but if no one has really bought into this then you have not spent the time building that openness and possibility. Then it is pure fiction what you have written. . . . I think that if you put together a project which says "we have very modest goals for this project, the reality of that country is that it is in dismal shape, but this will have a small effect on the conditions," why would the Board want to vote for that?[6]

Rajaram also pointed out that reform designers' personal incentives were often more closely linked to getting a project approved than to executing it successfully: "Unfortunately, the incentive system in a place like the World Bank is that you take the project to the Board and you are recognized. Whereas if you are the person who follows though, implementing the project and delivering it, there is much less structure." Kate Bridges and Michael Woolcock make a similar observation about projects being "overly ambitious" in their study of institutional reform in Malawi, citing World Bank research that found a "tendency to produce over ambitious plans at project design stage . . . for a [task team leader], what appears important when preparing the project is to make it as 'transformational' with a very ambitious agenda and please as many stakeholders as possible."[7]

The phenomenon of making projects overambitious to get the approval and resources necessary to undertake them is not restricted to civil service reforms or the operations of international donors but rather pertains to most large, complex public sector projects—and perhaps even to most major organizational change efforts in general. In his studies of infrastructure megaprojects, for example, Bent Flyvbjerg finds that nine in ten such projects have fewer benefits than forecasted and nine in ten overrun their anticipated costs. Examining the data, Flyvbjerg shows that this pattern isn't well explained by technical difficulties in forecasting or by simple overoptimism but instead that "planners and promoters deliberately misrepresent costs, benefits, and risks in order to increase the likelihood that it is their projects, and not those of their competition, that gain approval and funding."[8] Planners "spin scenarios of success and gloss over the potential for failure . . . this results in the pursuit of ventures that are unlikely to come in on budget or on time, or to deliver the promised benefits."[9] Similarly, Stefan Sveningsson and Nadja Sörgärde note in their textbook on change management that "To engage in organizational change can also be seen as an expression of drive and leadership, and can therefore enhance the status of those involved in it. Change attempts make it possible to profile oneself as a leader and to create an image of how you want to be perceived by others both within and outside the organization . . . hardly anyone wants to be seen as an ordinary supervisor or administrator of an existing organization compared to being seen as a change actor."[10]

Even within the context of civil service reform in Africa, setting overoptimistic reform goals was not solely attributable to donors. For instance, in one interview with Ghana's then-Head of Civil Service, Nana Agyekum-Dwamena, about the CSPIP reform, he explained how CSPIP had been adjudged to have fallen short of its goals because the project had included a number of highly ambitious "big-ticket items"—decentralization, public financial management reform, salary increases—among its deliverables. But the achievement of these was beyond the control of the Office of the Head of the Civil Service, and they did not happen within the project lifespan, so CSPIP was judged as having failed to deliver. I then began to ask a question about why the donors had been so overambitious in including these objectives in CSPIP, but Agyekum-Dwamena interrupted me: "No, no Martin, I disagree. In this particular case, with CSPIP, it was not the donors who set up those parameters." He then explained that these items were raised by domestic stakeholders during consultations in the design phase of CSPIP as being important for complementing and sustaining the performance improvement under CSPIP, and so including them within the CSPIP project had actually been the government's idea. "It was not an initiative of the DP [development partner], over a period of time it somehow then became a conditionality, not really imposed by DP, but by ourselves."[11]

Agyekum-Dwamena then carried on to explain that these system-wide, big-ticket changes were supposed to be undertaken under the umbrella of the broader National Institutional Renewal Program, which was governed by a National Oversight Committee. He said with a laugh, "My joke has always been that because they were called 'national oversight,' they lost sight of a lot of these things."[12]

To what extent did the projectization-induced incentive to set overambitious goals for reform explain the design and observed track record of civil service reforms? It's difficult to answer conclusively. The signs were all there—reform designers who talked about being ambitious and transformational and an abundance of reform plans that set out goals that were prima facie highly unlikely to be achievable. Issues of motivation, culture, and performance are always challenges for every bureaucracy in the world, so they are not problems that can be "solved" or "fixed," and certainly not in a few years. There is a lot of evidence that these dynamics exist with many types of public projects worldwide. At the same time, I encountered no "smoking gun" records of individuals saying that they consciously exaggerated the potential benefits or minimized the potential challenges of a specific reform, so it's hard to disentangle deliberate overselling from innocent overoptimism.

But the pattern of overambitious reform plans is certainly consistent with one of the more puzzling findings from chapter 3: that while most reforms achieved something, none of them achieved all the goals they set out for themselves. The dynamics of project design and approval processes are surely part of the explanation for this surprising pattern. Since it is nearly impossible to measure performance improvements civil service–wide in an absolute sense, the only available criterion for judging reform success is whether they meet their own goals. However, the goals, targets, and expectations for projects are endogenously determined, and reform designers have strong incentives to be overambitious in setting them—at least prior to the start of the reform. (Once the reform starts, of course, reform implementers' incentives might change, as the next section discusses.) So the more reformers think they can achieve, the higher they set their ambitions and vice versa. This practically guarantees that all reforms—from the most impactful to the least—will appear, from the outside, to be partial failures because they fell short of their own goals.

Another consequence of exaggerated expectations for reform is that it invites this glass-half-empty perspective, drawing attention toward reforms' shortcomings and away from what reforms do manage to achieve. Rajaram also reflected on this dynamic and what we should reasonably expect of reform efforts in complex bureaucratic systems:

> Even acknowledging that these things only achieve 50 percent of what they promised, that is fine. We should only expect 50 percent of what they promised to be achieved. I do not think they [can be] 100 percent with public sector reform, systems changes, behavioral changes, that would be difficult. Maybe only 20 percent even. . . . There are four components to this project, two went well and two did not. With the two that went well we met 60 percent or 70 percent [of] we thought we would achieve. That would not be a bad batting average for a public sector reform . . . [in] the evaluation of these projects, people do approach these projects like they are engineering projects. You say you [will] build 100 kilometers of road, but you only build five. You fall way short of the expectations. Building a road is something and building a system chain is quite different. It is way more complicated in some way . . . you won't get 100 percent [of] all these things [that] are there.[13]

HOW PROJECTIZATION SHAPED REFORM CONTENT

There is also reason to think that approaching reforms as one-off projects encouraged reformers to focus on making changes that were verifiable—in other words, on undertaking actions or outputs that could be specified in advance and measured afterward. Sometimes, this came in the form of creating or changing structures, rules, and processes, which exist on paper, and so are easy to explain in a strategic plan or annual report. Other times, it came in the form of undertaking countable actions, such as training sessions, organizational reviews, or purchasing tangible assets like computers. In this sense, the projectization of reforms compounded the tendency to focus on formal processes discussed in the last chapter, with similarly negative consequences for compliance with these processes and for eliciting important but unformalizable behaviors from civil servants.

The main factor driving this bias toward verifiable measures seems to have been the need to justify project budgets ex ante and account for how they were spent ex post. Getting either donors or finance ministries to approve budgets for unspecified reform activities is a challenge, and similarly, reporting on how resources were spent to donors or audit agencies is far easier for discrete, tangible outputs like new laws passed or workshops held than for harder-to-measure achievements like better implementation of existing processes or improved organizational culture.

These pressures have been widely noted by other researchers with respect to donor-funded institutional reform projects. For example, Lavagnon Ika has described an "accountability-for-results trap" in which implementers view results-based management tools as oriented toward external reporting and accountability rather than for use in internal improvement. Matt Andrews and colleagues have written about how projects tend to focus more on "form" rather than "function" in setting their targets and thus lead to changes in formal structures that are not matched by changes in actual behavior. Mark Buntaine and colleagues have shown that strong donor conditionalities push countries to adopt targets that measure "shallow" structural transformations rather than harder-to-achieve changes in outcomes. Kate Bridges and Woolcock have explored how donors' incentives to make disbursements on loans push them to adopt shallow targets in this mold.[14] In reflecting on Zambia's PSCAP-era reforms, Rajaram and colleagues ask, "is $10–20 million for a project in this area the best way to convince civil servants in a country to be more productive and change behaviors?" They go on to quote an anonymous Zambian senior official with experience designing and implementing reforms:

> In order to implement [reforms], I had been asked to provide cars to reforms teams, we did it; then, we were asked to provide computers, we did that too; then, we were asked to provide them formal training overseas, we did that as well; they came back and what happened? . . . Nothing! There was no greater capacity to reform despite these investments. Why is it so? Because reforming public sector requires a change in behavior and mindsets of people; cars, computers and formal training do not help in most cases. . . . The day a project is initiated, our problems begin.[15]

Most of this literature has placed the blame for this bias toward verifiable reform actions on the mindsets or incentives of donors. But similar dynamics also arose in cases where donors were not involved. For example, South Africa had relatively little donor funding for reforms (aside from technical assistance), but these tensions around the verifiability of reform achievements were very much present due to the threat of performance metrics being scrutinized or audited, and this sometimes pushed departments to focus these plans on activities and other easily measurable achievements rather than on outcomes. (Ironically, departments' five-year strategic plans were focused much more on impact and outcomes—because they were not subject to audit in the same way—and, thus, there was little articulation between them and the activity-focused annual plans.[16]) Similarly, South Africa had relatively few reforms with predefined end dates—perhaps due to not funding reform activities through donor projects— so, in that way, its reforms appeared to have been somewhat less projectized on average than in the other five countries. However, when I asked one senior official in South Africa whether he thought it was correct to say that the country had avoided taking a projectized approach to reform, he replied:

> I probably would disagree. . . . what we tend to do is we come up with new plans and we do tend to run it as projects. So unfortunately even a lot of our policies . . . what we tend to do is we start something and if we don't see immediate impacts we change it and give it a new name to try to create new energy around it. We tend not to show the patience to stick around and see it through. . . . My opinion is we have also very short-term focused projects and we don't see it through . . . we don't close these projects, we just slowly start putting them to the side and they become less and less visible.[17]

One specific way the bias toward verifiable reform activities manifested in both donor- and government-driven reforms was in the emphasis on trying to create new structures, rules, and processes rather than on trying to improve the implementation of existing ones. It is generally easier and more compelling (to most audiences) to say that a reform is going to revamp the country's annual appraisal system than to say that it is going to improve the execution of the existing one without making any formal changes. It is also easier to measure whether the new system has been formally adopted than how well it is being used. As one senior official in Ghana reflected, "Perhaps it's also the way we look at these reforms as projects. Projects come with money. Perhaps selling the idea that 'let's mend the old wineskin' is not so attractive."[18] For a whole range of stakeholders—from donors to finance ministries, audit agencies, voting publics, and even civil servants themselves—starting something new is easier to verify (and to claim credit for) than improving the operation of something that already exists. This bias in the content of reforms reinforced the existing tendency (discussed in the last chapter) toward formal reform measures and also had consequences for how projectized reforms were implemented.

HOW PROJECTIZATION SHAPED REFORM IMPLEMENTATION

The one-off nature of projectized reforms also directed energy and attention away from their effective implementation, institutionalization, and sustainability. Predefined timelines, the bias toward verifiable content, and a focus on introducing new processes rather than improving existing ones all contributed to far more attention being paid to making changes on paper than to embedding and sustaining them.

The senior official in Ghana mentioned above explained how this occurred in government. The combination of project timelines and pressure to disburse project funds meant that reformers spent most of their energy on the preparation and execution of the first phase of a reform initiative, often designing and introducing a new formal process. But by the time that was complete, either the funds and momentum had run out, or the project schedule stipulated moving on, and so the effective implementation of a reformed process was almost never the main focus of attention: "We have 3 phases, after we finish phase 1 instead of making sure this one is being used, we go onto phase 2." She blamed this implementation dynamic—rather than the content of the reforms, which she thought was largely good—for the pattern of disappointing reform impacts: "Probably we're not spending enough time cascading the ideas down, because as soon as the project ends it ends." She continued on to lament that individuals and governments tended to start one initiative, then move on to something new and forget about the older initiative instead of saying, "Wait a minute, let's make sure this one is being used before we go on."[19]

Similarly, Agyekum-Dwamena explained with respect to Ghana's Civil Service Reform Programme (1987–1993) how, as a junior officer working on the reform, he had "the impression later that there was going to be a review and the consultants are coming. 'We are to meet this deadline,' that was the message that was coming from OHCS [Office of the Head of Civil Service], MSD [Management Services Department], even our team leader that 'we needed to finish this thing by this date' so I did not really get the impression that we were doing it because it is good for the civil service." But when I asked a question about whether the donor-drivenness of the CSRP meant that its content was wrong for

Ghana, he replied, "No, no, no—I do not think it was bad, because all the things that we were supposed to do were good. But I think it was the timelines were more, we were doing because we have to deliver."[20]

This pattern of reform implementation—or nonimplementation—appeared across numerous sources, contexts, and reform efforts, both donor-supported and nondonor-supported. In Zambia, World Bank project completion reports from the Public Sector Management Program (2006–2012) state that service charters were "adopted and institutionalized" in eight ministries and pointed to the Ministry of Lands as a successful example.[21] But in an interview, a senior Zambian official who had been involved with supporting the adoption of service charters stated that he and his colleagues had observed that these tended to be adopted on paper and effective for one or two years but then rapidly drop off—even citing the Ministry of Lands as an example of this.[22] In Ghana, a different senior official observed a similar pattern of changes being put in place but then rapidly regressing in response to pressure brought to bear under the decidedly nondonor-driven Chief Directors Performance Agreement system since 2013.[23] An official in Nigeria described how SERVICOM evaluations of service delivery organizations were supposed to include periodic follow-up visits to check the implementation status of recommended changes but that this rarely happened.[24] In South Africa, another official explained that the raft of new laws and regulations introduced in the mid-1990s was accompanied by an initial burst of training and awareness raising, but, "I think it should have gone on for longer. Again, they assumed that the changes, I think they made assumptions about how, about the ease of implementing the changes, they made assumptions that things could be done in a relatively short period of time and that the initial capacity building that they did would be permanent. And they underestimated the extent to which it is difficult to implement changes like this and the length of time they take to implement properly."[25]

Why should it matter for implementation if a given process is introduced as a one-off intervention or project—particularly if such projects actually seem quite effective for designing and adopting new formal processes? Again, the answer goes back to the distinctions between nonperformance, perfunctory performance, and consummate performance from chapter 2. Formal processes are easy to adopt on paper, but if civil servants don't want to execute them—because they take time, create private costs, or perhaps are ideologically opposed to them—then they won't unless they expect that compliance will be enforced. So enforcement credibility matters for compliance. However, compliance alone only gets people to go through the motions, moving them and the organization from a state of nonperformance to perfunctory performance. For some types of processes, this might be adequate, but many important performance-related actions require individuals to do nonverifiable things that can't be formally prespecified and/or measured. Getting individuals to undertake these tasks as well—getting to consummate performance—requires that they expect other members of their team to also do so: bosses to recognize and reward it, and colleagues to match their effort so that it doesn't go to waste.

Expectations are about the future, about the continued emphasis on the implementation of these new processes. But approaching reforms as one-off, nonrepeated interventions, sometimes even with end dates, conveys the opposite message to workers who are the targets of reform: This is a one-time thing; it will not continue. Or at least, its effective implementation will not continue to be a priority for the people who authorize, lead, and manage reform efforts. Trying to achieve lasting changes with one-time interventions thus ignores the mechanisms that can lead to ongoing improvements in performance behaviors.

To illustrate this with a more tangible example, let's return to the case of individual-level performance management reforms that we discussed in chapter 4. Recall that these were intended to work via an annual process of setting performance targets, assessing performance, and delivering rewards or sanctions associated with that process. This is not a simple linear process where civil servants' actions follow in a direct and deterministic way once the system is introduced. Rather, it is a repeated cyclical process in which each step is shaped by expectations of how future steps of the process will unfold and by experiences of how the past steps have unfolded. Together, these experiences and expectations shape their perceptions of how credible the system is and how it will be implemented. As one Zambian official explained, civil servants' disappointing experience of previous reform waves meant that when new efforts came, they responded by saying, "'Ah we've seen it before.' . . . It can make a very toxic environment."[26]

Many processes introduced as reforms are intended to be ongoing and repeated, like annual appraisal systems. In their review for the World Bank about the worldwide evidence on such systems in both the private and public sectors, researchers Sabina Schnell and colleagues blame the frequent ineffectiveness of these systems on how they are often imposed as one-off reforms: "having a performance management system is not enough. . . . Yet more often than not, organizations approach the introduction or overhaul of their performance management systems as a one-off change in human resource (HR) rules and procedures, rather than as part of a broader set of long-term reforms of various core organizational processes."[27]

Thinking about the implementation of these systems as a matter of changing repeated processes, as figure 5.1 illustrates, rather than as the rolling out of discrete

Expectation

Experience

| Target Setting | | Assessment |

Expectation Experience

Experience Expectation

Incentives

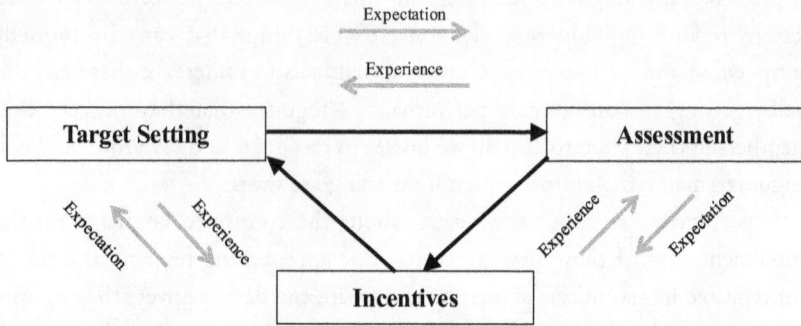

FIGURE 5.1 Performance Management Systems Are a Process, Not an Intervention

Source: Author's synthesis.

interventions helps explain why attempting to introduce them as part of one-off reforms often resulted in failure. Getting repeated processes to work properly requires not just creating them but ongoing efforts to support and reinforce their operation. But the dynamics of projectized reforms undermined reformers' incentives to do this and conveyed to the broader civil service that it probably wouldn't be done. Approaching the reform of ongoing processes as a discrete intervention thus undermined the effective implementation of such reforms.

HOW PROJECTIZATION SHAPED REFORM LEADERSHIP

Most reforms were characterized by top-down leadership models in which a central actor at the peak of the bureaucratic hierarchy designed and decided on the reform content and imposed it on the rest of the civil service. In some cases, this top-down reform approach was led by an individual like a president or head of civil service, in others by an organization like a cabinet office or ministry of public service, and often by some combination of the two. To some extent, this leadership model was identifiable by specific institutional and project features that were often present, such as the separation of reform from organizational processes and of design from implementation. But the dominant feature was an attitude held by those central actors who were primarily responsible for originating and delivering the reform about who was driving the reform and who "owned" it. This attitude was picked up and mirrored by rank-and-file civil servants, who generally perceived reform as something being done *to* them and their organizations rather than something being done *by* them.

This sentiment came through strongly in many interviews, especially with nonelite civil servants who were not involved in designing and implementing reforms but were affected by the rules, processes, and structures they introduced, many of whom specifically used the phrase "top-down" to describe how they experienced these reform efforts.[28] This pattern has also been noted by other researchers. For example, Abraham Rugo Muriu and Frank Kwaku Ohemeng both attribute the failure of individual-level performance management reforms to spur cultural change and meaningful performance improvement in Kenya and Ghana, respectively, to them being implemented in a top-down fashion and seen by civil servants as an imposition.[29] Similarly, Robert Dodoo (writing in 1997 as Head of Ghana's Civil Service), Stephen Adei and Yaw Boachie-Danquah, and Joseph Ayee all attribute the shortcomings of Ghana's Civil Service Reform Programme (CSRP, 1987–1993), in part, to the top-down fashion in which it was imposed on the civil service.[30] And with respect to institutional reforms in general, Matt Andrews has noted that donors tend to find it convenient to engage with a single reform "champion" within a government, leading to reforms often having only a very narrow support base.[31]

It is easy to see the top-down leadership model at work in reforms like Ghana's CSRP, which was oriented around cost-cutting, undertaken in conjunction with a structural adjustment program, and funded almost entirely by the World Bank. In such cases, reforms were clearly imposed on civil services by a combination of donors and a narrow set of elite actors within the government, such as project implementation teams and finance ministries.

However, the tendency toward top-down leadership of reforms was also in evidence in reforms that were definitely not donor-driven, such as the creation of Nigeria's SERVICOM, an agency that conducted service delivery reviews of other public sector organizations. Although it was inspired by a reform that happened in the United Kingdom and subsequently funded largely by a grant from the UK's Department for International Development, SERVICOM was created at the directive of President Olusegun Obasanjo and enthusiastically championed by him—supported by donors but not driven by them. But despite this high level of commitment from the presidency, SERVICOM initially struggled to be effective at spurring improvements in the ministries, departments, and agencies it worked with: "But at that time when the SERVICOM reform started, it was a top-down approach, [it] even started from the Presidency. He called the ministers and council and told them this is the directive, this is what you should do. And I think there was a little bit of . . . they felt they were being imposed

[on] ... well, there was compliance. But [also] the undertone of [we] really don't understand what this is all about."[32]

Similarly, development consultant and former head of Nigeria's Bureau of Public Sector Reforms, Joe Abah, described how SERVICOM's designers focused on getting changes mandated from the top down in ways that ended up undermining their ability to get cooperation from the service delivery organizations it worked with:

> I think the effect of [SERVICOM] has been limited. It hasn't been a complete waste of time but the effect has been limited ... there's this mentality of "all we need is power." That's the first thing they did, was go to the Federal Executive Council to ask that everybody must have a SERVICOM office. So of course everybody set up a SERVICOM office ... people stuck the SERVICOM banner on the nearest toilet, and nobody cared what was going on inside so it was just appearing to comply, which they did. The next thing they did was [say], "oh the nodal officer should report straight to the minister, period," so here is the permanent secretary rubbing his hands and thinking, "ok so you're a nodal officer, you are an assistant director, you're going to bypass me the permanent secretary to go report to the minister and you expect me to release funds for you to do any work ... never going to happen." So again, it antagonized the system against itself. ... Fine. Have a SERVICOM office [and] post to the most problematic person in the office in that place to get him out of the way. Make sure you don't release any funds to them.[33]

But despite these challenges, there is also evidence that SERVICOM did manage to get many organizations to implement some positive changes that improved service delivery, even if not to the extent that it desired. Support from above—both from the presidency and senior managers within each organization—was crucial to the setting up of SERVICOM and much of what it was able to achieve.[34] But it also illustrated the limitations of heavily top-down approaches for achieving and sustaining performance improvement.

Interestingly, SERVICOM has gradually evolved away from this top-down approach. After the exit of President Obasanjo in 2007 and the end of DFID funding in 2009, "Everything basically ground to a halt,"[35] and for half a dozen years, the organization struggled to sustain itself, retain staff, and continue its core work. However, the organization managed to cobble together funding from the government budget and international donors in order to maintain itself and operate on a more sustainable footing. While it arguably did not regain the political salience and centrality that it had during the initial Obasanjo years, it adjusted to this, in part, by pivoting its operations increasingly toward universities and hospitals rather than the higher-profile and more powerful (and, hence, potentially resistant) government ministries and agencies on which much of its early effort had been focused.[36] It also launched a weekly SERVICOM Help Desk radio program, in which SERVICOM's National Coordinator would listen to complaints about service delivery and human rights issues from callers, give advice, and follow up on cases with the relevant institutions—combining raising public awareness with generating legitimacy for its mission beyond the highest echelons of government. In this way, SERVICOM also serves as a model of what can be creatively achieved by working outside of a purely top-down paradigm.

HOW PROJECTIZATION SHAPED REFORM POLITICS

A truism among practitioners and researchers alike is that reforms require political backing and ownership at the highest levels to be successfully implemented. Numerous case studies and project reports have lamented the lack of political support for reforms and sought to explain the causes and consequences. The ways political support can be helpful for reform are obvious, and among the reforms examined in this book, there were certainly many whose shortcomings were, at least in part, attributable to a lack of political backing.

But even for reform efforts that did receive strong political backing or originated from politicians, this close association sometimes proved to be a double-edged sword. The same mechanisms that allowed politicians to channel their support into greater clout, attention, and resources for reforms also led them to be designed and implemented in more projectized ways that undermined their implementation, impact, and sustainability.

Where it occurred, the tight association of reforms with political leaders and parties seems to have arisen from a combination of two factors. First, bureaucrats, donors, and politicians alike often perceived vocal political support for a reform as necessary for its success and, thus, sought to create and channel it to support reform efforts. Second, politicians often sought to emphasize their association with a reform to claim credit with either voters or donors.

Both of these factors pushed all actors involved to find ways to make reforms more closely associated with their political sponsors. One obvious way was to separate reform activities from core bureaucratic processes by denoting reforms with their own acronyms, branding, and budget lines, all of which made it easier for politicians to attract attention to these reforms, make them more visible, and claim credit for them. Another way was to drive reform design and implementation through separate project teams or reform implementation units—often located in the presidency or otherwise close to executive authority—rather than through the mainstream bureaucracy, which gave politicians the ability to closely oversee reform activities and gave reform implementers greater access to their political sponsors. The association of reforms with political leaders strengthened the tendency toward both of these features of projectization (although they were not the sole cause of them). These same factors also reinforced the other submechanisms of projectization discussed above—more ambitious-sounding goals and expectations, more verifiable and publicly visible content, more one-off implementation, and more top-down leadership.

One of the ways these dynamics may have manifested was through a shortening of reform time horizons, as electoral pressures pushed leaders to not only want to demonstrate fast results but also to become risk-averse near elections. For example, Zambia's former Secretary to the Cabinet Roland Msiska lamented in an interview that reformers only had three years of any electoral cycle to work in because during the last two years, politicians would be campaigning and any complaint against a reform would sink it.[37] Similarly, a South African civil servant with experience implementing reforms reflected: "We've got to appreciate that politicians do not think longer than five years in advance. We've got elections every five years, so they are pressurized to show good, fast results. And then if you're not getting results from a specific initiative, then you can close it or just let it dwindle away."[38]

The incentive for politicians to create a perceived identification between themselves and specific reform efforts may also have undermined the likelihood that these efforts would be sustained after they left. For example, one interviewee involved in reforms in Ghana complained that politicians each wanted to start their own reforms once they came into office rather than continuing existing ones started by previous leaders.[39] This is consistent with the idea that political leaders' support for reforms is driven, at least in part, by a desire to claim credit for these initiatives. The more publicly a reform is identified with a given politician, the more likely their successors would likely be to discontinue it. Similarly, the researcher and experienced reform architect Tunji Olaopa remarked, "The backlash created by personalization of reform by [senior members of President Obasanjo's administration] . . . they made some statements at the time that offended the civil service. You know, 'that service has no brain,' 'most of them are archaic' . . . and this thing filtered into the press. . . . It eroded the service['s] support to some of the reforms that they did, so consequently when they exited the service was more inclined to pull down [some of] what they are doing [rather than] to drive it forward."[40]

How common is it for political backing to intensify the projectization of a reform, and how negative are the consequences for the reform's success? The answers are unclear. On the one hand, it is logical that greater personal identification of a reform with a political leader would lead to an increase in some of the features of projectization, and there is ample evidence consistent with these mechanisms across many reform efforts. On the other hand, the analysis in chapter 3 found little support for the idea that electoral cycles and leadership transitions were the main factors driving reform initiation and duration. It seems most appropriate to conclude that, while political time horizons do shape reform in at least some cases, they are not necessarily the main factor doing so—just as political incentives are only one of several channels through which projectization emerges and shapes reform efforts.

Similarly, while it seems plausible that politically driven incentives for projectization accentuate some of the negative consequences of projectization outlined above, it does not necessarily follow that greater political support is harmful overall for reform efforts. Rather, it points to a need to think in greater detail about the different ways political support can be expressed publicly and channeled bureaucratically during reform efforts. The challenge for reform leadership is to maximize the benefits of political support while minimizing the potential negative consequences of greater projectization, all while preserving politicians' incentives to offer support in the first place. We will return to this issue in chapter 7 when considering potential alternative approaches to reform that avoid the pitfalls of projectization.

• • •

This chapter has argued that governments' reform efforts were usually characterized by projectization—an approach that sees reform primarily as a one-off intervention that is separate from core processes, has distinct design and implementation phases, and/or has an envisioned end date. Projectization shaped reform and undermined its effectiveness through five sets of mutually reinforcing submechanisms that related to the expectations, content, implementation, leadership, and politics of reform. These patterns of projectization thus constituted the second main mechanism of reform failure I observed, and are summarized in table 5.1.

TABLE 5.1 How projectization shaped reform efforts

	Common features of projectization	Why?	With what consequences?
Expectations	• Overly ambitious goals • Framed as solutions to wide range of performance problems	• Need to exaggerate expected benefits to get buy-in and resources to undertake reform	• Reforms inevitably fail to achieve their goals, get viewed as failures
Content	• Focus on making changes that are ex ante specifiable and ex post measurable (i.e., verifiable)	• Design of project prior to and separate from implementation • Need to account for how project resources are spent	• Reforms focus on making formal changes rather than changing behavior • Reforms focus on introducing new processes rather than improving existing ones
Implementation	• Little focus on embedding and effectively implementing rules and processes	• Introducing new processes can be done as a one-off project or intervention; embedding them takes time and iteration	• One-off projects fail to improve compliance with formal processes or encourage informal supporting actions • Changes on paper but not in practice
Leadership	• Reforms designed and delivered in top-down fashion by a central actor	• Civil services conceived of as systems in bad equilibrium in need of a shock from outside/above • Separation of reform activities and teams from core organizational processes	• Reforms fail to get broad buy-in or trigger decentralized action, improvement
Politics	• Reforms closely associated with a specific political or bureaucratic leader • Greater separation of reform branding and activities from core bureaucratic processes	• Perceived need for high-level support and backing for reform • Desire to claim credit for reform (either vis-à-vis donors or voters)	• Higher salience makes it easier to push through formal changes but also decreases likelihood they are sustained after leadership transition • Shortening of time horizon of reform

Source: Author's synthesis.

Some clarifications and caveats are in order. First, projectization is not a single feature or variable but a linked set of mechanisms or submechanisms that frequently co-occur and stem from the same underlying factor: approaching reform as a one-off intervention. However, these mechanisms manifest to different extents and in different ways across different reform efforts, not only in the formal design features of the reform and its implementation structures but also in the mental models of the individuals driving the reform. So whether a reform has the features of projectization is not a simple yes/no question or even a linear spectrum but, rather, a hard-to-measure and interrelated set of qualitative judgments about how the reform is being approached. While the concept resists oversimplification, it is also abundantly evident in the data that essentially all reform efforts had some of the features of projectization, and many had all of them—with predictable consequences for how these reforms unfolded and consistently fell short of achieving the changes they aimed for.

Second, at the same time as projectization was clearly a mechanism of failure, it is not possible to conclude that projectization is always detrimental to reforms. Some of this is due to the empirical and methodological problems of measurement and the unavailability of counterfactuals that we've discussed previously, which make it impossible to conclusively estimate the impact of particular reforms. While we can observe reform features and approaches and trace through how they appear to be contributing to the failure and success of the reform, we need to be cautious about extrapolating from these mechanisms to the overall impact of the reform. More theoretically, it's also possible that projectization (or at least some features of it) is appropriate for some types of reforms. In particular, if a reform is trying to make a change that is highly verifiable and has predictable and deterministic consequences on performance—like flicking a light switch on or off—then approaching the reform as a one-off intervention might make sense.

However, what this book has found, over and over again, is that performance-oriented reforms in civil services are not like flicking a light switch, pulling a lever, or changing a line of computer code—they don't automatically and instantly translate into changes in behavior. This is because so much of what civil servants do is nonverifiable, and getting them to do nonverifiable things requires them to believe that their actions will be recognized and reciprocated, not just in the present but also in the future. This poses an inherent challenge for reform efforts that approach making change solely as a one-time intervention. So while some elements of projectized approaches might be appropriate or practical even in the most successful reforms, it's important to recognize the ways they risk undermining the end goal of reform: getting individuals to do the informalizable things they need to do to get to consummate performance.

It seems appropriate to close this chapter on projectization with a brief digression on the history of the term. The first use of the word *projectization* with respect to civil service or institutional reform that I have found comes not from an academic theorist but from the World Bank itself in a 1994 discussion paper entitled, "Projectizing the Governance Approach to Civil Service Reform," which was intended as a how-to guide for officials trying to package institutional reforms in ways that could be supported by project loans.[41] So from the term's beginning, *projectization* was understood as an effort to simplify and bound what was acknowledged to be the messy reality of systemic bureaucratic reform into something that was easier to administer and manage. Other practitioners and researchers have since remarked on what they term "projectitis," or the tendency to try (and fail) to achieve systems change through isolated projects with their own external funding streams in everything from health systems reform to solar system installation.[42] Also in the early- to mid-1990s, terms like *projectization* and *projectification* began being used in the literature on project management and IT investment in private firms in high-income countries—entirely separately from issues of development, donors, and public sector institutions—with *projectization* referring to "the extent to which a business is based on projects and the project way of working pervades."[43] The breadth of the term's usage is just one more piece of evidence that, while donors' involvement may exacerbate projectization, it is far from the sole factor driving it. Indeed, the negative consequences of projectized approaches to reform are also evident in much research on reforms, even in high-income countries where donors are absent. For instance, in their review of reform efforts in the United Kingdom, researchers Charlotte Pickles and James Sweetland write, "even where good ideas for reform are instigated and a serious implementation plan is in place, embedding and sustaining those reforms requires a different set of actions. Whitehall reform cannot be seen as a 'once and done' process."[44]

Having examined the two main mechanisms of reform failure, the next chapter turns to the main mechanisms of success that characterized reform histories across these six countries. While most reforms were designed to have an impact through the one-off introduction of new formal rules, structures, and processes, the most consistent benefits for performance occurred through a more informal and often unintended channel: getting civil servants to talk to one another, share information and ideas, and learn how to do their jobs better. Let's now explore how these unformalizable conversations unfolded, often in the shadow of (and sometimes despite) formal processes, and consider what lessons this yields for designing and implementing reforms.

6

Mechanisms of Success

Opportunities and Energy for Performance Improvement

Chapters 4 and 5 focused on the mechanisms through which reforms failed: trying to force performance improvements through formal processes and approaching reform as a one-off project or intervention. These mechanisms meant that reform efforts tended to yield perfunctory compliance with the new processes—just going through the motions—rather than meaningful changes in behaviors and performance. And even the perfunctory compliance often faded away over time.

However, many reform efforts also succeeded in spurring genuine improvements. In varying ways and to differing extents, they got civil servants to undertake unformalizable actions, changed expectations and norms, and made performance more prominent in organizational cultures. These weren't magic bullets that completely transformed civil services overnight. They were usually limited in scope, sometimes achieved their positive effects through unintended or unforeseen pathways, and had their own shortcomings and limitations. Still, they were promising examples of how system-level reforms can lead to meaningful change despite all the challenges they face in doing so. What were the mechanisms of success that explained how such improvements occurred?

This chapter argues that when reforms succeeded at improving performance, it was because they created *opportunities* and *energy* for civil servants to talk about performance and how to improve it.

Opportunities came from a mix of formal processes and informal spaces that led civil servants to have conversations about goals, roles, and performance that were not happening before. Providing these opportunities helped empower the many civil servants who already cared about performance and wanted to improve and gave them outlets through which to engage with their colleagues. This contrasted with the dominant paradigm of assuming that carrots and sticks were needed to force behavior change on unwilling civil servants. These forums and processes could help make performance and results more salient within organizations, and they also served as opportunities for civil servants to learn about their roles and how they connected to those of their colleagues, to give and receive feedback, and to generate and share ideas for improvement.

Energy meant making civil servants believe that the reform effort would actually lead to something tangible and wasn't just talk that would soon dissipate. It helped reformers surmount the credibility barrier that faced reforms, in which individuals did not change their behavior because they didn't expect their colleagues to change anything either. Energy came from leaders and was crucial for focusing attention on performance and building credibility and, thus, momentum for widespread changes in both nonverifiable and verifiable behaviors.

Even in the absence of energy from leaders, the intrinsic motivation and professionalism of individual civil servants still sometimes drove change at smaller scales when opportunities had been created. Similarly, energy for change in the absence of structured opportunities for discussing performance was also sometimes enough to spur improvements. But when reforms did succeed in making positive changes at scale, it was usually because these two mechanisms combined to catalyze conversations that helped managers and rank-and-file civil servants do their jobs better on a day-to-day basis and that contributed in small but meaningful ways to changing organizational cultures.

Before proceeding, an important reminder: In this book, I focus on analyzing not *cases* of success and failure but *mechanisms* of success and failure. Rather than classifying reforms as "successes" or "failures" and then trying to explain this variation, my main aim is to identify and understand the mechanisms through which each reform succeeded in some ways and failed in others. To recap, there are two reasons for this. First, the criteria for assessing reforms—their goals or targets—are set endogenously in the reform design process, so it is difficult to accurately measure and compare overall reform success. The fact that essentially all reforms are partial successes (or partial failures, depending on your view) is partially due to this. We can use qualitative data and careful triangulation to understand degrees of success and failure, but it would be misleading to try to formally code it. Second, and more importantly for this chapter, each reform is not wholly characterized by either mechanisms of success or mechanisms of failure but by multiple mechanisms coexisting together in various combinations and interacting. The reforms I discuss as exhibiting these mechanisms of success are not necessarily "success stories"; indeed, in past chapters, I have analyzed some of these same reforms in terms of their mechanisms of failure. So from an analytical perspective, the question is not so much whether each mechanism is present but to what extent and in what ways.

To investigate these mechanisms of success, this chapter begins by returning to the individual-level performance-linked incentive reforms discussed in chapter 4. It shows how they sometimes succeeded in creating opportunities for discussing and improving performance despite the near-universal absence of the rewards and sanctions that were intended to accompany them. The chapter then discusses how other types of reforms were also sometimes able to create opportunities for discussing and changing practices. It then turns to examining a set of reforms that succeeded in generating energy for change but created few opportunities for civil servants to actually discuss how to do it. Finally, the chapter considers how reforms did (and did not) manage to combine these two mechanisms of success—opportunities and energy—in various ways. The chapter closes by discussing some of the challenges of activating and sustaining these mechanisms and the ways projectization and a focus on purely formal changes often undermined them. Taken together, this chapter sets the stage for the third and final part of the book, which seeks to understand how reformers can maximize mechanisms of success and minimize mechanisms of failure.

CREATING OPPORTUNITIES TO DISCUSS PERFORMANCE

In chapter 4, we examined how individual-level performance management systems, like annual staff appraisals or leadership performance contracts, consistently failed to deliver differentiated rewards and sanctions. These systems' focus on using formal structures and processes to try to force or incentivize better performance constituted one of the main mechanisms of failure for reforms.

Despite the dismal record of formal incentives, however, it is not the case that individual-level performance management reforms had no positive effects. Across countries, interviewees pointed to the positive benefits that such systems sometimes brought by creating discussions around goals, responsibilities, and performance. For example, one rank-and-file civil servant in Ghana explained an effort in the mid-2010s to revitalize the annual performance appraisal system:

> The system gives everyone a specific focus and I benefit from that. I know what I am expected to do by the day, month and year. It makes me stay focused and more efficient. It makes me want to deliver and gone are the days where I sit about waiting for the work to come. . . . Before, there was no mutuality or

participation. . . . Now you sit with your supervisor. . . . Before you would set [targets] and there is no assessment until the end of the year . . . there is no way to see what has happened, [but] now there is a way to review. The old annual appraisal was sparingly used, only when people were due for promotion. Now there is care behind it. [Formerly the] head of department that would do [the assessment], now it is the one you are working with who will do the appraisal.[1]

Similarly, another midranking civil servant in Zambia said of their annual performance appraisals: "There has been a one-on-one interaction which has helped with understanding what gaps people have. It has helped me to understand at what level they are supposed to operate because at the end of the year, we find out if that has been met."[2] These discussions helped civil servants better understand how their work fit into that of their team and the broader organization. As one rank-and-file civil servant in Ghana commented about the country's Chief Director Performance Agreement system in the mid- to late-2010s (which had also begun to be cascaded down to directors), "You realise what you do is indirectly linked to the director. If I deliver, then the chief director is able to satisfy what he has to do. If I do not then my director and chief director are affected."[3] And a 2008 Zambian consultancy report evaluating Zambia's staff performance management systems noted, "The performance evaluation systems that both managers and employees rate highest are those that let managers and employees communicate—share ideas, opinions, and information whereas most 'traditional' systems put managers into the position of uncomfortable judges, telling employees that their work either was or was not 'satisfactory.'"[4]

These conversations and the clarity and understanding they brought were widely reported to have been useful, even though they did not always occur in each reform case or uniformly across organizations and teams. So while performance management systems were generally introduced with the idea that attaching incentives to formal performance measures was the key to improving performance, the main mechanism through which these appraisal systems actually improved performance was through the unformalizable processes of discussion and feedback, and civil servants then choosing to use this information to take largely informal, nonverifiable actions to improve performance. These discussions were largely nonverifiable—hard to prespecify exactly ex ante, hard to measure well ex post—because, while the formal rules of a performance management system could demand that such a meeting happen, they couldn't force the discussions to be honest and meaningful rather than perfunctory. So if the main mechanism of failure of performance-linked incentive systems was their focus on formal processes and formal performance measures, their main mechanism of success was their catalyzing of informal discussion and communication.

Of course, creating clarity around targets and feedback on performance was an explicit goal of many individual-level performance-linked incentive reforms. But in practice, this goal tended to sit in tension with these reforms' primary objective of creating a system of objective targets and performance measurements based on which incentives could be delivered. This was because trying to achieve full objectivity required squeezing out all the nonverifiable aspects of target-setting and performance measurement and feedback that inherently created ambiguity, subjectivity, and potential unfairness.

For example, individual appraisal and performance contracting systems universally demanded that targets be S.M.A.R.T.: specific, measurable, achievable (or attainable), relevant (or realistic), and time-bound. In other words, they should be verifiable: perfectly specifiable in advance and perfectly measurable after the fact. But this focus on measuring performance through verifiable targets fits poorly with the reality of civil service work. One South African civil servant involved in numerous reforms reflected on this mismatch:

> We try to be S.M.A.R.T., but I cringe every time I get feedback from my HR unit telling me my indicators are not S.M.A.R.T. A lot of people try to make performance management an objective system, and I tell them it cannot be . . . for me [discussion] is the most critical thing in this whole performance management system . . . [having] regular information about what's happening, and then having regular feedbacks. And you have to acknowledge that it's a subjective thing. Yes you can have some objective measures, but they should be to substantiate your subjective opinion as a manager and point towards indicators of that.[5]

This tension became more severe when stronger rewards, sanctions, and controls were applied to these processes. For example, in Kenya, linking hard incentives to performance contracts reportedly pushed permanent secretaries to start to seek out soft targets that they could control rather than aiming at improvement in final outcomes.[6] And in South Africa, the emphasis on measuring outcomes and results reportedly led not just to civil servants devoting a huge amount of time to an increasingly burdensome performance reporting system but also to performance agreements and annual work plans that increasingly focused on highly measurable short-term deliverables that were largely delinked from the broader five-year national plan—the implementation of which was the original rationale for the focus on outcomes.[7] Thus, while formal performance appraisal and performance contract systems had the potential to create discussion opportunities that could help improve performance via better communication, this benefit was easily erased when high-powered incentives were attached to these systems.

Aside from individual-level performance management systems, many other types of reforms also created opportunities for discussing performance and how to improve it. In South Africa, for example, the annual Senior Management Service conferences were "excellent" forums for managers to communicate with one another, share ideas, and shape culture.[8] "The speakers we brought to those, the exposure we had, it really benefitted [us] . . . talking to a number of senior managers, they seem to have really benefitted from that exposure that made a huge difference."[9] In Nigeria, the SERVICOM service delivery improvement agency conducted in-depth, participatory service delivery evaluations with scores of ministries, departments, and agencies to identify problems and ways to improve.[10] In Senegal, the Comité d'allègement et de simplification des formalités et procédures administratives (Committee on Reducing and Simplifying Rules and Administrative Procedures) regularly convened a rotating and cross-institutional set of officers to identify opportunities to alleviate both internal and client-facing administrative burdens.[11] In Kenya, Rapid Results Initiatives (RRIs)—one-hundred-day periods of intense action in a ministry aimed at changing a specific process or attaining a specific objective, with coaching (but generally not financial resources) from a central support team—brought organization members together to collectively diagnose and find ways to fix longstanding problems.[12]

What united these diverse reforms was the thoughtful use of formal processes to convene, enable, and encourage discussions about performance. The processes themselves were mainly formal in the sense that they could be specified and measured, but the discussions themselves were largely unformalizable. For example, annual staff appraisal systems could stipulate that supervisors and supervisees should have annual or quarterly meetings and talk about performance, and the completed appraisal template could be collected as proof that the meeting occurred (although even this could be faked, of course). But no one could force the content of these conversations to be meaningful, and efforts to do so via stronger incentives and control mechanisms tended to lead instead to gaming behavior and resistance.

Instead, the motivations that led civil servants to take advantage of these opportunities for discussion were intrinsic ones: the desire to do better for the country and the organization's clients and the professionalism that led people to want to get things done and feel proud of their teams and organizations. Of course, this meant that the take-up of these opportunities for performance discussion was far from the universal, homogenous, mechanistic ideal that many people envisioned for these systems and processes. Many supervisors and supervisees treated appraisal discussions as a formality or did not even have them, and many organizations treated SERVICOM evaluations as an imposition to be endured rather than a chance to improve, and so on. One interviewee remarked about South Africa's Management Performance Assessment Tool, which conducted annual reviews of organizational management practices and sought to use these to spark conversations around improvement, "It was more like a support measure than a regulatory measure, MPAT. And a support measure, support can be offered. But you can take a horse to water but you can't force it to drink. That was always going to be a limitation with it. And I think it was useful for those who wanted to participate and wanted to improve the administration across the board. It was useful for them."[13]

So creating these opportunities for discussion didn't automatically lead all people or organizations to do nonverifiable things. At the same time, neither did the use of rewards, sanctions, or compliance tools. But at least in some cases, the creation of these opportunities was a successful mechanism for getting civil servants to undertake important but nonverifiable tasks.

CREATING ENERGY TO DISCUSS PERFORMANCE

The other main mechanism through which reforms got people to change unformalizable behaviors was by creating energy around improving performance. More precisely, reforms sometimes managed to shift individual and collective norms and expectations about acceptable or encouraged behavior, how other colleagues were likely to behave, and whether unformalizable actions would be recognized and rewarded. A major common barrier to reforms was the sense of inertia and skepticism that often greeted them, both due to cynicism induced by past experience and because even the most motivated individuals would only want to put out the extra effort to perform consummately if they thought that other members of their team and organization might do the same. Creating energy in this way could help break out of this negative equilibrium, activating individuals' intrinsic motivation and desire for better collective performance and helping make them believe that taking important but unformalizable actions would not go to waste.

Perhaps the clearest example of this was South Africa's Batho Pele ("People First") initiative. Batho Pele was launched in 1997 as part of a postdemocratization raft of legislative and policy reforms that aimed at transforming the apartheid-era bureaucracy, which had been oriented around controlling and oppressing the majority population rather than being responsive to its needs and wellbeing. The white paper that inaugurated Batho Pele called it: "an approach which puts pressure on systems, procedures, attitudes and behaviour within the Public Service and reorients them in the customer's favour, an approach which puts the people first. This does not mean introducing more rules and centralised processes or micro-managing service delivery activities. Rather, it involves creating a framework for the delivery of public services which treats citizens more like customers and enables the citizens to hold public servants to account for the service they receive. A framework which frees up the energy and commitment of public servants to introduce more customer-focused ways of working."[14]

The Batho Pele approach was broken down into a set of eight principles, and it was these principles rather than a set of activities or outputs that comprised the core of the reform: "Batho Pele is not a single project. . . . Batho Pele is a characterisation of the nature and quality of service delivery interface that should obtain between government and the public."[15] The slogan rapidly became widespread throughout the civil service through consistent repetition by two successive Ministers of Public Service and Administration, Zola Skweyiya and Geraldine Fraser-Moleketi. Although the Department for Public Service and Administration did undertake a set of awareness-raising activities and developed some implementation guidelines and requirements—I'll return to these below—Batho Pele was mainly driven by leaders' rhetorical efforts to create energy around reorienting and improving the civil service's culture. One interviewee commented that "it was very much up to departments to implement it themselves. Obviously some departments saw the value in it and used it to guide the way they do things, but for other departments it was at best a compliance thing that we had to do and submit reports."[16]

Judging the impacts and success of Batho Pele as a reform is difficult due to its broad scope and ambition, its relatively decentralized implementation model, and its focus on difficult-to-measure culture change rather than the delivery of specific outputs. But there is general consensus that the Batho Pele slogan and rhetoric became widely recognized throughout the civil service down to front-line officers and even members of the public.[17] There is also consensus that some departments, such as the Department of Home Affairs, dramatically transformed their processes and client orientation through reforms under the Batho Pele banner. However, these successes in some areas were matched by lagging performance in others, both across departments and within them. For example, a set of service user surveys conducted by the PSC in 2012 found that majorities of Department of Home Affairs service users indicated satisfaction with the Department's levels of courtesy, information provision, and publication of service standards but that majorities also expressed being unaware of the Department's efforts on several other dimensions of Batho Pele standards.[18] But while its impact inevitably fell short of its hugely ambitious goals, as a reform, it seems to have been fairly successful in transforming deeply engrained norms around responsiveness to clients and service delivery—albeit, perhaps more widely so in principle than in practice—and in empowering civil servants with the motivation to make process improvements to do so.

Of course, part of what made Batho Pele successful in creating energy for change was not just the reform itself but also the moment of political and social transformation in which it was designed and implemented. Such moments sometimes helped reforms create energy for change within the walls of civil service institutions by linking them to wider changes and energy in society. For example, the most vigorous and successful civil service reforms in Kenya's modern history occurred in the years following the election of President Mwai Kibaki in 2002, which brought the country's first change in political leadership in decades and was widely seen as a clean break from the previous era of stagnation and economic crisis. This was as true for the civil service as for the country as a whole, with experts and former officials using terms like "euphoric" and "energized" to describe the enthusiasm within the civil service at this time.[19] This energy was channeled into change in policy and processes through reforms such as the Economic Recovery Strategy, Results for Kenya program, a Performance Contracting system for permanent secretaries and their ministries, and the aforementioned Rapid Results Initiatives.

While reforms were sometimes aided in creating energy by piggybacking off wider social and political momentum, energy from outside the civil service was neither sufficient nor necessary for creating energy within the service. For example, the coming to power of Abdoulaye Wade in 2000 in Senegal's first postindependence "alternance" (i.e., change in party control) created a structurally similar moment to Kibaki's election in Kenya but created relatively little new energy for reforms to the civil service—although a number of good governance reforms were implemented in other parts of the government, and civil servants themselves were fairly successful in carrying over and rebranding much of the reform activity from the previous administration. Similarly, Ghana's CSPIP reforms in the mid- to late-1990s were partially successful in creating energy and a new cultural focus on performance and service delivery despite being initiated and executed during a period not marked by major political change. Instead, reform energy came from the new Head of Civil Service, Robert Dodoo, and his team at the Office of Head of Civil Service, developing a "homegrown" reform agenda that empowered and supported organizations across the service to come up with their own ideas and initiatives for improvement. So energy for reform didn't necessarily need to come from a president or other political leader; it could also be built within the civil service.

The idea that creating energy for change is a good thing may sound simple and obvious, but these and other cases illustrate just how difficult it was for reforms to achieve it. For every instance in which genuine energy for reform spread throughout a civil service, there are many more where leaders declared the need for change—often using nearly identical rhetoric—but failed to shift civil servants' expectations about whether this was just another set of superficial changes that would fail to translate into real practices as opposed to a meaningful break with the past. Even when political leaders had energy for reform and wanted to convey it to civil servants, it was easy to miscalculate how such messages would land. The derogatory comments about civil servants made by some senior members of President Obasanjo's administration in Nigeria, for example, reportedly created resistance to reforms among civil servants at a moment when democratization and broader social change should have helped build momentum for reform.[20] Creating energy for change was not just a simple matter of top-down rhetoric but a more nuanced process of articulating a vision, building credibility around it, and creating space in that vision for civil servants to imagine themselves as agents of change rather than objects of it.

COMBINING OPPORTUNITIES AND ENERGY

There are obviously potential complementarities between these two mechanisms of success, ways in which the mechanisms are more effective in combination than on their own. Opportunities for discussing performance will be more likely to be seized and to translated into action if civil servants believe that things are really going to improve and that their leaders and colleagues also believe this. Likewise, creating energy for improving performance will be more effective if there are meaningful opportunities for civil servants to channel it into discussion of how to improve and tangible actions. How successful were reforms at bringing these two mechanisms together?

There are certainly some examples in which these two mechanisms appear to have complemented each other. In Kenya, for instance, the broader political and social energy for reform after 2002 was channeled into the civil service through (among other reforms) a Performance Contracting system that defined organizational goals, made them salient to leaders and staff of the organization alike, measured performance, and (for a few years) gave a group bonus to members of the top-performing ministry. This new salience of performance meant that when the Rapid Results Initiatives coaches turned up to offer their services, organizational leadership was more eager to accept their assistance and put effort into the one-hundred-day improvement initiatives that were framed in terms of the goals of the performance contracts. More broadly, many organizational performance review schemes brought together energy and opportunities to diagnose problems and identify solutions in participatory ways, including Ghana's beneficiary surveys, self-appraisal instruments, and performance improvement plans under CSPIP; South Africa's Management Performance Assessment Tool, which sought to evaluate not only if each management process was being formally complied with but also if it was actually being used to improve performance; and Nigeria's SERVICOM institutional diagnostics, which often received more welcoming receptions because of the high-level political backing for SERVICOM as an institution and service delivery improvement as a goal.

Further evidence in favor of the complementarity of opportunities and energy is given by instances where a lack of opportunities for discussing performance partially undermined the channeling of reform energy into actual change and vice versa. This is perhaps seen most clearly in the Batho Pele reform, the symbolic importance and awareness of which was not matched by processes to enable civil servants to actually translate changed attitudes into changed practices. As one interviewee reflected:

> The problem is that it was, it was very politically driven, and oddly enough, it wasn't managerialist enough, in that it assumed that making government organizations more customer-oriented and providing better quality services to the public was just a matter of attitude of the public servants and they completely ignored all the other stuff which needs to be in place for an organization to provide better quality services. . . . The [assumption was that] service delivery here will improve if you have the right attitude. That was the problem with Batho Pele, it stopped there. It didn't make sure that all the systems and much more managerialist stuff was in place to enable public servants to provide better services.[21]

The cases where reforms provided processes but little energy are even more numerous, leading to committees, reviews, and reporting mechanisms that achieved perfunctory compliance at best.

Despite the importance of bringing together energy and opportunities, reformers faced a number of challenges and limitations in doing so that were common across various types of reforms and contexts. Even in the best cases, implementation and impact tended to be uneven across the civil service, as some organizations enthusiastically took up the opportunities while others treated them as impositions to be avoided or perfunctorily complied with. It was also difficult to sustain. High-level leadership and the energy that came from it could easily vanish overnight with changes in governments, political crises, or shifting priorities. Opportunities for discussion were often in the form of one-off workshops, evaluations, or support, which could sometimes yield one-off improvements in specific areas but were harder to channel into sustained improvement.

One way that reformers attempted to address the challenges of sustainability and uneven engagement was by trying to link these improvement opportunities to other processes that created pressure, accountability, and/or incentives for performance. Kenya's combination of Rapid Results Initiatives and Performance Contracting was a somewhat successful example of this; Ghana's efforts under CSPIP to combine organizational performance reviews with performance contracts for chief directors and Zambia's similar efforts under PSCAP were largely unsuccessful. However, the more processes that created opportunities for discussion and improving performance were linked (or perceived to be linked) to potential rewards or sanctions, the more resistance they met and the less genuine engagement they received. For example, South Africa's Management Performance Assessment Tool experienced gaming as well as pushback from politicians and bureaucrats when they tried to link scores to incentives or published results publicly, which eventually contributed to the system's demise. Similarly, the only instances in which individual-level leadership performance contracting systems were sustained over a period of multiple years were those where the incentives associated with measured performance were relatively diffuse (e.g., Kenya's Performance Contracting system had only a group bonus for members of the top-performing ministry but no formal punishments or individual incentives) or weak (e.g., Ghana's Chief Director Performance Agreement system in the mid- to late-2010s, which had small and mainly symbolic awards for top performing chief directors). So institutionalizing top-down energy through high-powered formal incentive and accountability systems was rarely a successful route to sustained performance improvement.

The provision of financial resources to organizations was sometimes used to try to elicit energy from the organization. But this proved to be a double-edged sword: Resources generated interest from organizations in reform efforts, but this interest often became oriented around the resources themselves rather than on how they could be used to improve performance. This effect was compounded by accountability and budget-disbursement pressures that were more severe for donor-funded projects (but not solely restricted to them). For example, the Performance Improvement Funds (PIFs) in Ghana under CSPIP and Zambia under PSCAP each succeeded in not only generating some innovative and impactful initiatives but also led to many proposals that were only loosely linked to performance improvement and often focused purely on purchasing assets like cars or computers. In contrast, Kenya's Rapid Results Initiatives—which aimed at sparking similarly specific, short-term, innovative changes as Ghana and Zambia's PIFs—typically did not come with additional financial resources and largely avoided these distortions. Like carrots and sticks, resources were as often a hindrance as a help to efforts to combine and sustain energy and opportunities.

There was no simple formula for predicting when, where, and how energy and opportunities for discussing and making performance improvements successfully came together. Reforms that had formally similar designs and contexts often led to different outcomes in terms of whether these mechanisms of success emerged and amplified one another. Similarly, there were no design features of reforms or characteristics of reform context that guaranteed that these mechanisms would emerge or combine. Energy and/or opportunities could emerge in various ways and in different contexts as well as fail to do so.

On the one hand, this ambiguity is frustrating for reformers and academics alike, as it reinforces the idea that there are no simple, replicable, easily transferable, magic-bullet answers to the question of how to design and implement systemic performance-oriented reforms. On the other hand, it also seems appropriate and obvious that there wouldn't be a simple answer to the challenge of getting tens or hundreds of thousands of civil servants spread across hundreds of organizations to simultaneously undertake tasks that can't always be specified in advance or measured after the fact. Complex challenges like this don't usually have easy solutions.

However, the fact that there aren't simple, guaranteed-to-work solutions doesn't mean that there aren't patterns and empirical regularities to learn from. This chapter makes clear that when reforms did succeed in changing unformalizable behaviors, it was generally through one or of the two mechanisms of creating energy and creating opportunities—ideally both. There were also regularities in the proximate factors that enabled each mechanism to operate: Energy was successfully created and spread when civil servants' individual and collective expectations about the possibility and likelihood of meaningful change were shifted, and opportunities were successfully created when civil servants were given space and prompting to communicate with one another about goals, roles, feedback, and ideas for improvement. Neither mechanism could be forced or imposed top-down on a civil service, but both appeared in many diverse types of reforms and contexts. Together, they comprised the two main channels through which reforms managed to positively change bureaucratic behaviors and improve performance.

• • •

The end of this chapter begins our transition from part II of the book, on the diagnosis of how past reforms failed and succeeded, to part III of the book, on the prescription for how reformers can maximize the likelihood that their reforms are successful. It has argued that there were two main success mechanisms through which reforms consistently had positive impacts on behavior and performance: creating opportunities for civil servants to discuss performance and how to improve it, and creating energy for change. These mechanisms could each operate independently but reinforced each other when they were both present. While these mechanisms faced a range of limitations and challenges, they nonetheless recurred across a wide range of reform types and contexts.

One theme that unites part II's analysis of the mechanisms of failure and the mechanisms of success is the complex relationship between formal and informal processes and actions. On the one hand, the overfocus on changing formal rules and structures as an objective of reform and a way to improve performance was a clear and consistent mechanism of failure, and the actions sparked by the mechanisms of success were decidedly nonverifiable. On the other hand, these informal actions were still often undergirded or prompted by formal processes—or constrained and squeezed out by them. So any attempt to think about how reformers should approach designing and implementing reforms needs to grapple with both types of behavior and practices.

A second theme uniting the chapters in this section was the importance of civil servants' expectations about how their colleagues and supervisors will react to a reform effort and, thus, of the credibility (or not) of reform efforts. Expectations and credibility mattered both for whether civil servants complied with formal processes and for whether they undertook important but unformalizable actions to give meaning to these formal processes. So the implementation and impact of a reform were determined not just by its content and its designers' intent but by how it was perceived by the civil servants whose behavior it aimed to influence. Common approaches to designing and implementing reforms could inadvertently undermine this credibility—as could external factors like leadership turnover, the uncertainty of future funding, or a lack of support from key stakeholders. So finding ways to maximize the credibility of reform efforts and change civil servants' expectations is also crucial for thinking about to learn from these past experiences and approach future reform efforts.

Once again, these patterns are not restricted to these six countries or, indeed, to Africa in general. For example, the public administration scholar Donald Moynihan concluded in his study of performance information use in the United States that while organizational performance management systems almost never functioned as intended—they produced too much information, performance was too ambiguous to interpret, and elected officials ultimately didn't care very much about the formal performance ratings—they still often had positive impacts within agencies by enabling "interactive dialogue" about objectives and performance.[22] In their review of worldwide evidence on staff appraisal procedures for the World Bank, Schnell and colleagues recommend "that managers separate conversations focused on employee development from formal performance conversations that have primarily accountability and control functions" because linking conversations to rewards and sanctions triggered defensiveness, exaggeration, conflict avoidance, and behavioral biases among both supervisors and supervisees.[23] I imagine that most people reading this book have their own experiences of how useful conversations about goals, roles, and performance can be, as well as how difficult it is to be open and honest in such conversations when rewards and sanctions are on the line.

One obvious potential takeaway from this part of the book is this: Reformers should seek to minimize the mechanisms of failure and maximize the mechanisms of success. To do less of what hasn't worked and more of what has. For example, annual staff appraisal systems consistently failed to serve as the incentive delivery systems that reform designers envisioned, but they sometimes created useful opportunities for supervisors and supervisees to discuss goals, roles, and performance feedback. But the more burdensome these systems were and the more they threatened or promised incentives attached to these performance evaluations, the more that they were gamed or treated as tick-box exercises. What, then, would it look like to design annual appraisal systems that abandoned the failed premise of linking carrots and sticks to measured individual performance and instead sought to maximize energy and opportunities for supervisors and supervisees to share information, come up with ideas to improve performance, and put them into action? While the operation of these mechanisms and the interaction between them is, of course, more complex than just saying "less of A, more of B," these patterns of failure and success nonetheless provide a valuable starting point for thinking about how to design and implement more impactful reforms.

These are the questions that the next part of the book turns to. Building on the reform histories in the appendix and the analysis of past reforms from this part of the book, part III begins by building a theory of reform as an *ongoing process of catalyzing continuous improvement in actual practices*. It explores what this idea might mean not only in the abstract but also grounds it in past reforms that have exemplified aspects of this approach, both in Africa and around the world. While success can never be guaranteed for complex, systemic, large-scale reforms in an uncertain world, for a range of performance improvement objectives, this approach might offer reformers a better chance at success than past efforts have had. That's chapter 7. Chapter 8 then takes an in-depth, practice-oriented look at one version of what this theory of reform as process might look like. To do so, it examines how Nana Agyekum-Dwamena took a dramatically different approach to reform after he took office in 2014, an approach that exemplified this alternative approach to reform in many ways. Finally, the book closes by reflecting on the challenges and potential limitations of this approach and of the book's analysis, as well as how the optimal approach to reform might vary depending on reformers' objectives and contexts. With that in mind, let's move on to this third and final part of the book.

PART III

Reform as Process

7
Reform as Process

Theory

This book began with a question: If a senior leader asked you how they should approach reforms to improve the performance of their country's civil service, what would you advise them?

This chapter presents my best answer to this question using the language and style of academic theory-building. It is oriented mainly toward academics, students, and other readers who are interested in how this book contributes to scholarly research on civil service reform, organizational performance, and organizational change.

I argue that systemic, performance-oriented reform should be conceptualized as an effort to *catalyze* an *ongoing process of continuous improvement in actual practices*. This approach refocuses the goal of reform by focusing attention directly on changing the day-to-day work practices of rank-and-file civil servants and their managers rather than implicitly assuming that changes in behavior come from changes in formal rules. It reframes how reforms are implemented by viewing change as an ongoing process of many locally driven changes rather than a master plan rolled out through a one-off project or intervention. It also casts the role of senior leaders in a different light by seeing their task not as forcing or imposing reforms from above but rather as catalyzing, enabling, and inspiring decentralized local change efforts by thousands of staff spread across the whole civil service.

Chapter 8 then delves into what this theory of *reform as process* looks like in practice using the language of policy practice. It focuses on showcasing and learning from instances where similar ideas have been put into action, with a focused case study of Ghana from 2014–2019 and examples from other reform efforts in these six countries and elsewhere around the world. These two chapters complement and build on each other but can also be read in isolation. I encourage everyone to read both, but if you're mostly interested in the tangible takeaways rather than the underlying theory, you can skip ahead to chapter 8.

The theory-building in this chapter is the culmination of the abductive process of empirical analysis from the reform history appendix and chapters 2–6. Chapter 2 laid the conceptual foundations for the book's empirical analysis by defining consummate performance as requiring organizations to carry out a mix of verifiable and nonverifiable tasks and individuals to undertake a mix of verifiable and nonverifiable (formalizable and unformalizable) actions.

Chapters 3–5 found that most reforms largely focused their attention on designing and adopting new formal rules and processes and, on the whole, were fairly successful at making these changes on paper. However, they were far less successful at having them implemented in practice. This was because formal rules and processes were often not actually followed on a sustained basis or because they were complied with perfunctorily, without complementary informal practices. The one-off, projectized way many (perhaps most) reforms were implemented accentuated these limitations. These two mechanisms of failure—focusing on the formal and projectization—occurred, to varying degrees, across nearly all reforms and helped explain their near-universal pattern of falling short of expectations.

Chapter 6 then showed that when reforms did have some success at improving performance, it was typically because they managed to create opportunities and energy for civil servants to talk about performance and how to improve it. Formal processes were sometimes useful in providing opportunities for these discussions, but neither top-down mandates nor individual performance-linked incentives were sufficient to make these conversations more than perfunctory or to lead to the implementation and sustaining of changes. So unformalizable actions always played a crucial role in the performance improvements that did occur, even in reforms that envisioned formal processes, metrics, and incentives as the primary pathways to change.

What would it look like to approach systemic reform in a way that seeks to maximize these mechanisms of success and minimize the mechanisms of failure—to try to make large-scale change by foregrounding the centrality of the unformalizable parts of bureaucratic life for determining performance rather than wishing them away?

The chapter builds a theory of reform as catalyzing an ongoing process of continuous improvement in actual practices from the microlevel upward in three parts. To this end, I reverse the order of the phrase and break it down into three sections: (1) changing actual practices, (2) through an ongoing process of continuous improvement, (3) in which reform leaders' role is to catalyze decentralized change. In the first, I focus on exploring why workers sometimes undertake unformalizable actions that benefit the organization but that they can't be forced to do and what tools managers have to encourage them to do so and to build mutually beneficial relationships. In the second, I focus on characterizing this process of learning to build cooperation within teams and organizations, both in terms of the temporality of the change process as well as its substance. The third section then tackles the question of what a system-level reform leader can do to catalyze improvement simultaneously across the many teams and organizations that compromise a bureaucratic system. Separating the theory into three parts helps make it easier to present and digest but should not detract from the inter-connectedness of and complementarities between these aspects.

In developing and exploring this theory of reform as process, I draw exten-sively on existing research, evidence from past reforms discussed in previous chapters and the appendix, and on the experience and insights of many reform leaders themselves. So while I have referred to this theory as "new" or "alterna-tive" in order to contrast it to the approach that has dominated most reform efforts over the last three decades, it is emphatically not the case that nothing in this chapter has ever been said or tried before. Rather, many researchers and practitioners alike have recognized the limitations of dominant reform models and sought to grapple with a similar intellectual puzzle: If approaching reform as the simple unfolding of a top-down plan tends to yield disappointing results, what is the alternative? Efforts to experiment with alternative approaches have been hampered by the absence of a sustained academic articulation of the con-ceptual foundations of these alternatives. So nondominant approaches risk being defined more by what they are *not* than what they *are*. Or worse, not following the dominant approach may risk being perceived as doing nothing at all. In pre-senting this theory of reform as process, this chapter seeks to provide language and ideas for such reformers to structure their own thoughts, communicate with others, and legitimize their efforts to approach reform differently.

One final but important caveat: The theory of reform as process represents neither a blueprint, nor a one-size-fits-all solution, nor a guarantee of success. Deterministic answers aren't possible in the complex world of bureaucratic change, and the fine-grained work of translating abstract principles and theories into tangible actions will always have to be context-specific. Similarly, there will always be some instances when formal rules themselves do need to be changed or it makes sense to approach aspects of change as a one-off, top-down project—a topic we'll return to in chapter 9. Rather, this theory of reform as process is best viewed as a mental model for thinking about changing performance in large, professional bureaucracies. It is intended to be applicable as a midrange theory across a range of scenarios and contexts but will always require judgment and adaptation each time someone—a head of civil service, a researcher, an advisor, or a relatively junior team leader—attempts to translate it into practice.

With all that in mind, let's begin to lay out the theory of reform as process.

CHANGING ACTUAL PRACTICES

It might seem obvious to state that changing civil servants' actual day-to-day behaviors and practices should be the aim of reform. Certainly, few people go into a reform aiming *not* to change practices. Yet, we have so often seen reforms that resulted in little real change for rank-and-file civil servants or succeeded only at eliciting perfunctory compliance with new processes.

So how can reformers effectively aim to change actual practices in their change initiatives? Let's begin by thinking about the hardest part of this question: changing informal, nonverifiable practices.

To do so, we need to introduce the concept of *relational contracts* from organizational economics. As with organizational management processes, most contracts between parties (e.g., partnership agreements between firms or employment contracts between organizations and their employees) contain both verifiable and nonverifiable provisions. Ensuring that the other party carries out the verifiable parts of their side of the agreement can be done through a court, but carrying out the nonverifiable parts can't be forced in this way. In a one-off interaction, both sides have an incentive to "defect" and undertake only the verifiable parts since there is no penalty for not undertaking the nonverifiable parts. The key insight of relational contract theory is that parties can achieve consummate performance if they have ongoing, repeated interactions because the long-term benefit of a cooperative relationship can counteract the short-term incentive to shortchange the other party. So the relationship between parties—and all the actions, perceptions, and expectations that constitute that relationship—is the mechanism that might allow each party to get the other party to undertake the nonverifiable actions that they want but can't force them to do.

What might building positive relational contracts look like in the context of public bureaucracies? We can distinguish two main strategies available to public sector managers to get staff to undertake informal actions, each of which refers to a different type of relational contract.

First, managers can attempt to reward staff for undertaking informal actions or punish them for not doing so using either pecuniary incentives (i.e., those with monetary value) or nonpecuniary incentives. Chapter 4 showed that there are major practical limitations on efforts to do this. There were no examples of systemic reforms successfully delivering pecuniary incentives (i.e., those with financial value, like bonuses, accelerated promotions, or contract extensions for nonpermanent staff) to individuals at a system level, with the organization-level "13th-month" bonus payment to all staff of the best-performing ministry in Kenya under the Performance Contracting system being the only example of even a significant group-level pecuniary incentive that was actually delivered. These systems' failures derived from the fundamental challenges of attempting to impose formal incentive schemes and performance mesures on civil servants whose jobs comprised many nonverifiable tasks that couldn't be perfectly specified ex ante or measured ex post.

Nonpecuniary incentives, such as best worker awards or other recognition schemes, were more widely delivered. These were often delivered on an ad-hoc or organization-specific basis, as well as in selected systemic reforms (e.g., awards to top-performing chief directors under Ghana's Chief Director Performance Agreement system). These schemes also occasionally included small pecuniary rewards, but they were largely symbolic. On the punishment side, "naming and shaming" (e.g., via the publishing of rankings or singling out individuals in meetings for criticism) was sometimes used as a means of putting performance pressure on individuals or organizations. Both of these approaches seem to have had some positive effects in at least some cases, when used at a limited scale. But even without pecuniary incentives, trying to implement highly formalized and objective versions of such schemes at system level usually broke down due to perceptions of unfairness, backlash from bureaucrats, or politicians' desire to avoid negative press coverage. The more powerful the incentive, the greater the chance that managers responded by watering down or distorting their targets. So attempts to deliver nonpecuniary incentive systems with objective metrics also sometimes fell victim to the same implementability issues as with pecuniary incentives.

An alternative to these objective, mechanistic systems for delivering incentives would be to encourage managers to use discretion in delivering them. In other words, if it's not possible to specify ex ante what workers should do, but managers know who is performing well or not—even if they can't objectively prove it—then managers could decide ex post how and when to reward good performance or punish bad performance. In theory, this could be better suited to incentivizing informal actions since (by definition) these are observable by the parties involved but not verifiable by third parties. For example, some of the most reportedly meaningful nonpecuniary incentives reported by interviewees, such as commendation letters, were characterized by the managerial discretion inherent in deciding when and for what to give them. Similarly, a number of interviewees mentioned pecuniary incentives being successfully delivered in specific organizations or teams on a more discretionary, nonsystematic basis. While these discretionary pecuniary incentives were sometimes effective in these specific cases, it seems likely that attempts to scale them up and systematize them would have resulted in organizational, union, and political pressure toward more objective, nondiscretionary systems.

Another potential advantage of discretionary incentives is that they might actually be more effective at eliciting informal actions, at least in certain circumstances. This is due to the inherently social nature of manager-employee interactions. In a book chapter entitled "Employment as an Economic and a Social Relationship," James Baron and David Kreps point out that employees taking informal actions that are beneficial for the organization that employs them is akin to "giving gifts of consummate effort" to their organization, since they cannot be forced to undertake these actions and typically perform them without doing a full economic analysis of the costs and benefits of doing so. In this view, the best way managers can get their employees to give them "gifts of consummate effort" is to build the kind of reciprocal gift-exchange relationship that is so fundamental to human psychology and social relationships: You go above and beyond your minimum job requirements by performing consummately, and I will go above and beyond my minimal contractual requirements as your employer in how I treat you. Nonpecuniary rewards are the main types of gifts that public managers have at their disposal to give, but Baron and Kreps also point out that overly systematizing the process of earning and delivering nonpecuniary rewards risks turning these rewards from gifts into mere entitlements or extra compensation; gifts are most effective when they are personal or when the giver didn't have to give it (i.e., the gift is unnecessary or a surprise rather than a mandated monthly occurrence). They give the evocative example of a manager in a fictional U.S. company who gives his employees the gift of a turkey to cook for their family's Thanksgiving dinner but calculates the size of the turkey he gives according to an objective, numerical formula that takes into account their measured performance throughout the year. Such a nonpecuniary incentive would probably be perceived by his employees as something they had earned and would be unlikely to make them want to reciprocate by putting in more effort than they already were, whereas a more discretionary and unexpected gift might have been more likely to motivate his employees to reciprocate with informal (and thus also discretionary) actions of their own.[1] So while nonpecuniary incentives can be useful tools for managers to get staff to undertake informal actions, oversystematizing them in an effort to remove discretion and subjectivity might actually make them less effective.

At the same time, relying on managerial discretion to incentivize consummate performance is difficult for organizations to pull off in practice. Robert Gibbons and Rebecca Henderson describe how managerial efforts to reward employees for taking unformalizable actions suffer from a dual problem of clarity (in terms of what unformalizable actions managers want workers to undertake and what will be rewarded, neither of which can be perfectly specified in advance) and credibility (in terms of whether or not unformalizable actions will be rewarded).[2] Workers must trust their managers to recognize and reward them when they go above and beyond the minimum formal actions that can be required of them. Otherwise, they will just do the minimum required. Thus, workers cannot be told in advance exactly what to do or forced to do it, and managers can't credibly commit to rewarding them when they do. Gibbons and Henderson show how these clarity and credibility problems can only be resolved through the gradual building of relational contracts—i.e., of mutual expectations and understandings—over time through a complex, dynamic, and hard-to-pull-off process. So while discretionary incentives can potentially be used to encourage consummate performance in organizations, they are far from a simple, sure-fire solution.

The second strategy available to managers to get their staff to undertake informal actions is to leverage workers' intrinsic motivation to effectively serve the public and their professional desire to do their jobs well. To do so, they often need to find ways to strengthen not only the relationship between a worker and their manager but also among workers.

An enormous body of research has shown that intrinsic, public-spirited motivations can be powerful drivers for individual public servants worldwide, as recent works by authors like Marc Esteve and Christian Schuster, James Perry, and Dan Honig have surveyed and extended.[3] One implication of this literature is that civil services should try to hire intrinsically motivated workers. But once hired, how can managers best leverage these intrinsic motivations? Put another way, why might latent intrinsic motivation fail to translate into enacted consummate performance, and how can managers change this? This question is especially important for public managers who often have little control over who their team members are.

Whether bureaucrats act on their intrinsic motivations depends, in large part, on their feeling like they are being effective in their roles, achieving their goals, and making a difference in society. The realization of this linkage between individual effort and intrinsic rewards is not automatic since the achievement of these tasks and outputs usually depends not only on the effort of a single individual but also on the efforts of other individuals in their team and organization. That is, rather than individual members of an organization working separately on independent tasks, they typically have to collaborate to jointly accomplish important organizational outputs, even if some aspects of this can be subdivided. To the extent that workers' ability to effectively accomplish tasks and goals is dependent on team production in this way, individual public servants only get greater satisfaction from putting in the extra effort needed to perform consummately if other members of their team do as well.

The importance of team production has long been recognized in organizational studies and public administration theory.[4] While there is relatively little empirical measurement of the extent of team production in practice, what does exist emphasizes its prevalence. For instance, one study of hundreds of private firms from different industries in the United States asked managers to rate the extent to which a worker's job involves "teamwork" on a five-point scale, with 1 meaning "the worker functions entirely separately from other workers" and 5 meaning "the worker is such a crucial member of the team that the team's output or activity is wiped out by his or her absence". Only 12.6 percent of workers were rated 1, implying that 87.4 percent of workers' jobs involved at least some level of team production.[5] I am not aware of any comparable figures for public sector organizations, but one would expect team production to be at least as pervasive in these contexts. In such contexts, each individual's decision about whether to perform consummately will depend (in part) on whether that individual expects the other individuals with whom they work to also perform consummately—otherwise, their extra effort will be wasted. So individuals are not only embedded in relational contracts with their managers but also with their other colleagues.

Figure 7.1 summarizes these two types of relational contracts that matter for performance in teams in a stylized model. There are two basic types of actors: workers and managers. The actual work of the team is done by workers. Each individual worker undertakes tasks (verifiable and nonverifiable) that contribute collectively to performance via team-produced outputs. Workers can perform their tasks consummately, perfunctorily, or not at all, with the delivery and quality of outputs varying accordingly.[6] Managers can observe workers' performance both of verifiable and nonverifiable tasks but cannot objectively prove workers' performance of nonverifiable tasks to external parties and so are limited in their ability to systematically attach high-powered pecuniary incentives to their subjective perceptions of performance—following the trend observed across these six countries and, indeed, many civil services worldwide.

Team

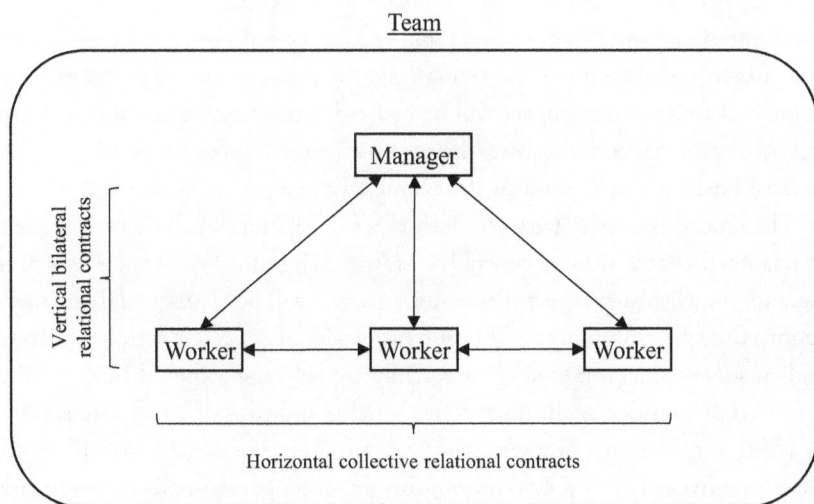

FIGURE 7.1 Relational Contracts in Teams

Source: Author.

Whether workers undertake the nonverifiable tasks necessary to perform consummately depends on the two types of relational contracts discussed above, which correspond to the two strategies available to managers for eliciting consummate performance. First, each worker has a vertical, bilateral relational contract with the team's manager. The key lever for change in this relational contract is an extrinsic one: "I will perform unformalizable tasks because I expect my manager will see it and I'll somehow benefit from that, even if this benefit may arrive in discretionary, ad hoc ways." This might be accentuated, in some cases, by the psychology of gift exchange: "My manager or organization did something to help me out that they didn't have to, so I will do something that helps them out that I don't have to."[7] These discretionary extrinsic rewards could be pecuniary (e.g., a small bonus, assignment to a project or training that entails extra compensation or desirable travel, etc.) or nonpecuniary (e.g., a letter of commendation, highlighting good performance in a team meeting, etc.).

Second, the workers in the team have a horizontal, collective relational contract among themselves in which the team as a whole can only produce its outputs and accomplish its goals if each puts in the extra effort needed for consummate rather than perfunctory performance. The key lever for changing this relational contract is rooted in the intrinsic motivations of job satisfaction, self-efficacy, and professionalism: "I will perform unformalizable tasks because I want to feel like I'm getting things done and having a positive impact on society." But workers know that this positive impact will be realized if their colleagues also perform unformalizable tasks. Otherwise, their extra effort will go to waste, which leads to these horizontal relationships also taking on a relational character.

The crucial similarity between both types of relationships—as with models of relational contracts more generally—is that each individual's choice of action depends on what they expect their counterpart(s) will do. This gives these interactions the self-reinforcing equilibrium properties of collective action problems and prisoner's dilemma-style games. Only by leveraging the "shadow of the future" (i.e., considering the prospective benefits and costs of future interactions in addition to the present interaction) can groups overcome individuals' short-term incentive to "defect" or shirk.[8] In this sense, cooperation must be built and sustained over time, with workers and managers alike updating their expectations iteratively based on past actions.[9] Similarly, in chapter 5, we saw the cyclical and mutually reinforcing process through which prospective expectations and retrospective experience shaped workers' engagement with performance management processes. So the question of how to change employees' expectations not just of their manager but of their colleagues is crucial for understanding how reforms can get bureaucrats to undertake beneficial informal actions.

So far, this section has focused on informal, nonverifiable actions. But these issues of expectations and credibility can also be central to getting individuals to comply with formal rules and processes—which is the other part of the puzzle of how reforms can affect actual practices. People don't necessarily comply automatically with rules, and, indeed, the norm, in many contexts, is that many rules and processes are inconsistently implemented and enforced (as discussed in chapter 2). So if individuals expect that formal rules and processes will be enforced and noncompliance sanctioned, they are likely to abide by them; if not, they are not. In deciding whether and when to comply with formal rules, individuals perform cost-benefit calculations where the costs of abiding by rules could be anything from going to jail to putting out a little extra effort, and the benefits anything from not going to jail to the satisfaction of better team and organizational performance. An enforcement problem arises, however, because managers, organizations, and systems are also making their own cost-benefit calculations: Is it worth our effort to try to enforce these rules? Will it be damaging to individual or team morale if we do? Will it invoke the wrath of politicians if I sanction a well-connected official? As with the case of individual performance-linked incentives, individual managers often find it less costly to ignore noncompliance because the benefits of enforcing a rule are often diffuse and in the future (i.e., sending a message to others, setting norms) and/or don't accrue to them personally, while the costs will fall directly on them. So even the enforcement of formal rules and processes—and, hence, the actual behavior and practices of the individuals these rules and processes seek to govern—depends on individuals' expectations and on the credibility of the rule (or of the effort to change it).

This section has argued that reforms' ability to change individuals' behaviors and practices—particularly informal but occasionally formal—depends, in large part, on their ability to change individuals' expectations about the future. An implication of this is that reform efforts that don't change expectations are likely to fail, not just in shifting nonverifiable practices but even in obtaining compliance with verifiable ones. This section has also distinguished between two different types of these expectations with associated levers for change: vertical, bilateral relational contracts between managers and workers, which might be amenable to extrinsic recognition, rewards, and/or sanctions; and horizontal, collective relational contracts among workers, in which change must be driven primarily by leveraging intrinsic motivations.

In placing the conceptual emphasis on how workers interpret and react to policies and processes, this focus on changing actual practices echoes a long tradition of policy implementation research.[10] For example, in one recent empirical study of education reforms in Delhi, Yamini Aiyar and colleagues argue that "the success and failure, and eventual institutionalisation, of reforms depend fundamentally on how the frontline of the system understands, interprets, and adapts to reform efforts."[11] At a conceptual level, Richard Elmore makes a conceptual distinction between "forward mapping" and "backward mapping" as approaches to making and implementing policy. Forward mapping involves a leader specifying a desired policy or set of outcomes and then specifying what workers should do to enact it (i.e., the standard, top-down approach to making policy). In contrast, backward mapping involves starting with a specific frontline behavior that leaders want to change, then working backward to consider what drives worker behavior and what tools are available to change it, thus building up a policy or reform in a worker-centered rather than a leader-centered way.[12] One way to read this section's emphasis on changing workers' actual practices, then, is as a relational contracts-inspired perspective on why performance-oriented reforms ought to take a backward mapping approach rather than the dominant forward mapping approach.

To understand how reforms *can* shift expectations, we need to think about change as a dynamic process rather than as a simple redefinition of rules and processes, a one-time managerial interaction, or the mechanical pulling of a lever on a machine. Let's now delve into this next piece of the puzzle.

REFORM AS AN ONGOING PROCESS OF
CONTINUOUS IMPROVEMENT

The second element of the theory is the conceptualization of reform as an *ongoing process of continuous improvement*. "Ongoing process" refers to the idea that the reform or change effort is open-ended and nontimebound in contrast to the dominant approach of conceiving a reform as a one-off intervention or project. "Continuous improvement" refers to the idea that the reform seeks to improve performance primarily through a multitude of gradual and iterative changes to practices, many of which are identified and executed in a bottom-up fashion. This stands in contrast to approaching reform as a discontinuous change in practices driven by the top-down rollout of a centrally designed, standardized set of processes and practices. Taken together, these ideas articulate a vision of how reforms can systematically induce meaningful and sustainable changes in individual practices while avoiding the pitfalls of projectized approaches to reform.

There are already substantial academic literatures both on process-based approaches to organizational change and on continuous improvement, as well as adjacent concepts like adaptive or agile management.[13] Some of these terms have become mainstays of management courses and books, sometimes almost to the point of being clichés. Thus, there is a risk that this book's theorizing of effective reform as an ongoing process of continuous improvement could be heard as a restatement of existing theories or even a statement of the obvious. Indeed, creating a culture of continuous improvement was articulated as a goal of many of the reform efforts studied in this book. Yet, few of these reforms succeeded in achieving this, with most efforts adopting the usual projectized approach. So even if these ideas are widely accepted as goals, there is evidently an intellectual and practical gap in understanding how to design reforms that embody them and stand a chance at achieving them, particularly in civil service contexts. Let me dive deeper into what I mean by this phrase and how it is inspired by but also differs from and extends existing theories of organizational change and reform.

I've already articulated—above and in chapters 2 and 5—why individuals' expectations of others' future behavior matter for their own enactment of non-verifiable practices and sometimes even for their verifiable compliance with formal rules. The basic idea is that individuals will only go above and beyond the minimum required of them if they expect either (a) that their manager will recognize and reward these unformalizable actions, typically also in unformalizable ways; and/or (b) that their colleagues will also carry out the nonverifiable practices necessary to effectively achieve collectively produced team outputs and goals. In both cases, if an individual thinks that a reform effort will trigger only a temporary change in the behavior of their manager and/or colleagues, they will be reluctant to also change their behavior—particularly because they will realize that their manager and colleagues will be thinking the same things about them. As with relational contracts more generally, the result is a collective action problem: We will each individually change behavior only if we expect others to also change theirs. The potential solution to this problem is the shadow of the future: If we expect our interactions to continue into the future, we might be able to build cooperation in mutually beneficial ways.[14]

A concerted application of leadership effort to change the dynamics of such interactions throughout a bureaucratic system—a performance-oriented reform—might shift an individual's expectations enough to get them to take a first step toward cooperation in the hopes that it will be recognized and reciprocated. However, if individuals perceive that it is only the application of leadership effort that is sustaining the behavior change, then an anticipated end to this effort—marked, for example, by a reform's predefined end date or some other expectation that it is temporary—may make them expect that others' cooperation will fall off at that time. Worse still, it may make individuals expect others to start shirking again as that end date approaches, potentially causing a backward-induction cascade of mutual shirking expectations that undermines the reform's ability to change behavior even at the start of the reform. So the conceptualization and perception of a reform effort as a one-off intervention that will eventually come to an end works against achieving and sustaining the very performance improvements at which the reform is aimed.

One might object to this argument that what matters is not whether individuals expect that the reform effort itself will be ongoing but if they expect that the reform (whether time-bound or open-ended) will permanently change the behavior of their manager and/or colleagues. In theory, after all, a one-off intervention into a collective action problem could induce a permanent switch from a negative, noncooperative equilibrium to a positive, cooperative one. Indeed, the use of the term *equilibrium* implies that the cooperative state is a self-reinforcing one once achieved. But there are good reasons that such situations are likely to be the exception rather than the rule.

From a relational contracts perspective, both theory and evidence suggest that individuals' expectations of one another's behavior tend to change through iterative cycles of action, reciprocation, and updating rather than through sudden, wholesale, irrevocable shifts. An actor who wants to break out of an existing negative pattern takes a small risk by taking an action that is personally costly to them but sends a signal to the other actor that they are willing to do more than the minimum expected of them. If the other actor responds with more than the contractual minimum required of them, they then take a slightly larger risk the next time, and so on. Through this process, a negative equilibrium can be gradually shifted to a positive one. Of course, the ease and speed with which these behavior and expectation changes happen depends, to some extent, on the broader political, social, and economic context within which these professional interactions are occurring. Even when individual expectations and actions do change rapidly as a result of broader contextual factors, though, they can easily sink back to previous levels if they are not reciprocated by action from others— or even cause disillusionment that makes changing expectations and behavior harder the next time. This reciprocation could hypothetically happen simultaneously and overnight across an entire bureaucracy, leading to a discontinuous shift from a negative to a positive equilibrium. However, the complex and constrained natures of bureaucratic systems would suggest that a messier, more iterative, gradual process seems a more realistic path of change.

We might go even further and question whether "positive equilibrium" is the best mental model with which to understand organizations characterized by cultures of consummate performance. *Equilibrium* implies behavior that is self-sustaining and self-reinforcing; once achieved, an equilibrium maintains itself in the absence of external interventions. But the picture that emerges from the management literature on high-performance organizations is not one of easy cooperation with minimal leadership effort but of a constant struggle to protect and maintain this culture. For example, in Peter Madsen and colleagues' study of how the leaders of a pediatric intensive care unit in a U.S. hospital created a high-performance culture of shared ownership and innovation, the authors describe the numerous and ongoing adaptations, interventions, and signals that the founding doctors had to undertake over the years to actualize the unit's mission. Positive organizational culture didn't stem automatically from clever organizational design and an initial investment of time and attention from the unit's founders; rather, "implementing their vision required continuous effort."[15] Similarly, Gibbons quotes the Google executive (and writer on organizational change) Shona Brown's reflection on the early days of building a high-performance culture at Google: "We were trying to build a new equilibrium. It was fragile; we had to reinforce it every day."[16] Haridimos Tsoukas and Robert Chia draw an analogy between organizations and acrobats balancing on tightropes. To an outside observer, the acrobat appears perfectly balanced and in equilibrium. But that balance is, in fact, continuously produced by the flexing, relaxing, and adjustment of every muscle in the acrobat's body; equilibrium is achieved not by effortless stability but by constant movement. So if what appears to be a positive equilibrium of persistently high performance in an organization is something that needs to be constantly adapted and reinforced, this suggests that high performance is not actually a stable equilibrium created by clever organizational design or a one-time leadership intervention. Rather, to borrow and adapt a phrase from Martha Feldman's work on organizational routines, high-performance cultures are "ongoing accomplishments"; they are built and sustained through processes of ongoing effort and reinforcement by reform leaders, not through one-off interventions.[17]

So far, the discussion has focused on the "ongoing process" part of "ongoing process of continuous improvement." Let's turn now to the "continuous improvement" part. These ideas fit intuitively together but are not always connected either in theory or in practice.[18]

Continuous improvement has been defined in many ways, but a good starting point is the definition used by Nadia Bhuiyan and Amit Baghel in their review of the literature—"a culture of sustained improvement targeting the elimination of waste in all systems and processes of an organization."[19] The emphasis here on "waste" reflects the origins of the idea in the manufacturing sector and the philosophy of *kaizen*, but we can generalize its applicability to different types of organizations by thinking of it as "the continuous search for opportunities for all processes to get better."[20] In this form, continuous improvement has been articulated as a goal and management philosophy in sectors from healthcare to education and government, more broadly, in Africa and around the world.[21] Indeed, the phrases "continuous improvement" and "learning by doing" have been so widely used over the past four decades that they can sound a bit like vague buzzwords, generic terms for good management. But they have specific meanings and implications that make them useful to invoke for the purpose of discussing systemic reforms.

These formulations almost all share three core ingredients. First, continuous improvement has to be a decentralized process, broadly owned and driven by (or, at least, not possible without) the active participation of all levels and types of employees, especially frontline workers. Second, this participatory, learning-by-doing approach is necessary because it is usually not obvious at the outset what changes should be made to improve performance—at least not to managers and senior leaders. Rather, "it is the worker who is on the shop floor [that] typically knows the best solution to an existing problem."[22] Third, continuous improvement is highly practice-focused, both as a goal of change and as a means of achieving it. So whereas "ongoing process" (and the associated process-oriented literature on organizational change) places the emphasis on the temporality of reform as occurring across time, "continuous improvement" places the emphasis more on the substance of what change looks like: a multitude of locally identified, broadly driven, and cumulatively built-upon changes to work practices rather than the top-down rollout of a predefined master plan.

"Continuous improvement" as an idea comes largely from the management literature but is a close cousin of other terms that have been widely used in the development and institutional reform literatures, such as "learning-by-doing" and "adaptive management." The main common thread is the idea that reform efforts should be focused on local problem-solving rather than on imposing pre-defined solutions and "best practices." Perhaps the most prominent work in this vein in the development sphere has been by Matt Andrews and colleagues, who show why the complexities and idiosyncrasies of specific reform contexts mean that it is often impossible for effective solutions to be designed from outside or above. Their concept of "problem-driven iterative adaptation" (PDIA)—in which change is driven by teams of individuals engaged in repeated, local experi-mentation and evaluation to find solutions that fit their local contexts—has been immensely influential in development circles.[23]

The idea of systemic reform as an ongoing process of continuous improvement shares with adaptive management the emphasis on decentralized problem-solving. But whereas adaptive management and related ideas tend to place emphasis on local experimentation being necessary because of uncertainty over *what* should be done to improve performance, I focus on its importance in enabling workers and managers to learn *how* to cooperate with each other. As discussed above, even in cases where it is obvious what practices need to be carried out to improve performance, the absence of positive relational contracts can prevent them from being taken. It is through many iterative behavioral changes, starting small and getting larger if reciprocation by other actors is observed, that workers and man-agers can surmount the relational problems of vertical bilateral credibility and horizontal collective action in achieving consummate performance. Grand, top-down reform plans offer fewer opportunities for teams to build cooperation with one another, focusing attention instead on compliance with imposed mandates. So an approach of iterative, decentralized learning-by-doing helps not only with discovering what to do but also how to get it done.

The importance of this collective, relational process of learning-how-to-do-together-by-doing-together is backed up by empirical studies of performance improvement efforts in organizations around the world. For example, Trish Reay and colleagues show how individual healthcare workers in a hospital achieved continuous change by leveraging their roles and relationships through "inter-dependent, recursive, situated 'microprocesses.'"[24] They observe that whereas actors' embeddedness in their organizations is often seen as a constraint or obstacle to change—which we can understand as being stuck in a negative equi-librium, though the authors don't use that term—the relationships that derived from their embeddedness were also the foundation of their ability to implement change. So making changes in actual practices was inseparable from the ongo-ing process of building relationships, and together, these enabled continuous improvement in the organization as a whole.

This emphasis on the centrality of everyday work practices and the relation-ships in which they are embedded also sheds new light on another concept that is central to both academic and popular discussions of reform and change: orga-nizational culture. Organizational culture is widely recognized as a key deter-minant of organizational performance because of the recognition that shared norms, expectations, and cognitive frameworks are powerful drivers of individ-ual behaviors.[25] But as the literature on continuous improvement (and practice theory more generally) emphasize, day-to-day practices are not only the result of organizational culture and change efforts, they are also constitutive of them.[26] For example, in his study of organizational socialization in the civil services of Nigeria and Ghana, Aung Hein finds that effective supervisors induct new recruits into the organization's culture not by talking to them about abstract concepts and values but by assigning and giving feedback on specific tasks—demonstrating norms and expectations rather than just talking about them.[27]

Thus, in the words of W. Warner Burke, "You don't change culture by trying to change the culture."[28] Since expectations and norms are formed by observa-tions of others' behavior, it is by changing these microlevel actual practices that larger changes in shared culture emerge. An implication of this is that rather than necessarily tackling the biggest problems first, they may often be better served by focusing first on the problems and associated practices that are easiest to change to initiate this cycle of mutually reinforcing changes in practices and expecta-tions. This could either be done through enforcing useful processes that already formally exist but are not being consistently executed or by focusing on simple, informal actions, depending on the context.

This mutually reinforcing relationship between actions and expectations in building culture helps explain the failure of so many reform efforts that rhe-torically espoused continuous improvement as a goal but then proceeded as if achieving it were merely the result of compliance with a preordained blueprint. Rather, a shared culture of continuous improvement can only be created by prac-ticing continuous improvement from the bottom up. Leaders have a crucial role to play in catalyzing this, as the next section discusses, but whereas continuous improvement is often viewed as an outcome of reform or a state of performance, it is also (and more importantly) the mechanism through which an ongoing change process is manifested and sustained. It cannot simply be decreed or rolled out in a top-down fashion.

Before continuing on, some clarifications. First, much of the theoretical and empirical literature on organizational change assumes that continuous change in organizations is marginal, small, or "incremental." Similarly, continuous change is often contrasted with "planned" organizational change, with the idea that continuous change is something that emerges from an organic process that is too complex to foresee or direct.[29] This can have the result of making continuous change as a model seem as if it necessarily entails lowering one's expectations of how much change is possible, meekly accepting the status quo. Viewed in this way, it is understandable why practitioners might see "incremental" approaches as uncompelling change strategies. From a theoretical standpoint, however, this perspective on continuous change also undervalues the extent to which a multitude of small changes can cumulate over time into major improvements in performance and also misses the point that high-performance cultures can only be built through the continued making of such small changes across the whole of the organization. So this book's goal in articulating a theory of systemic reform as an ongoing process of continuous improvement is not to suggest that reform leaders reduce their ambitions in how much they aim to improve performance but rather to lay out an approach to achieving major improvements that is better supported by theory and evidence than the dominant model of approaching reform as a one-off change to formal rules and structures.

Second, it is common in much of the existing practitioner and academic literature on bureaucratic reform to draw a sharp distinction between results-oriented management and process-oriented management. The refrain—familiar to much of the discussion of New Public Management as a management ideology—is that bureaucracies have historically focused too much on their own internal processes and not enough on tangible results like outputs and outcomes. This is a very different use of the term *process* than I am trying to invoke with the phrases "ongoing process" and "reform as process," which I intend to emphasize the central idea that reforms that aim to shift nonformalizable behaviors must be temporally ongoing and iterative processes rather than one-off interventions or projects. In my usage, treating reform as a process is theorized to be the best way to improve results, and the focus on shifting actual behaviors as the primary object of reform lends itself to an immediate focus on changing results—as opposed to imagining that results will improve after some new bureaucratic procedure has been created on paper.

Third, readers familiar with government reform efforts might see in this section echoes of Karl Weick's theory of "small wins," which has long been common in the discourse around development (and organizational change more generally).[30] In its use in institutional reforms, the theory of small wins (sometimes "quick wins") is generally interpreted as saying that reformers should start large reform programs by putting effort into achieving small but visible and tangible improvements as a way to demonstrate to skeptical internal and external stakeholders that it is actually possible to make change. This approach shares with this book's theory of reform as process the idea that credibility is important for reform efforts and that starting small can help build credibility. There are also differences, both in theory and in application. From a theoretical perspective, Weick argues that small wins matter through two mechanisms: the individual-level psychological effect of making change feel less overwhelming and more possible, and the system-level effect of aiding the building of political coalitions in favor of the desired broader changes and weakening opposition to them. In contrast, this book's theory of reform as process emphasizes the importance of building credibility not in terms of individual psychology or political interest groups but rather in terms of building cooperation within relationships and among teams. While seemingly minor, this difference has been consequential in practice: The theory of small wins has generally been deployed in bureaucratic reform not as a tool to help spur bottom-up improvements but as a first symbolic step in the rollout of larger top-down change initiatives—a way to encourage compliance, not a way to decentralize change and empower ordinary workers. So while these theories share an emphasis on the importance of building credibility, they differ in terms of how to do so and to what end.

With that in mind, let's now move to the final element of the theory of reform as process: If effective performance-oriented reform is an ongoing process of continuous improvement focused on changing actual work practices, what is the role of reform leadership?

LEADING BY CATALYZING

So far, this chapter (and, indeed, the book as a whole) has argued that leaders face major limitations in their ability to force widespread improvements in unformalizable behaviors, which must instead come from a decentralized, distributed process of teams of managers and workers iteratively building positive relational contracts among themselves. But if most meaningful improvements have to come to this distributed process, in what sense is planning and directing systemic reforms still possible? And what is the role of leadership in this?

Let's start by defining leadership in the context of systemic, performance-oriented reform. This book starts by putting you in the shoes of an advisor to a head of civil service—someone whose role puts them at the pinnacle of the pyramid of hierarchy that constitutes a bureaucratic system. However, reform leadership can also mean something much broader. In the sense I use it, a reform leader is someone whose role is to structure the work environment and interactions of multiple other individuals and teams. In other words, a reform leader is someone whose job is to influence (or try to influence) the performance of others. Such people can work in central management agencies like offices of heads of civil service, public service commissions, ministries of civil service, and cabinet offices that aim to influence performance across many organizations but can also work in line ministries and aim to influence performance across the multiple divisions of the organization. Similarly, a reform leader could be a senior executive like the head of civil service, an organizational CEO, or be in a technocratic role like an advisor or reform team member.

Figure 7.2 lays this out visually by zooming out from the single-team focus of figure 7.1 to consider a whole bureaucratic system. The basic building blocks are still worker-manager dyads and groups of workers that collectively constitute a team. In the absence of outside intervention, some teams are likely to develop

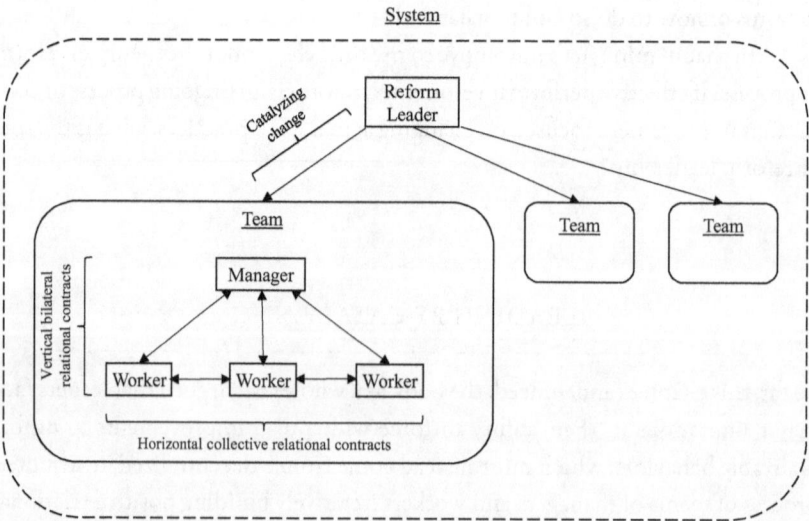

FIGURE 7.2 System Leadership Catalyzing Team-Level Change

Source: Author.

positive, cooperative relational contracts while others develop negative ones. But there is also a new type of actor—a reform leader—who sits outside this set of relationships and cannot control workers' or managers' actions directly but can apply effort to structure and influence interactions among manager-worker dyads and worker-worker groups. The reform leader can, thus, influence the likelihood of building positive relational contracts for manager-worker dyads and worker-worker groups in a setup that reproduces itself fractally across the many-tiered hierarchies and numerous lines of reporting and communication that together constitute a bureaucratic system.

Reform leaders have several types of tools at their disposal to influence these interactions among managers and workers within teams. Some of these tools are mainly focused on changing the formal structures, rules, and processes in an effort to change the incentives that underpin these interactions: performance-linked incentives, salaries, mandatory performance reporting and audits, and so on. But many other leadership tools are focused less on forcing or incentivizing people to behave differently and more on supporting, empowering, and enabling them to do so. Chapter 4 has already shown the limited ability of tools in the former category to make change, so here, I will focus on the latter category. Such supporting, empowering, or enabling actions include the following:

- **Creating opportunities for discussion and change.** Leaders can create forums and processes that bring teams together to discuss performance and how to improve it, as discussed in chapter 6. Such forums can't force teams to have meaningful discussions or to make changes based on them, and the more they try to force this with accountability and measurement mechanisms, the less meaningful and more defensive the discussions tend to become. But they can provide a setting and initiative for conversations to happen that might not happen otherwise, and therefore support the building of more positive relationships. They can also provide an institutional platform from which teams can begin the process of changing relational contracts by making small changes, observing each other's reciprocation, updating expectations, and iterating with slightly larger changes.
- **Creating energy and momentum for change.** Individuals and their teams can get "stuck" in negative equilibriums because of the mutually reinforcing nature of negative past experiences and future expectations. But if they believe that positive change is likely to happen in the broader organization or system, they might update their expectations of others' behavior and be more willing to put out extra effort themselves. This expectation of broader change might come from factors external to the civil service itself, such as

when Kenya's first electoral change of power took place in 2003 and the subsequent reforms took place in an environment that was "euphoric" and "energized."[31] But leaders themselves might also be able to generate this change in expectations through their own actions and speech. In particular, actions that are costly for the leader to take (e.g., in terms of their own time commitment) are likely to be especially effective at making the prospect of continued future change more credible.[32]

- **Providing information.** In the traditional hierarchical understanding of bureaucracies, information is usually understood to flow upward from workers to leaders to inform leaders' decisions, who then pass orders back downwards. But leaders can also provide information downward to help teams understand how their work fits into the broader system and how they are currently performing. In addition, leaders can provide information on practices that might potentially be helpful—for instance, practices that are in use in other teams around the civil service.

- **Escalation and authorization.** Teams might struggle to build positive relational contracts among themselves in cases where their ability to produce outputs depends on factors beyond their control, such as boundary-spanning problems or changes that require authorization or resources from above. Unresolved, such issues can demotivate teams and undermine continued effort, as Jillian Chown showed in her study of bottom-up improvement efforts in hospitals.[33] Similarly, Andrews and colleagues discuss the important role leaders play in authorizing and creating space for teams to undertake local change efforts.[34] An important role for leaders in catalyzing the building of positive relational contracts at team level is, therefore, to make themselves available to teams to help them resolve problems that are beyond their own control.

Each of these four categories of leadership tools comprises formal processes that can be codified on paper and officially adopted, as well as informal practices that cannot be. For example, a leader can create opportunities to discuss performance not only by mandating that each team should hold a monthly meeting and come up with new ideas to improve performance (formal) but also by unexpectedly dropping by workers' offices to chat about their performance or asking a manager a question about what new ideas the team has come up (informal). As with the types of management processes and practices discussed in chapter 2, it is often the unformalizable aspects of these leadership tools that breathe life into their formal manifestations. So reform leadership is not just about choosing the right set of tools to apply to influence teams' working out of relational contracts but also about knowing how and when to apply scarce effort to give meaning to these tools.

Shaping organizational culture is a responsibility normally associated with leadership and is a powerful shaper of behavior, as works by scholars like Judith Tendler, Merilee Grindle, Erin McDonnell, and Akshay Mangla—among many others—have shown.[35] However, it is not listed above as a category of reform tool for two reasons. First, all four of these categories of tools are important for shaping organizational culture, so it makes more sense to think of culture change as suffusing them rather than as a separate category of tool. Second, and more importantly, organizational culture—in the sense of shared expectations, norms, and cognitive frameworks—is something that emerges as an outcome of all these distributed processes of team relational contract building, not something that is decreed from the top down. Leaders undoubtedly influence culture through the above-listed categories of tools and their own actions that accompany them. But their most important impacts on culture result indirectly from their efforts to influence the building of positive relational contracts across the many teams that comprise the system they oversee rather than directly through the leaders' own unilateral actions. As discussed in the previous section, it is not by decreeing culture change that real culture change happens, but instead, by changing practices and expectations.

This view of leadership as catalyzing rather than driving reform connects with a number of existing strands of research on leadership, organizational change, and reform. Most obviously, the contrast between "top-down" and "bottom-up" approaches to reform is a well-established one. The distinction has been invoked by scholars such as Charles Polidano, Joseph Ayee, Christopher Pollitt and Geert Bouckaert, and Willy McCourt in their comparative studies of civil service reform, as well as in the organizational change literature more broadly.[36] While scholars use the term *bottom-up* in slightly different ways, it generally refers to change that initiates from within the bureaucracy that is incremental or marginal, unplanned, and/or determined and driven by a participatory consultative process. In most academic work, this terminology is used to describe and typologize change approaches rather than advocate for one approach or the other. The distinction is also frequently made in practice: For example, in the archived draft text of a speech from 1996, Ghana's then-Head of Civil Service, Robert Dodoo, contrasted the incipient Civil Service Performance Improvement Programme (CSPIP, 1994–2001) with its predecessor reform by saying, "Instead of the Top-Down approach we evolve an initial and essentially Bottom-Up orientation. Participation and consensus building is emphasized to allow each major stakeholder to co-determine aspects of the design and to interpret its own role in the process. . . . [CSPIP] places primary importance on individual Ministries, Departments and Agencies (Bottom-Up Approach) in the assessment of problems, their diagnosis and analysis and eventually in the formulation of reform plans) and the implementation of solutions."[37]

Similarly, the ideal of more bottom-up problem-solving approaches to reform has also been explored by (among others) McCourt and by Katherine Bersch in her comparative study of Argentina's top-down "powering" approach to policy reform and Brazil's more successful "problem-solving" approach.[38] In another empirical comparison, Andrews and colleagues contrast Malaysia's unsuccessful attempt to create internal audit functions by decree with Burkina Faso's slower but more sustained and successful approach.[39] These ideas also have a long history in public administration. Bersch traces her use of "problem-solving" to Hugh Heclo's 1974 work on "puzzling" versus powering in policy change, and Charles Lindblom's famous 1959 article defending "muddling through" as a bureaucratic problem-solving strategy is an even earlier argument in favor of decentralized, iterative, small-scale experimentation as a management strategy.[40] Applying this approach to actual reform initiatives has become an increasingly active area for practice-oriented experimentation in the last decade, with examples including the Doing Development Differently collective and the World Bank's GovEnable initiative for basing public financial management reforms on local problem-diagnosis and problem-solving.[41]

A complementary argument for the importance of delegating discretion and flexibility to work teams comes from the empirical literature on organizational performance. For instance, observational quantitative research by Imran Rasul and Daniel Rogger in Nigeria and in Ghana by Rasul, Rogger, and myself has found that the extent of autonomy and discretion that government organizations give their staff is positively correlated with organizational performance. Experimental work by Oriana Bandiera and colleagues found that procurement officers in Pakistan who are given greater autonomy and flexibility respond by obtaining better value for money on purchases.[42] Reviewing and analyzing a broad range of evidence across countries, Dan Honig argues that most bureaucrats are "mission driven," even in low- and middle-income countries characterized by relatively poor overall governance outcomes, and that organizations should use "empowering" management practices to activate this intrinsic motivation and leverage it in service of better performance. In a report on the future of public service, the OECD emphasizes the importance of meaning and autonomy in enabling workers to find fulfillment in their work and be effective.[43] Scholars like McDonnell have shown how the carving out of autonomy for teams within broader systems is crucial in enabling them to find ways to build performance-oriented cultures.[44]

While these studies each take differing theoretical perspectives, collectively, they and others provide empirical support to the idea that the decentralization of authority and action in government bureaucracies—rather than top-down and prescriptive direction from leadership—play an important role in supporting high performance.

The idea of catalyzing rather than driving change also echoes two important bodies of literature on leadership itself: on transformational leadership and on what is referred to variously as system leadership, shared leadership, or distributed leadership. The former is based in psychology and focuses on distinguishing transactional leadership—leadership by carrots and sticks—from transformational leadership—leadership by motivation and inspiration.[45] Transformational leadership theory shares with this chapter the focus on the limitations of extrinsic incentives and the importance of leveraging individual intrinsic motivations but tends to focus more on individual psychology rather than bilateral and collective relational contracts as the mechanism driving action. The idea of system leadership, however, derives more from complexity theory as well as practice-oriented research around improving performance, particularly in the education and health sectors, and emphasizes the need for change to be driven from many locations in a system—not just top-down.[46] This perspective on reform leadership is well illustrated by a set of articles in a journal special issue edited by Lucy Gilson and Irene Agyepong, which explores the effectiveness of and barriers to distributed leadership across a range of African health systems. For example, Thubelihle Mathole and colleagues compare two rural hospitals, one high-performing and the other low-performing, and find that leadership in the former was characterized as "supportive" and "approachable," while leadership in the latter was characterized as "authoritarian," leading to poor communication and demotivation.[47] While the literature on system/shared/distributed leadership refers to a wider range of types of leaders and contexts, it shares this book's emphasis on positive change as originating from many sources rather than from mere hierarchical compliance. Like the ideal of continuous improvement, achieving shared/distributed leadership can be understood as a goal, a means of the theory of reform as process, and of leadership as catalyzing rather than forcing change.

An even more radical way scholars have sought to transcend traditional models of leadership is by placing the decentralized, polycentric nature of systems front and center. The idea that many social systems are polycentric—governed simultaneously by multiple decision-makers rather than a single unitary authority—is perhaps best known through work by Elinor Ostrom and colleagues on collective natural resource governance, but it is equally applicable to bureaucratic systems.[48] A related strand on complexity theory explores the ways that change in such systems might be nonlinear, unpredictable, and emergent.[49] For example, the emphasis on learning-by-doing and experimentation as strategies for reform (rather than top-down, preplanned approaches) by scholars like Tunji Olaopa and Andrews and colleagues is motivated, in large part, by their foregrounding of the complexity of bureaucratic systems as their intellectual starting point as they explore how reform leaders might more successfully navigate situations "defined by high degrees of initial ignorance and uncertainty."[50] Similarly, the concept of "networked improvement communities"—decentralized groups of stakeholders collectively and iteratively trying to solve and act on common problems— has been an influential strand of thinking in the literature on education reform, mostly in high-income countries.[51]

So this book's emphasis on leadership's role in reform as catalyzing change shares with the literature on bottom-up reform, problem-solving, muddling through, PDIA, transformative leadership, system/shared/distributed leadership, polycentricity, and complexity, the core insight that top-down approaches to reform leadership are conceptually inadequate and have a poor empirical track record. They all share an inclination for avoiding comprehensive blueprints imposed from outside a system and embracing tinkering from within it, and an emphasis on seeing change as driven by many actors. They also differ from one another in their theoretical foundations, intended scope and topics of application, and the nature of the alternatives they propose, although these are often primarily due to differences in discourse across countries and disciplines rather than fundamental disagreements. So they—along with this book—are best seen not as rival theories but as allies in a common effort to challenge and reshape scholarly and popular mental models of bureaucratic change.

Having said that, it's worth restating what features collectively distinguish this book's approach to leadership. First is the focus on systemic change, in which a leader's goal is not to solve a specific problem or change a specific policy but rather to find ways to improve the performance of numerous teams that are each working on different types of tasks in different contexts. Second, whereas ideas of "incremental" or "emergent" change and of "muddling through" are often read as implying that change cannot be directed or planned—and, thus, giving reform leaders a passive or unambitious role—the idea that leadership is about catalyzing broad-based performance improvement across many teams implies an active role for leaders. Through their application of the tools of providing information, creating opportunities for discussion of performance and improvement, creating energy for change, and authorizing and escalating problems, leadership by catalysis allows leaders to exert significant control of the direction of change and potentially achieve ambitious goals.

Third, the idea of leadership as catalysis (and of reform as process more generally) is grounded in an underlying view of bureaucratic performance as driven by relational contracts and the challenge of getting people to take nonverifiable actions. In this view, the need for leadership to catalyze rather than force change is driven not (just) by uncertainty over *what* to do but by the insight that even simple actions are often not fully verifiable, and, thus, teams need to learn *how* to get them done. This clarifies the role of leadership in systemic, performance-oriented reform as neither being about trying to force compliance with predetermined blueprints nor about agnostically sitting back and letting teams and organizations experiment in a purely bottom-up fashion but rather as actively and consistently working to use their scarce time and attention to facilitate the building of positive relationships within and across teams throughout the system.

• • •

This chapter has put forward a theory of how systemic reforms can best be designed and implemented to improve performance. It has argued that reforms should usually be conceptualized and approached as efforts to catalyze an ongoing process of continuous improvement in workers' actual day-to-day practice. The dominant approach to civil service reform as a one-off change in formal rules and practices has continuously failed but persists, in large part, because of the lack of a compelling alternative mental model of how reform leaders can spark performance improvements at system scale. This chapter has tried to articulate how they can do so, starting at the level of relational contracts within teams and then building upward into change processes and the role of leadership.

An obvious question is: Does this theory of reform actually work? And the frank answer is: We don't know, and it's probably impossible to prove. To some extent, this is because the theory is propositional in nature, and so there isn't an extensive body of evidence on what happens when leaders try to put it into practice—although the theory built in this chapter has been shaped by the empirical evidence on patterns of success and failure from the previous chapters, including those that embodied elements of this approach and from research by other scholars. It's also because complex civil service reforms aren't mechanical interventions with predictable and consistent effects that we can causally identify, as chapter 1 discussed. So the theory of reform as process is best understood as a midrange theory of bureaucratic systems reform: neither a step-by-step blueprint nor an abstract framework universally applicable to every situation but rather a mental model of performance and change to help guide thinking and action across a wide range of bureaucratic contexts. The best test of such theories is not to try to evaluate whether they "work" or not in some universal, generalized sense, but to turn the question back on yourself and ask: Does this theory help me understand something important about performance and change in civil service organizations better? Does it help me see how I might be able to be a more effective reform leader—or manager, or worker—in the context in which I'm trying to improve performance?

Let's transition now from talking about these ideas as abstract theories to considering what it would look like to actually lead reform in a way that reflects this view of performance and change. To do so, let's go back to where this book started—Ghana in 2014, shortly after Nana Agyekum-Dwamena took over as Head of Civil Service—and examine, in practical terms, what it looks like to focus on changing actual practices rather than rules on paper, to treat reform as an ongoing process of continuous improvement, and to try to lead by catalyzing rather than forcing change.

8

Reform as Process in Ghana, 2014–2019

The previous chapter provided an academic answer to the question posed at the start of this book: How should a senior leader approach undertaking reforms to improve the performance of their country's civil service? It argued that rather than approaching reform as a one-off, top-down imposition of formal rules and processes, leaders should approach reform as an effort to *catalyze an ongoing process of continuous improvement in actual practices*. It traced how this approach helped answer the fundamental puzzle of reform: how to get workers to carry out important but unformalizable actions that they can't be forced to do. Doing this at system scale means reform leaders have to find ways to help workers and managers spread across numerous teams establish more cooperative and productive relationships with one another by encouraging, supporting, and enabling change rather than trying to force it.

This chapter tries to show what *reform as process* looks like in practice. It argues that the key insights of this approach can be captured in three simple rules of thumb for reformers:

1. **Focus first on what can be done within existing formal rules and processes so that changing formal rules and processes is a last resort rather than a first step.** Prioritize improving the implementation of existing processes that are useful but underutilized and getting people to undertake helpful informal practices that are possible within existing rules. Alternatively, if certain processes are being implemented too rigidly, find ways to relax or reinterpret their application. Working within existing formal structures minimizes the time delay and procedural obstacles to getting workers to change their behavior. Build up toward changing formal processes rather than starting anew.

2. **Approach change as a process of collective learning by doing, rather than as rolling out a predesigned blueprint.** The priority should not be to make the perfect plan upfront but instead to start changing actual practices—even small or apparently minor ones—as early as possible. This makes it possible to simultaneously and iteratively build up credibility around reform efforts while also defining their content in a participatory fashion. This allows work teams to take ownership of the changes, build better relationships with one another, and focus on what would be most useful in their specific contexts. Removing the "design phase" also lowers the barriers to starting the change process and treats reform and improvement as part of core operations rather than an add-on.

3. **Decentralize the leadership of reform as much as possible.** The role of the leader is to catalyze dispersed improvement across the system rather than drive it. This not only aids in broadening ownership and buy-in to changes but also reduces the risk that leadership turnover (which always occurs sooner or later) will undo everything the reform has achieved. Decentralizing reform helps create new tiers of future reform leaders who can sustain progress in the future and shifts the institutional culture from one of compliance to one of improvement and innovation. Leaders have a range of tools for achieving this, including creating opportunities for discussing performance and how to improve it, creating energy and momentum for change, providing information to teams, helping solve problems that are beyond each team's remit, and empowering lower- and mid-ranking workers and managers to initiate improvement efforts.

This chapter explores what these principles look like in practice. The starting point for this is Ghana's Civil Service from 2014–2019 under then-Head of Civil Service, Nana Agyekum-Dwamena—the period immediately following his conversation with me that motivated me to write this book. (He served in this position until his retirement in 2023, but, as with the rest of the book, this chapter focuses mainly on the years up to 2019.) Driven by his own experience with past reform efforts in Ghana, Agyekum-Dwamena—or Nana, as he is near-universally referred to within Ghana's Civil Service—tackled the task of reform in a way that embodied all three of the above principles.

The chapter lays out these decisions and practices in granular detail to help readers see one way that these abstract principles can be translated into day-to-day leadership actions. It is based on a series of five interviews with Agyekum-Dwamena, supplemented by data from other sources and the Ghana section of this book's appendix. My focus in this chapter is not on documenting and analyzing these changes but on recounting the decisions and approaches that Agyekum-Dwamena took from his perspective as a reform leader.[1] Wherever possible, I draw on other sources and interviews to triangulate and enrich his account and gauge the evidence on the effectiveness of these changes as best I can. For the most part, though, this chapter is the story of one leader's effort to approach reform differently than he had seen in the past—a story that I hope provides some inspiration and encouragement to other reform leaders around the world.[2]

At the same time, the story of civil service reform in Ghana during this time period is about far more than one person. Agyekum-Dwamena played a crucial role in initiating and leading many changes, but these reform efforts were fleshed out and implemented by others, and other initiatives were still proposed and led by his colleagues in the Office of the Head of Civil Service, Management Services Department, Civil Service Training Centre, and ministries, departments, and agencies throughout the service. Indeed, to the extent Agyekum-Dwamena was successful as a leader, it was not because he was a lone visionary champion but because he put a tremendous amount of effort into encouraging, supporting, and coordinating others to lead change efforts. While the majority of this chapter is framed for simplicity and brevity around Agyekum-Dwamena's perspectives and actions, the leadership of reform during his time in office is best understood as collective.

The chapter concludes by discussing some of the political and practical challenges to treating reform as a process: time horizons and turnover of political and bureaucratic leaders, incentives to projectize reform and focus on highly visible formal outputs, and accountability pressures to measure and demonstrate change. There are no easy solutions to these challenges, but there is often more space to work within and around them than we assume. This chapter begins the work of laying out these challenges and potential approaches to navigating them in an effort to help you think about how you might be able to do so in your own context.

BACKGROUND: AGYEKUM-DWAMENA AND GHANA'S CIVIL SERVICE IN 2014

Agyekum-Dwamena was appointed Acting Head of Civil Service on January 1, 2014, and confirmed in the role eight months later. Immediately prior, he had been serving as Executive Secretary of the Management Services Department (MSD), an organization under the Office of the Head of Civil Service (OHCS) that operated as a sort of in-house management consultancy for the government. He had come to this role after a career in MSD and OHCS that began in 1988 and had seen him either participating in or having a front-row seat for nearly all of Ghana's civil service reform efforts of the last three decades.

These experiences with reform shaped the mindset with which he took on the most senior role in the Civil Service. These lessons were garnered from tasks like conducting job inspections to inform retrenchment decisions under the structural adjustment era Civil Service Reform Programme (CSRP, 1987–1993), which allowed him, as a new recruit, to see how grand reform plans interfaced with the line ministries they were trying to reshape: "So from day one, I got to know that there were different routes to which organisations would respond to issues from the centre. . . . There were some people who had already prepared data to show us while others had nothing to show."[3] He then served as head of the Reform Coordinating Unit in OHCS during the Civil Service Performance Improvement Programme (CSPIP, 1994–2001), facilitating dozens of organizational performance improvement workshops and witnessing firsthand how the "maverick leader" Head of Civil Service, Robert Dodoo, generated huge energy through a homegrown reform program focused on participatory diagnosing and solving of performance problems—and how easy it was for this project to be dropped following a change in government and the end of donor funding.[4] He also benefited from formal training in organizational development, including completing a master's degree in organizational development at the University of Cape Coast in Ghana, which helped shape his subsequent thinking.[5]

Then, as Executive Secretary of MSD, he set out to improve the effectiveness of the organization by creating a culture of continuous improvement through initiatives like getting one worker each month to give a lecture to their peers on something they had been studying. "I learned that leadership is one of the key things, and that depends on getting people involved, building their capacity, creating an atmosphere of sharing. . . . Because we didn't have a lot of money, that was one of the ways of improving the skills of people on a regular basis. . . . So over time, a lot of capacity was built and I've learned that you can improve an organization without necessarily having all the resources."[6]

The Civil Service that Agyekum-Dwamena took over in 2014 was widely seen as poorly performing by politicians, citizens, academics, and even civil servants themselves. The litany of perceived problems was similar to those that were recited at the start of dozens of reform programs around Africa and will be familiar to frustrated public servants all over the world: Worker motivation and job satisfaction were often low; there was little link between performance and promotion, remuneration, sanctions, or career development opportunities; younger workers were frustrated by hierarchical organizational cultures and management styles that left little room for new ideas; managers were frustrated by workers' poor compliance with processes and perceived laziness; many workers had no work to do or only came to the office a few hours a day, while others were over-burdened and worked early in the morning and late into the night; issues with corruption were regularly reported; delayed budget releases meant workers often had to pay for office supplies or even operational expenses like workshops from their own pockets; and communication and record-keeping were spotty.[7] Even the Office of Head of Civil Service itself was sometimes wryly referred to as the "Office of Hardships, Complaints, and Sorrows."[8]

At the same time, there were some positive things that could be built on. While some parts of the service performed poorly, there were also teams and even whole organizations that were characterized by high levels of commitment, professionalism, and efficient processes.[9] The fact that some employees were working overtime and paying for expenses from their own pockets indicated that they cared deeply about their work. Indeed, a survey by Rachel Sigman found that 83 percent of civil servants said that they joined "to serve my community or my country."[10] Many rules and procedures—a code of conduct, a performance appraisal system, annual and medium-term organizational planning and report-ing cycles—already existed on paper, even if they were used inconsistently or perfunctorily in practice. So it wasn't as if everything in the service was dysfunc-tional and needed to be rebuilt from scratch.

The Civil Service was also faced with some important contextual pres-sures and constraints, which had the potential to both hinder and help reform efforts. On the positive side, there was broad consensus in society that the Civil Service needed to improve: Electoral pressures made at least some pol-iticians concerned with improving service delivery, and many civil servants were frustrated with the status quo. There was also fatigue and cynicism about the potential for change from civil servants who had seen numerous waves of reform come and go. The country had little fiscal space, partly due to the leg-acy of the costly Single Spine Pay Policy, implemented a few years previously as part of an earlier reform effort. Some international donors were willing to help fund public sector reform activities—in fact, the World Bank had approached Agyekum-Dwamena early in his tenure and indicated their potential willingness to support a multiyear reform program with a loan.[11] However, donor involve-ment would also entail additional administrative and reporting requirements, and the timebound nature of donor programs had arguably undermined the sustainability of previous reforms. Finally, legal protections and unions made it nearly impossible to fire significant numbers of workers, and budget constraints made it infeasible to hire new ones, so large-scale personnel changes weren't an option for Agyekum-Dwamena.[12]

The orthodox option would have been to follow the dominant approach to reform that this book has documented: to spend a year or two designing a new set of formal rules and processes that would then be adopted and rolled out across the service under a three-to-five-year reform program with its own acronym, budget line, and implementing team, supported in part by a grant or loan from donors. But Agyekum-Dwamena's experience with the shortcomings of previous reform waves that had taken this approach had soured him on "big-bang" approaches to reform that tried to design and then implement a grand plan to fix the Civil Service's perceived failings. Instead, he decided to take a different approach that he hoped would deliver faster and more sustainable improvement.

AGYEKUM-DWAMENA'S APPROACH TO REFORM

First, Agyekum-Dwamena focused on working within existing rules and processes rather than trying to create new ones: "Generally speaking, I think—talking about Ghana—we have more rules than we even need . . . if we could try and implement sixty—not even one hundred—sixty, seventy percent of the rules, we wouldn't even need new rules. I'm not saying therefore that we don't need new rules. But the problem is not the rules."[13]

More generally, he explained, "I'm skeptical about starting anything greatly new. I'm rather doing consolidation of things that we have started."[14]

One way Agyekum-Dwamena put this into practice was by trying to improve the functioning of the Civil Service's annual performance appraisal process. Introducing and reintroducing annual appraisal systems had been a staple of earlier reforms in Ghana, and another such effort had been initiated by the Public Services Commission in 2012, two years before Agyekum-Dwamena took office. But previous experience showed that the formal structure of these systems—the contents of the appraisal template, details of the scoring system, and so on—was secondary to the fact that the implementation of these systems was poor. The appraisal process was widely (though not universally) treated as a perfunctory exercise with no real consequences. In some organizations, workers didn't even do their appraisals annually, instead filling in and submitting multiple years' worth of forms just before they were due for promotion. Under Agyekum-Dwamena, OHCS began more diligently enforcing the requirement for these to be conducted annually. They also began occasionally writing letters to officers whose appraisals indicated exceptional performance. "I have been really focused on non-monetary incentives like resuscitating the Civil Service Week, recognizing people who perform. When the staff appraisals come and people have done well, instead of just allowing the ministries to write to them, we write from here encouraging them. So people are taking note of that and a couple of people . . . who have met me on the street and said, 'Nana the letter that you wrote was very good, I've been in the civil service 10 years, 15 years, 20 years and nobody has recognized anything.'"[15]

These letters were meaningful to the civil servants who received them because they signaled that OHCS and senior leaders were going above and beyond the minimum required of them by the appraisal process, and that they were taking the process seriously. In doing so, they also encouraged the receiving officers—and their colleagues who heard about the letter, their managers, and the OHCS staffers who helped identify the person and arrange for the letter to be sent—to take the process seriously in the future and treat it as more than just a compliance exercise. These letters thus signaled an intent to change expectations around performance within the service, saying to workers: If you go above and beyond the minimum required of you, we will recognize you for it.

Another area Agyekum-Dwamena focused on changing practices without changing rules was the lack of punctuality in starting meetings. This was not only an impediment to performance and a major waste of resources but also was symbolic of workers' expectations that many existing rules—from meeting start times to performance reporting requirements—could safely be ignored.[16] Changing this practice would be a simple but daily signal that "this time things are different." His inspiration for this came from working with the late President John Atta-Mills, who, when vice president, started an important meeting with chief directors and ministers at exactly 9 a.m. despite the fact that most of the ministers were not yet present. They even locked the doors so that the ministers were left waiting outside.[17] In his own meetings, Agyekum-Dwamena started to call out the people who arrived late and caused delays, including senior leaders. "Everybody knows in that if the meeting is organised by Nana, you have to be there on time."[18] The Civil Service saw some improvement in this area over time, though change was slow. "It's still a challenge when you have senior politicians or chiefs coming an hour late for meetings. I don't think we're fully there yet in terms of trickle down, but we're using every possible tool we can deploy."[19]

Another existing but underutilized tool for improving performance was the system of organizational service charters—public documents specifying services available, processes for accessing them, and processing timelines—that each ministry, department, and agency had. These had been introduced under the CSPIP reform of the 1990s and again under the Ministry of Public Sector Reform in the late 2000s, with extensive design processes, costly workshops, and great fanfare. Each time, they fell into disuse and became outdated soon after being written. Rather than seeking funds to revise and relaunch them, OHCS simply directed that each ministry conduct an in-house update of its service charter and do so regularly thereafter, and a line directorate inside OHCS began monitoring both the existence of the charter and, gradually and imperfectly, performance against these standards.[20] This reframed the act of setting and reviewing the standards not as a one-time, externally driven reform act but as a collective exercise within each organization that then became part of the ongoing, routine relationship between OHCS and that organization.

Agyekum-Dwamena sought to make use of the Civil Service's existing disciplinary tools when necessary to shift staff from an expectation that timeliness and process could safely be ignored to a new expectation that, if OHCS asked for something, it meant it. Agyekum-Dwamena gave the example of writing a letter or giving a query to ask why a report had been submitted late and even delaying promotions for a year for a ministry's staff when the ministry had not submitted its promotion register on time. Acts like these imposed real—but nonpermanent and relatively minor—costs for substandard performance. They were important not so much because of the delays themselves but rather for their symbolic value in signaling a change in performance expectations. Here were cases where someone had unarguably, verifiably failed to perform a task correctly and where tools already existed to signal to that person and their colleagues that improvement was needed. This approach even extended to more severe types of misbehavior and sanctioning:

> People say it takes a long time to sack a civil servant, so we need a new rule. No, you don't need a new rule. The civil service is a bureau, it's based on a certain system which says that everything must be evidence based, we have a court system that says you must have evidence. The rule says that you cannot capriciously exercise your discretionary powers. So you want to sack somebody . . . [but] you've never issued any query [to] that person. Then suddenly one day he does something extreme and you want to sack him. No. The rules will say no. But if when he did [it] the first time, there's documentation to that fact, then after three times you can start disciplinary proceedings and you can sack the person. So it's not an issue of [a] new rule.[21]

In other cases, Agyekum-Dwamena and OHCS sought to improve the implementation of existing processes by making operational tweaks—for example, by digitizing the process of submitting annual staff appraisals—to make it easier for officers and their organizations to comply with them.[22] Whether it was with carrots, sticks, or incremental process improvements, the primary focus was on working within existing institutional structures to try to achieve mutually reinforcing changes in actual behaviors and performance expectations. Changes in practice were leading to changes in formal processes rather than the other way around.

Second, Agyekum-Dwamena approached performance improvement as a process of collective learning-by-doing rather than as the design and roll-out of a grand plan: "We wanted to look at motivating people to improve over time and making incremental changes."[23] To do so, he took a learning-by-doing approach, prioritizing small innovations and speedy implementation over prolonged consultation. "We experimented with a lot of things—some other leaders would never have let that happen."

For instance, OHCS decided to modify how promotion interviews were conducted, moving from a rote process where candidates could supply abstract answers to one that demanded specific evidence and examples of skills and leadership competencies. "Normally we would develop a concept note, hire a consultant, think long and hard about how to do it. Instead . . . [working in a small team] we started to trial it in the Office of the Head of Civil Service. We sometimes would make mistakes, but we corrected them along the way. In two weeks, we did something that usually takes six months."[24]

This shift in interview approach effectively raised the standards demanded of promotion candidates, and there was a significantly greater number of failures. So OHCS responded by beginning to implement another existing process that existed on the books but was not being carried out:

> The development of [Personal] Performance Improvement Plans for those who fail interviews. Gradually it's catching up. In the past we were not even thinking about it at all, but now it's something that [the Career Management Directorate] has been mandated [to] do, that when people fail interviews we just don't leave them, let's develop these performance improvement plans. Let them send it to us, and let's see that directors and heads of organizations are actually working on that. [It was something that was on the books for a long time] but it was not being done, now we've started since last year.[25]

The determination to avoid the pitfalls of projectization also manifested in a deliberate decision to avoid basing reform decisions around external funding or resource availability more generally. Having seen the distortions that money introduced into previous reforms, Agyekum-Dwamena explained, "We are going for this [approach of] incremental but impactful, less expensive things, so we will not need any DFID or World Bank funding to get some of those things done. If they bring the money so be it, but we are not going to beg them for it."[26]

Third, and inextricable from the emphasis on learning by doing, was Agyekum-Dwamena's effort to decentralize the reform process by encouraging and empowering others to initiate change. "I go around directorates and speak to junior officers. I ask them: What have you been doing? Why are you doing it? Is there anything you want to change about it? What suggestions have you made to your Director or Chief Director? I do the same thing to staff of other ministries."[27] His focus in doing so was not just to counterbalance the hierarchical, bureaucratic culture that was often prevalent in the Civil Service but to try to get people to actually start undertaking small reforms to demonstrate to others how these could be impactful.[28]

Another small and subtle practice that was nonetheless an important signal was that Agyekum-Dwamena would frequently "cold call" junior officers in meetings to ask them for their opinions or analysis on the issue being discussed. In a context where junior officers were usually expected to listen rather than contribute, this simple act sent a dual signal. To junior officers, it flagged that their perspectives were important and valued, and they should always be actively thinking during meetings rather than passively listening. Perhaps more importantly, it signaled to senior officers that they too should care about what their subordinates had to say and invite them to take initiative, that strong leadership is not about always knowing the answers oneself but about bringing them out together as a team.

This was new and initially challenging for staff given the Civil Service's traditionally hierarchical culture, but over time, this modeling of the ethos of local micro-innovations and continuous improvement began to be embraced. "Now it's not just me bringing new ideas—Directors [in OHCS] bring up ideas, I [work with RCU to] sharpen them, and then we help implement them. Every two months they bring a new reform idea. That's how we institutionalise it. Every director, every two months. No matter how small."[29]

At another point in the interview, after explaining why he was so focused on trying to make improvements within existing structures rather than aiming for a "big-bang" reform, he quipped: "You know, through[out] the whole world, messiahs have always been killed. They are martyred." "So you're not trying to be a messiah?" I asked. "No, no," he chuckled, "I'm trying to be just working with people—facilitator, motivator, not a messiah."[30]

This effort to broaden reform ownership was linked to an approach that treated reform as part of the core operations of the Civil Service rather than as an add-on or separate activity. Agyekum-Dwamena viewed the failure of prior reform efforts as due, in large part, to having a central reform team that drove and coordinated every aspect of the reform. So while the OHCS under his tenure did have a permanent Reform Coordinating Unit, there was an emphasis on getting the organization's line directorates—operational divisions like Career Management and Policy, Planning, Monitoring, and Evaluation—to be the ones driving the changes in their relevant areas, so that the reforms were "mainstreamed" from the very start.[31] The Reform Coordinating Unit's role was primarily to support and monitor these changes, providing a weekly report to the Head of Service on what was going on.

Broadening the ownership and initiation of change efforts was also a strategic way to try to improve the sustainability of these changes in the knowledge that every leader and manager in the Civil Service would eventually retire or move to a different position. Agyekum-Dwamena explained that the goal was to develop "a critical mass in every ministry" of change-minded officers. "We realize that a particular Director or Chief Director may be interested in the reform and we'll do new things, but when he leaves or retires or dies or whatever things start to change. . . . So we are rather focusing on developing critical mass so that in every ministry we have . . . people who are interested and people who seem to make things happen, which is not necessarily from the top. In other words, spreading the ownership. So that when the person leading these administrations goes to another ministry they will continue with that."

To support this, OHCS's line directorates were also given more responsibility for engaging with sector ministries on reform and improvement. "In the past, it was a reform coordinator that was really working in the ministries but now it is rather the directorates, the departments, that are working with the ministries."[32] The main goals of giving line directorates responsibility for actively promoting improvement initiatives throughout the service—rather than just passively processing promotion requests, annual reports, and so on—were to decentralize ownership and leadership of reform, instill a culture of continuous improvement, and maximize the likelihood of improvements being sustained. Treating reform activities as part of ongoing core operations also served a very practical purpose in a resource-scarce context. Under previous reform efforts, staff in reform or project implementation units had expected to be paid extra allowances for their involvement, which they saw as above and beyond their standard duties. This was not only costly but also reinforced the idea that reform was something separate and temporary. In contrast, treating reform as something that all staff should contribute to as part of their core jobs not only sent a better cultural message but also meant that additional financial resources were not needed either to start reform or sustain it.

Much writing around reform emphasizes the importance of broad stakeholder consultations to build support for reform, and highly consultative approaches are often seen as an alternative to top-down reform. But here, Agyekum-Dwamena sometimes took a different view, and he and his team often started making de facto changes without necessarily preceding them with extensive consultations. "It's good to consult and it's good to partner, but try to find a ways of speeding up some of these processes . . . we engage them but we don't spend too much time. . . . So, I'll be honest, I'm not a key—I'll just be blunt, I'm not a key fan of having done so many of these stakeholder engagements. . . . What I do is design what I want to do and then as we go on we bring people [on board]."

Conducting extensive stakeholder consultations prior to acting would have been time-consuming and costly—under Ghana's CSPIP reform in the 1990s, for example, this consultative process was useful but took years, which meant that by the time the implementation of these plans started, the donor funding was ending and a leadership transition was approaching. It also would have introduced a separation between reform design and reform implementation, which Agyekum-Dwamena was trying to get away from with his approach of starting small and learning by doing. What made it possible for him to minimize stakeholder consultations prior to reform was his approach to working within existing rules and tools: Who could object to implementing or improving processes that had already been approved and were already on the books? In contrast, starting reform by seeking to rewrite these rules would likely have entailed more extensive consultations, with all the costs and delays these would entail.

At the same time, there were other instances and issues for which Agyekum-Dwamena undertook extensive consultations, which he saw as part of the process of basing reforms on research and evidence. Some of this took the form of consultations with key stakeholders from outside the Civil Service after his appointment in 2014–2015—although these were aimed more at shaping the longer-term reform agenda and were undertaken in parallel to his first phase of reform efforts rather than as a prelude to them. In other cases, it involved doing desk research to get ideas from other governments around the world or cooperating with outside researchers to undertake new studies.[33] What differentiated these consultations and research efforts was the way they rolled together action and learning as part of one internally driven process rather than as distinct exercises or phases.

Of course, Agyekum-Dwamena did introduce some new measures, including taking funding from the World Bank to digitize the performance appraisal and promotion interview processes, among other things.[34] However, donor funds were not driving reform efforts. "If the donors come, so be it. If they don't come, we're still going on."[35] He also championed a system of Chief Director Performance Agreements (later cascaded down to directors as well), which had been introduced under his predecessor, Woeli Kemevor, and was based on ideas first developed under CSPIP in the 1990s. This focused on defining and measuring a set of key deliverables as well as minimum administrative requirements for each chief director, with results published in a league table at the end of the year and the top performers receiving prizes. Rather than treating these performance agreements as a mechanical way to reward or punish performance, the prizes were largely symbolic. Instead, the system's focus was to signal the importance of performance; clearly communicate goals, roles, and responsibilities to chief directors as well as their staff; and create venues in which performance and challenges could be regularly discussed. Similarly, the target-setting part of the annual staff appraisal system was altered in 2015 to better link it to the organizational goals and Chief Director Performance Agreements.[36] But even where Agyekum-Dwamena did introduce new processes or utilize highly formal processes, it was not as stand-alone interventions but as supports and complements to a broader change effort that focused mainly on working within existing rules, making change through a collective process of learning-by-doing, and decentralizing reform leadership.

Reflecting in our final interview on what he had learned from his involvement in previous efforts at "big-bang" reforms, Agyekum-Dwamena said, "So if you want my honest opinion, with limited resources, get a bit of focus and push it. That's the way. Slowly, but consistently. The key thing is more about consistency, can you keep on pushing, can you keep on improving. Keep the people's feet to the fire. As distinct from seeing [reform as] an event, I think if we have the process approach then the chance of success is high."[37]

During another interview session, he captured it even more succinctly: "It's not a miracle, it's a process."

Table 8.1 catalogs these micropractices of reform as process along with the practical rules of thumb and linked theoretical principles with which they are most closely associated. Each practice in isolation appears simple, sometimes even obvious or unimpressive. But implemented together and consistently, with a great deal of informal stitching together, these practices amounted to something far more significant. Indeed, that these practices each appear trivial in isolation reinforces a key point from the last chapter: The "what" of reform as process is far less important than the "how" because the whole point is to build a mutually reinforcing cycle of changes in practices, expectations, and relationships. It is striking that Agyekum-Dwamena was—with only a handful of exceptions— quite agnostic about the specific types of changes or reform ideas that the people around him generated and that the service as a whole took. Rather, he cared

TABLE 8.1 Principles and practices of reform as process in Ghana, 2014–2019

Practical rule of thumb	Linked theoretical principle	Examples from Ghana 2014–2019	Illustrative quotes
Work first at improvements within existing formal processes	Focus on changing actual practices	• Enforcing completion of selected existing processes (e.g., annual appraisals); digitizing process to make it easier to track • Sending out letters of commendation for exceptional performance reported on annual appraisals • Starting meetings on time • Requiring ministries to review and update service charters • More consistent use of existing disciplinary tools in cases of clear malfeasance	• "I'm skeptical about starting anything greatly new. I'm rather doing consolidation of things that we have started."
Approach change as collective learning-by-doing	Ongoing process of continuous improvement	• Changing content and style of promotion interviews through in-house discussion, rather than contracting a consultant • Requiring personal performance improvement plans for individuals that fail promotion interviews (developed in consultation with their supervisor) • Integrating responsibility for coming up with innovations into operational directorates; part of people's core responsibilities • Focusing on changes that don't require any resources and avoiding relying on donor funding • Doing research and consultation alongside reforms (rather than before starting them)	• "We experimented with a lot of things—some other leaders would never have let that happen." • "The key thing is more about consistency, can you keep on pushing, can you keep on improving. Keep the people's feet to the fire."
Decentralize reform leadership as much as possible	Catalyzing rather than forcing	• Visiting staff offices and asking what suggestions they have made to their bosses for improvement • Cold-calling all levels of staff to ask their opinions in meetings • Asking each team to suggest a new reform idea every two months • Building networks and "critical masses" for change within and across each ministry • Putting responsibility for developing and leading reforms into OHCS line directorates rather than a separate reform team; reform coordinating unit just monitors and supports	• "I'm trying to be just working with people—facilitator, motivator, not a messiah."

Source: Author's synthesis. All quotes are from Nana Agyekum-Dwamena.

about what people were coming up with, suggesting, and putting ideas into action. Take care of the "how" and the "what" will follow.

Another important point about this table, and this chapter as a whole, is that readers' takeaway should not be that they should just go and copy this list of practices in their own context. This is both because the problems and levels of baseline performance might be different and because the lesson to take is the process and approach rather than the specific practices. What it means to focus on improvements within existing formal systems, approach change as a collective process of learning-by-doing, and decentralize reform leadership will obviously differ across contexts, across different leaders and their particular reform challenges and levers, and over time. The specific practices through which this approach is instantiated will only be meaningful if they are generated endogenously by a reform leader and their team themselves. Rather, the point of cataloging the changes made in Ghana in 2014–2019 is as an illustration, proof-of-concept, and inspiration for what reform as process (or something like it) *could* look like—a starting point for reform thinking, not a blueprint.

DID IT WORK?

An obvious question to ask is: Did it work? Was Agyekum-Dwamena's approach—which exemplified many aspects of the theory of reform as process while also differing in some ways—successful in changing behaviors and improving performance?

This is impossible to answer definitively both because not enough time has passed and because of the broader difficulties in evaluating systemic reforms that we discussed in chapter 1. However, we can look at the evidence that we do have—especially from interviews of rank-and-file officers throughout the Civil Service—to get some sense of whether any of these efforts seem to be translating into meaningful changes.

The evidence from these interviews is consistent with a perception that Agyekum-Dwamena approached leadership and reform differently than usual, both in general and with reference to specific practices. One interviewee (who had worked both in OHCS and in a line ministry) commented, "The current Head [of Civil Service], the way he approaches the work is different. . . . Head will demand that you deliver, he expects results. . . . For meetings if it starts at 9 a.m. he will lock the door and start at 9 a.m. Nana's time is not Ghana time. You will be sure to be there and the meeting will start."[38]

Other interviewees also commented (usually unprompted) on the changed expectations with respect to timeliness on everything from meeting start times to filing reports on time,[39] to the idea that OHCS and other parts of the Civil Service are increasingly trying to undertake reforms and improve performance without seeking additional financial resources to do so,[40] and that performance is generally increasing across the service.[41] A handful of officers did state that they had not seen any meaningful changes in recent years, but these represented a small minority of interviewees.[42]

With respect to changes in specific processes and practices, rank-and-file officers were generally positive about how the role of the annual staff appraisal system had changed in the years since 2014, making comments like, "The appraisal is so good now, you bring out the best in those who want to do well,"[43] and, "It has changed everyone and the way they work."[44] Interviewees perceived the appraisals to be helpful in introducing clarity around setting targets, sparking discussions with their supervisees and supervisors that wouldn't have happened otherwise, and providing a clear basis for holding themselves and their colleagues accountable for their performance:

> It helps me to know whether I am achieving my target. It is effective as it is tracking whether the ministry is doing well, and the Chief Director [too].[45]

> The re-introduction of the performance management system has affected not me alone but all HR practices. People before were just doing things the way they liked. If things are not done well then we will have to answer to the Head of Civil Service. . . . Now people are more serious about their work.[46]

> In those days, we would write our own appraisal and the boss signs it. Now we sit down with the bosses. If I say I will achieve four meetings there should be four meeting minutes. Now you can measure performance. Now you can set targets. This is from the Chief Director and down. If I fail, everyone fails.[47]

At the same time, interviewees emphasized that while the appraisal process increased perceived accountability for performance and thus effort, there were no hard rewards or sanctions attached—other than sometimes a vague sense that it might matter for promotion at some point or that it could be used as a basis for rewards or sanctions in future. Some felt that this lack of effective sanctions was a shortcoming of the system, while others reported that, in their ministries, the system was still not being treated seriously or discussed the difficulties in accurately measuring performance with them.[48] On the whole, though, there is strong evidence that the effort that went into making the appraisal system more effective was broadly successful in its goal of creating more discussion of performance throughout the service and bringing greater focus and energy to it.

Perceptions of the impact of the Chief Director Performance Agreements system (and, to a lesser extent, the Director Performance Agreements) were also mostly, though not universally, positive. The measurement of chief directors' performance, having these results shared within Civil Service, and the associated pressure from peers and superiors was seen to be making chief directors more focused on performance, with senior and junior civil servants alike making comments such as, "It's gingering the chief directors to get to work."[49] Many interviewees also made comments about how this focus on performance cascaded down to officers throughout each ministry:

If I'm [a head of an organization] I won't sit there and be made chopped liver because my directors aren't doing their jobs.[50]

When the chief director is preparing their performance agreement, some of the deliverables from me are going to impact the Chief Director's Performance Agreement. It puts directors on their toes.[51]

The Chief Director and Director's Performance Agreement has meant that they must deliver. Every year they are evaluated and they put you on your toes. . . . That affects everyone's performance. . . . There are deliverables in the Chief Director's Performance Agreements. In HR, I need to make sure all things the chief director does with HR are done and put them together. This affects my work . . . you have to make sure everyone delivers. Civil servants' attitude of sitting down has become people are on their toes. Because who wants their chief director to be last?[52]

Others remarked that chief directors having their performance measured also made them more attentive to supporting their workers' performance: "I think chief directors were doing whatever, but now they ensure they provide resources to do what you need to do."[53]

The mechanisms through which the performance agreement system was viewed as having positive effects were the clearer definition of targets and roles across all levels within each organization, the measurement and discussion of performance, and the "soft" accountability pressure of having the results published within the Civil Service and discussed: "The sanctions are seen by the announcement of which ministry is first and which is last which is announced."[54]

No interviewees mentioned "hard" rewards or sanctions, though one expressed concern that without hard sanctions, people would eventually begin to take it less seriously.[55] At the same time, no interviewees reported perceived gaming of targets or decreases in ambition as a result of the system, which would have been likely to occur if harder incentives had been in place (based on the observed track record of performance agreement or performance contract systems elsewhere).

There were also some voices of skepticism about the impact of the Chief Director Performance Agreements. One interviewee reported that the system had led to their chief director taking credit for all successes but casting blame on subordinates for all failures,[56] while another suggested that the impact had been greater for the compliance-oriented parts of the agreement system (which tracked the completion of mandatory processes, like reporting and audit requirements) than for the results and delivery parts of the agreements (which tracked the completion of specific outputs agreed with each chief director).[57] But even these concerns were couched within an agreement that the system had been at least somewhat successful, with many interviewees offering summary assessments along the lines of, "Overall it has helped."[58]

OHCS's reinvigoration of the service charter system was also viewed positively by interviewees. A number of them remarked that since 2014, OHCS had pushed them to update or revise their service charters and that they had done so, with some saying that they were now reviewing it annually.[59] Many also saw the charter as helpful for performance: "It makes it easier for external stakeholders to know what they can get from us and challenges us to be within a time boundary."[60] Another echoed the idea that the point of the service charter was not so much the existence of the document but its ongoing revision and discussion within the organization. "The service charter is one thing to change the service. We have key people behind that reform. . . . The service charter has to develop as it is a document to be used continuously. The service charter loses value and if [the] people who have developed it are no more there. . . . People are much more concerned with the [delivery of the] service and it should reflect the service charter and touch reality on the ground and align with services on the ground."[61]

However, several interviewees also made comments like "I have not read it before," "the service charter is good on paper but who has access to it?" or "it has not been very effective, as I do not even have one. I do not know how much we stick to the things in the service charter."[62] So the existence, awareness, and usefulness of service charters was more inconsistent across ministries than it was for the annual performance appraisals or Chief Director Performance Agreements.

Overall, then, the qualitative evidence from these interviews provides reasonably solid evidence both that other civil servants perceived a general change in attitude and approach to reform during Agyekum-Dwamena's tenure and that some of the specific practices and processes that Agyekum-Dwamena and OHCS tried to improve were, indeed, used and useful across large parts of the broader Civil Service. It was not unequivocally positive, though, as these changes were not felt and/or were not felt to be useful by a minority of interviewees.

Quantitative evidence of whether these changes have improved performance is hard to generate, both because of the data it would require and the difficulties of causally attributing any observed changes to Agyekum-Dwamena's actions. There is some suggestive quantitative evidence that practices and processes improved across the Civil Service as a whole during this period. In a 2019 policy brief, Imran Rasul, Daniel Rogger, and I compared the management practice quality indices that we compiled from large-scale surveys of thousands of officers across the Civil Service that we conducted in partnership with OHCS in both 2015 and 2018.[63] As discussed in chapter 2, these indices captured the actual use of both formal and informal types of management processes and practices within each organization and integrated the perspectives both of managers and rank-and-file officers. Comparing the management practice scores across these two survey waves—one occurring near the beginning of Agyekum-Dwamena's tenure, the other four years into it—can give us at least a suggestive sense of whether there was improvement during these years.

We found that the average quality of management processes and practices across the Civil Service improved by 0.11 standard deviations across these three years. This change was highly statistically significant (at the 1 percent level).[64] Whether one thinks that this is a large or small increase depends on one's perspective, and standard deviations are, unfortunately, not a very intuitive unit of measurement for nonstatisticians. The average increase also masks some heterogeneity across organizations, as some improved and others got worse during this time. It's also not possible to causally attribute this improvement to Agyekum-Dwamena's reform approach or to any other individual or factor. The quantitative data simply says that the processes and practices used to get things done in the Civil Service improved over these years without telling us why.

Taken together, though, the quantitative evidence shows us that things improved in the Civil Service during these years, and the qualitative evidence allows us to trace the ways Agyekum-Dwamena's reform approach was felt throughout the service and was linked with improvements in at least some actual processes and practices. So while it doesn't prove that Agyekum-Dwamena's approach to reform worked, overall, it provides suggestive evidence of positive impacts. Whether it succeeds in institutionalizing reform as an ongoing and sustained process, creating a collective culture of continuous improvement, and sparking decentralized leadership of future changes is a question that will have to wait for future researchers—and that depends on future generations of civil servants and reform leaders.

COLLECTIVE LEADERSHIP OF REFORM IN GHANA

So far, I have framed this discussion of reform in Ghana from 2014–2019 in terms of the perspectives and actions of one person—then-Head of Civil Service, Nana Agyekum-Dwamena. This is partly because he was influential and unusual in his approach, but it's also because it is easier for us humans to tell and remember stories with a single protagonist. But it risks doing a disservice to the many other individuals who were thinking and experimenting along similar lines during this time, all across the various organizations and levels of the service. I don't want readers to come away with the impression that this is a story of one visionary reform champion doing things that other mere mortals wouldn't be able to do. I can't tell the story of every individual who played a role in the collective leadership of reform and exemplified the idea of reform as process during this time, but let me highlight two.

The first person—a person in a senior leadership role who wished to remain anonymous—had also witnessed numerous reform efforts and had taken away similar lessons about their failings. "Perhaps it's also the way we look at these reforms as projects. Projects come with money. Perhaps selling the idea that 'let's mend the old wineskin' is not so attractive," she reflected during our interview. "If I were President for a day . . . I'd say stop creating new laws and policies, we have enough, let's just focus on implementing what we have. . . . If we could implement just forty, fifty, sixty percent, we'd be in a very good place." Instead, she emphasized that changing work habits and organizational cultures was about "simple things, like reporting requirements being maintained and enforced and verified . . . thinking small sometimes, and thinking out of the box. . . . I don't think we need a big big reform to do these things." She viewed improving civil servants' performance like training a mechanic: You want them to practice and get their hands dirty as much as possible, and the role of reform leadership should be "brought to how can we help you do this job as effectively as possible." "I am saying minimize the formal things, and focus on the informal," she said.[65]

Similarly, the longtime Principal of Ghana's Civil Service Training Centre (CSTC), Dora Dei-Tumi, described how she and her colleagues had built a culture of ongoing continuous improvement. While the institution had long been starved of resources, she remarked, "You don't need funds to take care of every-thing. It is just a paradigm shift."[66] While CSTC did receive funds from donor institutions—especially via a long-term partnership with the Japan International Cooperation Agency (JICA)—they placed a heavy emphasis on finding ways to do things themselves and viewing external support as temporary. "Any time we worked with a DP [development partner], we institutionalized what we had been doing before they pulled out."[67] For example, a key moment in the institution's journey was when JICA funded a training of trainers workshop for CSTC staff. But this training was important not because of the output of the workshop but because it "gave us the confidence to design these [trainings ourselves]." CSTC trainers began designing their own trainings in-house, over time experimenting with and improving them—but on an internally driven basis, not only when external support came. CSTC was also opportunistic in developing and offering new courses, for instance, designing a training on how to create service charters when this reform was introduced to the Civil Service in the late 2000s under the Ministry of Public Sector Reform—even though they were not formally part of the reform.[68] These and other steps exemplify the learning-by-doing ethos of the institution and, over time, have contributed toward CSTC dramatically improv-ing both the quality of its training and its perception within the Civil Service.[69]

As important as it is to highlight the ways in which other senior leaders also have experimented with and led reforms that took a more process-oriented approach, even this doesn't capture the efforts of the numerous other individuals—heads of organizations, middle managers, rank-and-file officers, even political leaders—who have also played important roles in making these changes. These individuals were located not only in central management bodies responsible for performance improvement, like OHCS, CSTC, and MSD, but also across Ghana's numerous sectoral ministries, departments, and agencies. It's important for leaders at the pinnacle of bureaucratic hierarchies, like Agyekum-Dwamena, to see themselves as catalyzing rather than driving change, to focus on decentralizing the leader-ship of change. However, decentralizing change leadership only works if there are other individuals across the system who are ready to seize the opportunity to make positive changes in their own organizations and teams.

The experience of Ghana's Civil Service during this period was that such indi-viduals existed all around the service. A great deal of research suggests that this isn't an exception: Many public servants around the world are driven by a com-mitment to the public good and are constantly trying to find ways to serve it bet-ter.[70] Individual, organizational, and societal characteristics obviously matter for how easy or hard it is for others to take up the baton of reform leadership when they are given the opportunity, and certain contexts or problems might require more or less effort, signaling, and authorizing of change or escalating of problems by senior leaders. But across most bureaucratic systems, most of the time, there are individuals who want things to work better and are waiting to be given the encouragement to do so.

NAVIGATING THE POLITICS OF REFORM AS PROCESS IN GHANA

Another natural question to ask is: How did Agyekum-Dwamena manage this unusual approach given all the demands and political pressures that so frequently have undermined or derailed reforms in other times and places? Weren't there pressures to launch flashy new initiatives or to demonstrate tangible results against predefined targets and outputs? How did he manage the relationship between the Civil Service and political leaders, not only with respect to getting political backing but also managing political interference?

One surprising part of the answer was that he consistently, deliberately, and publicly expressed disinterest in what politicians, donors, or other external stake-holders thought about what was happening within the proper domain of the Civil Service. For instance, during one interview, I commented to him that people often said that one factor driving the projectization of reform and the focus on introducing new formal processes was the pressure to be seen to be doing something, to demonstrate results publicly. He replied bluntly, "Martin, who cares about what people think outside of the Civil Service? That's to begin with. So, for me, that's a non-issue . . . So, as far as I'm concerned, yes, you may not see any target written, blah blah, [but] that is their problem."[71]

He continued, "So yes, I know, I understand. I've seen this so-called target thing, that says 'we've done twenty of this,' 'we've done . . .'—so what?! That is a mechanical approach, and once you've done that, you go and everybody forgets about that."[72] OHCS did set and use targets in setting expectations and monitoring progress but did not try to combine these all into a single master plan in the way that many formal-focused, projectized reform efforts did.[73] Implicit in comments like these were a mindset and message that improving performance and administration was the domain of civil servants and that they should focus on that rather than worrying about politics or other external things they couldn't control. He didn't say it explicitly, but I suspect that this attitude also served as a form of signaling to politicians that he wasn't interested in playing political games: I'll do my job, and you do yours.

At the same time, Agyekum-Dwamena didn't shy away from actively engaging with political leaders when it was consistent with the proper function and role of the Civil Service in implementing policy. For example, in December 2016—a little over two years into his tenure—Ghana's elections led to a change in political administration, with Nana Addo Akuffo-Addo of the New Patriotic Party taking over from John Dramani Mahama of the National Democratic Congress. As Head of Civil Service, Agyekum-Dwamena could be removed or retired by the new administration—as could any or all of the chief directors with whom he'd been trying to build momentum over the past few years—and such changes had happened after previous presidential transitions. While participating in the governmental committee that was managing the transition, Agyekum-Dwamena had heard mutterings from members of the new administration about how many of the chief directors were allegedly politically aligned with the previous administration and couldn't be trusted.

Rather than waiting and hoping, Agyekum-Dwamena decided to tackle the issue head-on. He wrote to the new President requesting a meeting—against the advice of several retired senior public servants he had consulted. His account of the meeting is worth quoting at length:

> So I wrote to the President asking him for meeting. Everybody was going to the President doing, you know, the usual congratulatory things, going to congratulate the President. So we went with all the chief directors and he said, "Oh, welcome," and I said, "Thank you Your Excellency. Congratulations. But that was not why we came, really we came to give you a brief and also to ask your opinion about how you want the Civil Service to support you." He said, "Oh, that is not what I was told. I was told that you just wanted to come and do the usual." I said, "No no Your Excellency, that's not why we came." He said, "Okay, I don't have enough time for that today, can you arrange [with] the Chief of Staff and come back in two weeks." We came back in two weeks and we had a two-hour meeting, and that meeting the Vice President was there [along with several other senior political leaders]. To cut a long story short, after the meeting the President called me to the side and said, "Thank you very much for this meeting, it has cleared a lot of things in my mind."
>
> Now, let me tell you one thing, why I think this meeting was so important. I had spoken to two [retired senior bureaucratic leaders] and they said, "No no no no no, don't go and have the meeting with the President, don't go don't go." I'd even spoken to [another retired head of one of Ghana's public services] and he said "No no." But I was convinced they were wrong. And we went. And that was what really saved . . . the chief directors. Because I was going to have a very

big problem on my hands, because listening to the comments being made during the transition period, it was going to be that. Because there'd been a lot of misinformation but that meeting cleared a lot of it. And at the end of the meeting the President said—I remember—he said, "I did not come to the office to remove any chief director. All that I'm asking is the Civil Service must support me. And Mister Head of Civil Service, I hope that I can get that support from you and your colleagues." And I said, "Sir, you can trust us we will do our best." And that was it. . . . Once the President said that it was finished."[74]

In the end, Agyekum-Dwamena and all the chief directors in the civil service retained their positions, while many other heads of services and heads of organizations in other parts of the Public Service were changed by the new administration. Of course, it is impossible to confirm that this meeting was the reason—or that a similar approach would have worked for other leaders or leaders in other countries. But it nonetheless illustrated the other side of Agyekum-Dwamena's approach to managing the political-administrative interference: to establish a clear boundary between bureaucratic and political roles but equally to not hesitate to engage actively with political leaders when appropriate.

Another way Agyekum-Dwamena was unusual in relating to politicians was that, unlike many reform leaders, he did not go out of his way to secure high-level political backing prior to undertaking reforms. In one of our interviews, I asked him what advice he had for other reform leaders, and he replied, in part:

> Try as much as possible to get political support, but that should not become the basis for your activity . . . [try to get] buy-in more on the peripheral level, not at the tactical level. Let me explain. A lot of people say, "Okay we want the President to come and launch this, and when the President launches it it will work." It doesn't work that way. You can get the President to launch it, but behave as if the President never launched that program and work with it yourself. Most of the people, people think that because the President launched it it will work, but it doesn't work.[75]

Another civil servant who had been involved in some of Ghana's past reform efforts, in discussing Agyekum-Dwamena's tendency to avoid (rather than seek out) external funding or high-level political involvement in reforms, reflected, "I think I support him. . . . It's better to go silently and introduce things piecemeal. . . . The big [project] names are more or less for the politicians."[76] Similarly, another civil servant commented, "Civil servants are championing change. . . . That has helped us to go through the [presidential] transitions. Because public servants were spearheading it, it was transcending transition and it is a good thing."[77]

Finally, Agyekum-Dwamena was strategic in when and how he dealt with the occasions in which either bureaucrats or politicians had tried to interfere in decisions—especially personnel decisions—that should have been the preserve of the Office of the Head of Civil Service.

> For instance, you won't get me directly engaging in political fights. You won't get me. I won't do that, because I don't think it's necessary to antagonize anybody. I have been a structures person, systems person, a process person, and that's what I focus my work on. And those ones nobody can question that. For instance, when we say that now postings must be done this way, according to the rules, there are people who don't like it. I don't have a problem. Let me give you an example. We have always had the rules that say that a person who has worked at a place for three to four years must move on. People get established, they don't want to move. I don't have a problem. We send a letter to a ministry saying you are supposed to be move to this, you don't go. I don't fight it. All that I do is we change your management unit which says that . . . they don't pay you from there, nobody backdates your salary, your name goes off the payroll, nobody will tell you to move. Or when you are due for promotion, it's just a simple thing, I say "Don't process that person, his Minister is now his human resource manager, so let the Minister process it." So that's the thing. Instead of fighting that process, we use the rules that we have, the systems to make sure that people will follow the rules. They may sound small, but they have big impacts, in the sense that once you refuse to follow the system we also use the tools that we have to work. So I could have written to the Minister to say that . . . it's against the rule so-so and so and all that, [but] it's [a] useless fight. [And] then you come to the problem [of] "Head of Civil Services fights Ministry of [redacted]." I'm not going to do that. I just go on with my work but soon, I know very soon, somebody will come to me and say they want to go on study leave, they bring the thing [and] I said "Oh, oh no no no, the ministry is now doing HR so let them go and do it, if they have the authority to do it"—until they address this issue. Because you can't say you should not do this in the HR and then you want to come to us at the same time and say you want us to do this in HR. No. So that is how strategically I choose my battles.[78]

Although dealing with interference in personnel decisions is, in some ways, a very different domain of leadership and management from performance-oriented reforms, Agyekum-Dwamena was strikingly consistent across both scenarios in using strategic (but not blind or rigid) enforcement of existing rules that were under his control as a tool for changing practice and perceptions. Rather than necessarily targeting bad practices head-on in fights that would be costly and possibly unwinnable, he found ways to address them indirectly using existing rules and tools in a fashion that would enhance the credibility of future directives and reform efforts from OHCS and gradually change people's expectations.

At the end of our final interview, I asked Agyekum-Dwamena what advice he would give to future reform leaders around the world. He replied, "I think consistency, tenacity is one of the things. Proper reforms take a long time, so you need to be consistent and let people know over a period of time that this is where we are going, this is what we are doing." He paused, chuckled, and added: "And don't get tired easily."

• • •

This chapter has told a story of how one leader—Nana Agyekum-Dwamena—tried to approach reform during his tenure as Ghana's Head of Civil Service. Doing so meant finding ways to improve mostly within existing rules and processes rather than creating new ones, treating reform as a process of collective learning-by-doing, and decentralizing change leadership as much as possible. The evidence available—though inherently limited—suggests that many of the things he tried contributed to improved performance and changes in organizational culture and civil servants' expectations of themselves and each other.

In a book about patterns of civil service reform, I think it's important to tell this story not because everything Agyekum-Dwamena did worked nor to imply that similar approaches would guarantee success elsewhere. Still less do I want to tell a story in which successful bureaucratic reforms are driven by the actions of a single heroic individual—that's not true in Ghana or anywhere else.

Rather, I think it's important because it's far easier for us to critique past efforts at reform than to imagine how we might do things differently in the future. This chapter is the story of how one leader recognized the pitfalls of the dominant approach to reform that he had seen and tried to do things differently. I present it not as a blueprint for others to copy or as a guarantee of success but rather as a tangible example of what it might look like to approach reform as an ongoing process rather than a project, to lead by catalyzing rather than driving, and to focus on changing actual practices rather than formal rules. My hope is that it can serve as an inspiration for other reform leaders in Ghana and elsewhere around the world to also experiment with these ideas—whether it's across the whole of a civil service or just within their own teams.

9

A Pragmatic Approach to Reform

I f I had to boil this book down into a single sentence, it would be this: Performance-oriented civil service reforms have usually been approached too much like one-off projects to change formal rules and processes, and not enough like efforts to catalyze an ongoing process of continuous improvement in actual practices. In chapter 8, I distilled what approaching reform as a process meant into three practical recommendations for reformers:

1. Focus first on what can be done within existing formal rules and processes so that changing formal rules and processes is a last resort rather than a first step.
2. Approach change as a process of collective learning-by-doing rather than as rolling out a predesigned blueprint.
3. Decentralize the leadership of reform as much as possible.

These summary sentences contain both analysis and advice, diagnosis of the past and prescription for the future. In search of clarity and simplicity, they strip away a great deal of detail and nuance—as with all summaries. It is impossible to adequately reduce the vast complexity of 131 large-scale reform episodes in six countries across the span of thirty years into a handful of digestible, intuitive, actionable insights. Yet this is what learning from history requires of us.

With respect to the "analysis" part of this advice and the simplifications it contains, I have tried to capture as much of the nuance of the histories of reform in these six countries as possible throughout the book. Chapters 3–6 and the appendix discuss the ways these mechanisms of success and failure were combined and intertwined in nearly every reform—the complicated calculations that reform designers, middle managers, rank-and-file civil servants, and other stakeholders made and the mixture of motivations, pressures, and ideas that drove them. In trying to balance clarity and nuance in this analysis and advice to would-be reformers, I hope to have done justice to the efforts of the many public servants who poured themselves into these reforms, the researchers around the world who have studied them, and my deep respect for them. I hope that you, as a reader, will take away not only some clarity but also an appreciation for the complexity that lies beneath it.

The remainder of this brief concluding chapter is devoted to unpacking and nuancing the simplifications contained in the "advice" part of the summary above. In particular, this chapter considers how four sets of factors might affect the generalizability of this book's advice:

1. The *purpose* of the reform, i.e., the type(s) of behavior or task whose performance the reform is trying to improve
2. The *context* of the reform, both geographic and organizational, and in particular the extent to which formal rules are typically complied with
3. The *people* designing and implementing reform and their location within or outside the bureaucracy
4. The *politics* surrounding reform, in particular, with respect to time horizons and the external pressures and constraints facing reformers.

This exercise in considering external validity and scope conditions is necessarily more uncertain than the analysis that has preceded it. I offer it in the spirit of "structured speculation."[1] While I hope this discussion makes it clear that I don't expect this book's analysis or advice to be universally true across every context, I also think that there is reason to think that its broad contours are applicable to many different places and moments. Throughout the book, I have presented evidence that these patterns of reform are not restricted to the six countries this book studies, to Africa, or to low- and middle-income countries generally. Rather, similar dynamics have been documented around the world, including in high-income countries and nonpublic-sector organizations. Perhaps some of what I've described has also resonated with some of your own professional experiences in the organizational contexts you've worked in. So if this analysis and advice is neither totally specific to these six countries nor completely universal, how should we go about assessing its generalizability?

This book opened by posing a practical question, so let's also conduct this discussion with a practical question as motivation: If you were charged with designing and implementing a reform to improve performance, in what circumstances might you want to take an approach that is more process and less project—or vice versa?

PURPOSE, CONTEXT, PEOPLE, POLITICS

Purpose: Targeting Verifiable or Nonverifiable Actions?

One factor in your choice would likely be the *purpose* of the reform. By "purpose," I mean the *type of behavior or task* that the reform is aiming to affect. In particular, are you trying to get people to take actions that are highly verifiable—that are predictable, easy to specify well ex ante and to measure objectively ex post, and individualized enough to be enforceable? Or are you hoping that the reform will lead people to undertake less verifiable types of behaviors or a mix of highly verifiable and less verifiable that is itself hard to specify exactly?[2]

The less-than-full verifiability of many of the day-to-day practices that were important for organizational performance underpinned both mechanisms of failure that this book described. Efforts to force behavior change through highly formalized processes, such as individual performance-linked incentive systems, typically fell quickly into a state of perfunctory compliance and often then into disuse. People and organizations followed the letter of the processes but not the spirit and then often stopped even following the letter. Similarly, projectized reforms failed to generate the credibility necessary to get individuals to put out the extra effort needed to undertake these nonverifiable behaviors and perform consummately. These two mechanisms of failure reinforced each other: Projectized reforms lend themselves to focusing on creating formal rules and processes as the main task of reform and vice versa.

If the disadvantage of project-style approaches is that they push reformers towards focusing on the formal, they also have some significant practical advantages over process-style reform approaches. Projects have clear goals and outputs and built-in timelines for measuring progress. They have end dates, clear deadlines, and separate budget lines—all of which make them attractive to people who make and fund budgets. They are highly visible, making them salient not only to bureaucrats but also to senior leaders and external stakeholders. Their visibility and tangibility also make them easier to claim credit for, and thus, leaders have more incentive to initiate them. Demarcating the work of reform and often the people driving it from the civil service's core work processes makes managing them simpler. Project-style reforms are undoubtedly easier to initiate and lead than process-style reforms, and given how hard senior public leaders' jobs are, it makes sense to opt for ease whenever possible.

So if the behaviors you are trying to change *are* highly verifiable, then relying on formal systems—and using project-style reforms to create them—might be an appropriate way forward. This might be the case for contexts where every aspect of what workers or organizations do is highly specifiable and measurable, and workers need to use little initiative or discretion. These are stereotypical assembly-line situations where exerting effort along a single well-defined dimension is enough. It might also be appropriate when the reformer's objective is simply to obtain compliance with a legal requirement. For example, performance rating systems, such as South Africa's Management Performance Assessment Tool, were often quite effective at getting individuals or organizations to fulfill administrative requirements like filing required reports on time or regularly holding committee meetings. (However, the same accountability pressures that made people responsive to these highly verifiable requirements also undermined their ability to spur people to take nonverifiable actions, as described in chapter 4.) So in contexts where the most important behaviors are highly verifiable and thus the difference between perfunctory and consummate performance is relatively small, the managerial ease of trying to change them through a project rather than a process might win out.

Context: Expectations of Rule Enforcement and Compliance?

Of course, the above discussion assumes that formal rules and processes are automatically enforced—that creating these systems in a one-off intervention will lead to at least perfunctory compliance with them. But empirically, we have observed that many formal rules and processes are *not* actually complied with, with variation both across countries and across different organizations within countries in compliance. And workers' compliance with rules also depends on their expectations about whether or not these rules will be enforced and violations punished. Whether rules are enforced or not, in turn, depends on a complex mix of political, legal, and managerial institutions and various actors' calculations about whether and when it makes sense to enforce formal rules.[3] There are some places where the norm is that people are rarely punished for violating rules, others where enforcement is so strict that public servants expect every rule's minutest detail to be enforced, and others—perhaps the majority of contexts—where compliance norms and enforcement expectations vary across different rules, different organizations, and different time periods.

So the extent to which formal rules are automatically complied with is another way in which the geographic or organizational *context* of the reform might guide your choices about project versus process. If you expect formal rules and processes to be implemented and complied with, then (all else equal) it makes relatively more sense to approach reform as a matter of changing what's written on paper. This might be the case in countries with very strong and active administrative law enforcement agencies, where fear of sanction means that people tend to follow at least the letter of the rules. To the extent that the implementation of these rules depends on the continuous application of managerial effort and attention to make the rules credible, then the reform can't be a one-off project. It might start with a big push to create the new system but then has to be followed up with an ongoing push for implementation.

Of course, many reforms studied in this book that created new formal rules and processes did contain phases or elements that focused on implementation—most sensible and experienced reformers understand that implementation matters. But even where the intent to ensure implementation existed, the projectization of reforms undermined its effectiveness because the dynamics of project funding and leadership meant that implementation was generally viewed as an afterthought. Most of the time, attention, resources, targets, and measurements were oriented toward creating the rules, with attention to implementation squeezed into whatever time was left over afterward. The effect of this was accentuated when projects had a formal end date or when reform leaders were expected to depart, as both factors undermined the credibility of this commitment to ongoing implementation. Projects tended to take on their own lives—their completion became their main purpose, even if that did not align with the good of the institution as a whole. So simply building an "implementation phase" into a project following its "design phase" was not sufficient to actually ensure implementation.

But variation across contexts in expectations around rule enforcement does matter hugely for this book's recommendations to focus first on making improvements within the existing formal rules rather than starting by changing them. This recommendation is most obviously applicable to contexts where at least some rules and processes that would be helpful for performance already exist but are not being implemented. Some reformers may feel that they are in the opposite situation: Either their existing rules are enforced so strictly that they wouldn't dream of changing their behavior without a prior change in the rules, or the existing rules are antithetical to good performance and shouldn't be fully implemented—or both.[4] Shouldn't this recommendation change in such contexts?

On a superficial level, the answer is obviously yes. There are surely contexts where the most important reform action needed to improve performance would be to change or remove a formal rule or where civil servants need some kind of formal authorization to introduce certain types of new ideas or practices. So this book's recommendation is certainly not that changing formal rules should never be a reform objective. Rather, it is to think of it as a last resort—something that should only be done if all other meaningful actions have been exhausted or if it is absolutely necessary to enable other meaningful actions.

This is partly because making changes on paper often fails to translate into practice, whereas making changes in practice helps build credibility and momentum to ensure that subsequent changes on paper are more likely to be impactful. It is partly because making formal rule changes is often slow and encounters resistance, whereas acting within existing formal rules can be faster and easier. It is partly because even when changes to formal rules do get complied with, the nonverifiability of many important behaviors often leads to perfunctory rather than consummate performance. Finally, it is partly because the mental bias runs so frequently in the opposite direction because it is so often assumed that formal rules are always the most important thing driving behavior and, thus, changing them should be the first step of any reform. So while contextual factors might mean that formal rule changes need to play different roles at different times in different places, the spirit of the process theory of reform is the recognition that there is often more room to maneuver within existing rules than we recognize and that—to the extent formal rule changes are necessary—they should usually be seen as enabling steps rather than ends in themselves.

People: Who's Doing the Reforming?

This brings us to a third set of considerations in choosing how to balance project and process: who the *people* doing the reform are. Are you a very senior reform actor, like a head of civil service or cabinet secretary? Or a more junior one, like a middle manager or technical officer? Or something in between, like a CEO of an organization or a director of a division? Are you a civil servant working within the bureaucracy itself, or are you a politician, donor, consultant, or representative of a civil society organization external to it? These factors might each influence what type of behaviors you aim to influence, what it looks like to approach reform as a project or as a process, and what blend of project and process you adopt.

On the one hand, the more senior you are, the more power you have to change formal rules, either by your own decree or by setting in motion some kind of broader legislative or rule-making procedure. So one could argue that senior leaders should focus their efforts on these formal rule changes since the people below them can't make them. In the same vein, the lower down the pyramid a reform leader is, the more day-to-day contact they have with their team, and presumably more ability to use informal management tools and practices to shape behavior change. So this perspective would seem to suggest that the higher up you are, the more you should focus on changing formal rules (and use projectized reform approaches), while the lower down you are, the more you should focus on using less formal reform tools as part of a longer-term process of building positive relational contracts within your immediate team.

On the other hand, one could take the opposite perspective: If informal cultures are more important than formal rules and if senior leaders are the people with the most power to change culture, then they should focus their efforts on that. They are the ones with the most ability to catalyze the decentralized changes in expectations, relational contracts, and, thus, nonverifiable actions that are necessary to improve performance. So approaching reform as a process is arguably even more important the more senior you are.

This debate is an unresolvable one because the correct answer in each situation is likely to be highly contextually dependent. Senior and junior leaders alike have both formal and informal management tools available to them. Both formal and informal tools can shape both verifiable and nonverifiable actions, albeit in very different ways. And both verifiable and nonverifiable actions are important for performance, albeit in different measures for different types of tasks. So while the specific reform actions and approach one should take does depend, in part, on one's seniority, this recognition doesn't lend itself to a universal, one-size-fits-all recommendation about how seniority affects optimal reform approach. The calculation is an important one but must be answered in each case by the reform leaders themselves—by you, as you puzzle through what each situation requires.

How might your approach differ if you are external to the system rather than internal to it? By this, I mean: If you work outside the civil service but you care about improving its performance, what approach should you adopt? Let's set aside the role that external actors play in demanding improvements in performance—which is hugely important but beyond the scope of this book—and focus on their potential role in the actual process of reform and change.

One key difference is that actors outside the bureaucracy are likely to be less able to observe or influence the nonverifiable aspects of bureaucratic performance than actors within it. So if you are a member of parliament, a donor official, or an NGO worker, it probably makes relatively more sense to focus your attention, resources, and influence on making changes to formal rules and processes than it does for public servants inside the bureaucracy. But you should also be conscious of the ways focusing on the formal so often distorts reform efforts, drawing attention and resources away from the nonverifiable aspects of performance. And you should also remember that formal rules and processes were typically less successful than expected in forcing people to behave differently (a mechanism of failure), but often more successful than anticipated in creating opportunities for public servants to talk about performance and how to improve it (a mechanism of success).

So even if it makes sense as an outsider to focus relatively more on formal processes, that doesn't necessarily mean approaching your role in reform as one of trying to force change or drive reform. Rather, in many (perhaps most) cases, outside actors should ask themselves how they can play a supporting role in creating and supporting opportunities for discussing how to improve performance and in building and sustaining momentum. A great deal has been written about how such external interventions, especially by donors, can lead to perverse consequences and the positive roles that donors can play in large-scale civil service reform.[5] There are also unexpected ways that they have sometimes been able to support change and the difficulties in doing so. For example, the researcher Dana Qarout has written about how international donor involvement in education system reform in Jordan was a double-edged sword: It complicated goals and lines of accountability but also helped sustain reform efforts across frequent leadership turnovers.[6] Smaller and more nimble actors like foundations or NGOs may be able to play an important role in supporting innovative reform efforts with less need to demonstrate preplanned and verifiable results than would be demanded by large donors or finance ministries. At the same time, though, if this support takes the form of financial resources, then such actors should be mindful that injecting resources into reform efforts can risk focusing attention on spending money rather than on changing behavior, and they should find ways to avoid inadvertently distorting productive efforts in this fashion. So while the specific roles that external actors can play in reform might differ from those of internal actors, the goal—catalyzing an ongoing process of continuous improvement in actual practices—should remain the same.

Politics: Time Horizons and External Pressures

A final set of considerations involves the *politics* of reform. While the political economy influences and constraints on reform are numerous and have been discussed previously in this book and in great depth elsewhere,[7] two factors seem especially important to discuss here: time horizons and the influence that external factors like unions, patronage politics, or political opinion might have on the feasibility of differentiating rewards and/or sanctions to civil servants.

The limited time horizons of political and bureaucratic leaders are often cited as a reason why reformers focus on making formal changes through time-bound projects. If you may only be in office for a few years, the logic goes, why not focus on changing tangible things that can be changed in a limited time span rather than investing in changing intangible things like relational contracts that are hard to measure, take a long time to influence, and might be undone by your successors anyway? While there is an intuitive appeal to this idea, the track record of such reforms is clear: Meaningful performance improvements very rarely come merely from the one-off imposition of new formal rules and processes. However, approaching reform as a process can be undermined by short or uncertain leadership time horizons, as this makes changing expectations and relational contracts more difficult. But this risk is part of why the recommendation to decentralize reform leadership is so important: Even if a senior leader leaves or is removed, the ideas and momentum they catalyzed can be sustained by others who remain. So while short time horizons can also undermine process-style approaches to reform, they may still offer more hope for meaningful change than project-style approaches that have their mechanisms of failure baked in.

Political contexts also differ in the possibilities they offer for formal differentiation of incentives, rewards, sanctions, and/or career progression opportunities across public servants. Efforts to restrict patronage hiring or diminish bias, the desires of unions for due process and protection of their members, and the risk of public or media backlash to efforts to reward or punish civil servants are all factors that push reformers toward seeking highly formal and regimented personnel management systems. In focusing on verifiable or objective performance metrics and squeezing out nonverifiable or subjective performance metrics, such systems become misaligned with the actual work context and are increasingly perceived as unfair, and this—among other factors discussed in chapter 4—often contributed to nondifferentiation in performance assessments and thus nondifferentiation in incentives, and eventually the collapse of these systems. At the same time, the politics of patronage and clientelism also created opposition to formal systems for measuring and rewarding performance from another side: In places like Kenya and Ghana, as researchers Sylvester Obong'o and Daniel Appiah and Abdul-Gafaru Abdulai document, politicians opposed bureaucratic efforts to use measured performance to guide hiring and promotion decisions out of fear that it would undermine their patronage powers.[8]

Of course, the extent to which external factors limit the possibility of formally differentiating rewards and sanctions according to measured performance is only a meaningful constraint on reform activity if one assumes that such a linkage is desirable in the first place. This book provides relatively little direct evidence on whether linking individual incentives to measured performance is a good thing simply because none of the thirty-four efforts I examined actually succeeded in doing it. But between the empirical evidence of how hard such systems are to implement on a large scale and the conceptual reasons to doubt how effective they can be at improving informal behaviors in civil service contexts, I think it would be reasonable to come away from this book with a fair degree of skepticism about the potential for high-powered individual incentives to be a meaningful lever for positive change in civil services. All that said, though, in contexts where external political economy factors are relatively weaker constraints on the ability to use differentiated incentives, then it may make relatively more sense to focus on such instruments. In contexts where such constraints are relatively strong, it may be even more necessary to rely on the informal approaches to recognizing and rewarding performance that the reform-as-process approach emphasizes.

These four sets of factors and questions you might ask yourself when deciding how to balance project and process approaches to reform are summarized in table 9.1. These considerations are presented as questions rather than as conclusions or recommendations because there are typically multiple factors at play. The implications of the answers to these questions are also likely to be highly contextual; they are not simple if-then statements. The evidence and analysis of this book have argued that reforms in the six countries studied tended to err too much toward approaching reform as a project, and I have presented theory and some evidence that process approaches might be more promising. The discussion above has hopefully been helpful to you in thinking whether the same is likely to be true in other contexts—particularly the ones that are most relevant to you.

A PRAGMATIC APPROACH TO REFORM

Of course, the idea that there is a binary choice between project and process approaches to a reform is false. While it is useful to distinguish them conceptually and consider when each might be most useful, every existing reform effort is a mix of the two. Projects can contain or aim to catalyze ongoing processes, and long processes can be punctuated by discrete projects. Rather than being driven by an ideological choice for one or the other, reformers should be *pragmatic* in applying and combining them in order to suit their purpose, context, people, and politics.

But being pragmatic doesn't necessarily mean doing what is easiest. It means doing what is most likely to succeed. Approaching reform as a project to change formal rules and processes is undoubtedly easier: It is time-bound and highly visible, it lends itself to clear goals and progress measurement, and it is easier

TABLE 9.1 Potential considerations in balancing project and process

Type of factors to consider	Potential considerations
Purpose: targeting verifiable or nonverifiable actions?	• Are the types of behaviors you are aiming to change highly verifiable or mostly nonverifiable?
Context: expectations of rule enforcement and compliance?	• Can formal systems be expected to be complied with and enforced, once put in place on paper? • Is overzealous enforcement of existing formal systems getting in the way of innovation and important informal practices? • Are there existing formal practices that need to be changed or removed before any other actions to improve performance are possible?
People: who is doing the reforming?	• Do you occupy a relatively senior and powerful position within the bureaucratic hierarchy, or a more junior one? • Are you acting as an insider (i.e., a civil servant) or an outsider (i.e., a donor, politician, consultant, or civil society representative) with respect to the bureaucracy?
Politics: time horizons and external pressures	• What is your time horizon, and how much uncertainty is there around it? • How strong are the external pressures against formal differentiation of rewards, sanctions, or career progression based on performance?

Source: Author's synthesis.

for political and bureaucratic leaders to manage and take credit for. This book has shown over and over, though, that the same features that make projectized reform approaches convenient often undermine their success—projects are easier, perhaps, but not necessarily more pragmatic. In contrast, approaching reform as a process and focusing change efforts on nonverifiable practices might seem difficult, even unrealistic: It is hard to specify exactly what is being done, hard to measure progress, and hard to claim credit for. Yet, reforms that exemplified aspects of this approach also represented key mechanisms of success for many reforms across diverse contexts while lacking the built-in mechanisms of failure that plague projectized reforms.

Approaching reform as a process isn't a guarantee of success nor is it necessarily always the best way to improve performance. However, it may often represent reformers' best chance of success. Despite being difficult, it may be the most pragmatic choice more often than we realize.

Helping reformers to better understand how, why, when, and where this is true—and unpacking what actions and approaches that implies—is a crucial role for researchers. There exists a far greater wealth of research on reform efforts in Africa and around the world than many people realize, and this book has aimed to help contribute to this. But the breadth and depth of this literature pales in comparison to the gaps in our knowledge, the demand for greater evidence and insight, and the urgent importance of improving performance in civil services worldwide. Many researchers have shied away from studying systemic reforms because they are too big, complex, and endogenous to lend themselves to the sort of narrow questions, closed-ended answers, and airtight impact assessments that are increasingly valued in much of modern academia.

While this book's findings and recommendations still leave a great deal to the judgment of you, the reader, I hope that the evidence and analysis presented here have also helped demonstrate why such research is important. I hope it has advanced a conversation being held among innumerable reformers and academics around the world, and I hope its contributions and limitations will inspire even more researchers to take up the challenge. Most of all, I hope that you have found it useful in thinking through what you will say the next time you are asked for advice on how to improve performance in a bureaucratic system—or try to do it yourself.

APPENDIX

Country Reform Histories

BACKGROUND, DATA, AND METHODS

This appendix presents short narrative histories of civil service reforms in each of the book's study countries. These summaries have two purposes. First, they give interested readers a better understanding of the full set of reforms on which the descriptive and analytical work of the book is based. Whereas the main text of the book draws selectively from these reform histories to evidence and illustrate particular themes or support arguments, this appendix presents a more comprehensive view of reforms. Thus, it gives readers a more systematic view of the nature of the source material on which the book's analysis is based. That said, the book is based on far more data—from primary interviews, existing literature, and secondary data—than can be presented in this appendix, so even these histories should be viewed as summaries rather than a complete corpus of evidence.

Second, this appendix will be useful for readers who are interested in the reform trajectories of particular countries and in the cross-cutting themes and patterns across them. This book takes the reform case as the unit of analysis and does not seek to perform a comparative analysis across countries. For clarity, the main text is thus organized by themes rather than by countries. However, there is value nonetheless in presenting these findings in a more narrative format, particularly for readers with a special interest in one of these six countries. These country summaries can serve as useful entry points into further reading and research for readers who want more detail about a given country.

The summary histories presented here cover the period from roughly 1990 to 2019, with slight variations in start dates depending on each country's particular history of reforms (and, in some cases, the date of democratization). Each country's summary in this appendix has three components: a short narrative history summarizing the main reforms undertaken, a graphical timeline of these reforms, and a table showing the types of policies each major reform aimed to put in place or change. These should be read and interpreted together.

In this appendix, as with the book as a whole, I define a reform as a strategic and intentional structural or managerial change to the internal administration of civil service organizations, whether de jure or de facto, aimed at improving bureaucratic performance. I focus exclusively on reforms in central/federal government (as opposed to state/provincial/local/municipal governments or decentralization reforms) and on reforms that were systemic in nature (as opposed to focused on a single organization or sector). I include only reforms that had performance improvement as a primary goal and exclude reforms that focused exclusively on financial management, anticorruption, and other adjacent topics. These distinctions were sometimes difficult to apply, as these types of reforms were often intertwined, and almost everything governments do could conceivably affect performance. Where such challenges emerged, I prioritized consistency of application while also trying to reflect the idiosyncratic circumstances of each country and reform effort. As a result, some reforms that were highly salient to civil servants and that greatly affected their working lives—such as public financial management reforms or efforts to increase the regularity of salary payments—are left out of these historical narratives. But these distinctions were blurry in practice, and so, in each country, there are reforms that I left out but could have justified including and reforms that I included but arguably could have excluded.

The process of compiling each country's reform history began with two types of systematic searches for existing literature.[1] The first stage entailed searching two existing multicountry databases of international aid projects and extracting a list of all donor projects in the six countries that were coded as being related to core public sector reform.[2] For each program, an online keyword search was conducted to gather documents (e.g., donor plans, reports, evaluations) about the program. These were then used to assess whether the program fit within this book's definition of reform, and documents for qualifying reforms were saved and filed. The second stage entailed undertaking systematic keyword searches of academic research databases and internet search engines based on country names and keywords, as well as names of relevant institutions.[3] These structured searches were then followed up flexibly with more targeted searches and citation tracing until a point of saturation was reached. This process eventually yielded a total of around one thousand books, articles, theses, government and donor documents, think tank and NGO reports, newspaper articles, and other material.

This secondary material was then supplemented for all six countries by interviews with elite individuals who were directly involved in the design and implementation of reforms in each country as civil servants, donors, and/or consultants. These were undertaken in a semistructured fashion, with a common set of questions and themes but tailored to each individual's experience. Potential interviewees were identified and approached through a combination of existing networks, snowball sampling, and targeted outreach. In Ghana and Zambia, these were supplemented by interviews with rank-and-file civil servants who were not directly involved in reforms in order to gauge how and to what extent systemic reforms affected their day-to-day work.[4] These interviewees were drawn from a common set of ministries and divisions across both countries to maximize comparability.[5] Interviews comprised a mix of open-ended questions about how these individuals perceived reforms in general, with a set of standardized questions about how specific recent reform efforts had (or had not) affected them. Interviews were undertaken between 2018 and 2022, in person in Ghana and Zambia and remotely via video call or telephone for the other four countries after the onset of the COVID-19 pandemic. In Ghana, I also draw on semistructured interviews on de facto organizational management practices undertaken in 2013 with sixty civil servants across forty ministries, departments, and agencies. Altogether, I am able to draw on data from 144 primary interviews across the six countries.

Finally, with the permission of Ghana's Office of the Head of Civil Service (OHCS), I also draw on dozens of boxes of OHCS's public records and internal archives, held both at Ghana's Public Records and Archives Administration Department and at OHCS itself. These cover reforms from the 1980s to the present and provide additional factual details on reform design and implementation as well as an inside perspective on the civil service's discussions and stakeholder interactions surrounding these reforms.

The country histories presented in this appendix draw on all these data sources. On its own, each data source has its strengths, limitations, and potential biases. Triangulating across them allows for combining many of these strengths while overcoming some of these limitations. The strengths include the use for each reform episode of contemporaneous and retrospective perspectives; both primary and secondary data; and official, personal, and academic sources. It also highlights differences in perspectives—between official program documents and the perspectives of individuals involved in the reforms, for instance, or between reform designers and rank-and-file civil servants—that are often revealing in themselves.

At the same time, there are undoubtedly biases and limitations remaining in these histories. Some reform episodes have more data sources than others, and it was harder to assess the implementation and impacts of more recent reforms because not enough time had passed. Having conducted rank-and-file interviews in Ghana and Zambia means that I am more able to assess the extent to which reforms actually affected day-to-day practices in these two countries than in the other four. Similarly, having access to OHCS's archives in Ghana gave me a richer picture of contemporaneous reform thinking within the government than in the other countries. This was especially important for earlier reform periods in the 1980s and 1990s, as many of the individuals who occupied senior positions during those periods have now retired or passed away, and so, retrospective interviews about the thinking behind these reforms sometimes occurred with interviewees who were relatively junior at that time.

The threshold for what constitutes a reform (by my definition) also proved a challenge in two main ways (in addition to the issue of scope discussed above). First, some reform efforts barely or never got off the ground, while others lasted for years. There is naturally more secondary literature on the latter than the former, and the longer-lived reforms were also more likely to be remembered by interviewees. Second, both documents and interviewees were almost certainly more likely to pick out high-profile reforms that generated lots of attention and documentation (such as multiyear donor reforms) than lower-profile, internally driven efforts that did not have large-scale funding or did not lead to legal or structural changes. While I tried to mitigate these potential biases by specifically searching for shorter-lived or less-prominent types of reforms, it is likely that these reform histories undercount the true number of reform efforts and especially undercount less prominent types of reforms—biases that likely apply to any effort to study civil service reforms in any country. Awareness of these potential biases and limitations is one reason (among several) that I am cautious with my empirical claims and do not couch my analysis in terms of hypothesis testing or causal inference.

The main goal of this appendix is to present histories of reform in each country that are as comprehensive as possible and are consistent in format and coverage across countries. But I do not claim, nor do I want readers to think, that these appendix sections represent comprehensive or definitive histories of each reform or of each country. Still less do I claim to be an expert on all six countries—no scholar could be—or to be able to capture all the varied perspectives, details, and nuances of each context. Other scholars and practitioners have written about many of the reforms I discuss here in far more depth than could possibly be included in this book. In particular, it is important to note that many of these works have been written by African scholars and practitioners, many of whom were or still are working in universities, think tanks, and governments in these six countries. These works are crucial for documenting, understanding, and learning from these reform efforts but do not always receive the attention or credit that they should.

In this appendix, I cite this existing literature to indicate where I have drawn on it for specific facts or analytical perspectives, and also to highlight these contributions and point readers who are seeking even more depth on particular reforms, periods, or countries toward them. However, there were hundreds more documents that were reviewed in the process of writing the book and that related to some of these reforms but which I do not reference specifically in this appendix or the main text and, hence, are not listed in the references. I have compiled many of these into an extended bibliography in an online supplementary appendix to give them due recognition and so that other researchers can easily find and consult them.

These short narrative histories are subject to many of the same challenges of delimiting, measuring, and making inferences about reforms that I discuss in the main text. I have strived to present histories that are as accurate as possible, but there were many instances in which sources conflicted or lacked information on aspects of reforms, so it is almost certain that some of these details are inaccurate or incomplete. Usually, these uncertainties pertained to relatively minor details, such as the exact year a formal process ceased to be carried out regularly, that would not affect the overall patterns or findings. Similarly, people who lived through or worked on these reforms might present the stories differently or have different judgments about how to interpret the same set of facts, or may have had differing experiences of a reform due to differences in how it unfolded in different parts of the civil service. In this appendix, as in the rest of the book, I have aimed to strike a balance among the (often divergent) views of those who were involved in the reforms and the various researchers and policymakers who have previously written about them, all while maintaining consistency of presentation and analysis across cases. I have tried to reflect these inherent ambiguities, challenges, and differences of perspective in the text where relevant by indicating variable levels of confidence, noting conflicts between sources, and discussing challenges of interpretation.

GHANA

The first installment in Ghana's history of modern civil service reforms, the Civil Service Reform Programme (CSRP), emerged in 1987 during a period of political and economic turbulence. Military coups had occurred in 1979 and 1981, and a structural adjustment program beginning in 1983 saw the government implement numerous measures related to fiscal restraint and economic liberalization.[6]

This period also saw the beginnings of a series of structural reforms to government ministries and an extensive decentralization program under the aegis of the Public Administration Restructuring and Decentralisation Implementation Committee (PARDIC).[7] This era of fiscal and bureaucratic retrenchment was the context in which Ghana's modern history of performance-oriented civil service reforms emerged.

The 1987 CSRP was created as part of a structural adjustment program that aimed to reduce the size of the public sector through the reduction of staff numbers, job reevaluations and organizational restructuring, and a pay scale regrading and decompression. While primarily fiscally motivated, this reform also aimed to improve performance and modernize performance management[8] and improve "value for money,"[9] including by conducting a functional review of staffing, adopting "an incentive-oriented public service salary policy"[10] and introducing Manpower Units in all ministries to strengthen staff planning and control.[11] It also aimed to revise the civil service law to adopt a common divisional structure for all ministries, strengthen the Office of the Head of the Civil Service, and introduce a "high-flyer" scheme to fast-track promotion for a small cadre of new hires.[12] Funded by the World Bank and United Kingdom's Overseas Development Administration (ODA) mainly via the Structural Adjustment Institutional Support (SAIS) project, the CSRP ran until 1993—the same year that Ghana returned to multiparty democracy. The CSRP was, in the words of an internal Civil Service document that recorded the minutes of a meeting of senior civil servants, "designed abroad."[13]

While the government nearly reached its target for staff retrenchment, with almost fifty thousand positions eliminated in the first three years of the CSRP, actual payroll reduction was much less due to rehiring of some retrenched workers and other new employees.[14] The reform succeeded in developing new salary policy guidelines, but their implementation was partial and delayed amid political and bureaucratic opposition,[15] and there is no evidence that Manpower Units were ever introduced at a significant scale. A new Civil Service Law was passed into place in 1993, which consolidated some of the structural reforms made during CSRP and the pre-CSRP PARDIC era, but these were mainly administrative and procedural changes with little direct bearing on performance. Both the OHCS and Management Services Department (MSD) emerged as strengthened institutions,[16] which would be important for the design and direction of future reforms but had little direct effect on performance.

The main performance improvement component of CSRP was the introduction of a new staff appraisal system. The preexisting Annual Confidential Report (ACR) system was untransparent, and ratings had little association with performance, with then-President Jerry Rawlings lamenting that "confidential reports on individual performance are just a matter of routine; almost everybody, that is, the hard-working and the lazy, get a good confidential report."[17] Similarly, an internal government evaluation of the ACR at the time found that:

> One major problem with it is that no provision is made under it for agreeing on objectives and tasks to be performed. Consequently, there is no formal objective basis for assessing the performance of workers under it. The result has been the tendency to place emphasis on personal qualities and attributes of individuals, and not on their perforamcne [*sic*] on the job.
>
> In practical terms, no use has been made of the ACR to identify the worker's specific weakness and also for determining his training needs. Nor has it been used as major support for promotion decisions. In other words, workers that have been promoted or gone for training have not done so because of the annual confidential report on them. Perhaps, this was the better thing to do, especially since the ACR system has never been rigorously applied: one year a report is made, another year nothing is written. The lack of seriousness surrounding the ACR system is noticeable from examining some of the returns. Invariably, most workers are graded "satisfactory." Under such circumstances, the ACR system has lacked confidence, no one being certain of its uses and benefits.[18]

Under the CSRP, this appraisal system was redesigned and replaced in 1992 by a more interactive Performance Evaluation System (PES),[19] which comprised joint target-setting and assessment by supervisors and their subordinates and was intended to provide an objective basis for linking performance to rewards and sanctions.[20] This performance management system was intended to provide an objective basis for increasing pay for the remaining (and, hopefully, better-performing) civil servants after fiscal space had been created by staff reduction.[21] Indeed, an internal circular with organizations being directed to set aside 10 percent of their personnel budgets for merit-linked cash awards starting in 1992, giving guidance that: "For this purpose, cash awards should be at least 5 percent of the Officer's consolidated gross annual salary. Non-cash awards which should not exceed 5 percent of the Officer's consolidated gross annual salary may be in the form of tangible objects, eg. Clock, cloth, wrist-watches, furniture, set of books, radios, scholarship for a child for one year."[22]

While the World Bank rated the delivery of the SAIS project that funded the CSRP as "satisfactory" overall and asserted that the "conduct and implementation of management reviews and job inspections has contributed to major increases in Civil Service productivity,"[23] most sources are considerably more skeptical of significant performance improvements. Indeed, Ghana's subsequent Head of Civil Service, Robert Dodoo, wrote in an archived draft of a 1996 speech that, "The reforms did not enhance overall performance and achieve the expected transparency, accountability and good governance in public management, in service to the people and the private sector. It was also limited in scope and coverage hence its limited impact and lack of commitment on the part of Civil/Public Servants. Most of the essential reform outputs are, as a result, yet to become an integral part of the culture of management and result in increased productivity and performance improvement in the Civil/Public Services."[24]

Similarly, the new staff appraisal system was enacted on paper, but even several years later, internal civil service documents reported that the system had not been effectively institutionalized: "Even though a new appraisal and reporting system had been introduced into the human resources management system of the Civil Service five years earlier, it was found during the consolidation period (1994/95), that it had not become an effective part of the culture of management in the civil service,"[25] and appraisals were not being linked to rewards and the envisioned merit pay had not materialized.[26] At the same time, several interviewees agreed that the new PES appraisal system brought transparency, mutuality, and a better understanding of roles to many workers who were, for the first time, having routine conversations with their supervisors about their responsibilities and performance.[27] However, this sentiment was not unanimous among interviewees.[28]

In 1993, as the CSRP was drawing to a close, planning began for what would become its successor program: the Civil Service Performance Improvement Programme (CSPIP), designed explicitly to "correct [CSRP's] shortfalls."[29] In response to the perception that the CSRP was driven by donors and merely imposed on the broader civil service, the CSPIP was designed as a "homegrown" reform—a term that almost all interviewees, academic studies, and official documents invoked. Whereas CSRP had focused almost exclusively on high-level structural changes that were mostly intended to improve performance indirectly, CSPIP aimed directly at engaging individual ministries and civil servants in search of improved performance. In the words of Head of Civil Service Dodoo, who took office during the design of CSPIP:

> Instead of the Top-Down approach we evolve an initial and essentially Bottom-Up orientation. Participation and consensus building is emphasized to allow each major stakeholder to co-determine aspects of the design and to interpret its own role in the process.... Output and performance orientation is also emphasized as a guiding principle of the CSPIP design. Participants collectively own the problems and the solutions as well as the strategies through which they are reached....

Administration

- PNDC - Rawlings
- NDC - Rawlings
- NPP - Kufuor
- NDC - Atta-Mills
- NDC - Mahama
- NPP - Akufo-Addo

Reform Era

- Civil Service Reform Programme (CSRP)
- National Institutional Renewal Programme (NIRP)
- Ministry of Public Sector Reform (MPSR)
- "New Approach"
- Performance Management
- Nat. Pub. Sect. Ref. Str. (NPSRS)

Reform Programs

- Civil Service Reform Programme (CSRP)
- Struct. Adjustment Institutional Support Project (SAIS)
- Priv. Inv. and Sust. Dev. Promo. Cred.[1]
- Economic Management Support (EMS)
- National Institutional Renewal Programme (NIRP)
- Civil Service Performance Improvement Programme (CSPIP)
- Public Sector Mgmt. Reform Project (PSMR)
- Ghana Central Governance Program
- Performance Agreement System
- Policy Coordination, Monitoring, and Evaluation Unit (PCMEU)
- Pov. Red. Strat. Cred. (PSRC I-III)
- Public Sector Reform Agenda (PSRA)
- Ministry of Public Sector Reform (MPSR)
- Perf. Mgmt. Policy (PMP)
- Single Spine Pay Policy (SSPP)
- "New Approach"
- Performance Management Policy for the Public Services of Ghana
- Chief Director Performance Agreements (CDPA)
- Min. PCs[2]
- Capacity Development Mechanism
- Policy Monitoring and Evaluation Unit (PMEU)
- Presidential Delivery Unit
- Nat. Pub. Sect. Ref. Str. (NPSRS)

Years: 1987 1988 1989 1990 1991 1992 1993 1994 1995 1996 1997 1998 1999 2000 2001 2002 2003 2004 2005 2006 2007 2008 2009 2010 2011 2012 2013 2014 2015 2016 2017 2018 2019

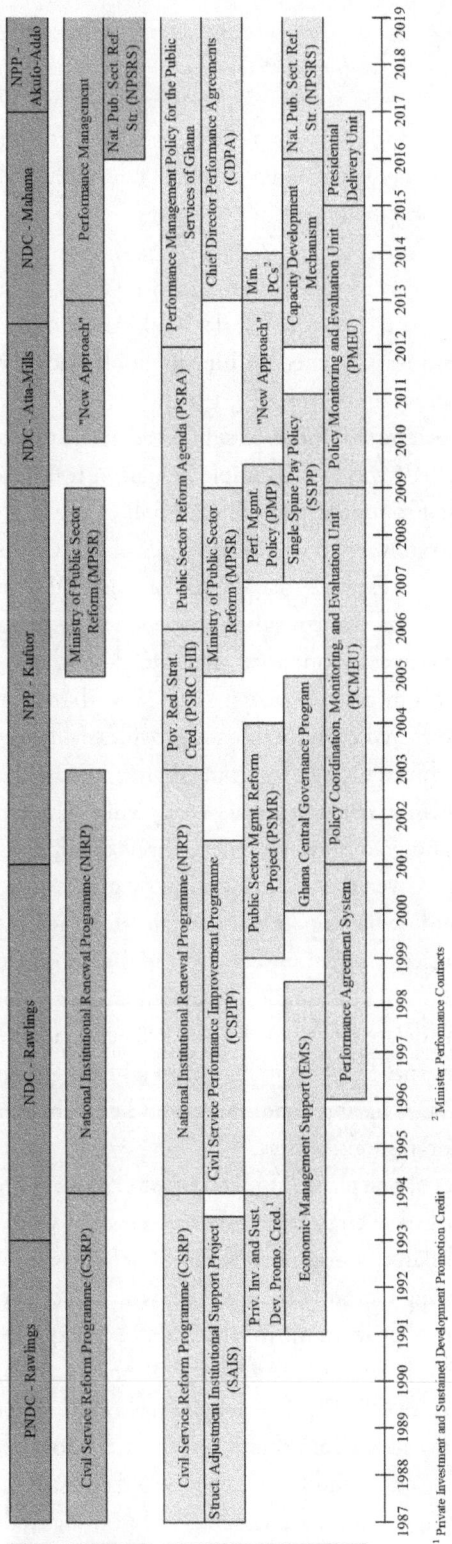

[1] Private Investment and Sustained Development Promotion Credit [2] Minister Performance Contracts

FIGURE A.1 Timeline of Civil Service Reforms in Ghana

Source: Author's synthesis based on document review and interviews.

It is now not a situation in which a group of experts, Committee and Commission Members formulate a programme and then pass it on to the majority or the Government for implementation.[30]

CSPIP was funded largely by the United Kingdom's ODA, although it also received some early support from the World Bank's Economic Management Support (EMS) loan and was couched within the public sector-wide National Institutional Renewal Programme (NIRP), which was aimed more at making fiscal savings through structural reforms to subvented agencies like state-owned enterprises. Like the CSRP, the CSPIP implementation team did involve foreign consultants—most prominently Hugh Marshall of the UK's Royal Institute of Public Administration, who was in residence at OHCS throughout the project[31]—and archival records show that World Bank and ODA staff were periodically involved in meetings and consultations around the design of the program.[32] However, interviewees emphasize that the design and leadership of CSPIP were driven mainly by civil servants in OHCS, with foreign staff in advisory capacities only.[33] Archived correspondence provides evidence in support of this. For instance, an archived 1994 letter from Ghana's Head of Civil Service to the British High Commission's First Secretary (Aid) Mike Wood, begins with an informal "Dear Mike" and goes on to comment about the draft CSPIP memorandum of cooperation: "Given that CSPIP is a 'home-grown' product involving our full participation and ownership, it is important that the ODA advisers fit into my office structure clearly under my control and direction. Decisions about UK Consultants' inputs would be handled by myself and my team. . . . I believe that the connotation associated with an 'ODA Project Manager' implies too high a profile for an external IT consultant within a home grown project such as CSPIP. . . . We see ODA having a monitoring and guidance role for CSPIP rather than 'management' responsibilities."[34]

Similarly, the minutes of one planning meeting for CSRP's continuation project noted, "In his remarks the chairman [previous Head of Civil Service E. A. Sai] thanks the [World Bank] consultants for finding the time to be present at the meeting of the Steering Committee on CSRP which had reached the stage of evolving a 'home-grown' programme for the CSRP. . . . The three consultants departed soon thereafter."[35] Similarly, Agyekum-Dwamena explained why the World Bank withdrew from CSPIP: "I remember one of the very first meetings with the World Bank, the idea [from them] was 'how far down can we go further?' [in terms of staffing cuts], and Dr. Dodoo looked and said that was not on the card. The next reform era he was envisaging had nothing to do with downsizing, reduction in numbers and all that. So, after a bit of back and forth, the

World Bank did not directly participate in supporting CSPIP. So, we had DFID who bought into our methodology."[36]

The substantive core of CSPIP was an elaborate system of organizational performance diagnostics and reviews that aimed to build institutional awareness of and commitment to performance improvement, both in the immediate term and as part of a broader culture change.[37] The organizational reviews were highly participatory and included the constitution of an internal capacity development team, a survey of beneficiaries and stakeholders, an organizational self-appraisal, and the development of a Performance Improvement Plan (PIP).[38] These were facilitated by a project team housed in OHCS, which also operated a Performance Improvement Facility (PIF) for small grants to support organizations' PIPs. CSPIP also mandated and supported the development of service charters (detailing services available, timelines, application steps, and costs) and client service units (one-stop front offices for stakeholders to access services and information) to improve service delivery and client orientation.[39]

The organizational reviews and PIPs were often successful in creating meaningful conversations around performance, sometimes for the first time, and the organizational PIPs brought forward numerous examples of impactful ideas.[40] One officer who was involved in delivering CSPIP explained that civil servants participating in these workshops were often defensive at first, both about the beneficiary surveys and the workshops, to discuss the findings of the survey and organizational self-appraisal, but that this attitude gradually reduced as they received assurances from OHCS that the exercise was not intended to be punitive.[41] This initial reaction may also have been influenced by the functional reviews and manpower hearings that occurred during CSRP just a few years earlier that also focused on productivity issues but from the perspective of forcing organizations to justify their operations and trying to reduce or reallocate resources. Agyekum-Dwamena gauged the rate of implementation of PIP actions at "between 45 and 55" percent and highlighted that many of the ideas surfaced in the PIP development process went on to become cornerstones of ministry-level reform trajectories in the following decades, such as the Ministry of Defense's relocation from a military base to a civilian office area and the Ministry of Lands and Natural Resources beginning to streamline and digitize land titling processes.[42]

At the same time, some rank-and-file officers reported seeing little impact from these activities on their day-to-day work, with one explaining that, while he remembered engaging with the CSPIP organizational reviews, he had seen no real effects from them: "I think they were just mere formalities."[43] While some of these PIP ideas were implemented under CSPIP and others stayed on organizations' agendas and were implemented in later years, the deeply participatory process was also very time-consuming, which delayed the onset of actual implementation. By the end of 1997, three years into the reform, 154 of 182 target institutions had started the PIP process by taking the first step of creating internal Capacity Development Teams, but only twenty-nine had actually produced a PIP, and only twenty had actually begun implementation of their PIP.[44] Ministries and departments also encountered structural barriers to changing processes, such as rigid personnel rules (that, for example, prevented the Driver and Vehicle Licensing Authority from keeping its offices open after 5 p.m. to better serve clients) and persistently delayed and reduced budget releases, that were beyond the scope of CSPIP to change.[45] At a joint review meeting in 2000, Ghanaian and British participants alike praised the achievements of CSPIP while also spending much of the workshop discussing "system-wide issues" that hindered the full achievement of the PIPs.[46] Other organization-level outputs of the CSPIP reform, such as service charters and client service units, were created by most institutions, but there were few monitoring or enforcement mechanisms, impact varied across institutions, and, while they continued to exist on paper after the end of CSPIP, they generally lost institutional commitment after donor funding ended.[47]

In terms of individual-level performance management, the CSPIP era also saw the institution of a Performance Agreement System (PAS) as a performance management tool for chief directors (the bureaucratic heads of organizations equivalent to permanent secretaries).[48] As with individual-level (PES) appraisals, this started with the definition of a schedule of targets at the start of the year (albeit with more detail and structure than the PES), which were intended to correspond to the organization's work plan and would be evaluated at the end of the year—again, with the intention of using these as the basis for allocating rewards and punishments.

The performance agreements for chief directors were developed and finalized as intended, and OHCS's internal logbook records sixteen signed agreements in 1997 (with an evaluation in March 1998), none for 1998, forty for 1999 (for both chief directors and some directors, with an evaluation in March 2000), and sixty-one for 2000.[49] The first round of nonpilot ratings (from 2000) were supposed to be published in 2001, but the new presidential administration decided against publishing them, after which, the review of chief directors' performance ceased and the agreement system faded away.[50]

CSPIP ended when the expiration of the five-year UK donor funding agreement in 2001 coincided with a transition in the presidential regime and in Civil Service leadership, despite positive discussions in 2000 aimed at extending CSPIP into a second phase.[51] While CSPIP thus succeeded more than CSRP both in terms of implementation and impact, and introduced several ideas that would be taken up again by future reforms, it nevertheless failed to outlast the end of donor funding and leadership transitions and fell significantly short of its ambitious visions of transforming performance and culture in the civil service. At the same time, its actual impacts were much more limited than envisioned, and the momentum it successfully built was not sustained beyond its lifespan.

Presidential elections in 2000 were won by the opposition New Patriotic Party (NPP), which spent its first years in power focusing on economic growth and poverty reduction through Ghana's first Poverty Reduction Strategy Plan. Civil service reform came back on the agenda in earnest in 2003 when the Public Sector Reform Secretariat (PSRS) was created under the Office of the Senior Minister and commissioned a team of consultants to review NIRP.[52] In 2005, a Ministry of Public Sector Reform (MPSR) was created under the Office of the President, with a high-profile minister, Paa Kwesi Nduom, and staffed by a mix of civil servants and consultants.[53] The creation of the MPSR was reportedly at the insistence of the World Bank, which wanted a permanent institution to oversee the reforms, while its location in the Office of the President was an effort by its minister to increase the ministry's political clout.[54] The MPSR created a five-year Public Sector Reform Agenda (PSRA) with an associated work program, beginning in 2006.[55] Much of the PSRA focused on making deep structural changes, from the establishment of a senior management service to decentralization, pay and pension reform, restructuring of central management agencies, and ICT reforms, while the service delivery-oriented aspects mainly repackaged and reintroduced CSPIP's work program of ministerial client service units and service charters.[56]

These client service units and service charters were reintroduced and rewritten by many ministries, with a range of training and sensitization workshops conducted in support of this and some perceived impact on civil servants' mindsets.[57] However, they were reportedly perceived as "owned" by the MPSR, which paid for the development of the charters and the equipping of the client service units, and so the energy behind them disappeared with the departure of Nduom as minister and the downgrading of the MPSR in the wake of the 2008 electoral alternation.[58] OHCS itself reportedly benefited from some restructuring and internal strengthening under the PSRA.[59]

However, by far, the most salient component of the PSRA was the harmonization and rationalization of pay scales and negotiating processes across the public service through the Single Spine Pay Policy (SSPP) that would be administered by the newly created Fair Wages and Salaries Commission (FWSC).[60] The SSPP was seen both as a financial management reform as well as a step toward performance-linked pay, as reflected in FWSC's dual mandate: first, pay scales would be harmonized and increased, and then salaries would be linked to performance.[61]

This agenda also brought the issue of staff performance management back to the fore, and from 2007, the Public Services Commission began the development of a new Performance Management Policy to revisit the appraisal process,[62] although its goals remained substantially the same and there is no evidence that the system was significantly changed or implemented in more meaningful ways as a result. In 2008, the opposition National Democratic Congress (NDC) won the presidency, as a result of which, the MPSR was downgraded back to a secretariat (the Public Sector Reform Secretariat), and the performance management policy—as well as many other activities initiated by MPSR—lost steam.

The MPSR era saw a great deal of activity, but its main lasting legacy was the initiation of the SSPP salary reform process. The FWSC and the salary review it oversaw outlived the MPSR and the NPP administration that initiated it, with the implementation of the SSPP beginning in January 2010 under President John Atta-Mills of the NDC.[63] The new pay scales and grading system were implemented across the whole of the Public Service (including the Civil Service) and did lead to a greater degree of harmonization as well as a general uplift, albeit at a much greater cost than anticipated.[64] Part of the explanation for why the cost "ballooned" so much more than the reform architects anticipated was the 2008 presidential campaign, during which public sector salary increases became a subject of political debate and campaign pledges.[65] The envisioned and all-important final step—the linkage of pay to measured performance—never happened due to a combination of fatigue after the years-long regrading process, the ballooning cost of the higher pay levels that eliminated fiscal space for performance bonuses, and turf wars between the FWSC and other statutory personnel management bodies like the Public Services Commission.[66] While the SSPP thus reduced salary inequalities within the public service and may have contributed to greater long-term staff retention through higher pay levels, there is thus little evidence that it (or other MPSR reforms) contributed directly to improved performance.

Under the new government of President John Atta-Mills in 2009, a "New Approach" to public sector reform was instituted under the leadership of Secretary to Cabinet Ben Eghan. Rather than coordinating a government-wide reform strategy of internal administrative reforms, the New Approach encouraged ministers to develop sector-specific reform programs that focused on improving service delivery in a number of priority sectors.[67] This approach to reform aimed to focus not on internal bureaucratic processes but specifically on job creation and food security as outcomes.[68]

While some ministries undertook new job creation activities under the New Approach, with the Ministry of Defense cited as one ministry that introduced significant new initiatives during this time period,[69] there is little evidence about

TABLE A.1 Content of civil service reforms in Ghana

	Civil Service Reform Prog. (CSRP), 1987–93	NIRP & Public Sector Mgmt. Reform Project (PSMR), 1994–2002	Civil Service Perf. Impr. Prog. (CSPIP), 1994–2001	Policy Coord., Mon., and Eval. Unit (PCMEU), 2001–08	Public Sector Reform Agenda (PSRA) & Single Spine Pay Policy (SSPP), 2006–11	Perf. Mgmt. Policy (PMP), 2007–09	Policy Mon. and Eval. Unit (PMEU), 2009–14	Presid. Delivery Unit, 2015–16	"New Approach", 2009–12	Perf. Mgmt. Policy for the Public Services of Ghana, 2012–	Minister Perf. Contracts	Chief Director Perf. Agree. (CDPA), 2013–	Nat. Pub. Sect. Ref. Str. (NPSRS), 2016–
Individual performance mgmt.													
Leadership performance agreements			✓		✓						✓	✓	
Individual staff appraisal & performance management	✓		✓		✓	✓				✓			✓
Org. mgmt. and capacity													
Org. reviews/ perf. improv. plans/ perf. mgmt.			✓										
Performance improvement funds			✓										
Service delivery-focused reforms													
Client-focused reforms			✓		✓								✓
Sector-driven reforms									✓				✓
Salaries and structures													
Staff redundancies & org. restructuring	✓	✓											
Pay regrading/ reform	✓	✓			✓								
Other reforms													
Cross-government coordination				✓			✓	✓					
Other													

Source: Author's synthesis based on document review and interviews.

whether the system-level intervention of the New Approach drove new initiatives or performance impacts more broadly.[70] The New Approach was eventually interrupted by the sudden death of President Atta-Mills in 2012, and its overall impact on the internal administration of the civil service was limited, with no evidence that the focus on better service delivery improved bureaucratic efficiency.[71]

From 2013, the public sector reform agenda came to be dominated not by reforms driven by political leadership or sweeping donor programs but by the revitalization of performance management programs. These took three forms: (1) a revision and revitalization of the staff appraisal system for rank-and-file officers; (2) a system of Chief Director Performance Agreements for top-level bureaucrats; and (3) performance contracts for ministers announced by the president.

At the rank-and-file level, the Public Services Commission began developing a new Performance Management Policy for the Public Services of Ghana.[72] Three academic studies conducted around this period found that the existing appraisal system continued to be implemented either perfunctorily or only occasionally and without any systematic rewards or punishments, albeit with some variation across and within organizations.[73] The new Performance Management Policy introduced a simplified appraisal template and slightly more elaborate target-setting and performance-review processes but maintained the same approach to improving individual productivity by combining annual target-setting and assessment as the basis for allocating rewards and punishments.

The new process was introduced in 2015 and received praise from many civil servants.[74] One interviewee explained that prior to 2015, "We would write our own appraisal and the boss signs it. Now we sit down with the bosses. If I say I will achieve four meetings there should be four meeting minutes. Now you can measure performance. Now you can set targets. This is from the chief director and down. If I fail, everyone fails."[75] This new system also featured (for at least some civil servants) greater training on performance awareness and how to set better targets.[76] However, there was still significant variation within Ghana's Civil Service in the extent to which these conversations were actually happening,[77] and there were still no formal rewards or punishments associated with measured performance. (Toward the end of the 2010s, OHCS did begin to renew its efforts to make promotion interviews more meaningful and differentiated in terms of outcomes, but these efforts occurred mainly after the time period examined in this book.)

At the same time, in 2013/2014, the Office of the Head of Civil Service began working to reintroduce Chief Director Performance Agreements (CDPAs). The CDPAs were rolled out initially with French and Canadian donor support but subsequently funded from the general budget.[78] This was consciously modeled on the performance contracting system that had been created under CSPIP but fell away after 2000—unsurprisingly perhaps, as then-Head of Civil Service, Nana Agyekum-Dwamena was a junior member of the CSPIP design and implementation team during the 1990s—with even the three sections of the template (institution-specific deliverables, general requirements, and personal development) remaining the same. The revitalization of these two key performance management systems complemented a range of other incremental revisions to promotion and training procedures.[79] At their core, though, they still shared the vision that "every individual including Heads of the Public Services Chief Executive Officers/Chief Directors, Heads of Departments and Directors are to have annual performance targets whose attainment will be enforced by appropriate combinations of incentives and sanctions."[80] Directors have also been increasingly brought into this performance agreement system over the years, albeit with a less formalized performance evaluation and scoring system.

The CDPAs during this period were more regular and successful than their predecessor performance contracts in the 1990s under CSPIP while still not resulting in the envisioned linkages between measured performance and rewards or sanctions. The CDPA target-setting and evaluation exercise was routinely carried out annually from 2013/2014 through the end of this book's coverage in 2019, with high-profile signing ceremonies and an internally published scorecard for each chief director, and was widely viewed as successful in establishing discursive accountability mechanisms and increasing pressure on chief directors to improve, particularly on basic deliverables.[81] One public servant who had been a part of the evaluation team for the performance agreements gave an example of a case where a chief director had signed an agreement, but his directors had not taken it seriously, so his performance was poor. The next year, however, the chief director applied pressure on his directors and other middle management to make sure they delivered on their work that fed into his targets. As the interviewee remarked, "If I'm CEO, I won't sit there and be made chopped liver because my directors aren't doing their jobs."[82] A junior rank-and-file officer also perceived that the CDPAs had led chief directors to be more responsive to what their staff need in order to perform well, remarking, "I think chief directors were doing whatever, but now they ensure they provide resources to do what you need to do."[83] Another junior officer remarked that the clarity and linkage of deliverables between the performance agreements of the chief director and the director of their division have helped them see the connection between their work and overall organizational performance.[84] However, there was also concern among at least some interviewees that the lack of hard incentives attached to the CDPA results could eventually undermine the seriousness with which they were taken,[85] and that there was limited visibility of the CDPA process and results for rank-and-file staff.[86]

In mid-2013, President John Mahama announced the creation of a system of performance contracts for government ministers.[87] These set out delivery targets and aimed to "maximize the performance of ministers" and "make Government transparent and accountable to the people."[88] Ministers went through performance evaluations with the president in December 2013,[89] although the results of these do not seem to have been published, and the exercise does not appear to have been repeated in 2014 or subsequent years.

Overall, the performance management initiatives for rank-and-file civil servants and senior bureaucratic leadership during this period appear to have had largely beneficial effects—albeit mostly through clarifying goals and spurring performance discussion, and without the sticks and carrots that were envisioned. It is also notable that, unlike CSPIP and the MPSR performance management reforms, this phase of reform effort persisted despite a change in presidential administration in 2016. However, the politically driven performance contracts for ministers had no apparent effects and were not sustained.

The most recent wave of reform in Ghana (prior to the end of this book's study period in 2019) was triggered by the government's 2015 approach to the IMF for a program loan in the face of a worsening fiscal situation, which coincided with a latent demand from a range of stakeholders for improvements in the effectiveness of public service delivery.[90] However, the IMF left the details of the administrative reforms to be developed by the government, which conducted extensive stakeholder consultations with these various stakeholder groups.[91] The resulting National Public Sector Reform Strategy (NPSRS) was initially developed and approved by the Cabinet in 2015/2016, but after the 2016 change in the presidential administration, the NPSRS was subsequently reviewed and some details revised (while retaining the thrust of the original document).[92]

The main focus of the NPSRS reforms returned to sector-focused efforts to improve public service delivery efficiency across a range of priority sectors. The NPSRS itself aimed to be a strategic framework for coordinating a wide range of preexisting and planned sectoral reforms, rather than originating new reforms itself,[93] with most program funds being channeled through ministry budgets rather than a centralized reform budget line.[94] The cross-sectoral internal administrative reform agenda aspects of the NPSRS, for the most part, were drawn from previously defined work programs in the public sector that were ongoing during the design of the NPSRS and a renewed emphasis on reestablishing service charters for ministries.[95] At the time of research, the idea of instituting 360-degree evaluation as part of the performance appraisal process had been mooted as part of the NPSRS reforms,[96] and the goal of developing performance-related pay was reiterated,[97] but neither of these had progressed as of 2019. The implementation and impacts of this reform fall largely outside the time window of this book, so they are not assessed here, although a 2022 academic study was critical of the NPSRS's goals and design, arguing that it represented a continuation of past unsuccessful patterns of reform rather than a new reform paradigm and that it was insufficient "to turn around the performance of the bureaucracy."[98]

KENYA

The era of civil service reforms in Kenya covered in this book began as part of its transition from authoritarian rule into multiparty democracy, marked by the contentious December 1992 elections in which Daniel arap Moi retained the presidency—although there had, of course, also been important reform efforts in the prior decades.[99] The civil service had played a key role in exerting social control and serving as a vehicle for patronage, marking it as "an exemplification of authoritarian rule in Kenya, and a target for reform" for Kenyan pro-democracy activists.[100] This movement occurred in the context of an economic crisis during the 1980s and a set of structural adjustment programs and associated fiscal restraints beginning in 1986 that gave international donors substantial leverage over the government, culminating in a 1991 aid embargo aimed at forcing democratization and deeper reforms.[101]

Under these pressures, in May 1992, the Kenyan government published the Kenya Civil Service Reform Program and Action Plan (KCSRPAP), a diagnostic study it had commissioned from the Directorate of Personnel Management in the Office of the Presidency.[102] This document became the basis for the donor-supported Civil Service Reform Programme (CSRP), launched in 1993 after the elections, which became the umbrella and driving force for civil service reform in Kenya until the end of the Moi administration in 2002.[103] The KCSRPAP and CSRP identified a litany of challenges facing the civil service that echoed those facing other governments in Africa during the structural adjustment era, including organizational duplication, overstaffing (in large part due to patronage hiring), low salary levels, and the lack of linkage between performance and pay or career progression.[104] The CSRP envisioned addressing these challenges through three phases: downsizing and cost reduction (1993–1998), performance improvement (1998–2001), and consolidation (intended to run 2002–2006 but never occurred).[105]

The early years of the CSRP were aimed at carrying out a large-scale staff retrenchment program, which included restrictions on new and replacement hiring and the creation of a Voluntary Early Retirement Scheme (VERS) in 1993, which gave staff financial payouts for leaving the service early. The aim of this was to reduce staffing levels, with the rationale that the associated cost savings would allow for greater spending on service delivery and operations and maintenance of infrastructure and thus improve efficiency.[106] This was followed by an effort to consolidate a number of government ministries from 1996 and, in 1999, by a revised VERS that included compulsory retirements for officers from overstaffed cadres and eliminated departments.[107] The aim of these cost containment measures was to reduce staffing levels, with the rationale that the associated cost savings would allow for greater spending on service delivery and on the operation and maintenance of infrastructure.[108] In parallel, the government envisioned decompressing pay scales and monetizing allowances with the aim of transitioning toward a leaner, more efficient civil service with more competitive and performance-linked compensation packages.

The staff retrenchment measures were broadly successful in reaching their reduction targets but resulted in less-than-anticipated cost savings. Sources differ on the exact number of staff retrenched, with different sources reporting figures of 52,781, 69,877, and 81,502 staff during Phase I of the CSRP due to voluntary retirement and natural attrition.[109] These were significant reductions relative to the 1991 civil service staff strength of 271,979[110] and the CSRP target of 80,000 redundancies.[111] However, actual fiscal savings from these departures were limited due to significant replacement hiring, the burden of severance payments and ballooning pension costs, unplanned patronage-driven hiring of and pay raises for teachers by the government prior to the 1997 election, and pay scale and allowance reform during 1994–1997.[112] Meanwhile, the organizational restructuring component stalled after the planning stage.[113] Perhaps most damagingly, there is also consensus among sources that the VERS resulted in the loss of many of the best civil servants and deficiencies in key technical areas. As one retired civil servant reflected, "We did not ringfence the critical cadres, so what happened was that a lot of the people who took the package were some of the best people . . . we were probably left with some people who were not necessarily the best people."[114] A World Bank evaluation concluded that the VERS and associated reform measures had minimal effect on the fiscal deficit, did not result in better compensation for remaining civil servants or higher operations and maintenance allocations, led to "a number of ministries being deprived of essential services," and did not have "any positive effects on performance, efficiency or service delivery."[115]

Under strong donor pressure again, the second phase of the CSRP (from 1998, integrated into the broader Public Sector Reform Programme) doubled down on cost containment measures by renewing the push to decrease the number of ministries and adding a compulsory retirement redundancy program for staff from abolished ministries and other targeted groups, alongside a watered-down VERS. A six-member Change Team of noncivil servants—nicknamed the "Dream Team"—was placed in charge of key positions for pushing this agenda in order to assuage donor concerns about patronage, corruption, and lack of ownership undermining the reforms.[116] Again, nominal successes were achieved, such as the consolidation of twenty-seven ministries to fifteen in 1999 and the compulsory retirement of 23,448 civil servants through 2001.[117] However, these politically painful reforms met with strong resistance from within the government (reportedly due to concerns about losing patronage powers, and with an eye on the upcoming 2002 election) as well as from civil servants.[118] This led to a deluge of court cases and even reemployment of some terminated civil servants.[119] In May 2001, the Moi government fired three of the six Change Team members, bringing an effective end to the CSRP reform era.

In parallel to these cost-oriented reforms, the KCSRPAP and CSRP also envisioned reforming personnel management policies to link individual performance with pay and career progression.[120] These reforms began in 1992, even prior to the CSRP, with the reform of the staff Performance Appraisal System. Under the old confidential system, the appraisal "was by your supervisor, and it was confidential, and you did not set up targets at the beginning of the performance period. So, what happened really, it was about more of your relationship with your supervisor . . . he would do an appraisal at the end of the year, not based on targets that you have agreed, but based on [his] own feeling."[121] This system was implemented perfunctorily, with the outcome being conveyed in an impersonal letter that merely conveyed the absence of any adverse findings.[122] The new system increased the intended frequency of appraisal meetings from twice-yearly to quarterly and created a participatory target-setting process at the beginning of the period. The CSRP aimed to leverage this newly introduced system as part of a broader transition from an overstaffed, underpaid, patronage- and poor-performance-ridden civil service to a smaller, better-paid service that tied performance to promotion and training.[123] However, the CSRP did not take any meaningful steps to create the intended performance-promotion-pay linkages beyond the 1992 Performance Appraisal System reform. Though most officers reportedly welcomed the transparency of the new system, the target-setting process was still largely rhetorical.[124] The process as a whole "was being taken as a routine thing . . . even if your performance was not very good, nothing would happen to you. You would still be getting your salary, you still even get promoted, and so on. So it wasn't really taken very seriously."[125] This performance management aspect of the CSRP reforms, therefore, also resulted in little, if any, improvement in performance.

Many historical accounts treat the CSRP as an externally imposed set of reforms with no political ownership that failed to improve performance. There is a good deal of truth to these claims, with most civil servants perceiving CSRP as donor-driven,[126] and one expert noting that under the Moi administration, civil service reform initiatives were "in many ways symbolic."[127] But while fiscal crisis and donor dependence did drive Moi to take actions (such as compulsory redundancies and reduction of the number of ministries) that were half-heartedly implemented at best, many senior public servants were also concerned about the country's trajectory and saw a need for reform.[128] Similarly, one former civil servant involved in implementing the CSRP emphasized that both it and the KCSRPAP were actually written by civil servants, not donors, with a career civil servant directing the reform effort.[129] Although funding was received from a UN basket fund and the World Bank, the only interaction the implementing team had with donors was reportedly occasional sharing of thoughts with a Swedish government official and quarterly update meetings with the UN team, although "they did not direct where those funds should go."[130] While the more politically painful components of CSRP were certainly resisted both by President Moi and many rank-and-file civil servants whose jobs were under threat, there were also internal constituencies thinking about and pushing for reform.

The next and most vigorous era of civil service reform in Kenya kicked off with the election of President Mwai Kibaki in 2002 and the subsequent launch of his government's Economic Recovery Strategy (ERS) in 2003. Section 4.1 of the ERS laid out an ambitious agenda for civil service reform and performance improvement, including organizational rationalization, undertaking ministerial service delivery surveys, "developing, introducing and institutionalizing performance based management practices in the public service," and pay reform to ensure that (by June 2004) pay and benefits would be "rationalized, market oriented and performance based."[131] Kibaki's election was widely seen as a clean break from the inertia of the Moi era for the country as a whole as well as the civil service, with experts and former officials using terms like "euphoric"[132] and "energized"[133] to describe the enthusiasm within the civil service at this time.

The driving philosophy of the Kibaki era was results-based management, enshrined in 2004 by the creation of the Results for Kenya program, a cabinet decision, and the creation of the Public Sector Reform and Development Secretariat (PSRDS). These were collectively intended to translate the ERS's vision into a set of tangible reforms. The process of developing the Results for Kenya program included not only elements of new thinking and rupture with the past but also important continuities. The 2003–2004 period during which Results for Kenya was formulated included a set of study trips to the UK, Sweden, and Canada, whose Results for Canadians program directly inspired the Results for Kenya name.[134] At the same time, there were important elements of continuity: the introduction of multiyear strategic planning under CSRP II provided the foundation for defining and measurement results;[135] a precursor document on performance improvement was published in 2001;[136] and conversations around results-based management started as early as 1999 among public servants who would go on to serve in leadership positions under the Kibaki administration.[137] Similarly, while the flagship performance contracting system is now closely associated with the Kibaki administration due to the high level of political sponsorship it received, the idea of introducing such a system had actually been circulating within the civil service since the precursor documents and activities in the late 1990s and early 2000s, during which hundreds of senior officers were sent for performance-oriented training in South Africa: "So then when the issue now of performance contracts now came in 2004, at least the staff, I mean the heads of ministries and heads of department were not . . . it was not a new thing as such to them, because they were already quite familiar with [the] reform."[138] The 2003–2007 era in Kenya thus combined change and continuity, external and internal influences, in its ambitious reform program.

This era saw three main sets of performance-oriented reforms in the civil service: (1) the Performance Contracting system; (2) Rapid Results Initiatives; and (3) another effort to use the Performance Appraisal System to link performance to rewards and sanctions for rank-and-file staff. In addition, there were a handful of other reforms planned for this period, such as the creation of ministry-level Results Units/Ministerial Management Units, ongoing pay scale and organizational rationalization efforts, the creation of institutional service charters, a broader management accountability framework, and another voluntary redundancy scheme.

The Performance Contracting system consisted of an annual "contract" signed between the Head of the Public Service (representing the government) and each ministry's permanent secretary (representing that ministry).[139] This contract consisted of a set of performance targets set through a negotiation process at the start of each fiscal year that constituted the ministry's obligations, as well as a set of agreed inputs (mainly budget) that constituted the obligations of the center of government and Ministry of Finance to enable the ministry to deliver.[140] Each ministry was then ranked at the end of the year, with the intention that the staff of the top-rated ministry would be awarded a "thirteenth month" salary bonus.[141] The process of introducing performance contracts began in 2003

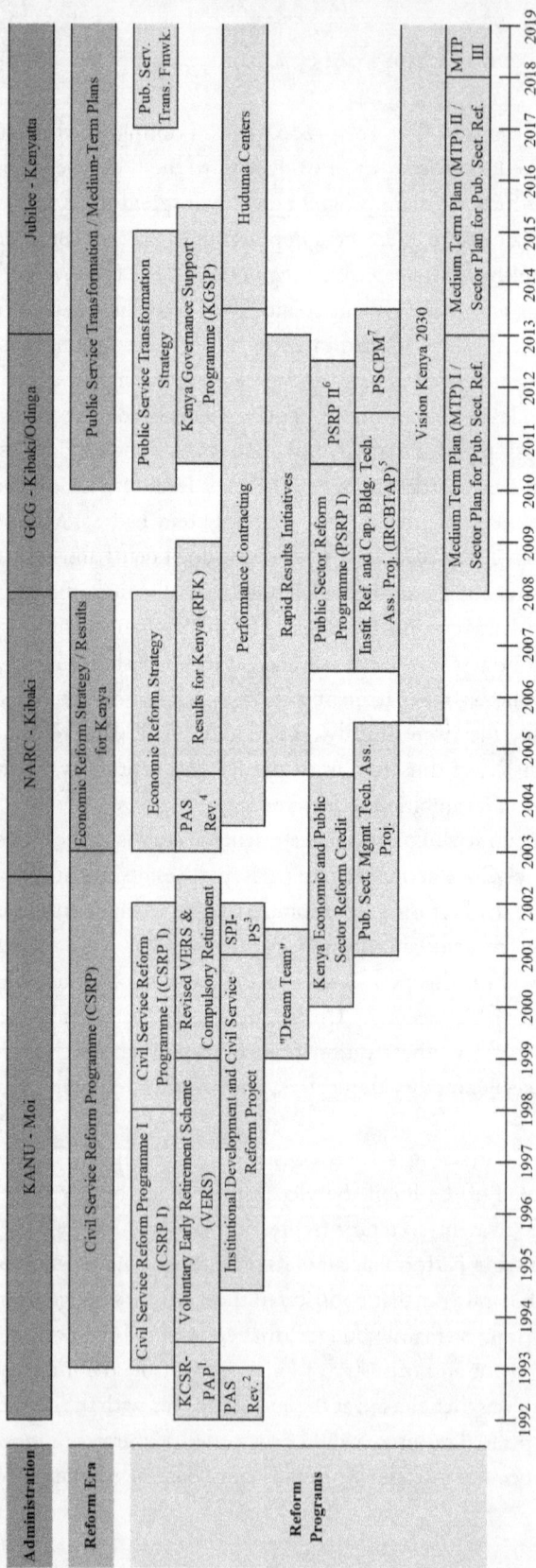

FIGURE A.2 Timeline of Civil Service Reforms in Kenya.

Source: Author's synthesis based on document review and interviews.

1 Kenya Civil Service Reform Programme and Action Plan
2 Performance Appraisal System Revision
3 Strategy for Performance Improvement in the Public Service
4 Performance Appraisal System Revision
5 Institutional Reform and Capacity Building Technical Assistance Project
6 Public Sector Reform Program II
7 Policy Steering Committee on Performance Management

with the creation of a steering committee, with associated tools, regulations, and training rolled out over the subsequent years.[142] After piloting the performance contracts with sixteen state-owned enterprises in the 2004/2005 fiscal year, they were first rolled out to government ministries and departments in 2005/2006.[143]

The performance contract system for permanent secretaries was widely (though not universally) viewed as a success, albeit with a number of limitations. The contracts were generally signed by each ministry and department each year (thirty-five of thirty-eight in 2005/2006[144]) and continued to be used in the central government consistently for years afterward,[145] albeit more as a "routine thing" from 2013, as President Uhuru Kenyatta's administration placed less emphasis on the process,[146] and the secretariat was repeatedly moved and attention shifted away from central government ministries to using performance contracts as part of Kenya's devolution process.[147] During the system's heyday, however, the setting of performance targets was quite a rigorous process that pushed the ministries to set precise targets that stretched their ambitions and clarified lines of accountability,[148] and thousands of staff participated in workshops about the system.[149] The very strong political sponsorship of the Performance Contracting system, particularly in its early years, created a strong incentive to perform well on the assessment to receive favorable attention and avoid public criticism.[150] The thirteenth-month salary bonus was actually paid to staff of the top-performing ministry (although one source reports that this practice ended after two years), but no formal sanctions were ever levied against low performers.[151] It is also widely agreed that the system was effective in channeling the enthusiasm and political pressure of the period into an impetus for bureaucratic action and helping to focus organizational cultures more toward results.[152]

That said, in practice, the application of Performance Contracting still fell somewhat short of the systematic means of delivering performance-linked incentives its designers had envisioned. Despite a relatively propitious fiscal environment that minimized budget disruptions, delayed budget releases and other exogenous factors often prevented the achievement of targets; although the assessment included space for discussion of mitigating factors, this undermined the perceived objectivity of the resulting scores.[153] Some officials perceived that the incentives built into the system pushed organizations over time toward setting easy targets[154] or said that it was taken "quite seriously in the beginning until people knew how to play the game."[155] Others reported that there were "a lot of accusations about soft targets" in centralized ministries with administrative remits, whereas service delivery-oriented ministries, such as Health or Agriculture, faced targets that were more tangible and harder to affect.[156] A government-appointed expert review panel found in 2010 that the "setting of targets had not been well coordinated and that the PC process was not in tandem with the budget process hence impeding on performance improvement efforts."[157] A 2011 survey of 108 officials in one ministry captured both the salience of the Performance Contracting system and the ambivalence of attitudes about its effectiveness: while a majority (57 percent) of respondents felt that performance contracting "played a significant role in service delivery," only 38 percent agreed that the public ranking system enhanced performance, while an almost equal share (37 percent) disagreed.[158]

The second key component of the government's results-based management strategy was its rollout of Rapid Results Initiatives (RRIs). Based on a model developed by a private consultancy that the World Bank had previously introduced in several other countries, each RRI consisted of a concerted effort by a government institution to achieve a measurable improvement on a priority target within one hundred days.[159] These targets were selected by institutional leadership, who received significant technical support from externally hired coaches based out of a central secretariat (selected and trained by the private consultancy firm) in both design and implementation.[160] The RRIs were introduced on a pilot basis in 2004 based on the externally defined, private-sector-oriented model but were adapted to Kenya's governmental context. The former national coordinator of the RRI program explained that the initial pilots of the RRI were expensive (largely due to the use of external coaches) and required adaptation: "I looked at the tool and reshaped it reconceptualized it to fit the public service environment. I had to change a lot of basic working approaches. There are a number of things I introduced to ensure that it worked within a public sector environment, I changed the nomenclature, I roped in the Minister in the process, and roped in the highest level of the bureaucracy and that made it work."[161]

With these adaptations, strong backing from senior political leadership, and eventually a circular enshrining RRIs as government policy and mandating institutions to adopt them, RRIs were soon scaled up and implemented widely throughout central government.[162]

The RRIs and Performance Contracting system were intended to complement each other: RRI targets were often chosen from the targets listed on the institution's Performance Contract (which were, in turn, drawn from its annual work plan), and the pressure to achieve these targets exerted by the Performance Contracting system helped generate demand and willingness from institutions to work with the coaches and PSRDS on the RRIs.[163] Although the process was designed to be driven as much as possible by demand for support from the implementing institutions and to articulate with the Performance Contracting system, the coaches and PSRDS staff—who were not involved in Performance Contracting—also pushed them to select suitable targets for their RRIs. As one former official involved in implementing RRIs described: "So the process of RRI was: do you have a PC—a defined performance contract? What are the targets in that performance contract? And you then pick the targets and see how you break them down into 100-day initiatives where we see progress towards achieving that target. So the [performance contract] targets were not taken as gospel truth . . . even if they'd been set in the PC, [the coaches would] try and make them as results-oriented as possible."[164]

Once these targets were agreed upon, there would be both a technical-level and a political-level launch for each RRI as part of a broader communication strategy before, during, and after the initiative.[165] This communication strategy also included the public celebration of successful initiatives. The steps taken to achieve the target varied from case to case but often included action within the organization as well as the convening of stakeholders from outside the organization.[166] The RRIs also typically aimed to take actions that did not incur significant additional costs for the organization (beyond already budgeted staff and operations), so significant expenditures or transfers of resources did not feature prominently in RRIs.[167] One former official described how staff assigned to the project would work seven-day weeks and skip public holidays throughout the one-hundred-day period; such was the intensity of the work.[168]

The RRIs are widely viewed as having been successful in many respects. There were numerous instances when organizations made significant improvements in various service delivery metrics, from increasing antiretroviral drug uptake to reducing passport delays and reducing water leakage and theft.[169] One donor review in 2011 reported that sixty-five central government institutions had run RRIs.[170] Another, in 2012, reported that the one-hundred-day objectives had been delivered in 90 percent of RRIs (although this figure also includes local governments[171]). Over time, the initial cohort of private sector trainers conducted training-of-trainers sessions, leading to over two hundred individuals being trained in how to coach RRIs with the intention of enabling organizations to run RRIs themselves without external prompting or support.[172] Yet, while broadly successful, one expert also expressed skepticism about the potential gains from focusing on short-term improvements: "You don't change the culture through [an RRI] . . . you require changes in the systems. And the systems . . . just don't happen overnight."[173] An evaluation of the Results for Kenya program as a whole (including both RRIs and Performance Contracting) found positive but incremental improvements in the use of results-based management practices, staff attitudes and behavior, and service delivery over the course of the program.[174] Kenya also received several awards from the UN, African Union, and Harvard University Ash Center between 2007 and 2010 in recognition of the performance improvements associated with the Performance Contracting system and RRIs and its results-based management reforms more broadly.[175] These two reforms were also relatively inexpensive, with one donor report stating that the "average cost per RRIs exercise or PC adoption was around £5,300"—although it is unclear what costs are included in this estimate.[176]

The enthusiasm for RRIs in central government peaked in 2007, shortly before the violence-plagued 2007 elections disrupted reform momentum, occasioned a change of government, and eventually shifted most reform energy to local governments and devolution after the new constitution of 2010.[177] While both RRIs and Performance Contracts nominally continued to be in use in central government for years following the 2007 election, the intensity of their use reportedly dropped off significantly.[178] After the Jubilee administration took office in 2013, a new cycle of Performance Contracts were signed for 2013/2014, but no annual evaluations were published, and even public signings appeared to have ceased subsequently.[179] Both tools did, however, play a significant role in devolution reforms, with RRIs (from 2009) and Performance Contracts (from 2014) being rolled out as tools for improvement at the local government level throughout the 2010s.[180] While the use of these tools in local government falls outside the scope of this book, their spread speaks to the generally positive views of them during the Results for Kenya reform era.

The third major plank of this reform era was a renewed effort to reinvigorate the Performance Appraisal System (PAS). In 2003–2004, the structure and content of the appraisal system for rank-and-file officers were reviewed, and in 2006–2007, it changed again, with an emphasis on linking individual targets to departmental work plans and to the Performance Contracts of the institution's leadership, and on attaching rewards and sanctions to measured performance.[181] The PAS and Performance Contracts were thus envisioned as part of an integrated National Performance Management Framework and human resources management strategy.[182]

However, this effort at revitalizing the PAS met with little success. Muriu found that while some managers reported that the content of appraisals was consulted during promotion decisions, there were widespread perceptions that the information in them was manipulated or subjective, that poor ratings were almost never given, and that rewards and sanctions were nonexistent, with one manager reporting that "sometimes officers only fill the PAS forms when there is an advertisement for a promotion that they are interested in applying for."[183] Interviewees and donor reports also echoed the sentiment that there was little differentiation in appraisal scores and few consequences for poor performance,[184] and that this was due to the nature of civil service work:

What happened with that new system is that not everything deliverable ended up in the appraisal. . . . some people ended up setting targets on very easy things achievable, which are then measured. But you also end up doing a lot of other things which are not actually in your performance [appraisal] . . . 90 percent of what I do, and what I'm engaged in is not in part of those targets by nature of the public, so really . . . the whole thing is . . . mechanical. . . . So I'm more or less saying that at the end of the day, really, it doesn't really make a lot of sense to have these targets at the beginning of the year, which you put two or three, but what you end up doing is not what you . . . what you have planned to do. Theoretically it makes good planning sense . . . but by the nature of the actual practice in the office, it's not. That's why at the end of the day, everybody ends up getting 100 percent.[185]

This state of broad compliance with little meaningful impact continued into the following decade. A survey carried out in 2012 found that, while 88 percent of respondents said they had written descriptions of the criteria on which their performance was evaluated and 82 percent said they had a written performance appraisal at least once a year, only 15 percent broadly agreed that their organization "reward[ed] excellent professional achievement" (answers of 4 or 5 on a 5-point Likert scale; 69 percent broadly disagreed), 40 percent broadly agreed that "disciplinary actions have been impartially applied" (40 percent broadly disagreed), and 38 percent broadly agreed that "disciplinary action have been effective tool [sic] for motivating staff to perform well" (35 percent broadly disagreed).[186]

The intended linkages between the PAS and the strategic planning and Performance Contracting systems also failed to materialize, with one donor report stating, "The Government's own review of performance contracting carried out in 2010, revealed that there is disparity between PC and other performance management tools."[187] Another explained that "a National Performance Management Framework was developed and approved by Cabinet but critically was not fully implemented."[188]

The Results for Kenya program also included several other minor components. It envisioned the creation of Ministerial Management Units to serve as ministry-level hubs for performance improvement and reform implementation. A handful were created, but most were not. Those that were created had unclear roles, failed to attract good staff, overlapped with the authority of other units, and lacked champions.[189] Government institutions were required to create service charters outlining the services they offered, how to access them, and timelines for delivery.[190] By 2010, it appeared that these largely existed but with little public

TABLE A.2 Content of civil service reforms in Kenya

	Civil Service Reform Prog. I & II, 1993–2002	Economic Recovery Strategy / Results for Kenya (2003–2007)	Public Service Transf. Strategy (2010–2014)	Public Service Transf. Framework (2017–)
Individual performance mgmt.				
Leadership performance agreements		✓	✓	
Individual staff appraisal & performance management	✓	✓	✓	✓
Org. mgmt. and capacity				
Org. reviews/ perf. improv. plans/ perf. mgmt.		✓	✓	✓
Performance improvement funds				
Service delivery-focused reforms				
Client-focused reforms		✓	✓	✓
Sector-driven reforms		✓	✓	
Salaries and structures				
Staff redundancies & org. restructuring	✓	✓		
Pay regrading/ reform	✓	✓		
Other reforms				
Cross-government coordination			✓	✓
Other				

Source: Author's synthesis based on document review and interviews.

awareness or compliance with the standards.[191] The program also envisioned the further reduction of staff numbers, salary reform, and reduction of the number of ministries,[192] but none of this actually happened.[193]

The disputed 2007 election and the violence that followed brought a sudden halt to the momentum that the 2003–2007 era of civil service reforms had built. At the political level, the postelection settlement involved the creation of a coalition government, with Kibaki continuing to serve as President and Raila Odinga serving in the newly created office of prime minister. This led to the promulgation of a new constitution in 2010, which (among other changes) mandated a sweeping wave of decentralization reforms that would consume most reform attention for the coming decade—and are outside the scope of this book. The coalition government ended with the 2013 elections that brought Uhuru Kenyatta into office as president at the head of the Jubilee Alliance. He would remain president for the remainder of this book's study period (through 2019).

Civil service reform efforts during this 2007–2013 transitional period were marked both by rupture and continuity. The successes of 2003–2007 were facilitated by strong and relatively undivided support from the highest political levels and a prioritization of central government reforms. After 2007, there were no formal policy changes, but central-level civil service reforms implicitly took a backseat to the negotiations around the new constitution, the devolution process that followed, and campaigning in the run-up to the 2013 election. The bureaucratic units responsible for driving the 2003–2007 reforms were reorganized twice and shifted from the Office of the President to the Office of the Prime Minister for the 2008–2012 period,[194] further disrupting momentum and diluting the unity of political sponsorship of reforms.

Despite these changes, implementation of both the Performance Contracting system and the Rapid Results Initiatives continued during this period, as discussed above. Key planning and strategy documents—the long-term Vision 2030 Strategy (created in 2005), the Medium Term Plan I (2008–2012), and the Results for Kenya/Public Sector Reform Programme I (2006–2010)—remained essentially unchanged with respect to central government reforms, and programmatic activities related to them continued (if at a somewhat reduced intensity).[195] Perhaps most importantly, in 2010, a Public Service Transformation Strategy (PSTS) was released by the Public Service Transformation Department (PSTD), a unit housed within the Office of the Prime Minister that had become the driving unit behind civil service reforms.

Covering the period 2010–2014 and complemented by the donor-funded Public Sector Reform Programme II (2010–2013), the PSTS both sought to institutionalize and continue the reforms of the results-based management era and to map out the next generation of reforms. Its architects saw it as linking backward to Vision 2030 and forward to the new constitution, which was being developed in parallel and came into force in the same year.[196] In terms of institutionalizing previous waves of reforms, both Performance Contracting and RRIs continued to be implemented at lower intensity in central government but with the focus shifting increasingly toward rolling them out to local governments. A Policy Steering Committee on Performance Management was created in 2011 to continue to try to connect the institutional strategic planning, Performance Contracting, and PAS systems,[197] which had not been attempted but not achieved in the previous reform wave.[198] As discussed above, the use of Performance Contracts and RRIs tailed off in central government, especially under the new administration from 2013, and there is little evidence that the PAS became more effective. During this period, the government did, however, manage to establish Ministerial Management Units in all central government institutions,[199] although little information is available on their effectiveness. It also consolidated existing government training institutions under the umbrella of the Kenya School of Government in 2012 as part of a broader effort to improve training in results-based management as well as transformative leadership and public service ethics,[200] although, again, little information is available on its effectiveness.

In the years following the 2013 elections, most reform attention shifted to devolution and the county governments, with relatively less focus on reform at the central level.[201] However, this period also witnessed the rollout of one of the most successful reform initiatives: Huduma Centers, or one-stop shops for accessing a range of services from both central government institutions and county governments. The Huduma Center initiative was formally launched in 2013 by President Kenyatta but originated in discussions within PSRDS around 2008–2009, was influenced by a training on alternative service delivery methods by the Commonwealth Secretariat, a study visit to Brazil, and was included in the 2010 PSTS plan.[202] The name Huduma, which means "service" in Swahili, also referenced the subtitle of the Results for Kenya program, which was "Huduma Bora Haki Yako," meaning "good service is your right."[203]

Huduma Centers were intended to increase the accessibility of services to citizens by providing physical access points for a range of services under one roof, with clear procedures and a customer-centric management and culture. Located in dozens of sites nationwide, often in post offices, the centers were to be managed by a dedicated management team with a central secretariat, with each government institution that offers services responsible for staffing and managing its own counter at the center.[204] Centralized monitoring by closed-circuit cameras, public counters, and payment by mobile money transfers reduce the scope for corruption.[205] The centers themselves included automated feedback mechanisms for clients, center managers reported weekly on performance to the central secretariat, and the secretariat produced quarterly rankings both of centers and of the government institutions that offered services within them.[206]

The rollout of Huduma Centers during this period was widely viewed as successful, albeit with some challenges. Centers were operating in forty-one of forty-seven counties as of 2017, with five in Nairobi,[207] and were subsequently rolled out to all counties,[208] as per the initial target.[209] Staffing, budgeting, and coordination challenges with the government institutions that offer services in them reportedly proved challenging, with some centers understaffed or able to offer fewer services than they would like, but by 2017, around thirty thousand transactions were being conducted per day nationwide, with steps being taken to make more services available online and via mobile.[210]

The remainder of the central government reform agenda for 2013–2019 was relatively low-key, with most major new initiatives, such as a Capacity Assessment and Rationalization of the Public Service program and the 2017 passing of a new Public Service Commission Act being driven mainly by the requirements of the devolution process.[211] The key institutions for designing and delivering reforms were repeatedly moved and restructured, being housed in the Ministry of Devolution and Planning from 2013–2015 and eventually settling in the Ministry of Public Service, Youth, and Gender Affairs from 2015 onward.[212] A President's Delivery Unit was created in 2016 to oversee the delivery of key policy priorities but delegated all central government reform oversight to this ministry.[213] A wide range of other reform activities were outlined in the 2013–2017 Sector Plan for Public Sector Reforms (part of the second Medium-Term Development Plan) and its successor plan, the 2017–2022 Public Service Transformation Framework, ranging from improved training and leadership to better record management, harmonization of service conditions, business process reengineering, and institutionalization of results-based management.[214] While spanning a wide range of planned activities and functions, at the time of writing, there was relatively little available information about their implementation or impact, with the bulk of reform attention during this period being put into the devolution process.

NIGERIA

Nigeria's history of federal-level, performance-oriented reforms in its democratic era began in 1999 with the election of President Olusegun Obasanjo after a transition from military rule. While the period from 1999 to 2019 is the main focus of this book's analysis, Nigeria had also undertaken two important sets of reforms to its federal civil service under the military government in the late 1980s and 1990s that serve as important context for the postdemocratization reforms.

The first of these reforms began in 1988 with the establishment of the Dotun Philips Reform Commission and the Civil Service Reorganization Decree of 1988 (widely referred to as Decree 43), which codified its recommendations. While drawing on some managerialist ideas that dated back to the 1974 Udoji Commission, the overriding theme of the Decree 43 reform was a push from then-head of state General Ibrahim Babangida to transition from a British-style parliamentarian civil service that was centrally regulated but formally quite independent from political leaders to a more American-style, presidential system with more direct control of ministries by the president.[215] The reform combined a set of linked measures: the abolishment of the Office of the Head of Civil Service of the Federation (OHCS-F) and the transfer of recruitment and career management functions to ministries; restricting individual career paths so that each bureaucrat would remain within a single ministry for their whole career to encourage specialization; and increasing political control of the bureaucracy by making ministers (rather than permanent secretaries) the accounting officers for their ministries and making the appointment of permanent secretaries at the president's discretion.[216]

The Decree 43 reforms were largely reversed after 1994 when the new head of state, General Sani Abacha, created the Ayida Review Panel. The Decree 43 reforms were widely perceived as driven by political imperatives, vulnerable to corruption, and detrimental to merit-based hiring—perceptions that were subsequently echoed by the Panel's diagnoses of poor morale and widespread ineffectiveness in the civil service—and were heavily resisted by many civil servants.[217] Unconvinced of the need for the reforms and needing support from within the Civil Service, General Abacha's view was reportedly to "let the old people who understand come and help us to re-jig the system."[218] He chose a traditionalist civil servant to lead the Panel, which subsequently recommended the reversal of the Decree 43 reforms as well as some pay reforms and a set of new accountability and integrity measures.[219] However, many of the recommendations were "neither firm nor assertive," as they frequently employed language that was unclear or potentially interpreted as permissive of existing policies.[220] Aside from the reversal of Decree 43 and an increase in minimum wages for civil servants, the Ayida Panel reforms were not widely implemented.[221] Though it helped restore the more familiar personnel management structures, there is little evidence that the Ayida Panel led to improvements in the performance-related deficits it and earlier reviews had diagnosed. While both Decree 43 and the Ayida Panel were initiated prior to democratization in 1999 and are out of this book's scope of analysis, the issues they raised regarding bureaucratic structure and the political-administrative interface became recurring themes and fed into reform debates in the following years.

After President Olusegun Obasanjo took office in 1999 in democratic elections, an intensive process of reflection and reform formulation began that comprised both internally driven thinking and external advice and benchmarking.[222] This would last until the start of Obasanjo's second term in office in 2003, when his renewed mandate finally lifted some of the political constraints that had hampered his scope for action during his first administration.[223] However, some reform activities did occur during this period aimed at resetting and reorienting the civil service's day-to-day operations after the period of military rule, which had caused a range of deep dysfunctions. This included the appointment of new permanent secretaries and orienting them toward improved service delivery, weekly meetings with permanent secretaries, some organizational restructuring to avoid duplication of functions and streamline communication channels, establishing clear political-bureaucratic relationships after the period of military rule, and (nonperformance-linked) pay and pension reforms. These measures reportedly led to some improvements in discipline and performance, beginning the process of restoring the Civil Service after years of military rule.[224] Overall, though, these four years were a period dominated by thinking and planning rather than major new reforms.

The internal aspect of the reform planning process began with a review committee appointed by President Obasanjo shortly after taking office and led by Professor Adebayo Adedeji to recommend reforms to improve the performance of the public service.[225] These commenced with a series of lectures during a weeks-long retreat for groups of permanent secretaries and directors from across the civil service aimed at beginning the process of reorienting the public service toward stronger public service delivery, integrity, and work culture and continued with the compilation of a harmonized report detailing areas needing reform.[226] In parallel to this, by mid-2000, the Ayida Panel finished its implementation of the first phase of reforms and presented a memo to the Federal Executive Council proposing a second phase that would involve some additional "tinkering with the structures," but this was rejected as not ambitious enough.[227] Under Head of Civil Service Alhaji Yayale Ahmed, the Management Services Office and OHCS-F then led a planning process which resulted in another memo being submitted to the Federal Executive Council in June 2001, which led to the Head of Civil Service being given a mandate to design and implement a new reform strategy.[228]

During these planning processes in 2000 and 2001, Nigeria also received technical support and high-level visits from the Commonwealth Secretariat, World Bank, and UK government, and conducted study tours to various Commonwealth countries as well as Brazil and the United States.[229] Among the most important elements of this support was a visit from Wendy Thomson (then head of the UK's Office of Public Sector Reform) to discuss her experience reforming service delivery in the UK[230] and a panel discussion in London with Nigerian academics and experts from various Commonwealth countries.[231] These interactions were influential in shaping the thinking of the technocrats in charge of designing Nigeria's reform approach during these years. This thinking merged into the research and thinking happening internally within the Civil Service, eventually leading to a Public Service Reform Strategy document that was finalized and adopted in May 2003, shortly after Obasanjo's reelection.[232] The implementation of this Strategy, with high-level political backing from Obasanjo and his high-profile Economic Management Team, would make 2003–2007 the most active period of reform in Nigeria's modern history.

The centerpiece of these reform efforts was the creation of the Bureau of Public Sector Reform (BPSR) in 2003. The BPSR was created with the aim of professionalizing and institutionalizing the initiation of reforms within the government.[233] One official closely involved in creating the Strategy attributed this approach, in part, to lessons from the external engagement during the reform planning phase, which impressed on Nigerian officials the limitations of once-a-decade commissions as a strategy for driving performance improvement.[234] The BPSR immediately got to work on a set of challenges related to organizational structure and personnel policy, including eliminating or merging a number of organizations; standardizing the internal structure of ministries; retrenchment of staff in outdated or redundant roles or with poor disciplinary or performance records; removal of ghost workers; creation of an Integrated Personnel and Payroll Information System to reduce corruption and delays in payment of salaries; a series of pay reforms to monetize fringe benefits, link compensation to evaluation of job criteria, and increase minimum salaries; pension reform and introduction of a contributory pension scheme; and introducing a National Health Insurance Scheme in which public sector employees were encouraged to enroll.[235] In a direct sense, these changes were mostly aimed at fiscal savings but with improved performance—via freeing up funds to spend on service delivery and improving job satisfaction and conditions of work for public sector employees—as the ultimate goal.

These reforms were successfully implemented, for the most part, and did address many of the underlying challenges facing public organizations and employees (as well as making fiscal savings)—as documented by a detailed 2015 review of past reform efforts conducted by the BPSR itself.[236] However, there is little evidence that they contributed directly to an improvement in performance. For instance, the review concluded that: "Many public servants still feel that there is wide disparity in pay scales. . . . There is no link between pay and performance and also no clear link between job evaluation and grading . . . the pay reform has not appreciably increased the purchasing power of public servants and has not reduced corruption in the Service."[237] Similarly, even the process of retrenching staff resulted in fewer savings than anticipated due not just to severance payments but also to industrial and legal action that resulted in some terminated staff being brought back on the payroll, creating a "slightly dysfunctional" chemistry in the system.[238] Other aspects of these reforms, such as reducing the number of organizations with duplicative functions, were only partially successful and would continue to be significant concerns for subsequent generations of reformers.

In parallel to these system-wide reforms, this period also saw a large number of sector-specific reforms driven both from the center of government and from organizations themselves. The BPSR not only helped design and drive some of these but also attempted to support endogenously driven efforts by organizations themselves to improve by creating guidance for organizations on how to design and implement their own reforms—"so it was not a question of everybody must move at the same pace."[239] By 2007, this had led to a number of emerging "oases" of excellence—albeit still perceived as isolated success stories rather than system-level change—and this experience would help shape the formulation of the next phase of reforms towards the end of Obasanjo's administration.

Another major reform—linked to the BPSR but institutionally separate from it—was the creation of SERVICOM in 2004 to try to drive a citizen-centric approach to service delivery across the government. The idea was initiated after a conversation between President Obasanjo and Prime Minister Tony Blair of the UK, which led "to Thomson's visit to Nigeria in 2001.[240] In 2003 a diagnostic study on service delivery challenges in five institutions was undertaken by a joint British-Nigerian team led by Thomson and published in early 2004 under the title "Service Delivery in Nigeria: A Roadmap," with damning findings about the difficulties faced by people trying to access services and recommendations for improvement drawn, in part, from the UK experience.[241] In March 2004, a presidential retreat led to a "service compact" declaration and the creation of SERVICOM as an organization housed within the presidency.[242] UK DFID provided technical assistance as well as the bulk of the organization's funding from its inception through 2009.[243]

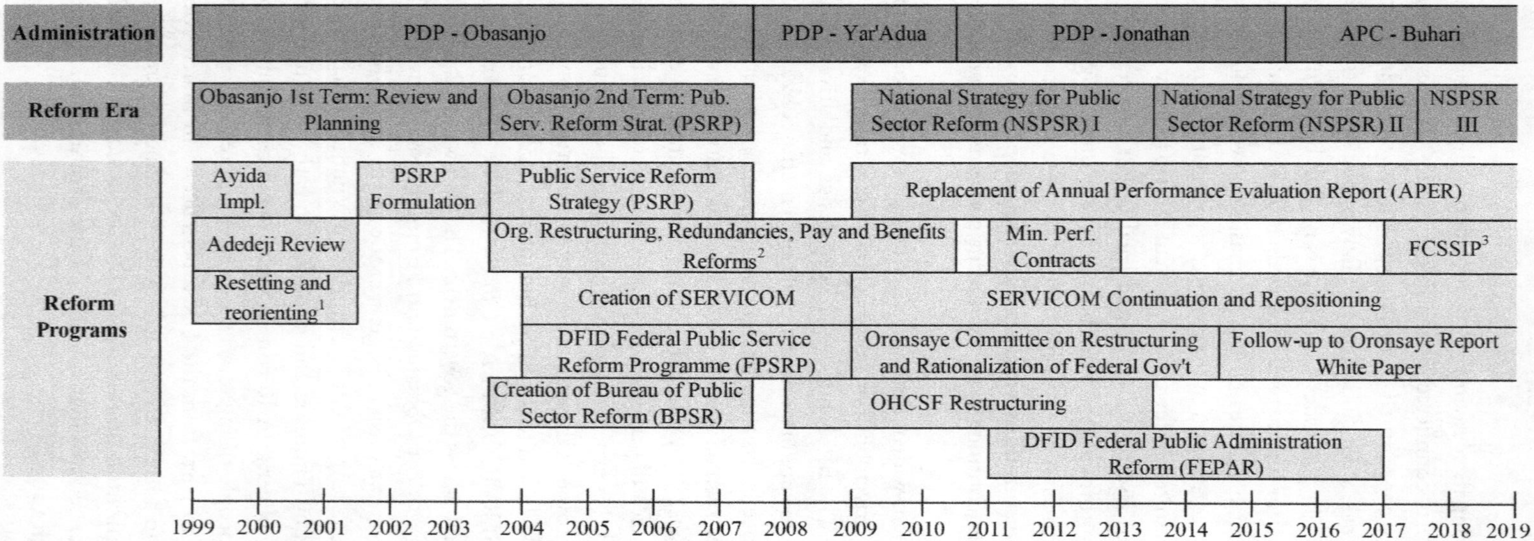

FIGURE A.3 Timeline of Civil Service Reforms in Nigeria

Source: Author's synthesis based on document review and interviews.

[1] Post-military rule changes in day-to-day operation of civil service, including appointment of new permanent secretaries and new political-bureaucratic communication routines

[2] Includes: Monetization of fringe benefits (2003); Pension reform (2004); Edozien Panel (2004); Shonekan Panel (2005); Integrated Personnel and Payroll Information System (IPPIS, 2007); Belgore Committee (2009); Diejomaoh Committee (2010)

[3] Federal Civil Service Strategy and Implementation Plan (FCSSIP)

In its first few years, SERVICOM combined several main tools to try to improve service delivery. First, ministries, departments, and agencies (MDAs) were mandated by the president to create service charters that identified their mandate, vision and mission statements, a list of services provided, and standards (cost, timelines, documents required, etc.) for the provision of each service. These were to be posted publicly and had the dual aim of focusing managerial attention on service delivery and improving public awareness and ability to demand their service delivery entitlements.[244] Second, SERVICOM established a system of nodal officers in Ministerial SERVICOM Units who would function as SERVICOM liaisons in each ministry to drive implementation, monitor progress, and report back to SERVICOM.[245] Within each ministry, these officers reported directly to the minister—rather than the permanent secretary, as would be standard—to give them more direct access to political leadership.[246] Third, SERVICOM created a process of organization-specific service evaluations in which SERVICOM staff would identify a particular service window within an organization; write to them to inform them that a team would come to conduct a diagnostic study; gather data through interviews, surveys, visual observation, inspection of records, and/or mystery shopper exercises; suggest "quick-win" immediate improvements; write a formal report for the ministry, including a performance rating and recommendations; and present the report back to ministry management before making it public.[247] Fourth, from 2006, a training center— the SERVICOM Institute—was set up to provide training on enhancing service delivery.[248] While SERVICOM also conducted some other activities, like public awareness campaigns and providing office facilities for nodal officers, these four sets of interventions comprised the core of its work in its first five years.

During the period from 2004 to 2009, SERVICOM was mostly successful at implementing these core activities but seems to have been only moderately successful—albeit with perceptions varying across individuals and sources—in improving service delivery. In terms of implementation, the majority of relevant institutions established their service charters and appointed nodal officers within a year or two of SERVICOM's establishment, even if they were sometimes only short documents.[249] The BPSR reported that (as of the later date of 2015) 80 percent of organizations with citizen-facing services had service charters, eighty-four organizations had established nodal offices, evaluations had been conducted on 202 service windows in twenty-four organizations, and over ten thousand individuals had been trained by the SERVICOM Institute.[250]

There is mixed evidence about how successful SERVICOM was at improving actual service delivery outcomes during its first few years. Several showcase pilot interventions demonstrated significant improvements, and the issue of citizens' experiences of service delivery became a central consideration for the government where previously it had been absent.[251] Outside of these pilot interventions, there were many specific cases of improvement that can be pointed to, "but these are largely unreported and have not yet been taken to scale. . . . In most cases, the improvements have endured, but the gains have been reversed in some other instances."[252] One former head of the BPSR stated, "I think the effect of it has been limited. It hasn't been a complete waste of time but the effect has been limited."[253] He went on to explain that the approach of using presidential sponsorship to create mandates for ministries evoked a compliance mentality in many places:

> That's the first thing they did, was go to the Federal Executive Council to ask that everybody must have a SERVICOM office. So of course everybody set up a SERVICOM office . . . people stuck the SERVICOM banner on the nearest toilet, and nobody cared what was going on inside so it was just appearing to comply, which they did. The next thing they did was [say] "oh the nodal officer should report straight to the minister, period," so here is the permanent secretary rubbing his hands and thinking, "ok so you're a nodal officer, you are an assistant director, you're going to bypass me the permanent secretary to go report to the minister and you expect me to release funds for you to do any work . . . never going to happen." So again, it antagonized the system against itself . . . Fine. Have a SERVICOM office [and] post to the most problematic person in the office in that place to get him out of the way. Make sure you don't release any funds to them . . . [SERVICOM] developed some really good tools. They developed a service delivery assessment tool which was quite good but again, they didn't manage to connect that to the purpose of the organization and where the leadership of the organization is going. So you can do a kind of assessment that says, "ok service delivery is poor in such and such a place," but then if you don't address it at the policy and leadership level that sees service delivery as a key measure of how well an organization is doing then you have a disconnect, period, and that's exactly, I think, what has happened with SERVICOM.[254]

This perspective was echoed by another official:

> At that time when the SERVICOM reform started, it was a top-down approach, [it] even started from the presidency. He called the ministers and council and told them "this is the directive, this is what you should do." And I think there was a little bit of . . . They felt they were being imposed. . . . It came from the British and . . . well, there was compliance. But [also] the undertone of "[we] really don't understand what this is all about." . . . So, it took a little bit of time,

to educate, to communicate . . . stakeholder engagement at that time was not very, very strong. Instead, the focus was on trying to establish the unit, set up charters . . . so yes, people went ahead to do it, but the minute the president, that is the president who brought in the initiative, left, it now became a struggle to try to explain to the incoming government every time there is a change of administration that this is what SERVICOM stands for.[255]

Another officer who had interacted with SERVICOM through their role in a service delivery organization reported, however, that the external scrutiny provided both useful ideas and information as well as providing leverage for improvement-minded individuals within the organization. But this officer also felt that their organization was more advanced in its own reform activities than what SERVICOM was demanding and also perceived that SERVICOM focal officers around the service were struggling to do more than serve a minimal reporting function: "Where SERVICOM wanted us all to be, you couldn't do it without strong push and support. If I was a focal officer in a big ministry where people don't even care about service it will be difficult for me to, just depending on my level, to push through for change. I would definitely need senior management support and a stronger voice at the top to make any real change happen."[256] There is, thus, considerable uncertainty about how much impact SERVICOM had on actual measures of performance in service delivery during this period.

SERVICOM's operations suffered a dramatic drop-off following the exit of President Obasanjo in 2007 and the end of DFID funding in 2009—"Everything basically ground to a halt."[257] This was, perhaps, compounded by the dependence on political support from the president to push organizations to be responsive to SERVICOM and a lack of coordination and an implicit degree of competition between SERVICOM and the BPSR.[258]

Overall, the reforms embarked on during this period made some significant improvements and set the stage for many of Nigeria's later reforms, but with limited scope of impact and poor sustainability after the departure of the Obasanjo administration. While high-level political support and pressure for reform had been an important driving force during 2003–2007, it also undermined the ownership and sustainability of reforms from within the bureaucracy.[259] As part of its pressure for reform, some senior members of Obasanjo's administration sometimes made harsh public criticisms of civil servants, which "eroded the service['s] support to some of the reforms that they did, so consequently when they exited the service was more inclined to pull [the reforms] down."[260] One senior civil servant and scholar involved in driving reforms during this period captures the ambivalent effects of these reform efforts: "By and large, our sense [was] that as at the time that Obasanjo was going, these oases of excellence were more aligned to the personalities that were driving the reform. Secondly, [the oases of excellence] were too few and far between, so it didn't quite create that significant, if you will, systemic change that the system requires in order to move. But so much really changed and so much has been built on ever since."[261]

The post-Obasanjo direction of reforms was meant to be guided by the 2009 National Strategy for Public Sector Reform (NSPSR), developed by the BPSR as the successor plan to 2003's Public Service Reform Strategy. The NSPSR was intended as an overall coordinating mechanism for reforms ongoing across the public service, compiling many reforms ongoing at the sector level as well as a broad set of activities rolled over from previous reform efforts.[262] However, the NSPSR was never considered by the high-level Steering Committee on Reform (SCR), nor was it sent for approval to the Federal Executive Council.[263] Its successor document, the National Strategy for Public Sector Reform (NSPSR) II, was commissioned in late 2013 and only given approval in early 2015, just before the 2015 elections, which saw a change in administration.[264] This was indicative of a broader floundering and fragmentation of the reform agenda in the post-Obasanjo years. Selected sector-driven reforms did proceed during this time. OHCS-F and associated agencies underwent a restructuring, and in 2009, term limits for permanent secretaries were introduced (a reform that was subsequently reversed in 2015 upon the election of President Muhammadu Buhari).[265] However, the coherence that had characterized the 2003–2007 period dissipated somewhat, and reform efforts were fragmented across different parts of the federal government.

One strand of this next phase of reforms was a set of performance management policies announced in 2009 by the Federal Civil Service Commission (FCSC). The main component of this was the replacement of the preexisting Annual Performance Evaluation Report (APER) with the new Automated Performance Appraisal System (AUTOPAS). APER was a standard annual appraisal process for rank-and-file civil servants used as an input into the promotion process run by FCSC but had been criticized for nepotism and corruption[266] as well as for near-universally positive reviews.[267] As one senior official and researcher lamented, "APER is not useful, it does not assess anyone."[268] While the new system was intended to be operational by 2014, APER remained in place through 2019[269] (the end of this book's study period) and continued to be subject to the same flaws that had motivated the announcement of its replacement.[270]

Alongside this, in 2012, the FCSC, OHCS-F, and National Planning Commission (NPC) instituted a system of ministerial performance contracts that committed ministers to achieve a set of negotiated targets and were

TABLE A.3 Content of civil service reforms in Nigeria

	Post-Military Rule Resetting and Reorienting, 1999–2001	Bureau of Public Sector Initial Phase, 2003–2007	SERVI-COM Initial Phase, 2003–2009	OHCSF Restruct., 2008–13	Replace-ment of Annual Perf. Eval. Report (APER), 2009–	SERVI-COM Continua-tion and Reposition-ing, 2010–	Oronsaye Committee Review and White Paper and Follow-up, 2009–	Minister Perf. Contracts, 2011–2012	Federal Civil Service Strategy and Impl. Plan (FCSSIP), 2017–
Individual performance mgmt.									
Leadership performance agreements								✓	
Individual staff appraisal & performance management					✓				✓
Org. mgmt. and capacity									
Org. reviews/ perf. improv. plans/ perf. mgmt.		✓	✓			✓			
Performance improvement funds									
Service delivery-focused reforms									
Client-focused reforms			✓			✓			
Sector-driven reforms		✓	✓			✓			
Salaries and structures									
Staff redundancies & org. restructuring		✓		✓			✓		
Pay regrading/ reform		✓							✓
Other reforms									
Cross-government coordination	✓			✓		✓			
Other	✓	✓							✓

Source: Author's synthesis based on document review and interviews.

countersigned by the president. These were based on a balanced scorecard model developed by consultants KPMG for the government[271] and took into account experience with performance contracts in Kenya and other countries.[272] However, it was discontinued after one year after it was found that "not one minister met the targets that they had agreed to."[273] Ministers objected to the system's premise, making arguments along the lines of, "How can we meet these targets when you didn't release all the money for the budget, and we have no control over our staff . . . we can't hire and we can't fire, so how can you hold us accountable to something that we have no control over?"[274] This failed attempt at performance contracting had been preceded by an effort by the BPSR to create an organization-level performance management system based on a system of institutional self-assessment validated by the BPSR, which had proceeded on a pilot basis with a handful of organizations but was then superseded by the failed performance contracting system.[275]

Another main strand of reform effort in the post-Obasanjo years has been directed toward consolidating the number of government ministries, agencies, and parastatals. The main vehicle for this was a committee led by Stephen Oronsaye, inaugurated under President Yar'Adua and renewed by President Jonathan in 2011, which was charged with making recommendations on the organizational restructuring of government.[276] The Oronsaye Committee recommended a threefold reduction in the number of ministries, departments, agencies, and parastatals, many of which were argued to be redundant or no longer relevant.[277] The motivations for this reduction were partly fiscal but were also driven by an effort to avoid interinstitutional conflicts and duplication of functions.[278] These recommendations were largely accepted in a 2014 government white paper but were not implemented—in large part due to the large-scale staff redundancies and elimination of senior roles that it would entail, particularly with the 2015 election looming.[279] Upon taking office in 2015, the Buhari administration pledged to implement the Oronsaye Report, as it is widely referred to, and the BPSR began working with some of the ministries destined to be consolidated in order to map out institutional and individual roles and responsibilities in the realigned institutions.[280] However, the proposed organizational mergers and eliminations were never actually effected despite repeated pledges to implement the report.

SERVICOM also continued its efforts throughout this period after something of a lull in activity following the departures of its chief backer (President Obasanjo) and chief funder (DFID) in 2007 and 2009, respectively. During this transitional period, "most people thought the office had closed, activities were very, very low, you know at a low ebb. We basically didn't have much funding to conduct evaluations."[281] There was a five-month gap during which staff worked without salaries, as they were trying to be moved onto the regular government payroll (as salaries were previously funded mainly by DFID), with a senior officer during that time remarking, "We were left thoroughly orphaned. There was a huge gap because it didn't transit to the government."[282] The ensuing years for SERVI-COM were dominated by this effort to ensure institutional continuity, with staff lobbying and writing memos to political leaders. This resulted in a degree of rhetorical support and modest financial and administrative backing but not in the high-level political legitimacy the institution had previously enjoyed, with many staff leaving as a result[283] and "reduced activity . . . on key SERVICOM activities, due to lack of funding and political commitment."[284] As of 2015, the BPSR reported that "SERVICOM is perceived as ineffective and lacking in most quarters, therefore, it is unable to amass the momentum required to create an effective service delivery culture in MDAs."[285] SERVICOM nevertheless managed to sustain itself and eventually began to receive a (much smaller) level of financial support from DFID's Federal Public Administration Reform program from 2011. Another important step toward SERVICOM's revitalization took place in 2017 with the National Policy Dialogue on Strategies for Improving Service Delivery in Government Parastatals, Agencies and Commissions hosted by the Office of the Secretary General of the Federation, which helped reelevate its profile and led to substantive agreement on a number of next steps for the institution.[286]

Operationally, during the post-2009 period, SERVICOM maintained many of its preexisting activities, such as the institutional evaluation process, its emphasis on establishing service charters, and targeted training. However, it adjusted to its reduced level of inter-institutional authority by increasingly focusing its operations on universities and hospitals rather than the higher-profile and more powerful (and hence potentially resistant) government ministries and agencies on which much of its early effort had been focused.[287] It also launched a weekly SER-VICOM "Help Desk" radio program, in which SERVICOM's national coordinator listened to complaints about service delivery and human rights issues from callers, gave advice, and followed up on cases with the relevant institutions—combining raising public awareness with generating legitimacy for its mission within government. While SERVICOM's level of activity and prominence has not quite returned to the initial levels reached during the Obasanjo administration, it has nevertheless managed to sustain and adapt itself across a longer period than many other donor-supported initiatives.

While there were several important strands of reform effort during the period from 2007 to 2019, there was relatively limited coherence and coordination to these efforts. As noted above, the initial NSPSR and successor NSPSR II were both slow to be implemented and served more to compile stalled systemic reforms and already ongoing sector-level reforms than to launch new efforts. The NSPSR III, inaugurated in 2017, also rolled over many of these initiatives. The general sense of slow progress is revealed by the parallel sets of goals and delayed timelines in the NSPSR I and NSPSR III. NSPSR I "proposed a three-stage reform program. These stages are: (1) a rebuilding phase (2009–2011); (2) a transformation phase (2012–2015); and (3) world-class public status phase (2016–2020)."[288] Almost a decade later, the NSPSR III was also organized into nearly the same "three main phases:

- **Reinvigorating** the public service with emphasis on critical institutional changes, restoring professionalism and client focus, and delivering effective basic services by 2018.
- **Transforming** the public service into an efficient, productive, incorruptible and citizen-centred institution by 2021.
- Attaining **world-class** level of service delivery in the public service by 2025."[289]

Meanwhile, in 2017, the OHCS-F launched its own reform strategy entitled Federal Civil Service Strategy and Implementation Plan (FCSSIP, 2017–20), which aligned closely with the civil service reform pillar of the NSPSR III. This included a broad range of activities, mostly aimed at implementing previously mooted efforts that had been stalled or drifted (such as salary review, strengthening the integrated human resource database, and implementing a new performance management system), as well as a handful of new initiatives, such as training.[290] It also proposed that the individual-level performance management policies be linked to incentives, envisioning that "implementation of more effective performance management and incentives systems, and restoration of meritocracy in appointments will be accorded high priority in strategy implementation," and "a stick and carrot approach to personnel management will be adopted, whereby poor performances are sanctioned and exceptional/outstanding performances are recognised and rewarded."[291] As of the end of this book's period of coverage in 2019, these had not been implemented, and it was too early to assess the extent of progress toward the other elements of FCSSIP.

SENEGAL

As with many other countries, the fiscal crises and structural adjustment programs of the 1980s provided the context for Senegal's recent history of performance-oriented civil service reforms. Earlier reform efforts from 1960–1980 (prior to this book's temporal scope) focused primarily on questions of organizational structure and restraining personnel costs, albeit with some consideration of organizational capacity and efficiency.[292] By the early 1980s, fiscal crisis had spurred the government of Senegal to create two bodies charged with reducing and rationalizing staffing and salary expenditure in the public service, the Cellule de Contrôle des Effectifs et de la Masse Salariale (CCEMS, Workforce and Salary Control Unit), created in 1981, and the Commission de Rationalisation des Structures et des Emplois Publiques (CORASEP, Commission for the Rationalization of Public Bodies and Employment), which was created by decree in 1979 but only became operational from 1984.[293] The onset of formal structural adjustment programs soon after that saw the privatization and liberalization of much of the state, and CCEMS and CORASEP became key actors for operationalizing this within the civil service itself. One civil servant described the philosophy of the time as "less government, and better government."[294]

The CCEMS, based in the presidency, focused exclusively on controlling hiring and reducing the wage bill primarily through a hiring freeze and exercising strict powers of approval over hiring.[295] In parallel, CORASEP began to develop restructuring plans and undertook strategic organizational audits to search for sources of redundancy and possible efficiency improvements across the civil service, beginning with a mandate for all institutions to develop organograms to be used as the basis for this analysis and restructuring.[296] These activities also encompassed initial efforts at process restructuring and digitalization within the government.[297] It also ended the practice of the public service automatically hiring all the graduates of the national training schools that had historically fed their cohorts directly into government employment.[298]

These personnel management reforms also included the creation, in 1986, of Conseillers en Ressources Humaines et Organisation (CRHOs, Human Resource and Organization Councilors) and, in 1987, of Cellules de Gestion des Ressources Humaines (Human Resource Management Units) as officers and units responsible for coordinating human resource management and training within each line ministry.[299] Under its inherited French-style administration system, all human resources issues had previously been handled centrally by the Ministère de la Fonction Publique (MFP, Ministry of Public Service), which administers personnel management, and the Bureau Organisation et Méthodes (BOM, Organization and Method Bureau).[300] The BOM, in particular, was an elite unit within the civil service—one of the rare organizations in Senegal that hired using an exam-based competition[301]—that was the primary government institution responsible for introducing new reform initiatives. This reform was an effort to deconcentrate the handling of these processes by creating units that would work with the MFP and BOM to create training plans. The creation of

CRHOs was part of a broader effort to improve human resource quality and training practices across the economy (including the civil service as well as the private sector), which led the government, in 1987 and 1988, to create a set of linked institutions: the Office National de la Formation Professionnelle (ONFP, National Office of Professional Training), the Conseil National des Ressources Humaines (National Human Resource Council), and the Commission Nationale des Ressources Humaines (National Human Resource Commission).[302] Together with CORASEP, these aimed to create a system of continuing training and professional development within the civil service where none had existed previously.

The payroll reduction efforts were the most salient of these reforms, particularly in the context of structural adjustment and fiscal crisis, and these efforts encountered resistance from staff and ministers.[303] While they were largely successful during the mid-1980s in halting the increase in public employment,[304] the overall wage bill actually increased by 20 percent during this time.[305] The net effect was that CCEMS "hardly made a difference in reducing public spending."[306] CORASEP was successful in some of its programmatic activities, such as creating organograms and conducting personnel audits in large ministries, but fell short of its transformative vision—although a number of the ideas created under it would go on to inspire future strands of reform.[307] Writing for the International Labor Organization in 1995, Tall called it a "relative failure," reflecting:

> At the theoretical level, CORASEP had a mission based on an appealing plan. In reality, it has only partially responded to the objectives that were assigned to it. In effect, while it has succeeded at limiting the number of organizations and at rationalizing the allocation of tasks by putting in place organograms in all ministries, on the other hand it has not succeeded at creating an organizational culture shared by all officers in the service; one applies the measures dictated by CORASEP not out of conviction, but because they are necessary to get the ministry's budget approved. This perception has resulted in the emptying of CORASEP of all its substance.[308]

The CRHOs suffered from a range of challenges, from limited human and financial resources to being bypassed in personnel management decisions due to a lack of authority, leading CRHOs to be viewed as "secondary, even subsidiary"[309] and "marginalized"[310] in their work. The national human resource development bodies created during this time to promote human resource development also saw "more or less disappointing" results.[311] While a plan for continuing training and professional development was put in place during the late 1980s, and a version of the ONFP remained in existence, the Conseil National des Ressources Humaines had reportedly met only once as of 1995, and the Commission Nationale des Ressources Humaines was reported to lack the resources to undertake its core missions.[312] One World Bank report concluded that, altogether, "the results of civil service reform [in Senegal] have been very disappointing . . . institutional reforms in the civil service have only been partially or provisionally implemented."[313]

A new wave of reforms began in 1990, coinciding with Senegal's fourth structural adjustment program, which combined further structural personnel reforms with a set of efforts to "modernize" the state. The push to reduce payroll expenditures was renewed, driven by a combination of a voluntary severance scheme and hiring restraints, and aimed to "create the conditions simultaneously for better administrative effectiveness and better resource utilization."[314] In addition, the government put in place a program designed to push out poorly performing or underqualified officers who could not be terminated: "We can't fire you, but we are telling you that you needn't bother, you no longer have a post in the administration, we'll keep paying you if it's necessary but you won't come into the service and step on people's toes. . . . The majority of them understood and proceeded into the voluntary severance program."[315] Over the course of three years, this effort did see 3,747 public employees leave (compared to an initial target of 4,806), with limited replacement recruitment, although this represented only around 5 percent of the estimated total public workforce of approximately seventy thousand.[316] The staff reductions were intended to go hand-in-hand with a refocusing and retraining of the remaining workforce to improve productivity, which one government document described as "collective psychotherapy in the civil service."[317] However, the institutional rationalization and realignment component of the reform that was central to the productivity improvement thrust "was only partially or provisionally implemented", with the number of ministries actually increasing from nineteen in 1987 to twenty-seven in 1993.[318] In addition, one official involved in designing and implementing reforms during this time reflected: "There too, errors were committed. . . . We had the emergence of a highly performing digitalization system, lots of IT specialists were recruited and knew that they had the ability to find roles for themselves in the private sector, so they left en masse with the voluntary severance [program]. That, unfortunately, we did not anticipate, and it meant that we lost some quality officers."[319]

The voluntary retirement program was envisioned to be accompanied by a restructuring of the salary system for remaining workers, with salary increases to come exclusively through bonuses "based on the productivity and output of workers."[320] In 1995, however, Tall wrote, "In reality, we are today far from this theoretical plan. The results obtained so far do not seem to respond to the objectives

FIGURE A.4 Timeline of Civil Service Reforms in Senegal

	PS - Diouf	PDS - Wade	APR - Sall
Administration	PS - Diouf	PDS - Wade	APR - Sall
Reform Era	Human Resources Rationalization and Reform / Modernization of the State	Programme Nationale de Bonne Gouvernance	Reform Master Plans (Schemas Directeurs / Plan Senegal Emergent (PSE))

Reform Programs (timeline, years 1984–2019)

- Cellule de Contrôle des Effectifs...(CCEMS), Comm...de Rationalisation...(CORaSEP)[1]
- Voluntary Retirement & Org. Restructuring
- Introduction of staff appraisal system
- CIP-PIRSP[6]
- Programme Nationale de Bonne Gouvernance (PNBG I)
- Prog. Nat. de Bonne Gouvernance II (PNBG II)
- SDRE[8]
- Schema Directeur de Modernisation de l'Administration Publique (SDMAP)
- Conseillers en Ressources Humaines et Organisation[2]
- CME[3]
- MME[4]
- Ministère de la modernisation de l'État et de la Technologie
- Comité d'allegement et de simplification des formalités...[5]
- Creation of CGHR, ONFP, CNRH, CNRH[2]
- Poverty Reduction Strategy Paper (PRSP) I
- Poverty Reduction Strategy Paper (PRSP) II
- Performance contracts
- CMAP[11]
- Structural Adjustment Programs I-III
- Structural Adjustment Prog. IV
- European Development Fund - Support to PNBG I & II
- UNDP Support to PNBG I
- PRECABG[7]
- Development of PSE
- Plan Senegal Emergent (PSE)
- Bureau Organisation et Methodes (BOM)
- Delegation au Management Public (DMP)
- DREAT[9]
- DGR-EAT[10]
- Bureau Organisation et Methodes (BOM)

Years: 1984 1985 1986 1987 1988 1989 1990 1991 1992 1993 1994 1995 1996 1997 1998 1999 2000 2001 2002 2003 2004 2005 2006 2007 2008 2009 2010 2011 2012 2013 2014 2015 2016 2017 2018 2019

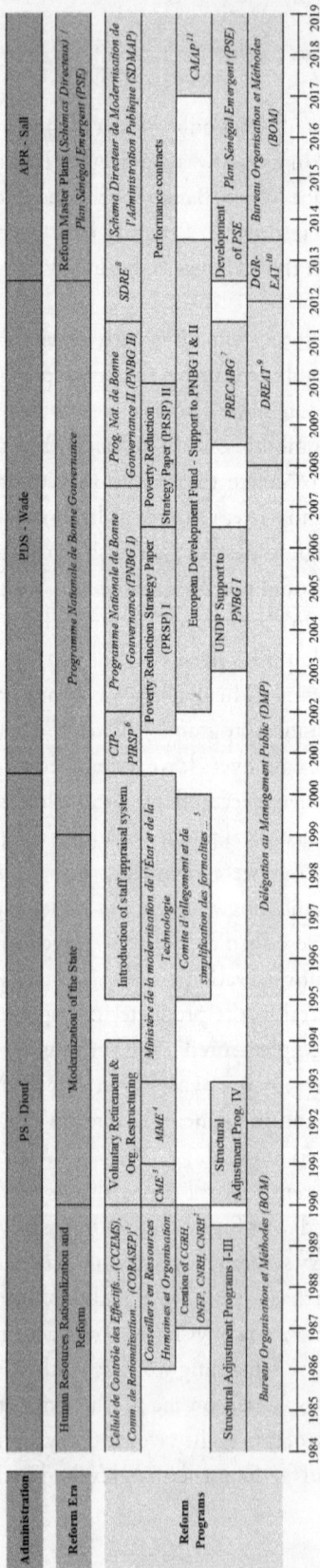

[1] Cellule de Contrôle des Effectifs et de la Masse Salariale, Commission de Rationalisation des Structures et des Emplois

[2] Cellules de Gestion des Ressources Humaines, Office National de la Formation Professionelle, Conseil National des Ressources

[3] Comité de modernisation de l'État

[4] Ministère de la Modernisation de l'Etat

[5] Comité d'allegement et de simplification des formalités et procedures administratives

[6] Comité Interministériel de Pilotage du Programme Intégré de Réforme du Secteur Public

[7] Programme de Renforcement des Capacités de Bonne Gouvernance

[8] Schema Directeur de la Réforme de l'Etat

[9] Délégation à la Réforme de l'Etat et l'assistance technique

[10] Délégation générale à la Réforme de l'Etat et à l'assistance technique

[11] Comité de modernisation de l'administration publique

FIGURE A.4 Timeline of Civil Service Reforms in Senegal

Source: Author's synthesis based on document review and interviews.

that were initially set. The voluntary severance program has not yielded the expected results, the financing of bonuses has not ensued."[321]

This period also saw performance become more central as a goal of civil service reforms in Senegal, with significant reforms to the institutions charged with leading reform and personnel management regulations. A Comité de modernisation de l'État (State Modernization Committee) was created in 1990, was subsequently upgraded to a ministry in 1991, and had its portfolio extended further in 1993 and became the Ministère de la modernisation de l'État et de la Technologie (MMET, Ministry of State Modernization and Technology), with the government seeing information technology as integral to improving internal administration as well as improving relationships with service users.[322] The early 1990s also saw the first of what would become a series of renamings and reshapings of the core institution in the Presidency responsible for introducing new civil service reforms and launching performance improvement activities. In 1992, the Bureau Organisation et Méthodes (as it had been known since its creation in 1968) was renamed the Délégation au Management Publique (DMP, Public Management Delegation), a naming shift that reflected the unit's gradual shift in focus from issues of organizational structure to human resource management and information technology,[323] and the DMP was later shifted to the MMET in 1995.

A core element of these reforms was an effort to link pay and promotion to measured performance through the creation of a new staff appraisal system. This system was to become operational in 1998, with the "definition of a performance rating scale for each employee, based on appropriate performance indicators,"[324] to create "an administration operating on the basis of clearly defined mechanisms to ensure transparency, responsibility, control, merit, and sanctions in order to increase effectiveness and reduce costs."[325] This system also had the tacit goal of eliminating "clientelist relations" within the bureaucracy[326] and was a cornerstone of the Ministry of Modernization and Technology's grand vision of gradually phasing out the career-based system of public employment in favor of a position-based system characterized by more merit-driven promotion and salary systems.[327]

The Ministry of Modernization and Technology also drove a set of reforms aimed at organizational performance. In 1995, the government created the interministerial Comité d'allègement et de simplification des formalités et procédures administratives (CASFPA, Committee on Reducing and Simplifying Rules and Administrative Procedures) spearheaded by the MMET. This committee aimed to simplify both internal and client-facing procedures,[328] many of which were left over from the colonial era and unnecessarily burdensome,[329] and "agencify" service provisions in keeping with the broader drive to liberalize the state and make it less interventionist.[330] The committee had no permanent members but was composed of a mix of BOM officers and officers from other organizations who were not paid for their work—"it was just people with a bit of good sense."[331] The Committee's work was also connected to the government's broader drive for digitalization of processes.[332] Finally, the Ministry of Modernization and Technology also led a series of seminars with other ministries that aimed to create mission statements and service delivery targets for these ministries to serve as a basis for organizational performance measurement.[333]

Most of these reforms made some progress, but the overall impacts were generally disappointing. For the staff appraisal and career progression reforms announced in 1995, the formal processes and associated training were put in place on schedule, but the system only operated as intended for two years,[334] and suffered from problems in its implementation: It was not clearly communicated, most people in the public sector did not know it existed, and "even the evaluations were not systematic," as some officers were evaluated and others were not.[335] A 2002 government document noted that the system "has shown itself to be too cumbersome and incapable of objectively assessing officials' performance, merit, and aptitude, to prepare for the changes of the modern world. The inadequacies revealed relate to the absence of a performance contract signed between the two parties (the evaluator and the evaluated) and the non-systemization of the assessment interview."[336] One of the reform architects reflected, "Unfortunately, we have continued to gangrene our administration with the logic of a career-based service."[337] With respect to the broader modernization and simplification agenda, mission statements and service charters were put in place,[338] but the same 2002 government document stated, "The results attained, in terms of modernizing the state and improving the quality of public services, have been weak."[339] The IT-oriented reforms of the 1990s may have been more effective, at least in the long-term, as the government's digitization efforts have been among its most successful reforms, and these initiated that process,[340] although there is little information on the shorter-term impacts of this first set of digital government reforms.

The next landmark set of reforms were launched in 2002 with the Programme Nationale de Bonne Gouvernance (PNBG, National Good Governance Program) of President Abdoulaye Wade's government, which had come to office in the 2000 elections in Senegal's first postindependence "alternance" of power. But many of the civil service-oriented aspects of the PNBG actually had their genesis in thinking, research, and piloting that began in the mid- to late-1990s under the government of Abdou Diouf. Reflections began within the bureaucracy in 1995,[341] and in 1997, the Ministry of Labor and Employment undertook a productivity study of the state bureaucracy.[342] In 1998, Senegal presented preliminary plans for a national governance program to a World Bank Consultative Group,[343] and in 1999, an effort to introduce a "results culture" was announced[344] (albeit with few specifics) that presaged the Wade administration's later focus on results-based management. Following the 2000 elections, these plans were reviewed, and a national stakeholder meeting on public service quality and good governance was held,[345] leading to the establishment of the Comité Interministériel de Pilotage du Programme Intégré de Réforme du Secteur Public (Interministerial Steering Committee for the Integrated Public Sector Reform Program) that would finish laying the groundwork for the PNBG.[346] While the PNBG was thus closely linked with the Wade administration, the civil service reform aspects of it were largely a continuation of existing efforts.

The PNBG was a comprehensive governance program with components covering everything from local government to the judiciary, but the first and most prominent component was focused on core civil service reform and delivery of services to citizens.[347] It set out a broad agenda for continued institutional streamlining (with a New Public Management-inspired focus to "reduce the size of the State, and recenter it on its sovereign functions"[348]) and reduction of burdensome administrative rules,[349] continued "modernization" of human resource management along the same lines as the reforms of the early/mid-1990s (including a focus on performance-linked individual appraisals),[350] and emphasis on the adoption of digital tools.[351] It also stated a desire to transition to a more participatory and goal-centered management style in line ministries,[352] albeit without any details on what this would entail. The PNBG was also closely linked to international trends and donor support: It was institutionally tied to Senegal's 2001 Poverty Reduction Strategy Paper and founding of the New Partnership for Africa's Development (NEPAD),[353] received significant financial support from the United Nations Development Program (UNDP) and European Commission (EC), and, over time, increasingly adopted the "results-based management" rhetoric of the 2005 Paris Declaration[354] (although this was also prefigured by internal thinking in the late 1990s). The implementation of the PNBG was overseen by the Délégation au Management Publique (DMP), which was moved to the Office of the Prime Minister in 2000, then back to the presidency in 2001, before being renamed the Délégation à la Réforme de l'Etat et l'Assistance technique (DREAT, Delegation for State Reform and Technical Assistance) in 2008 in an effort to strengthen the cross-sectoral coordination of reforms.[355] The PNBG also received extensive donor support, mainly from the UNDP and European Commission. The PNBG was renewed for a second phase from October 2007[356] with the same core components.

TABLE A.4 Content of civil service reforms in Senegal

	Cellule de Contrôle des Eff. et de la Masse Salariale (CCEMS), Comm. de Rat. des Struct. et des Empl. Publiques (CORA-SEP), 1984–1990	Conseillers en Ressources Humaines et Organis-ation, Cellules de Gestion des Ressources Humaines, 1986–1990	Voluntary Retirement Program and Org. Restructuring, 1990–1993	Modern-ization of the State, 1990–1999	Prog. Nationale de Bonne Gouvern-ance I and II, 2002–2011	Perf. Contracts, 2010–2019	Reform Master Plans (Schémas Directeux) / Plan Sénégal Emergent (PSE), 2011–2019
Individual performance mgmt.							
Leadership performance agreements						✓	
Individual staff appraisal & performance management				✓	✓		✓
Org. mgmt. and capacity							
Org. reviews/ perf. improv. plans/ perf. mgmt.	✓			✓			
Performance improvement funds							
Service delivery-focused reforms							
Client-focused reforms				✓	✓		✓
Sector-driven reforms					✓		✓
Salaries and structures							
Staff redundancies & org. restructuring		✓	✓	✓	✓		✓
Pay regrading/ reform				✓			
Other reforms							
Cross-government coordination					✓		
Other	✓	✓		✓	✓		✓

Source: Author's synthesis based on document review and interviews.

The PNBG I and II had mixed success both in terms of implementation and impact, although the evidence is relatively thin. The first phase of the program, through 2008, ended up focusing more on the formulation of reform plans than their implementation.[357] The core civil service reform component was reportedly the part of the PNBG that worked the best, with the digitization and e-government component especially central and effective in improving performance.[358] By 2011, the government web portal had four hundred digitized processes accessible online with an average of five hundred users per day.[359]

There is mixed evidence on the effectiveness of the PNBG's efforts to focus on results: While one former official viewed it as just "rhetoric,"[360] another viewed it as a "necessary" step in the long-term process of inculcating a mentality in officials that their job was to serve citizens.[361] More broadly, much of the work of reorienting service delivery procedures around citizens' needs and streamlining procedures continued during this period with some successes.[362] However, the institutional reorganization and "rationalization" elements of the PNBG (which continued a trend ongoing since the late 1980s) were arguably counterproductive. In his study of administrative modernization, Gaye observes that frequent structural reorganizations weakened the institutional anchoring of many service provision agencies, with 80 percent of agencies lacking legal frameworks (as of 2006) and one directorate having been moved between ministries five times between 2001 and 2005.[363] Similarly, the number of ministries rose from twenty-six in 2000 (itself up from fifteen in 1990) to thirty-seven by 2007, with even larger increases in the number of other agencies, directorates, and services.[364] This organizational fragmentation and greater decentralization of personnel management also enabled more hiring outside the civil service system and weaker overall control of staff numbers, "so we got the contrary of what was thought before."[365]

The linking of rewards and career progression to individuals' measured performance continued to be unsuccessful in practice during the PNBG years despite the existence of formal rules and processes. One contributing factor was the fear of confrontation with Senegal's powerful civil service unions—a common constraint from the 1980s through the 2010s.[366] Another factor was the Wade administration's perception that the civil service had been politicized by Diouf and staffed largely with PS sympathizers, which led the administration to a great deal of upheaval and replacing of existing personnel with new, trusted individuals, along with significant pay increases that "disarticulated the salary policy" developed during the 1990s.[367] The use of the performance appraisal system to drive promotions and rewards was thus "put between parentheses, it was put on standby" during these years.[368]

The electoral transition in 2012 of the presidency from Abdoulaye Wade to Macky Sall resulted in a nominal rupture of reform strategies on paper, but—as with Wade's own transition in 2000—the substantive direction of reforms was marked by strong continuity from the previous administration. The Wade administration had developed the Schéma Directeur de la Réforme de l'Etat (SDRE, State Reform Master Plan) as the successor to the PNBG II to run from 2011–2015; under Sall, it was relaunched as the Schéma Directeur de Modernisation de l'Administration Publique (SDMAP, Public Administration Modernization Master Plan) to run from 2013–2017, with verbatim identical components and summary diagram.[369] The SDRE and SDMAP were both centered around the idea of results-based management, with three main components that strongly echoed the PNBG and even the reforms of the 1990s: improving the quality of public management (including modernization of human resource management and a focus on operationalizing the existing performance measurement and management systems), improving the quality of service delivery, and "rénovation" of the administrative state through reorganization of organizational structures.[370] As with the PNBG, the SDMAP was nested within a broader cross-sectoral national development plan—in this case, the Plan Sénégal Emergent (PSE, Emerging Senegal Plan). Many of the core personnel involved in designing and driving reform within the government remained in place across this transition (despite a degree of upheaval across the service).[371] The combination of nominal changes with substantive continuity even extended to the institution leading these reforms, with the DREAT being renamed the Délégation générale à la Réforme de l'Etat et à l'Assistance technique (DGREAT, General Delegation for State Reform and Technical Assistance) in 2012 by the Sall administration before reverting, in 2013, to its original name: the Bureau Organisation et Méthodes (BOM).[372]

One of the most significant new elements was the introduction of performance contracts between the minister of finance and the director-general of each ministry or agency—a process that was originally announced in 2010 under Wade but was maintained under Sall's SDMAP/PSE. These three-year contracts defined performance objectives and associated financial rewards or (unspecified) sanctions,[373] and were an extension to senior leadership of the broader focus on measuring and evaluating individual officers' performance. However, there is little evidence that these operated as envisioned, with one senior official stating that they had never seen any director-general held accountable for performance, with keeping political leaders happy being the driving factor: "There is no other criteria, that's the reality."[374] Similarly, the use of the performance appraisal system reportedly remained largely perfunctory throughout this period: "We evaluate in a routine, mechanical way. One does the evaluation, gets a rating, and gets promoted. . . . But in reality, we haven't sufficiently integrated the dimension of officers' performance to improve the quality of services. It's still a challenge that we must manage."[375]

Other significant new elements included the 2017 creation of ministry-level reform committees and an interministerial Comité de modernisation de l'administration publique (CMAP, Public Administration Modernization Committee) to facilitate the modernization of human resources and administrative procedures within each ministerial department and encourage a "culture of innovation and efficiency of modernizing activities within the ministries."[376] More broadly, the direction of reforms under the SDMAP and PSE reflected the underlying continuity and progression of a number of the reform threads initiated in the early 1990s—digitization, improved service accessibility and citizen orientation (including through the creation of client service units within selected line ministries), and performance-driven human resources management and the creation of a results culture as the "leitmotif" of reform.[377] However, aside from the continued progress of Senegal's digitization reforms,[378] as of 2019, there was little available evidence on the degree to which this most recent set of reforms had been implemented or had impacted the behavior or performance of civil servants.

SOUTH AFRICA

South Africa's first phase of civil service reforms in the postapartheid era comprised a set of legislative and administrative changes aimed at integrating the parallel, racially defined civil services that had been administered to the country under the apartheid system. This was done primarily by merging personnel from the separate civil services into the former white civil service to create a unified administration, accompanied by an "aggressive" affirmative action campaign to bring new and formerly excluded talent into government at all levels.[379] At the same time, the government also emphasized the importance of changing individual and organizational norms and processes "to facilitate the transformation of the attitudes and behaviour of public servants towards a democratic ethos underlined by the overriding importance of human rights."[380] (Although these reforms targeted the central, provincial, and municipal levels of government, here, I focus solely on central government.)

To integrate the country's separate civil service into a unified civil service, the legislative framework for public personnel and organizations was overhauled with a series of linked legislation, regulations, and white papers, including the Public Service Act (1994), White Paper on the Transformation of the Public Service (1995), Public Service Conditions (1996), White Paper on Human Resource

Management in the Public Service (1997), White Paper on Affirmative Action in the Public Service (1998), and Public Service Regulations (1998). A Presidential Review Commission on the Reform and Transformation of the Public Service in South Africa, recommended by the 1995 White Paper, tied together many of these documents and made a series of recommendations for their implementation.[381]

These reforms established new pay scales, job grading and evaluation, hiring procedures, and other administrative changes necessary to integrate personnel into a unified civil service. They also took steps to democratize and decentralize what had been a very hierarchical institution under the apartheid regime, giving central government departments significant autonomy over their own personnel management, creating greater lateral entry opportunities to enable noncareer civil servants to join at all levels and splitting the powerful Public Service Commission into a Department of Public Service and Administration (DPSA) with active responsibility for transforming the service and a much smaller Public Service Commission (PSC) to serve more of an oversight and adjudication role.[382] These reforms also established an annual staff appraisal system in an effort to ensure employees had performance targets, received regular feedback, and that good performance could be rewarded through practices such as performance-based pay increments and bad performance could be managed and eventually lead even to "dismissals on grounds of inefficiency."[383] A similar system of performance contracts was also envisaged for senior managers.[384]

In tandem, these reforms also aimed to effect a significant demographic and ideological transformation of the civil service. On one side, the government introduced a Voluntary Severance Package scheme (1996–1997) to reduce payroll and facilitate the exit of officials from the previous administration, which was "dominated by white Afrikaner males"[385] who were often (though not universally) ideologically aligned with the former apartheid regime.[386] As Cameron explains, "There was genuine concern that old-guard bureaucrats would thwart the implementation of the policies of the new government."[387] This structural integration—referred to as "transformation"—was envisioned by the government "as a dynamic, focused and relatively short-term process, designed to fundamentally reshape the public service for its appointed role in the new dispensation in South Africa."[388] On the other side, the government adopted a wide-ranging affirmative action plan that mandated the use of numerical targets for race, gender, and disability. It also stipulated the integration of affirmative action measures into all aspects of public personnel management as well as a core aspect of organizational processes: "affirmative action is not an isolated function carried out only by specially appointed staff, but rather an integral element of every aspect of the organisation's management practices."[389] The government included "productivity and improved service delivery" as a core principle and objective of these reforms, stating, "Affirmative action programmes must promote the development of more innovative work practices which maximise productivity and increase customer-responsiveness."[390]

The integration-oriented "transformation" reforms are widely viewed as the most successful of South Africa's postapartheid history. Although the timescale stretched significantly beyond the "short-term process" initially envisaged and not all targets were met, the reforms were broadly successful in integrating the separate apartheid administrations into a common one and creating a more demographically representative national civil service—albeit more so for race than gender or disability.[391] There is also some evidence that having a more representative bureaucracy may have led to performance improvement, at least in some domains.[392] The Voluntary Severance Packages were largely successful in facilitating the civil service's demographic and ideological transition, but also resulted in the loss of many highly skilled individuals—"some [of whom] later returned to the public service as consultants."[393]

The other performance-oriented aspects of these structural reforms—namely, the effort to make institutions less rigid and hierarchical by delegating greater managerial authority downward and the use of staff appraisal and performance contracting systems—seem to have been less successful. One review of the evidence, for example, noted some progress but commented that "most departments are still centralized . . . departments, by not delegating authority to the appropriate levels, experienced delays in decision-making."[394] It attributed this to "the intransigence of politicians" but also argued that "managers are not willing to manage," blaming this on the rigid, rule-bound bureaucratic culture instilled by apartheid.[395] At the same time, the push for greater flexibility and delegation of authority also ran up against concerns from the control authorities within the government, who were concerned about corruption and other organizational hygiene issues and were trying to introduce stricter procedural rules.[396] Individual-level performance management and performance-linked incentive reforms, meanwhile, focused on the adoption of performance contracts for senior managers. These were in place for directors-general during the late 1990s and from 2001 for all senior managers with the creation of the Senior Management Service, albeit with generally weak linkages to actual performance.[397] The implementation and effectiveness of these are discussed in more detail later.

With respect to the transformation of bureaucratic culture envisioned in the mid-1990s wave of reforms, though, the centerpiece was undoubtedly the Batho Pele ("People First") initiative and set of principles laid out in the 1997 White Paper on Public Service Delivery. Inspired both by the moral and political

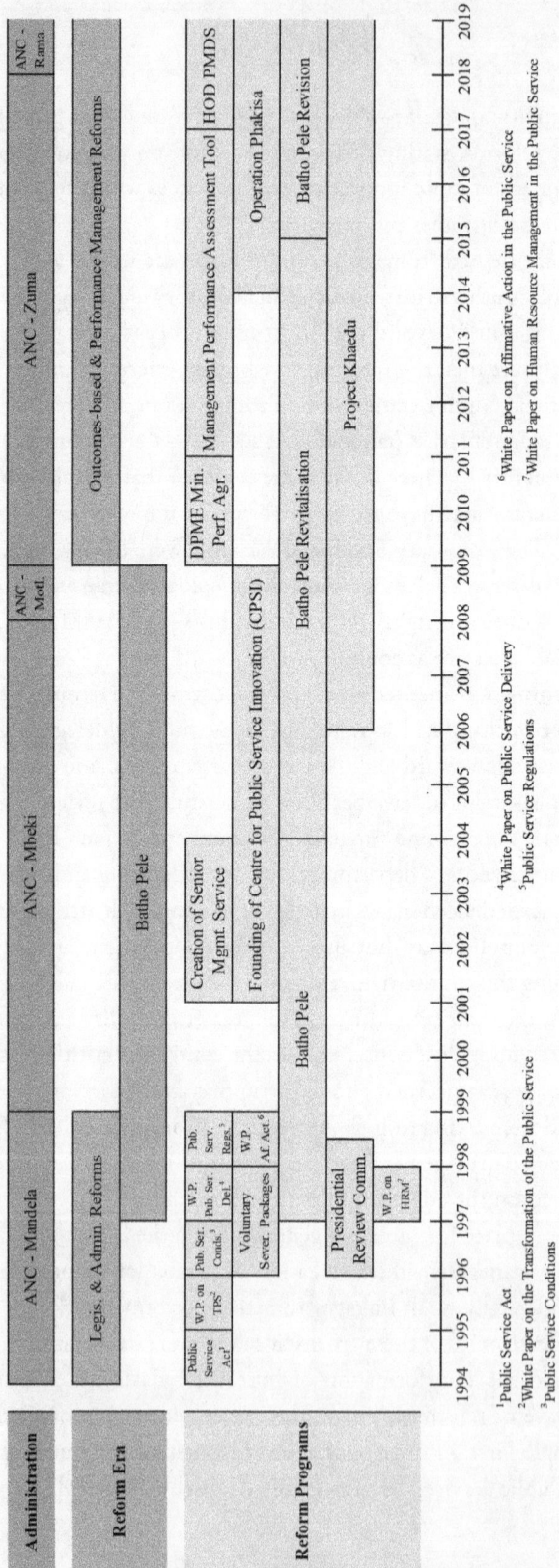

FIGURE A.5 Timeline of Civil Service Reforms in South Africa

Source: Author's synthesis based on document review and interviews.

imperatives of the new democratic dispensation and by similar reforms from the United Kingdom,[398] this White Paper outlined the government's plans to counteract the apartheid era's rigid, exclusionary, social control-oriented approach to public management:

> This White Paper on Transforming Public Service Delivery therefore, urgently seeks to introduce a fresh approach to service delivery: an approach which puts pressure on systems, procedures, attitudes and behaviour within the Public Service and reorients them in the customer's favour, an approach which puts the people first. This does not mean introducing more rules and centralised processes or micro-managing service delivery activities. Rather, it involves creating a framework for the delivery of public services which treats citizens more like customers and enables the citizens to hold public servants to account for the service they receive. A framework which frees up the energy and commitment of public servants to introduce more customer-focused ways of working. The approach is encapsulated in the name which has been adopted by this initiative—Batho Pele (a Sesotho adage meaning "People First").[399]

The White Paper elaborated the approach into a set of eight principles and mandated the development of service charters, routine citizen consultations, and complaint-handling mechanisms. It also mandated the creation of organization-level Batho Pele implementation committees. It was unusual in explicitly emphasizing the importance of broad-based cultural change as its core objective rather than the implementation of any particular project or process: "Improved service delivery cannot only be implemented by issuing circulars. It is not only about rule-books and 'prescripts,' because it is not simply an 'administrative' activity. It is a dynamic process out of which a completely new relationship is developed between the public service and its individual clients."[400] Indeed, one public servant at the time wrote that "Batho Pele is not a single project. . . . Batho Pele is a characterisation of the nature and quality of service delivery interface that should obtain between government and the public. It found formal expression through the 1997 policy framework but is given effect through a number of efforts whose collective impact leads to public service that puts people first."[401]

As a reform, Batho Pele can be understood as trying to change culture through two mechanisms: (1) changing officials' mindsets through its rhetorical force as a high-profile slogan, which would lead them to change their behaviors and create and adopt improved service delivery processes; and (2) a set of activities undertaken by the DPSA to more directly push line ministries to improve their service delivery processes. The former was driven by strong political backing, especially through the long-serving Minister of the DPSA from 1999–2008, Geraldine Fraser-Moleketi. Over its first five years, the latter gradually grew to include such measures as an awareness campaign and events; annual reporting and monitoring of line ministries' fulfillment of Batho Pele mandates like service charters and complaint handling systems; and a periodical newsletter circulated across the service, the Service Delivery Review, that communicated reform initiatives and highlighted success stories.[402]

By the early-to-mid-2000s, the Batho Pele slogan was widely recognized within the service. While a 2000 evaluation by the Public Service Commission found significant deficits in openness, consultation, and service standards across the government, its 2005 evaluation found much higher levels of implementation—although still only 52 percent of departments had actually developed service standards and were using them.[403] There had also been some success stories, such as the dramatic overhaul and automation of service delivery processes at the Department of Home Affairs.[404] A Centre for Public Sector Innovation was created in 2001 and was producing innovation case studies and a journal and running annual awards ceremonies.[405] Overall, though, there was a sense that departments' progress in taking tangible steps to actualize these principles was slow and uneven:

> In parts of the administrative system, it was treated as an "add on" to the core programmes of government departments rather than the catalyst ensuring the implementation of those programmes within a changed service delivery ethos ... it is not surprising that Batho Pele has not invariably exerted the hoped-for impact in every corner of the South African public administration. . . . In the early years of the introduction of the Batho Pele programme, the public service directors general and heads of department failed to adequately integrate Batho Pele into their strategic plans or their performance management plans and as result the policy were left largely unimplemented and only recognized for its symbolic value.[406]

At the same time, the DPSA's limited staff capacity and approach to institutionalizing Batho Pele may also have contributed to its limited implementation during this period.[407]

The DPSA, therefore, launched a "revitalisation" of the Batho Pele reform beginning in 2003–2004, which sought to encourage departments to focus more on tangible processes and behavior change. This came in part from "a general frustration by the minister at the time about how it was being done and also a frustration, I think from communities that she as a politician was very well aware of, a frustration that service delivery did not change."[408] As part of this revitalization, the DPSA issued a detailed Batho Pele Handbook that collected step-by-step guides to topics like "How to delegate," "How to consult," "Wayfinding and signage," and "Handling complaints."[409] While still preserving Batho Pele's original approach of allowing departments to decide on the steps they would take in a decentralized way, the handbook highlighted potential actions and ideas from four different strategy "pillars": "re-engineering and improving the back-office operations of government; re-engineering and improving the front-office operations of government; internal communication; and external communication."[410] Reviews were undertaken by the DPSA, the Public Service Commission, and Cabinet; reform "Champions" were identified and profiled; and a Change Engagement Program was elaborated.[411] Perhaps most saliently, the DPSA also launched Project Khaedu, an initiative in which midlevel managers spent a week at a service delivery site to gain a better understanding of the day-to-day challenges facing frontline bureaucrats.

The Batho Pele principles would remain as a pillar of government policy for the remainder of the study period (i.e., through 2019), with DPSA continuing to conduct activities like monitoring, awards ceremonies, and periodically reviewing and relaunching the principles. However, from 2008–2009, their role as the central driving force of civil service reform in South Africa faded somewhat due to the end of Minister Fraser-Moleketi's tenure and the creation of a new reform agency under President Jacob Zuma in 2009 (more below).

Judging the impacts and success of Batho Pele as a reform is difficult due to its broad scope and ambition, relatively decentralized implementation model, and focus on difficult-to-measure culture change rather than the delivery of specific outputs. There is consensus, however, around the rhetorical success of the policy in changing at least the normative ideal of public service behavior if not always its practice. The Batho Pele name and rhetoric have also been frequently referred to in public statements, exhortations, and criticism by political and bureaucratic leaders as well as citizens and the media since the late 1990s. For example, Fraser-Moleketi reported that "At a public meeting in the Eden district municipality (9 December 2005), in George—Southern Cape, both officials and residents referred to 'batho pele' as they talked about the provision of services. This reflects that the rhetoric has reached the different corners of the country."[412] The invocation of Batho Pele principles as core to service delivery standards and bureaucratic performance persisted all the way up through 2019—over two decades since Batho Pele's launch.[413] Similarly, the DPSA continued conducting routine monitoring of the implementation of Batho Pele mandates and principles at the departmental level, as well as occasional targeted intensive workshops and remediation processes with selected departments.[414]

There is also a general consensus that some organizations dramatically transformed their processes and customer orientation through reforms under the Batho Pele label. The Department of Home Affairs is often cited as an example that, under apartheid, had been a rule-bound and control-oriented hierarchy that successfully transformed itself through process reengineering and digitalization into an efficient and customer-oriented bureaucracy.[415] However, these successes in some areas were matched by lagging performance in others, both across departments and within them. For example, a set of service user surveys conducted by the PSC in 2012 found that the majority of Department of Home Affairs service users indicated satisfaction with the department's levels of courtesy, information provision, and publication of service standards—although, at the same time, majorities also expressed being unaware of the department's efforts on several other dimensions of Batho Pele standards.[416] The picture was similar across other departments, with strong citizen ratings on some dimensions and weaker satisfaction in other areas.[417]

Of course, using these success stories and citizen ratings to assess the success of the Batho Pele reform itself is difficult due to the lack of counterfactuals and unclear anchoring of citizen perception surveys. Another way to get at least a partial window into this attribution issue is by looking at the extent to which departments were complying with the Batho Pele mandates and whether Batho Pele reform activities actually drove changes in processes and management activity within departments. Here, the picture is also mixed. One interviewee, speaking of the 2009–2010 time period, stated: "At that stage we had an environment where compliance to the basic administrative policies was minimal. So then let's take the Batho Pele prescripts saying you've got to have a Batho Pele officer, you've got to have a little committee, and you must report on it. Then it wasn't uncommon that we had a 20 percent compliance rate, so 80 percent of departments didn't comply with this"[418] The same interviewee commented:

> All our intent is brilliant, I think we've probably got some of the best intent in the world, but it's about how do we implement. Batho Pele is about how do we start institutionalizing this into people's everyday lives and delivery, and I think that's where we've failed. . . . And that's probably why some of it hasn't gone in, because we haven't made it part of doing the business, because it hasn't been institutionalized, it's always been sitting on the side somewhere and then we remember we have to report on Batho Pele. . . . It was a compliance, tick-box approach to change.[419]

Another interviewee remarked:

> DPSA were very weak in actually assessing how departments conformed and complied with the regulations around Batho Pele. . . . A lot of time was put into the development of the policy and the tools, but then it was just given over to the departments to implement with no real monitoring or support. So it was very much up to departments to implement it themselves. Obviously some departments saw the value in it and used it to guide the way they do things, but for other departments it was at best a compliance thing that we had to do and submit reports.[420]

Another commented that the program "was all very well on paper, it just never translated into practice," attributing this mainly to a lack of real follow-up, enforcement, and accountability pressure from the DPSA.[421]

In a 2012 report, the PSC also noted that the three major national departments it studied had implemented 85–89 percent of the recommendations that the PSC had made in previous reports over the preceding five years.[422] Although it is not possible to link these process changes directly to changes in outcomes or service delivery performance, it does at least suggest that the Batho Pele program was driving some process changes within departments and that this was linked, to some extent, to efforts by the DPSA and PSC to support departments to actualize these principles.

The same gap between good intent and limited actual impact was also visible with the Project Khaedu managerial study visits to frontline offices. One manager stated, "I think it almost felt like it was forced on departments and individuals, I think most senior managers kind of reluctantly participated in it. I think the intent was a good one, to get people to go back and look at improving systems, but yeah, I don't know if it really achieved what it wanted to."[423] Another former senior civil servant replied to a question about Project Khaedu's impact by saying, "Let me put it this way, I've never attended that program."[424] One factor that limited the program's success was its one-off nature, which meant that potentially valuable relationships and insights were rarely sustained or implemented.[425] Each study visit led to the creation of a report on suggested process improvements, but an ex post analysis by the DPSA of the "stacks and stacks of those reports" found that "very few, if any" of the recommendations contained in these reports were actually implemented.[426]

While there is thus significant uncertainty over Batho Pele's actual impacts, it seems clear that it was at least partially successful in shifting both culture and actual bureaucratic processes and behavior—at least within some organizations and domains—while also falling far short of its highly ambitious vision of transformation. These mixed results and the perceived gap between its achievements in the realms of rhetoric versus action are summed up well by one senior civil servant:

> Well, I think the problem with Batho Pele was that it was about . . . trying to make the public servants and the managers more customer-oriented and more people-oriented. But the problem was . . . it was very politically driven, and oddly enough, it wasn't managerialist enough, in that it assumed that making government organizations more customer-oriented and providing better quality services to the public was just a matter of attitude of the public servants and they completely ignored all the other stuff which needs to be in place for an organization to provide better quality services. . . . The [assumption was that] service delivery here will improve if you have the right attitude. That was the problem with Batho Pele, it stopped there. It didn't make sure that all the systems and much more managerialist stuff was in place to enable public servants to provide better services.[427]

From 2009, the newly created Department of Planning, Monitoring, and Evaluation (DPME) sought to address these perceived failings by taking a more directive and top-down approach to improving performance across the civil service. Inspired by ideas of results-based management,[428] the DPME was created as a unit within the presidency. The DPME's flagship management intervention was the Management Performance Assessment Tool (MPAT), which it launched in 2011. The MPAT was inspired by the Canadian civil service's management accountability framework, which South African officials had seen on a study visit.[429]

The MPAT's primary aim was to improve departmental management practices by defining, measuring, and reporting on a set of good management processes using a standardized assessment. It was envisioned that this would improve performance in several ways. On one hand, the MPAT emphasized its use as a tool for supporting managers and helping them learn.[430] In this spirit, and building on the thrust of the reforms of the late 1990s, much of MPAT's rhetorical focus was on recognizing and valorizing managerial autonomy.[431] In addition, a behind-the-scenes motivation of focusing attention on management and organizational processes was to help build "autonomous, independent, free-standing departments away from political influences. . . . The thinking at that stage was to clearly define, what is my role, what is the administrative role and what is the political role."[432]

On the other hand, the highly structured, quantitative MPAT rating system also provided a framework for measuring departmental performance, which could easily be used for accountability purposes. The MPAT was defined into four "key performance areas" (KPAs) that each sought to capture different aspects of process quality: strategic management, governance and accountability, human resource management and systems, and financial management.[433] These four KPAs were further subdivided into two to three dozen "performance areas", each of which were organizational processes that corresponded to a specific statutory or administrative requirement. The content of the MPAT thus focused more on basic compliance rather than learning and innovation per se.

The MPAT was assessed on an annual basis for each national and provincial department through an intensive process. This six-step process involved the use of secondary data from the auditor-general and other bodies, a departmental self-assessment, validation of the self-assessment against documentary evidence by DPME and sectoral experts, discussion of findings with each department, and the development of a plan to address identified shortcomings.[434] While this thorough process was burdensome for departments and the DPME alike,[435] it was also viewed as necessary in order to generate rigorous assessments that departments could not ignore and that could be used to hold departments accountable.

The MPAT defined four levels of performance for each performance area. As one senior official explained, there were "four levels of standards. 1: they don't know what to do and aren't doing anything. 2: we can see they have awareness of what they should do but they're not there yet. 3: they are totally complying but not yet using compliance info to manage. 4: we see evidence they're using compliance info to improve and management their performance in that specific area."[436] Thus, scores of one through three could be achieved through mere compliance with the letter of the policy, while achieving a score of four required the department to go above and beyond the letter of the policy by taking action to actually use the process to improve their performance in that area. As another official explained, "At level three the assumption was that departments were compliant, but it was just a tick-box. Level four was where we needed departments to go: 'once we comply, is it changing our department?' "[437]

In addition to overseeing and verifying the departmental MPAT assessments annually, the DPME undertook a range of activities to support departments to improve and implement identified actions. While these were varied in nature, a partial list includes collaborating with the National School of Government to use MPAT results to guide capacity development and use case studies for teaching material; working with the National Treasury, DPSA, and other center-of-government stakeholders to provide support to departments to improve their performance in specific areas; undertaking sector-specific investigations and root cause analyses;[438] publishing a thrice-yearly internal journal, the *Service Delivery Review*, which was still in publication as of 2019; and running learning events, such as a Learning Laboratory for Middle Managers in 2004.[439] The importance for DPME of collaborating with other institutions in support of the MPAT reflects that DPME was reliant on authorizing power from the presidency and legal frameworks from the DPSA and the National Treasury, since DPME lacked statutory authority of its own[440] and often relied on its proximity to the presidency to get departments to cooperate.[441]

In addition to these learning-focused mechanisms, the DPME also sought to leverage accountability pressures to spur departments to improve. While the MPAT scores themselves were not directly attached to benefits or sanctions, the DPME did report the scores to the cabinet and in Parliament, as well as in the media.[442] One official remarked that "naming and shaming was probably our biggest motivator for MPAT."[443]

There is good evidence that the MPAT led to some positive changes but also that it fell short of its ambitions. One interviewee remarked:

[In] the first few years the MPAT had quite a big impact on the public service.... I think we were quite successful because prior to that, human resource matters would never get attention from the DGs and the executive of the department, they were saying, "I don't have time for this stuff." ... That's why we built in the self-assessment part, we subscribed to the [principles of] AA [Alcoholics Anonymous] and say you have to get people to admit to having a problem before they address it.... But I think the big thing we were successful in was getting them to give some airtime to this administrative stuff.[444]

Similarly, one study highlighted improvements in culture change around evidence use and improvement in audit findings due to better record-keeping, noting that the MPAT empowered constituencies within departments (such as internal audit) to use the MPAT results to push for change.[445] Departments that scored well on the MPAT also valued the recognition that it brought, and the MPAT scores were sometimes used to determine how to allocate morale-boosting non-financial awards.[446]

As with Batho Pele, there is also agreement that the MPAT's impact varied significantly across departments. For example, one former DPME official remarked that "some departments really took hold of it and ran with it."[447] The DPME published thirty-four good practice cases (from both national and provincial departments), which were organizations that had significantly improved on one indicator between the 2012 and 2013 MPAT iterations.[448] In 2016, the DPME identified fourteen departments that had improved and eleven departments that had regressed since 2011.

At the same time, the magnitude of these tangible improvements relative to the identified shortcomings was relatively small. One former DPME official remarked of the MPAT that "it was effective to some extent, but if you put it on a scale of one to 10, where 10 is the problem is completely fixed on one is the current situation, it maybe moved the dial from 1 to 3, 1 to 2 or 3."[449] This perception appears to be borne out by the DPME's own analysis of the evolution of MPAT scores, which found that while scores steadily improved year-on-year from 2013–2015 in national departments and in every province, this represented a net change of only 0.1 points (from 2.6 to 2.7 on the four-point scale) for national departments over these three years.[450]

One reason for the mixed impact was the difficulty in getting departments to treat the MPAT as a real opportunity for learning and improvement rather than just an externally driven compliance exercise.[451] One interviewee explained:

> In many areas, a large number of departments were at level 1 or level 2. So you know, just getting everybody to level 3 was deemed to be progress. So over the years when MPAT was running, we saw a gradual improvement in moving from level 1 to level 3. But I suppose if the program had to continue, you had to strive to get everybody to level 4 and get everybody to recognize that level 4 was where you had to be. But when departments compared themselves to the other departments, level 3 looked good. . . . There were some departments that would try and game the system, but generally we had a thorough system. . . . You couldn't really game level 4, you could game level 3, you could comply and tick-box and get level 3, but the moment that you asked about impact you couldn't game that.[452]

Another reflected that it was "always going to be challenging with a voluntary thing and where it's not done with any legal authority. So, it was more like a support measure than a regulatory measure, MPAT. And a support measure, support can be offered. But you can take a horse to water but you can't force it to drink. That was always going to be a limitation with it. And I think it was useful for those who wanted to participate and wanted to improve the administration across the board. It was useful for them."[453]

In a similar vein, another former official explained that she had witnessed many departments that genuinely treated the MPAT as an opportunity to improve, particularly for officers in administrative roles, such as human resources, procurement, planning, and internal audit, "who often felt that their issues weren't seen as important . . . [it] elevated their importance in the department."[454] However, "there were others who it was simply . . . not so much ticking the boxes, but we just want to look good . . . if you scratched further, there are lots of things that were not going right, but they just wanted to make sure that things look good."[455]

Another factor that limited MPAT's impact was the tension between its dual goals of increasing managerial autonomy and increasing compliance with prescribed management practices. "But I think all our reforms, I think the one big mistake we made is that we didn't adjust our systems to be able to implement these new reforms. So our HR system is this very administration-based system, our IT and payroll systems and all that. We wanted people to go for more management and more decision-making powers but our operational systems were all based on this very prescriptive environment."[456]

A final limitation on the MPAT's impact was the pushback from powerful political and bureaucratic actors that was generated by the publication of the ratings and their use in naming-and-shaming.[457]

> But then the kickback—and we were fortunate that it had quite high profile [backing] from the President so people took it seriously—but then people started learning the system and started playing us, because then it became about the rating and the scoring. We did initially introduce competition and give awards out and say who's the best and who's the worst to try to motivate people to make the change, but unfortunately it then became about the score. So we tried to give awards about who's the most improved department, but it became a lot about the scores, not about "am I improving," "are we getting better." . . . Then we started getting a huge amount of pushback from the departments and the DGs and that, saying "why are we focused so much on compliance and we should rather focus on outcomes and all that."[458]

Similarly, one researcher reported an interviewee saying, "When MPAT results were presented in Parliament, 10 minutes after, my phone goes off with people at the highest level concerned about scores and ratings."[459] Some cabinet reshuffles were also undertaken in departments subsequent to poor MPAT performance; although it is not clear whether the MPAT itself was the driving factor with these, it is also clear that attention was being paid to department MPAT scores at high levels.[460] One official explained that "it didn't go well with the ministers and the departments that were at the bottom. We also went public with the results which put further pressure. And politically it wasn't liked by some, the approach, and that's kind of why it died a quiet death, because maybe we were too transparent and pushed too much."[461] Another interviewee explained, "we published the results and that became an issue . . . it was an external instrument that was now showing up where you are failing as a department, [but] because people didn't like that, it eventually got scrapped."[462] The 2015 MPAT round appears to have been the last.[463]

While MPAT was focused on performance improvement in line departments, the process also led to some unintended benefits at the center of government. A former official remarked that the process of pulling together expert moderators from across departments each year to evaluate departmental self-assessments "itself was an important learning process" that generated insights about good practices that moderators could take back to their home organizations and DPME could follow up on.[464] Similarly, DPME's engagement with numerous other departments over MPAT reportedly created a rare culture of innovation and risk-taking within DPME, which was both reflected in and enabled by its flexible, learning-by-doing approach to developing and adapting the MPAT over time.[465]

In parallel to the Batho Pele and MPAT reforms, South Africa also undertook a series of structural personnel and performance management-oriented reforms, beginning in 2001 with the creation of the Senior Management Service (SMS). Enacted by an amendment to the public service regulations, this reformed the hiring, tenure, and evaluation system for top managers (from directors to heads of department), enabling greater lateral entry and making all appointments under a three- to five-year contract.[466] The aim of this system was to increase flexibility, improve salaries to be more competitive with the private sector, and tie tenure and promotion to performance through the use of annual performance contracts under the Performance Management and Development System (PMDS). The PMDS evaluations were based on mutually agreed Key Performance Indicators (KPIs) that were tailored to managers' specific responsibilities and deliverables and, after the advent of the MPAT, sometimes included MPAT ratings for the department as a whole or relevant indicators.[467] While this system potentially gave politicians more discretion in appointing top managers—a contentious step during a period when issues like politicization and rent extraction were major concerns in the country[468]—the intention behind introducing the system was primarily to professionalize and improve the quality of senior management rather than to increase political control of the bureaucracy.[469]

While the hiring, salary, and temporary contract provisions of the SMS were rapidly implemented, the envisioned linkage of salary, retention, and promotion with measured performance did not materialize. Some of this was due to simple implementation and logistical failures.[470] As of 2009, only "slightly more than half of senior managers typically signed a contract in a given year."[471]

TABLE A.5 Content of civil service reforms in South Africa

	Legal and Admin. Reforms and Voluntary Severance Packages (1994–1998)	Batho Pele (from 1996)	Creation of Senior Mgmt. Service and Perf. Mgmt. and Develop. System (2001–2003)	Founding of Centre for Public Service Innovation (2001–2008)	Project Khaedu (2006–)	Ministers Perf. Agree-ments (2009–2010)	Mgmt. Perf. Assess. Tool (2011–2016)	Operation Phakisa (2014–)	HOD Perf. Mgmt. and Devel. System Relaunch (2017–)
Individual performance mgmt.									
Leadership performance agreements	✓		✓			✓			✓
Individual staff appraisal & performance management	✓								
Org. mgmt. and capacity									
Org. reviews/ perf. improv. plans/ perf. mgmt.		✓					✓	✓	
Performance improvement funds									
Service delivery-focused reforms									
Client-focused reforms		✓			✓				
Sector-driven reforms		✓		✓	✓			✓	
Salaries and structures									
Staff redundancies & org. restructuring	✓								
Pay regrading/ reform	✓		✓						
Other reforms									
Cross-government coordination								✓	
Other				✓					

Source: Author's synthesis based on document review and interviews.

One researcher explained that "The reasons for this delay range from documents not being submitted to the PSC, the HOD [head of department] not occupying the post for a full financial year, PAs [performance agreements] not reaching finality, and both, the HOD and EA [executive authority] are in an acting capacity."[472] The PMDS also ran into challenges with objectively measuring performance. "A concern expressed by HODs, is that a poorly formulated and designed PA may result in an appraisal outcome that may be unfairly biased towards or against the HOD. Another concern that emerged was the appraisal process may not reflect adequate correlation between individual performance and overall organizational performance. It is generally accepted that an outstanding rated performance of an HOD means, that he/she is leading an organization which performs optimally. However, the PMDS does not provide an instrument to deal with the potential disjuncture between individual performance and organizational performance."[473]

The difficulty in identifying KPIs that are both objectively verifiable and are good measures of individual managers' performance has led to the collapse of any link between measured performance and rewards or sanctions:

> So yes our PMDS system has three categories . . . not fully effective (and then there's meant to be some corrective actions taken, and if non-performance is persistent ultimately it can lead to dismissal or demotion or other sanctions). And then our system also has what we would call fully effective, who earn their salaries and get an annual notch increase, and then the highly efficient ones who qualify for an annual increment as well as a cash bonus. So over time the cash bonus part has been becoming less and less. . . . [A] normal distribution would say 5–15 percent of people are good and same is bad. We saw that happening in early days but then with budget pressures and all that we've seen less and less becoming highly effective. Now we've lost the bell curve and we just look at how much money we have to distribute and decide rewards based on this. Also our management style is that we're afraid to face conflict, so you don't find a lot of people being assessed ineffective.[474]

To hedge against the risk of being held personally responsible for failures by their own or other organizations, managers were naturally strategic designing their KPIs. One interviewee explained:

> The way they design it, is that it's not something that comes back to them and I mean you can write your indicator in such a way that " . . . that I am not responsible if I don't meet that target." For example, a simple one would be you need to build X number of houses per year, so you receive a budget of X billion rand,

you need to build so many houses, the manager was simply right there to oversee the building of houses so whether we build ten when we were supposed to build twenty, I have overseen the building of the houses, I didn't put a target on building twenty houses although I received funding for twenty houses and therefore when you do the assessment, ". . . I did oversee it, these are the reports . . ." so it's the manipulation of the system to a large extent. [475]

While these performance agreements were taken seriously in some departments, in general, there quickly became an assumption that the performance bonus component was an entitlement and expected part of a salary package, simply for doing one's job. "So everyone signed the agreement, everyone did the assessment after six months, everyone did the annual assessment, and if you look at the most of those assessments, everyone got their average assessment, so they got their performance [increment] on an annual basis and they were quite happy with that."[476] As one former official with a senior role in a personnel management institution said, "People were just getting our performance increases irrespective of their performance . . . so I don't think that overall the performance management system worked very well because there are no consequences for poor performance."[477] This official could name only one instance when poor performance led a manager on probation to be refused a permanent appointment, while another former official stated: "I don't think there was a single public manager dismissed from the public service because of poor performance."[478] Staff below the SMS grades used a different annual appraisal system, but with similar dynamics.[479] Overall, "lots of these things were put in place with good intentions, [but] they were simply just watered down to an extent that they just became tick-box exercises . . . yes we did the recruitment process, sent people for competency assessments, [but] no matter what the outcome is if I have decided I am appointing [this person], I am appointing [this person]."[480]

Some interviewees perceived that the strength of South Africa's audit system was another factor that pushed managers' KPIs toward compliance-style indicators that were short-term and easy to measure but less meaningful. One former official described how the increasing emphasis on outcomes from 2009 led to increasing scrutiny on departments' reports of their results and achievements, but there was a misalignment between the rigid standard of evidence and procedure applied in financial auditing norms and more inherently ambiguous data on performance.[481] Another interviewee also remarked on the challenge posed by differences between financial audits and performance data: "But Cabinet then said, 'Why are people getting qualified audits but bonuses on their performance agreements?' "[482] Over time, this led not just to civil servants devoting a huge amount of time to an increasingly burdensome performance reporting system, but also to performance agreements and annual work plans focusing increasingly on highly measurable short-term deliverables that were largely delinked from the broader five-year national plan—even though the implementation of this plan was the original rationale for the intense focus on outcomes:

> So because the APP annual performance plans, they focus on activities that can be done within a year, whereas the five year [national development plan] focuses more on longer term things which had more impact and outcome. So the five year targets [in] the five year plan doesn't get audited, so basically it gets written because it's a requirement and then it gets put on the shelf, published and put on the shelf, and no one looks at it again and then everyone focuses on the annual APP [that] they report against. But if you look at all the content, APPs and targets and everything is all very activity-based, and it's . . . almost impossible to find a link to any cogent links between progress with those activities and actual impacts and outcomes. So you can have a situation where across the board you can make an argument that the performance of the South African government has been deteriorating, and at the same time we've had this very strong strategic plan, APP system [that] so many people spend all their time on and where the performance information is audited . . . that kind of performance system is actually having no impact on improving performance.[483]

Another interviewee explained, "I sometimes think the performance management system itself undermines the approach to thinking beyond yourself and beyond your bonus at the end of the year . . . the long-term trajectory is missing and it is not being followed, even the National Development Plan, it was written and everyone raved about it and no one goes back . . . they were supposed to cascade back so in theory the system should work like that but in practice it is about short term gains."[484]

These challenges were compounded by legal and political tensions and ambiguities. Since politicians had a role in appointing senior managers, political connections made it difficult to sanction underperforming managers and led to pushback when the PSC, DPSA, or DPME tried to do it.[485] "So managers then sit back and say, 'But why do I need all that stress?' so you just rather not get involved."[486] Appointing people into the SMS reportedly became a way of rewarding favored individuals and doling out perks, which led to an explosion of very junior directors who often lacked the skills to be effective managers.[487] Even beyond political connections, one interviewee explained that "it's sometimes inter-personal issues. So sometimes contracts are terminated and [managers are] redeployed somewhere else or the minister sits it out and doesn't renew their con-tracts, so because of those relationships we're losing some good DGs."[488] Other factors also impinged on the PMDS's intention to use measured performance as the sole criterion for retention, promotion, and transfer decisions, with union resistance and equality considerations[489] as well as legal ambiguity about who has the authority to fire directors-general[490] both playing a role.

In 2016, the responsibility for undertaking PMDS assessments was moved from the PSC to the DPME, and in 2017 a new set of guidelines was approved that began implementation with the 2018 cycle. This involved rebalancing rat-ing systems so that individual ratings included a broader set of factors, with only 40 percent of the assessment based on one's individual performance.[491] The aim of this change was to focus less on individual performance in isolation and more on value-added, collaboration, and creating an enabling environment for others.[492]

Linked to this was a growing recognition by at least some officials that many key aspects of performance for senior managers were difficult to measure objec-tively and that this might require adopting different approaches to performance management:

> We try to be SMART, but I cringe every time I get feedback from my HR unit telling me my indicators are not SMART. A lot of people try to make perfor-mance management an objective system, and I tell them it cannot be . . . it prob-ably comes back to this unwillingness to manage. I want a system that manages people's performance without having to do anything, so I can say, "It's not me saying you're not performing, it's the system." . . . For me [discussion] is the most critical thing in this whole performance management system. . . . Firstly to have regular information about what's happening, and then having regular feedbacks. And you have to acknowledge that it's a subjective thing. Yes you can have some objective measures, but they should be to substantiate your subjective opinion as a manager and point towards indicators of that. . . . You think the system can manage performance for you. An old colleague in [organization name] used to say, "We shouldn't talk about performance management systems, we should talk about managing performance."[493]

This different approach to achieving impact through the performance manage-ment system was also linked to dropping the effort to use high-powered formal incentives as the system's main lever for change: "On the performance man-agement system, what DPSA is trying to do at the moment—and I know the Namibians tried it—is to try to delink rewards from performance assessment.

People are saying, 'to get a bonus is nice, but it's actually more about the recognition. At least you're recognizing I'm doing good work.' "[494]

While the PMDS's linkage of measured performance to hiring, retention, and pay did not materialize as envisioned, some interviewees noted positive effects from the repeated definition of roles and discussion of performance. For example, one former official stated that the system "definitely led to people being more conscious of [their] performance as an individual and their responsibility as a manager."[495] The SMS was also successful in other aspects. In addition to the rapid restructuring of salaries and conditions achieved early on, there were a number of complementary efforts to build the SMS as a true cadre oriented toward professionalism and performance. These included annual SMS conferences, which were "excellent" forums for communication and culture shaping, as well as public service awards to recognize good performance.[496]

An effort was made in the early years of President Zuma's administration to create a performance agreement system for ministers as well. However, these were largely ineffective:

> What really struck me is that when the President signed with all the ministers, he didn't read a single one of them . . . there was no process at all for performance reviews against those agreements. So to be frank, it was a publicity stunt. It might have had a bit of impact for some of the more conscientious ministers [who] might have actually studied that performance agreement in detail and might have focused on those areas that we put in there. That might have had some positive impact. But . . . the President himself never used it as a performance tool in any way whatsoever in his management, or his interactions with the ministers. [497]

After their signing in 2009, these performance agreements for ministers were not renewed in subsequent years. While a new set of performance agreements for ministers were signed more recently under President Cyril Ramaphosa, they fall outside the temporal scope of the book.

Another attempt to implement an outcomes-focused reform occurred in 2014 with the launch of Operation Phakisa, which was modeled on Malaysia's PEMANDU system that combined a small number of high-profile targets with mechanisms for facilitating cross-sectoral collaboration to achieve them.[498] While this garnered a high degree of attention, "The problem we ran into there is that it became the sexy thing to do. Operation Phakisa. Everyone wanted to have a Phakisa project, so rather than having a few highly focused projects we started having multiple proliferation of projects and then we lost that focus . . . but the President only has time and capacity to focus on a few."[499]

As with the SMS and ministerial performance agreements, Operation Phakisa also encountered the problem that, while the delivery of many key public sector tasks required collaboration across institutions, resources and other accountability mechanisms (such as reporting to Parliament and auditing) were all based on individual departments.[500] While Operation Phakisa was still formally in existence through 2019 (the end date of this study), most initiatives seem to have ceased after the first few years of implementation, and there is little available evidence on its impacts on performance in the civil service.

ZAMBIA

Zambia's recent history of civil service reform began shortly after the 1991 transition from a single-party state under Kenneth Kaunda's United National Independence Party (UNIP) to a multiparty democracy under Frederick Chiluba's Movement for Multi-Party Democracy (MMD). The new government faced the dual challenges of making significant budget cuts to cope with a fiscal crisis (having been under structural adjustment programs since the mid-1980s) and of professionalizing and depoliticizing a public service that had become bloated and patronage-ridden under Kaunda.

The main vehicle for reform was the Public Service Reform Programme (PSRP), which ran from 1993–1999. Work on developing the PSRP had begun in 1990 under Kaunda's administration, but Chiluba's new administration paused it and revamped it.[501] International donor agencies were closely associated with the PSRP, particularly the UNDP and the World Bank,[502] and some reform activities that would eventually fall under the PSRP began in 1992 with the Privatization and Industrial Reform Adjustment Credit from the World Bank.[503] The PSRP was composed of three components: (1) downsizing of staff and organizational restructuring, (2) performance management of staff, and (3) decentralization.[504] I discuss components one and two below (decentralization is outside of the book's scope).

The overarching emphasis of PSRP was on the reduction of staff numbers, which was to be achieved through a combination of organizational restructuring that imposed institution-by-institution employment caps, mandatory staff retrenchments, a voluntary severance package for senior employees, and the imposition of minimum educational qualifications that many existing staff did not hold.[505] Enacted within the context not only of fiscal consolidation but also a broader economic liberalization and privatization, the aim was to create a "more efficient but smaller public sector."[506] The headline goals were "to reduce public employment by 25 percent within three years and to improve the conditions of service of personnel"[507] and to "link pay and performance in a way that would attract and retain skilled professionals in the civil service."[508]

The PSRP was somewhat successful at the narrow goal of reducing staff numbers but without achieving its broader intended impacts. Some "ghost workers" were eliminated early in the process, and total public service employment reduced from a high of around 140,000 in 1992 to 104,000 in 2000.[509] However, payroll cost was reportedly larger in 1995 than in 1991,[510] and by the early 2000s, it was dubbed "out of control,"[511] with staff numbers starting to increase again from late 2000.[512] The process of rationalizing and reducing the number of state organizations went similarly unimplemented, and by 2000, all there was to show was a list of thirty-five state organizations that should be abolished, merged, or privatized but had not yet been altered.[513] By the end of the 1990s, some pay reforms had been undertaken, and salaries improved for some high-skilled positions.[514] However, most staff groups faced lower real terms salaries, and the broader picture was one of decreased motivation and declining standards of service delivery[515] with no pronounced impact on bureaucratic performance.[516]

There were at least four reasons why these downsizing and pay reforms did not result in the positive transformation that the PSRP envisioned—some more predictable than others. First, the threat to livelihoods and patronage networks provoked resistance from politicians and bureaucrats and perceptions of politicization. The Chiluba administration had made campaign promises to improve the civil service[517] and saw mass redundancies as a way to purge the civil service of what it perceived as unqualified patronage hires by the preceding UNIP government and replace them with people loyal to him.[518] Some experts perceived a degree of political bias in who was retrenched and who was brought in during this time.[519] However, these redundancies were also politically painful, and many bureaucrats and politicians perceived the retrenchments as having been imposed on them by international donor institutions, leading to even more negative attitudes about the reforms.[520] Donors, in turn, perceived the faltering pace of payroll reductions as a sign of limited commitment on the part of the government, leading to an attempt to accelerate the pace of redundancies in the late 1990s by bringing in a private sector executive to serve as director of the PSRP, which lasted just a year before bureaucratic resistance forced him out.[521]

Second, the combination of expensive severance payouts and the proliferation of retrenchment-related lawsuits meant that even painful redundancies did little to reduce personnel costs. Severance payouts totaled as much as twelve years' worth of pay for retrenched staff, so many "public officials identified for retrenchment were sent home while they kept getting paid."[522] The PSRP and associated firings were also reportedly undertaken without consulting the civil service union, and some retrenched staff filed lawsuits and won significant judgments against the government for procedural irregularities in the conduct of the redundancies.[523] As of 2019, the government was still making payouts related to these lawsuits from two decades earlier,[524] and some court cases were reportedly still ongoing.[525]

Third, the imposition of minimum educational qualification requirements is widely perceived to have reduced rather than improved the quality of the workforce. These requirements were intended as an objective way to purge unqualified patronage hires from the preceding decades and bring in younger people with better educational qualifications who (it was assumed) could better deliver public services.[526] But this resulted in the loss of many of the most experienced staff who knew how to do their jobs despite their lack of formal education.[527] As one civil servant working during that time explained, "We ended up with people that were qualified, but surprisingly not competent."[528] Another explained that his institution at the time had been very concerned about losing institutional memory as a result of retrenching its most senior staff who had a lot of experience but no university qualifications,[529] which necessarily undermined the extent to which they could reduce payroll costs.

Fourth, the redundancies that did occur had a negative impact on service delivery. Under the voluntary retirement scheme, many of those who left were those with the best private-sector employment options, such as nurses.[530] When pressured to reduce staffing, management often targeted "nonessential" staff, which they interpreted to mean employees in lower grades such as cleaners and porters.[531] However, this resulted in hospitals that had surgeons but no staff to clear operating rooms or mortuary attendants, and boarding schools with no cooks.[532] This caused service delivery to "hit a disaster level, especially when it came to the frontline services like health and education."[533] In another case, the retrenchment of agricultural monitoring and vaccination officers in western Zambia led to the failure of a cordon that had been preventing the entry of contagious bovine pleuropneumonia from Angola into Zambia's economically important cattle industry, necessitating the costly imposition of a livestock quarantine on the entire region.[534]

These retrenchments and salary reforms were intended to be complemented by the second major component of the PSRP, its Performance Management Package. This aimed to introduce a new Performance Management System, the most notable element of which was a shift from the longstanding Annual Confidential Report (ACR) system of staff appraisal to the more modern Annual

FIGURE A.6 Timeline of Civil Service Reforms in Zambia

Administration	MMD - Chiluba	MMD - Mwanawasa	MMD - Banda	PF - Sata	PF - Scott	PF - Lungu

Reform Era

- Public Sector Reform Programme (PSRP)
- Public Service Capacity Building Programme (PSCAP)
- Public Service Management Programme (PSMP)
- Public Sector Transf. Strategy (PSTS) I & II

Reform Programs

- Privatization and Industrial Reform Adjustment Credit (PIRC) I & II
- Public Sector Reform Programme (PSRP)
- Econ. & Soc. Adj. Cr. Proj.
- Public Service Capacity Building Project (PSCAP)
- Valentine Report[1]
- Performance Contracts
- Public Sector Management Program Support Project (PSMP)
- EM-GC[2]
- Pay Policy
- Poverty Reduction Support Credit I-II-III
- Pay & Allowance Reforms
- Public Sector Transf. Strategy (PSTS) I
- PSTS II
- Public Sector Performance Project (PSPP)
- Performance Contracts

Years: 1991 1992 1993 1994 1995 1996 1997 1998 1999 2000 2001 2002 2003 2004 2005 2006 2007 2008 2009 2010 2011 2012 2013 2014 2015 2016 2017 2018 2019

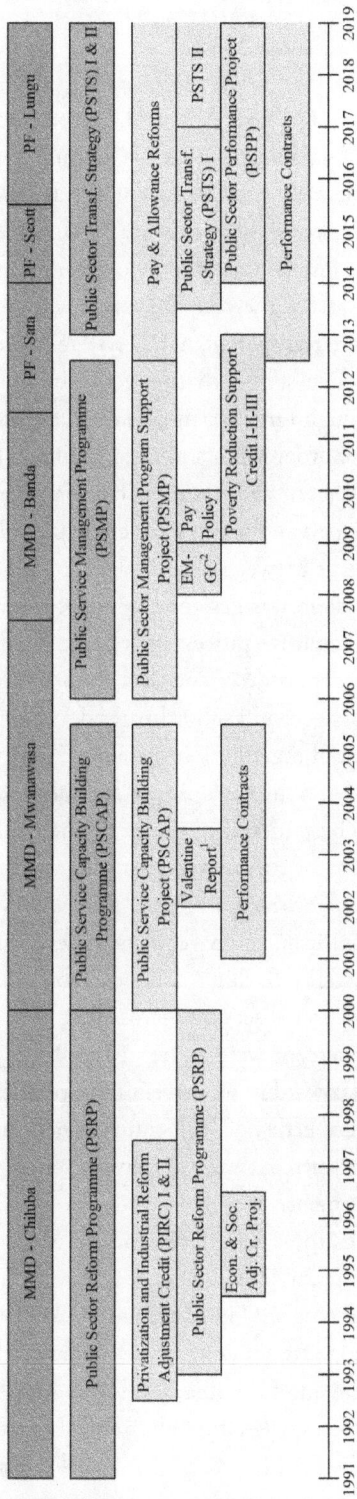

[1] Medium-Term Strategy for Enhancing Pay and Conditions of Service

[2] Economic Management and Growth Credit

Source: Author's synthesis based on document review and interviews.

Performance Appraisal System (APAS).[535] The ACR consisted solely of a supervisor scoring each subordinate without discussing their performance with them—as one interviewee exclaimed, "that Annual Confidential Report was so confidential you wouldn't even know what is in it!"[536] Under APAS, subordinates and their supervisor were instead intended to jointly undertake work planning and target-setting at the start of the year and assessment of performance at the end of the year.[537] The more transparent APAS system was thus envisioned as the mechanism through which staff activities would be linked to national and organizational plans (through target-setting) and incentivized (by linking performance appraisal to career progression and pay increments), neatly nesting individual performance management within strategic management.

The APAS system was designed and began to operate under PSRP but without actually achieving any linkage between measured performance and any type of reward or sanctions. The system was designed by 1996, and each institution gradually undertook the time-intensive process of creating job descriptions and performance standards.[538] One report described the APAS as follows: "In short, the program required that managers and subordinates develop work plans that would support the achievement of organisational goals and performance evaluation based on the achievement of results against pre-set, agreed upon targets."[539] Although appraisals began to be undertaken under the new APAS system, an external review reported that as of the early 2000s, there were no rewards or sanctions attached to the results of the appraisal.[540] A civil servant at the time remarked, "There were no significant improvements in performance. The new performance management systems couldn't function objectively."[541] For the PSRP as a whole, a survey of 102 civil servants across four ministries published in 2001 found that, while 91 percent were aware of the PSRP and 73 percent had positive initial sentiments toward it, 62 percent of respondents felt that the PSRP had brought "little", "very little", or "nil" improvement in the quality of service delivery, against only 18 percent who perceived "much" and none who perceived "very much" improvement.[542]

The second wave of reforms took place from 2000–2005 under the Public Service Capacity Building Program (PSCAP), a successor project to PSRP.[543] PSCAP had a total anticipated cost of US$45 million, backed by a World Bank project loan of US$28 million, US$16 million from DFID and other donors, and US$1 million from the government of Zambia.[544] It was planned to run in three phases over a thirteen-year timeframe—although it ended up running for only five years (through 2005).[545] The British government was also heavily involved in designing PSCAP, and inspiration for some elements was drawn from reforms undertaken in Ghana.[546]

PSRP had been driven by the assumption that bringing in more qualified staff with better salary structures would improve civil servants' performance, but when this did not materialize, it was argued by some (including many civil servants) that perhaps they lacked the necessary equipment and resources to improve. PSCAP's mantra and core goal was, therefore, to improve individuals' and institutions' "capacity to deliver."[547]

The main vehicle for directly trying to increase capacity was a Performance Improvement Fund (PIF) to which service delivery organizations in priority areas could apply to fund discrete, "quick win"-type projects to demonstrate that reforms could yield tangible results.[548] PIF applications were formulated by the organization itself, and this bottom-up process led to several innovative ideas for projects such as mobile hospitals and mobile education labs, including a UN award for a grant addressing the scarcity of medical facilities for deliveries in the Copperbelt.[549] These PIFs were intended to be embedded within the broader organizational strategic plans that began to be developed under the PSRP, serving as a small-scale accelerant and demonstration of success.[550]

Despite these initial successes, PIFs did not catalyze the broader impact they were intended to. Whereas the funds were meant to be targeted toward seven priority service delivery organizations, the World Bank reported, "in the early stages of the project, PIF funds were made widely available to all restructured ministries, regardless of whether they had a direct public service delivery orientation or not."[551] After a refocus on service delivery, an internal review of the PIF found that only fifteen of thirty-eight projects funded under the PIF had "an observable impact on service delivery," indicating "a disconnect between the service delivery and strategic planning basis for PIF funded projects and the projects actually funded."[552] Of the innovations introduced, reportedly only the mobile labs in education were sustained after the end of the project funding.[553] Another study found that the PIF "has not lived up to expectations. The logic of PIFs and quick wins was not sufficiently embraced by the MDAs. PIFs were seen as supplementary financing to government allocations. As a consequence, most applications for PIF funding were inappropriate (for example, cars and computers), lacked both innovation and a focus on performance improvement, and were not linked to MDAs strategic plans."[554]

Slow progress in the development and implementation of the broader planning and budgeting systems in which PIFs were meant to be embedded accentuated the disconnect between PIF-funded activities and the core work of ministries. One consultant pointed out that while "it is essential that the work planning process proceeds in line with the budgeting process so that the organization can accurately estimate its resource requirements (money, staff, etc.) to achieve the objectives and also ensure that the resources will be available, this requirement seems to be more honoured in its breach than in its attainment."[555] Given this, it is no surprise that there is little evidence of PIF grants fulfilling their catalytic "quick win" function, having served, instead, as one-off resource injections for discrete activities or assets.

At the same time, the severe spending restraints in place meant that there were real shortages in equipment within the government. As one former civil servant involved in designing and implementing the reforms explained, ministries would approach the implementing secretariat and say, "We are incapacitated because we don't have a vehicle," so there was some service delivery rationale for these purchases—even if there were also abuses.[556] Similarly, while the core PIF grants that were at the center of PSCAP did not function as intended, some sector-specific reforms that occurred during these years (e.g., in health and agriculture) were reportedly very successful—although these sectoral reforms were only loosely linked to PSCAP itself. Nonetheless, disappointing progress meant that the World Bank curtailed its support after just five years (which itself constituted a two-year schedule overrun on what had originally been intended to be a three-year first phase).[557]

Alongside its organizational performance component, PSCAP also undertook a set of staff and pay reforms that followed on from the PSRP. While the PSRP had been successful at reducing total staff numbers, resistance to cuts was growing due to the personal and political costs of retrenchments and a growing awareness of the negative effects on some aspects of service delivery. PSCAP continued the organizational restructuring and associated retrenchments but reframed this as "rightsizing" rather than downsizing and increased hiring in some areas, particularly in frontline social service delivery roles.[558] Despite this rhetorical change of tack, staff numbers continued to decrease, with a net reduction of 24,000 staff between 2000 and 2003.[559] Although there were some hiring increases for teachers and nurses, ongoing fiscal challenges with overall payroll figures meant that staff strength was sometimes increased on paper (through higher establishment numbers) but financial clearance was not given to actually hire people, resulting in positions being left unfilled for many years.[560]

At the same time, PSCAP also reiterated the PSRP's aim of establishing performance-linked incentives for individual civil servants. The government's 2002 Medium-Term Strategy for Enhancing Pay and Conditions of Service ("Valentine report")—written by a consultant as part of the PSCAP reform—was unequivocal about the importance placed on incentives for improving performance: "The newly articulated pay policy should as much as possible, aim at explicitly linking pay to performance, signalling a major change in the incentive system and in

performance expectations. Rewards and penalties are both vital for a well functioning incentive regime. . . . Meaningful performance incentives are a must."[561]

The government aimed to achieve this goal of instituting performance-linked
incentives through two channels: the proper implementation of the APAS annual
appraisal system for rank-and-file civil servants up to the level of director and the
creation of performance contracts for permanent secretaries (bureaucratic heads
of ministries).

The mechanics of the APAS system were established during the latter stages of
the PSRP reform. PSCAP did not change these substantively but sought to actually attach incentives—such as differential pay increments, accelerated or delayed
promotion, and meaningful sanctions—to the results of officers' APAS appraisals.
This effort was not successful. External reviews in both 2005 and 2008 reported
that there were no rewards or sanctions attached to the results of the APAS
appraisal,[562] with the 2005 report stating that "good performance is not rewarded
while poor performance goes unpunished" and remarking that many employees
do not even go through the appraisal process on an annual basis.[563] These faults
were blamed not on the system itself, which was considered "adequately designed",
but on the system's implementation and "low commitment of its users."[564]

One set of reasons highlighted for the non-delivery of rewards or sanctions
is that "targets are not set properly and are not always SMART [specific, measurable, achievable, relevant, time-bound]."[565] While the 2008 report puts some
blame for this on a lack of training and "an attitude that whatever is written will
be accepted,"[566] it also noted more fundamental challenges in establishing precise
and comprehensive targets: "The Job Descriptions are not updated on a regular
basis to take into account changes in job performance requirements. Moreover,
the Principal Accountabilities in many cases appear to be vague (e.g. 'undertake
appropriate measures to ensure security and safety'; 'manage effectively the laboratory'; 'General management to ensure that the office runs efficiently') and require
close scrutiny to be used effectively. For these reasons, job descriptions are not very
useful tools for supporting the application of APAS."[567] These challenges were
compounded by the inherently unpredictable nature of much civil service work.
As the evaluation noted: "The best laid work plans can be de-railed when urgent
and pressing work duties displace work plan targets. This displacement often
results in the work plan being compromised, and in some instances, rendered use-
less as a planning document. Political directives from above, and outside of the
scope of the work plan, must be recognized as part of the working culture."[568]

This uncertainty was further compounded by unexpected budgetary shortfalls or nonreleases of budgeted funds. One architect of Zambia's PSCAP reform
explained that individual targets were usually taken from organizational work

plans, but since the Ministry of Finance would frequently give ministries budget ceilings of only 65 percent of the cost of these work plans, it was inevitable that many activities would never be completed—how, then, could an individual be blamed for not meeting their targets?[569]

In addition, managers were often reluctant to score their subordinates poorly, even in cases where their performance merited it. "Sometimes the evaluation is confusing and even contradictory as the supervisor will rate the overall performance of the subordinate as high but then targets are marked as not being met. In other cases people are rated as highly skilled in an area where they are recommended for training as well as people being rated as not having the required skill but have met all targets."[570]

Skepticism about fairness in evaluation also created a great deal of acrimony and resentment, which further discouraged managers from rating subordinates anything but positively.[571] While some managers reportedly actively used the system in support of performance improvement, this was largely based on individual initiative and was far from systematic.[572]

Furthermore, while one intended improvement of the APAS system over the older confidential appraisal system was to stimulate dialogue and feedback between managers and subordinates, this did not happen in practice:

> The APAS System is not feeding back vital information to the appraised and the appraisers. . . . The APAS should have an end result that people are aware of; unfortunately, nothing seems to happen as a result of APAS other than the filing of the document . . . little effort has been made to commit line managers in Ministries to play a lead role in performance management through the use of APAS. This responsibility has been relegated to the HR department with little realisation that this department is simply a support mechanism to ensure that things happen in the Ministry in accordance with the requirements of this system. . . . The APAS process is not being used to constantly monitor performance of personnel and remind them of what is expected of them in the course of performing their duties but as one-time per year activity.[573]

The evaluation's overall assessment of the implementation of the APAS system was that the system "results in little individual or organizational performance improvement" and was unusually frank about the situation: "As time has passed the real purpose of the APAS report has become the justification of pay increments and promotions. This has led to the a [sic] view that completion of the form is a necessary evil to which one should devote as little time and thought as possible. The result in many instances is a report replete with inconsistencies, contradictions and very little assessment of performance that bears little relation to a real work plan and virtually none to the organisational and strategic plan."[574]

In addition to the APAS, PSCAP saw Zambia's first effort to put permanent secretaries (the bureaucratic heads of ministries) onto performance contracts. This was reportedly based on a suggestion by an expatriate consultant from New Zealand and a subsequent consultancy report.[575] These performance contracts were intended to become the primary means of performance management for permanent secretaries, who were not covered by the APAS appraisal system.[576]

However, while the subsequent Kasanga review had proposed a comprehensive performance contracting system, what ended up happening was that permanent secretaries were put onto fixed-term three-year contracts at the end of 2001 (rather than the permanent and pensionable civil servants they had been) but without meaningful setting of targets, assessment, or incentives.[577] Permanent secretaries were willing to accept the temporary contracts because it promised to be a lucrative three years prior to retirement,[578] and the arrangement was also "user-friendly" to politicians in that it gave them greater discretion and leverage over permanent secretaries.[579] However, permanent secretaries lacked not only annual targets but also basic job descriptions, so in practice, there was no formal linkage between performance and incentives.[580] These problems were easily foreseeable, with a World Bank-funded consultancy reporting in 2002, "it is unclear at this point on what basis performance will be measured. What benchmarks will be used to objectively distinguish between levels of performance, particular[ly] since the MDAs have not completed the strategic planning process and thus do not have clear performance targets."[581]

Taken together, these major components of the PSCAP reform—the Performance Improvement Fund, "rightsizing" redundancies, pay reform, the institutionalization of APAS, and the creation of performance contracts for permanent secretaries—fell short of the transformative impact on service delivery that they envisioned. The overall sentiment regarding the limited performance impacts of the PSRP and PSCAP reforms is well-captured by a 2008 review of Zambia's linked performance management reforms to date, which found that they resulted in "only marginal impact on the effectiveness and efficiency of the public service and result[ed] in little individual or organizational performance improvement."[582] As a result of these perceived shortcomings, the PSCAP program was terminated in 2005 at the end of the first of its envisioned three phases.

PSCAP's successor was the Public Service Management Programme (PSMP), which ran from 2006 to 2012.[583] PSMP was, in some respects, a new project with new objectives, but the World Bank (again the lead donor funder) referred to it as a "change of name" of its support.[584] It had two main areas of focus: establishing

TABLE A.6 Content of civil service reforms in Zambia

	Public Service Reform Prog. (PSRP), 1993–99	Public Service Capacity Building Project (PSCAP), 2000–2005	Public Service Mgmt. Prog. (PSMP), 2006–2011	Public Service Transf. Prog. (PSTS) I & II, 2013–
Individual performance mgmt.				
Leadership performance agreements		✓		✓
Individual staff appraisal & performance management	✓	✓	✓	✓
Org. mgmt. and capacity				
Org. reviews/ perf. improv. plans/ perf. mgmt.		✓		
Performance improvement funds		✓		
Service delivery-focused reforms				
Client-focused reforms			✓	
Sector-driven reforms				
Salaries and structures				
Staff redundancies & org. restructuring	✓	✓	✓	
Pay regrading/ reform	✓	✓	✓	✓
Other reforms				
Cross-government coordination				✓
Other				

Source: Author's synthesis based on document review and interviews.

service charters to improve the standard of service delivery and continuing the pay and performance management reforms of PSRP and PSCAP.[585]

The service charters were introduced in Zambia's civil service in 2009. For each ministry or agency in which they were adopted, they aimed to specify the services offered to the public, establish clear requirements for what documents or steps were required, and indicate the timelines on which each service should be delivered. These standards would then serve as frameworks within which business process reengineering could be undertaken. Modeled on the UK government's Citizen Charters,[586] by 2012, eight service charters had been adopted,[587] and at least some other ministries continued to adopt them after the formal end of PSMP.[588] Some successes were noted with these, with the Department of Immigration reportedly reducing passport processing times from three months to five to seven days and an information center established at the Ministry of Lands.[589] There is also evidence that the service charters had positively affected the work of some rank-and-file civil servants. One stated that their ministry's service charter "has improved service delivery. Service charters will help the ministry toward doing the right thing for the citizens and address these things in a realistic way,"[590] while another told of how the service charter brought about "a change from employees" with respect to the "needs of their clients" and "how people regarded the ministry."[591]

In other instances, however, service charters do not appear to have had an effect on practice, with rank-and-file interviewees making remarks like "some may not even know of its existence"[592] and "people do not understand it."[593] One interviewee attributed this to a lack of follow-up and institutionalization of the document. "The problem with the service charter is that it is not a document stating ownership of the objectives. After launching the service charter, directors do not really emphasise how things should be done. There is a detachment with how something should be done and then it is not owned."[594] Another person involved in implementing reforms echoed this, explaining that there was a general pattern of service charters having some effect in their first year or two but then decaying.[595]

The pay and performance management components of PSMP were essentially a continuation of the directions charted under PSRP and PSCAP. One aspect of this was mainly retrospective in that it aimed to pay for redundancy expenses that had been incurred under previous reform waves but for which the government lacked the funds, meaning that these laid-off employees continued to pose a fiscal burden.[596] More directly related to performance, it continued the effort to establish a more rationalized pay scale that would integrate performance-linked rewards and sanctions. Work on a new pay policy had begun in the 1990s under

PSRP, and the outlines of this policy were made clear in 2002 by the Valentine report, funded by the World Bank and written by an international consultant, with the changes partially codified through a Medium-Term Pay Reform Strategy under PSCAP.[597] Under the PSMP, this report was translated into a new official Pay Policy in 2009—although this did not begin to be implemented until mid-2012, at the end of the PSMP.[598]

PSMP's aim of linking pay to individual performance failed almost entirely. Against the target set in 2006 (at the start of the reform) of establishing a "performance based pay salary component in 10 of [sic] ministries linked to the strategic and work plan processes", the World Bank's report in mid-2012 stated frankly: "Indicator will not be met."[599] Although some progress was made—strategic plans were finally established in all ministries during the PSMP[600]—the broader picture was that interest in civil service reform during this period petered out both on the parts of government and donors.[601] This was likely due, in part, to leadership turnover, as the death of President Levy Mwanawasa in 2008 was followed by President Rupiah Banda's election loss to Michael Sata in 2011, but it also seemed to represent a culmination of frustration with the perceived limitations of successive waves of reform.

Civil service reform was then revitalized in 2013 by the first Public Sector Transformation Strategy (PSTS I, 2013–16), subsequently succeeded by PSTS II (2017–2021). In contrast to previous reform waves, the PSTS received little financial support from donors and was an internally developed and driven reform program originating from the Cabinet Office under Secretary to Cabinet and Head of Civil Service Dr. Roland Msiska.[602] Under the PSTS, the government tried to implement some reforms that had been put onto paper but not institutionalized under previous reform waves (the new pay policy and the APAS staff appraisal system), tried to reintroduce others (performance contracts for permanent secretaries), and adopted others anew (balanced scorecards for ministries).

The new pay policy that was approved in 2009 focused mainly on trying to rationalize a pay structure that had become rife with a complex system of allowances that reinforced perceived unfairness across institutions and staff grades. From 2013 onward, the government tried to put these changes into effect. The most salient part of these pay reforms was bringing the myriad of allowances that existed—at least twenty-four different types in 2002, most of which still existed[603]—into officers' base salary. Two decades of fiscal restraints on salaries (as well as a legacy from colonial times of generous allowances for senior officers) had incentivized institutions to compensate their staff increasingly through nonsalary allowances for things like housing and transportation. Similarly, donor agencies' practice of offering sitting allowances for civil servants to attend meetings had bled over into the government so that many civil servants expected to be offered sitting allowances for every meeting they attended.[604] This led to a situation where some staff received allowances worth up to five or even twenty times their base salary,[605] officers would refuse to do work that did not involve a linked allowance,[606] and abuses were rife—such as one officer who reportedly claimed to have attended 1,800 meetings in a single year.[607] Civil servants were also being paid across eight different pay scales and negotiating working conditions across multiple different venues, which created perceived unfairness, difficulties in managing the negotiations, and a lack of clarity about how much the government was spending on wages.[608]

The pay and allowance reforms implemented beginning in 2013 eliminated almost all of these allowances—in particular, the use of sitting allowances for meetings—by integrating them into core salaries. The sitting allowances were highly salient and contentious, and these changes had to be phased in by initially allowing officers to collect allowances for up to four meetings per month for four hours prior to full elimination.[609] This was accompanied by selective graded salary increases for groups of workers who were deemed to be underpaid relative to their colleagues in other institutions or classes by job evaluations and plotting of salary rates of each group. Since no officers' salaries could go down, equalization happened by giving significant net increases to some groups while slowing growth in the salaries of high-outlier groups.[610] Salaries were also increased for lower-level workers explicitly to reverse the salary decompression that had happened under previous reforms under pressure from international donors.[611] By the end of these changes, eight different public sector pay scales had been integrated into one,[612] and provisions on public sector salary negotiations had been built into the constitution in 2016.[613]

These pay reforms largely succeeded in producing a "clean [i.e. transparent and comprehensive] wage bill."[614] The abolition of sitting allowances was also widely seen as a success,[615] with one senior officer remarking, "Meetings still take place. And the beauty is, now the unnecessary meetings don't take place."[616] This also reportedly changed the composition of who attended meetings, with senior officers reportedly now more likely to send junior officers to meetings in their place—with obvious potential downsides but the benefit that junior officers got to engage more.[617] Rank-and-file officers reported mixed perceptions on the pay and allowance changes, with some reporting improved productivity, motivation, and peace of mind,[618] but others complained about the loss of allowances, difficulties making ends meet, and demotivation.[619] From a fiscal perspective, however, these reforms were problematic. In addition to the selective percentage increases to base pay, the bringing of allowances into base pay massively increased final-salary pension entitlements, particularly for senior officials.[620] Zambian law required a large portion of the pension to be paid as a lump sum on retirement, but the fiscal burden imposed by this meant that funds were not always available to pay these lump sums on time, so retirees sometimes stayed on payroll for years until they were able to be pensioned—further increasing fiscal strain.[621]

The PSTS also reiterated the importance of performance-linked incentives, with the strategy document that outlined PSTS I lamenting the lack of "effective rewards and sanctions" that had been attached to the results of the APAS staff appraisal system since its creation in the 1990s.[622] Despite yet another push to attach rewards and sanctions to the outcome of end-of-year APAS appraisals, however, there was little progress in this. Nearly all interviewees—from senior management to trade union leaders to rank-and-file officers—agreed that the appraisals continued to be treated as simply a formality required for promotions, confirmation of positions, and annual pay increments without any linkage to performance.[623] One rank-and-file officer commented, "APAS has mainly been used for administrative convenience. . . . I have never seen someone be demoted due to bad performance."[624] Only one interviewee reported seeing any type of sanctions applied during their time in the public service—the demotion of three officers—although it is unclear whether these demotions were actually based on the APAS itself.[625]

Many interviewees expressed the view that the lack of incentives undermined the seriousness with which the end-of-year assessment process was approached by supervisors and subordinates alike, with some officers simply filling it out themselves without any discussion with their supervisor, only filling it out immediately before promotion procedures, or not filling it out at all.[626] There was also little variation in reported performance, with analysis from the government finding that nearly all officers were rated excellent,[627] and even rank-and-file officers making remarks like, "Every appraisal form is above target."[628] While cultural issues were often cited as a potential reason for this, one senior officer questioned this explanation, arguing that similar staff appraisals were "ruthlessly applied" in the private sector in Zambia.[629] This pattern of high scores across the board undermined the informational value of the appraisals for employees and HR managers and also obviated the possibility of using the scores to administer incentives since rewarding nearly everybody would be prohibitively expensive. Indeed, fiscal constraints imposed by the Ministry of Finance were reportedly another factor preventing the payment of bonuses and the provision of training based on training needs identified in the appraisal system.[630]

With respect to the information sharing and dialogue promotion aspects of the staff appraisal system, during the PSTS era, the APAS continued to be largely ineffective for most rank-and-file staff. On the one hand, a handful of officers reported positive experiences with it, with one middle manager explaining that under APAS, "there has been a one-on-one interaction which has helped with understanding what gaps people have. It has helped me to understand at what level they are supposed to operate because at the end of the year, we find out if that has been met."[631] On the other hand, officers much more commonly expressed experiences such as, "APAS is not a two-way thing. There should be feedback and interactions on performance. . . . The problem is not getting feedback or me talking [with my supervisor] about my ratings. It would have been impactful if you could discuss performance."[632] Another lamented the lack of investment in the process, which undermined its potential benefits: "Sometimes these interactions do not happen because they are not taken seriously. Why should you fill in something which does not work?"[633] One officer summed up, "The APAS is excellent if you follow it through but without interaction it is not as effective."[634]

The PSTS also saw the reintroduction of performance contracts for permanent secretaries, this time technocratically driven by Zambian civil servants who wanted to see the system implemented in full as proposed by the Kasanga review of the early 2000s.[635] Work on establishing these began in 2012, with the rollout of performance contracts for permanent secretaries in 2015–2016.[636] Performance contracts began to be cascaded down to directors in 2019, with the aim of eventually cascading them down to all levels of staff so as to achieve a harmonized performance management and appraisal system through the civil service[637]—a direct echo of the initial vision of the PSRP's Performance Management Package in the 1990s. This unified vision was summarized by one individual involved in these reforms in Zambia: "We're trying to create a line of sight from the PS down to the last person."[638]

One major reason for the failure of PSCAP's earlier effort to introduce performance contracts was that permanent secretaries had lacked clear targets against which to measure performance, and, indeed, as of 2013, permanent secretaries still had no job descriptions.[639] The PSTS-era effort to introduce performance contracts thus made this a priority. Job descriptions for permanent secretaries were introduced in 2016, and performance contract targets were taken from each organization's annual work plan, which, in turn, were linked to the National Development Plan.[640] However, since the National Development Plan itself was highly ambitious—a "wish list"[641]—each permanent secretary's target was unrealistic, and so almost everyone scored poorly.[642] Another challenge encountered was how to define the scope of accountability for the purpose of the targets. The push from ministers was to focus targets on service delivery outcomes rather than organizational outputs, but technocrats noted that outcomes were affected by numerous factors outside the permanent secretary's control, making it too complex for a personal appraisal.[643] One such factor (resource sufficiency) was built into the contracts as part of a section on obligations of government to the permanent secretary, with the idea that they would be discharged from their obligations if budgeted resources were not delivered as promised,[644] but in a context where resource availability was frequently unpredictable, this likely also made the contracts harder to use as an objective basis for evaluation.

While (imperfect) targets for permanent secretaries were thus created by the system, as of this study's end date of 2019, there had been no linkage of any type of incentive to the result of the performance contract evaluation.[645] At the permanent secretary level, a challenge to the credibility of the contracts emerged from the fact that the president (rather than technocratic leadership or the formal measurement system of the performance contracts) held the ultimate say over appointments and contract renewals.[646] With the cascade of performance contracts to directors from 2019, a different challenge was presented—whether the conditions of service of permanent and pensionable civil servants (which directors were, unlike permanent secretaries) could be changed as a consequence of performance contracts.[647] Finally, the evaluation of permanent secretaries presented a logistical challenge because high-level employees like permanent secretaries could only be appraised by someone more senior—of whom there are few in the government. As one officer pointed out, as of May 2019, there were fifty-seven permanent secretaries in the government, and if each performance contract appraisal took just one to two hours of time from someone at the level of deputy secretary to Cabinet or higher, that would still be very time-consuming.[648] Overall, the PSTS-era adoption of performance contracts managed to assign clear (albeit somewhat contentious) targets to permanent secretaries but did not institutionalize the other elements of the performance contracting system (incentives, meritocratic appointment and contract renewal, and resource guarantees) that had been proposed by the Kasanga review.[649]

Despite these limitations, however, rank-and-file civil servants in Zambia expressed generally positive sentiments about their superiors' performance contracts. These stemmed largely from the perception that improved clarity of goals would spark both the intrinsic and extrinsic motivation of rank-and-file officers:

> If I do not perform then the Permanent Secretary will not perform. I do not want to see my permanent secretary fail. That is why we set goals and targets, we need to show if we met the target. We need to prove we shine. . . . It is about time people realized they are being paid for something.[650]

It has made me a lot more alert and cognisant. It helps to portray permanent secretaries in a positive light. Apart from knowing my mandate, I am contributing to the permanent secretary. There is double the motivation. . . . It will put people on edge and impact productivity.[651]

A final element of the PSTS that was in the early stages of its rollout as of 2019 was the introduction of Balanced Scorecards for ministries, which were a response to the challenges of using the National Development Plan as a basis for setting targets for performance contracts.[652] The idea was that the scorecards would provide not only a retrospective measure of performance but also a strategic map for the future[653] and clearer prioritization than the National Development Plan.[654] In practice, though, as of 2019, the rollout of the Balanced Scorecards was proving to be deeply time-consuming, and some institutions still did not have them created despite there being just two years until the end of the National Development Plan.[655] Given this, it is not possible to say whether the development of these scorecards had any effects on performance.

Although the PSTS era of reforms was driven and funded almost entirely by the government, there was one donor project that aimed to contribute toward performance improvement in central government: DFID's Public Sector Performance Project (PSPP). Initiated in 2014, the PSPP was focused mainly on decentralization and support to monitoring and evaluation and also included a component that aimed to help the Cabinet Office push performance improvement in ministries. This would have helped the Cabinet Office identify a set of priority reforms and work with the ministries responsible for delivering them.[656] However, this component of the project was dropped after the scoping phase due to a personnel issue.[657] The PSPP did, however, support study visits to the UK and Ghana that informed the passing of a new Public Service Commission Act in Zambia, which aimed to allow the Public Service Commission to play a more active role in encouraging individual-level performance improvement through streamlining, delegation, and a broadening of the institution's goals.[658] However, shortly after the passage of the new act, the commissioners were all replaced, which undermined cooperation between the commission and other reform actors, so as of 2019, there was little evidence that this had yet led to significant performance improvements.[659]

Notes

1. THE PUZZLE OF REFORM

1. Among a range of important multicountry studies on civil service reform in Africa, see for example: Ladipo Adamolekun, ed., *Public Administration in Africa: Main Issues and Selected Country Studies* (Westview Press, 1999); Brian Levy and Sahr Kpundeh, eds., *Building State Capacity in Africa: New Approaches, Emerging Lessons* (World Bank Institute, 2004); Joseph R. A. Ayee, *Reforming the African Public Sector: Retrospect and Prospects* (CODESRIA Green Book, 2008); Gelase Mutahaba, ed., "Human Resource Management in African Public Sector: Current State and Future Direction" (African Public Sector Human Resource Managers' Network, 2013); Benon C. Basheka and Lukamba-Muhiya Tshombe, *New Public Management in Africa: Emerging Issues and Lessons* (Routledge, 2017); as well as numerous other studies cited elsewhere in this book.

2. I am grateful for Henry for describing his own impossibly ambitious but important project in these terms and for allowing me to borrow the phrase.

3. A full review of this vast literature is beyond the scope of this book, but see, for example, recent reviews by: Frederico Finan et al., "The Personnel Economics of the Developing State," in *Handbook of Economic Field Experiments*, ed. Abhijit V. Banerjee and Esther Duflo (Elsevier, 2017), 467–514; Thomas Pepinsky et al., "Bureaucracy and Service Delivery," *Annual Review of Political Science* 20 (2017): 249–68; Timothy Besley et al., "Bureaucracy and Development," *Annual Review of Economics* 14 (2022): 397–424. For a focused application of this literature to the challenges of bureaucratic reform in a particular context, see Karthik Muralidharan, *Accelerating India's Development: A State-Led Roadmap for Effective Governance* (Penguin, 2024).

4. See, for example, Imran Rasul et al., "Management, Organizational Performance, and Task Clarity: Evidence from Ghana's Civil Service," *Journal of Public Administration Research and Theory* 31, no. 2 (2021): 259–77; Martin J. Williams and Liah Yecalo-Tecle, "Innovation, Voice, and Hierarchy in the Civil Service: Evidence from Ghana's Civil Service," *Governance* 33, no. 4 (2020): 789–807; Margherita Fornasari et al., "Ideas Generation in Hierarchical Bureaucracies: Evidence from a Field Experiment and Qualitative Data" (Working paper, June 2025).

5. See, for example, on measuring performance see: Colin Talbot, *Theories of Performance: Organizational and Service Improvement in the Public Domain* (Oxford University Press, 2010). On multiple competing goals: James Q. Wilson, *Bureaucracy* (Basic Books, 1989); Avinash Dixit, "Incentives and Organizations in the Public Sector: An Interpretative Review," *Journal of Human Resources* 37, no. 4

(2002): 696–727; Young Han Chun and Hal G. Rainey, "Goal Ambiguity and Organizational Performance in U.S. Federal Agencies," *Journal of Public Administration Research and Theory* 15 (2005): 529–57. On the differential measurability and joint production of bureaucratic tasks: Imran Rasul and Daniel Rogger, "Management of Bureaucrats and Public Service Delivery: Evidence from the Nigerian Civil Service," *Economic Journal* 128, no. 608 (2018): 413–46; Rasul et al., "Management, Organizational Performance, and Task Clarity"; Muhammad Yasir Khan, "Mission Motivation and Public Sector Performance: Experimental Evidence from Pakistan," (Mimeo, September 14, 2023). For more generalized discussions on methodological challenges of evaluating systemic reforms: Jonathan Boston, "The Challenge of Evaluating Systemic Change: The Case of Public Management Reform," *International Public Management Journal* 3 (2000): 23–46; Yuen Yuen Ang, *How China Escaped the Poverty Trap* (Cornell University Press, 2017).

6. "On the macrohistorical determinants of governance quality, see for example: Timothy Besley and Torsten Persson, *Pillars of Prosperity: The Political Economics of Development Clusters* (Princeton University Press, 2011); Daron Acemoglu and James A. Robinson, *Why Nations Fail: The Origins of Power, Prosperity, and Poverty* (Crown, 2012); Martha Wilfahrt, *Precolonial Legacies in Postcolonial Politics Representation and Redistribution in Decentralized West Africa* (Cambridge University Press, 2021). On geographical determinants of state capacity: Jeffrey Herbst, *States and Power in Africa: Comparative Lessons in Authority and Control* (Princeton University Press, 2000). On the impact of political economy context on reform: Brian Levy, *Working with the Grain: Integrating Governance and Growth in Development Strategies* (Oxford University Press, 2014); Daniel Appiah and Abdul-Gafaru Abdulai, "Competitive Clientelism and the Politics of Core Public Sector Reform in Ghana," ESID Working Paper 82 (March 2017); Sam Hickey and Naomi Hossain, eds., *The Politics of Education in Developing Countries: From Schooling to Learning* (Oxford University Press, 2019).

7. This is referred to as research about "the effects of causes" and the "causes of effects," respectively, in Gary Goertz and James Mahoney, *A Tale of Two Cultures: Qualitative and Quantitative Research in the Social Sciences* (Princeton University Press, 2012).

8. The distinction between core and frontline civil servants is blurry both conceptually and in practice. There is also significant variation across countries in the extent to which frontline staff like nurses or teachers are part of the same organizational structures and personnel management systems as administrators or technical experts sitting in ministry headquarters, and, hence, variation in whether such frontline staff are covered by the reforms I study. I try as much as possible to maintain the conceptual distinction in my data collection and analysis, although official documents and interviewees do not always make this same distinction. This notwithstanding, my analysis should be read as applying directly to reform of the core civil service only.

9. See Talbot, *Theories of Performance*, for a discussion on debates around the definition of performance and the nuances of conceptualizing it in civil service organizations.

10. By "whole civil service" I mean the whole of the core civil service, subject to the conceptual and practical blurriness discussed above.

11. This distinction builds on the concept of verifiability, introduced by Oliver Williamson, *The Economic Institutions of Capitalism* (Free Press, 1985) and subsequently foundational to much of contract theory and organizational economics, and adapts it to a public sector bureaucracy context in which the undertaking actions and tasks is a more suitable basis for analysis of performance than transactions (to which the terminology was originally applied).

12. On mimetic pressures and the transplantation of models that are inappropriate fits for context, see for example (within a large literature): Matt Andrews, *The Limits of Institutional Reform in Development: Changing Rules for Realistic Solutions* (Cambridge University Press, 2013); Matt Andrews et al., *Building State Capability: Evidence, Analysis, Action* (Oxford University Press, 2017); Rosina Foli and Frank L. K. Ohemeng, "The Role and Impact of International Bureaucrats in Policymaking in Africa," in *Routledge Handbook of Public Policy in Africa*, ed. Gedion Onyango (Routledge, 2021),

117–27. On political resistance to reform, see for example: Nicholas van de Walle, *African Economies and the Politics of Permanent Crisis* (Cambridge University Press, 2001); Sylvester Odhiambo Obong'o, "Political Influence, Appointments and Public Sector Management Reform In Kenya, 1963–2014" (PhD diss., University of Newcastle, Australia, 2015).

13. On the political economy of reform, see for example (in addition to works cited earlier): Frank L. Kwaku Ohemeng and Felix K. Anebo, "The Politics of Administrative Reforms in Ghana: Perspectives from Path Dependency and Punctuated Equilibrium Theories," *International Journal of Public Administration* 35, no. 3 (2012): 161–76; Vivek Srivastava and Marco Larizza, "Working with the Grain for Reforming the Public Service: A Live Example from Sierra Leone," *International Review of Administrative Sciences* 79, no. 3 (2013): 458–85; Mai Hassan and Ahmed Kodouda, "Dismantling Old—or Forging New—Clientelistic Ties? Sudan's Civil Service Reform After Uprising" (Mimeo, 2022).

14. On bottom-up reform approaches, see for example: Charles Polidano, "Why Civil Service Reforms Fail," *Public Management Review* 3, no. 3 (2001): 345–61; Christopher Pollitt and Geert Bouckaert, *Public Management Reform: A Comparative Analysis* (Oxford University Press, 2004); Ayee, *Reforming the African Public Sector*; Willy McCourt, "Models of Public Service Reform: A Problem-Solving Approach," World Bank Policy Research Working Paper 6428 (2013). On relational contracts approaches to management practices: Robert Gibbons and Rebecca Henderson, "Relational Contracts and Organizational Capabilities," *Organization Science* 23, no. 5 (2012): 1350–64; James N. Baron and David M. Kreps, "Employment as an Economic and Social Relationship," in *The Handbook of Organizational Economics*, ed. Robert Gibbons and John Roberts (Princeton University Press, 2013), 315–41. On backward mapping: Richard F. Elmore, "Backward Mapping: Implementation Research and Policy Decisions," *Political Science Quarterly* 94, no. 4 (1979): 601–16. On continuous improvement: Donald M. Berwick, "Continuous Improvement as an Ideal in Health Care," *New England Journal of Medicine* 320, no. 1 (1989): 53–56; Nadia Bhuiyan and Amit Baghel, "An Overview of Continuous Improvement: From the Past to the Present," *Management Decision* 43, no. 5 (2005): 761–771; Maxwell M. Yurkofsky et al., "Research on Continuous Improvement: Exploring the Complexities of Managing Educational Change," *Review of Research in Education* 44 (2020): 403–33; Anthony S. Bryk et al., *How a City Learned to Improve Its Schools* (Harvard University Press, 2023). On process approaches to organizational change: Andrew M. Pettigrew, "Longitudinal Field Research on Change: Theory and Practice," *Organization Science* 1, no. 3 (1990): 267–92; Wanda J. Orlikowski, "Improvising Organizational Transformation over Time: A Situated Change Perspective," *Information Systems Research* 7, no. 1 (1996): 63–92; Martha S. Feldman, "Organizational Routines as a Source of Continuous Change," *Organization Science* 11, no. 6 (2000): 611–29; Haridimos Tsoukas and Robert Chia, "On Organizational Becoming: Rethinking Organizational Change," *Organization Science* 13, no. 5 (2002): 567–82. On muddling and problem-solving: Charles E. Lindblom, "The Science of 'Muddling Through,'" *Public Administration Review* 19, no. 2 (1959): 79–88; Hugh Heclo, *Modern Social Politics in Britain and Sweden* (Yale University Press, 1974); Andrews, *Limits of Institutional Reform*; Katherine Bersch, *When Democracies Deliver: Governance Reform in Latin America* (Cambridge University Press, 2019). On bureaucratic cultures, autonomy, and organizational effectiveness: Merilee Grindle, "Divergent Cultures? When Public Organizations Perform Well in Developing Countries," *World Development* 25 (1997): 481–95; Judith Tendler, *Good Government in the Tropics* (Johns Hopkins University Press, 1997); David Leonard, "'Pockets' of Effective Agencies in Weak Governance States: Where Are They Likely and Why Does It Matter?" *Public Administration and Development* 30 (2010): 91–101; Michael Roll, ed., *The Politics of Public Sector Performance: Pockets of Effectiveness in Developing Countries* (Routledge, 2013); Dan Honig, *Navigation by Judgment: Why and When Top-Down Management of Foreign Aid Doesn't Work* (Oxford University Press, 2018); Erin McDonnell, *Patchwork Leviathan: Pockets of Bureaucratic Effectiveness in Developing States* (Princeton University Press, 2020); Akshay Mangla, *Making*

Bureaucracy Work: Norms, Education and Public Service Delivery in Rural India (Cambridge University Press, 2022). On agile government: Ines Mergel et al., "Agile: A New Way of Governing," *Public Administration Review* 18, no. 1 (2020): 161–65. On complexity and problem-driven iterative adaptation: Tunji Olaopa, *Managing Complex Reforms: A Public Sector Respective* (Bookcraft, 2011); Andrews et al., *Building State Capability*. Chapter 7 discusses these areas of literature more extensively.

2. THEORY AND EVIDENCE ON ORGANIZATIONAL PERFORMANCE

1. For an excellent review and discussion, see: Colin Talbot, *Theories of Performance: Organizational and Service Improvement in the Public Domain* (Oxford University Press, 2010).
2. Of course, issues can arise from the tensions among bureaucracies' multiple goals or between goals and rules. As these are the focus of a great deal of existing research and are not core to my study, I do not discuss these in the abstract here but instead discuss them as they arise in the context of specific reforms in the subsequent empirical parts of the book.
3. See, for example, Oliver Williamson, *The Economic Institutions of Capitalism* (Free Press, 1985); George P. Baker, "Incentive Contracts and Performance Measurement," *Journal of Political Economy* 100, no. 3 (1992): 598–614; George P. Baker et al., "Relational Contracts and the Theory of the Firm," *Quarterly Journal of Economics* 117, no. 1 (2002): 39–84.
4. James Q. Wilson. *Bureaucracy* (Basic Books, 1989).
5. Lant Pritchett, and Michael Woolcock, "Solutions When the Solution Is the Problem: Arraying the Disarray in Development," *World Development* 32, no. 2 (2004): 191–212; Matt Andrews et al., *Building State Capability: Evidence, Analysis, Action* (Oxford University Press, 2017).
6. See, for example, Herbert Kaufmann, *The Forest Ranger: A Study in Administrative Behavior* (Johns Hopkins University Press, 1960); Wilson, *Bureaucracy*; e.g., Canice Prendergast, "The Limits of Bureaucratic Efficiency," *Journal of Political Economy* 111, no. 5 (2003): 929–58; Young Han Chun and Hal G. Rainey, "Goal Ambiguity and Organizational Performance in U.S. Federal Agencies," *Journal of Public Administration Research and Theory* 15 (2005): 529–57.
7. See, for example, Avinash Dixit, "Incentives and Organizations in the Public Sector: An Interpretative Review," *Journal of Human Resources* 37, no. 4 (2002): 696–727; Muhammad Yasir Khan, "Mission Motivation and Public Sector Performance: Experimental Evidence from Pakistan" (Mimeo, September 14, 2023).
8. See, for example, Gwyn Bevan, and Christopher Hood, "What's Measured Is What Matters: Targets and Gaming in the English Health Care System," *Public Administration* 84, no. 3 (2006): 517–38; Steven Kelman and John N. Friedman, "Performance Improvement and Performance Dysfunction: An Empirical Examination of Distortionary Impacts of the Emergency Room Wait-Time Target in the English National Health Service," *Journal of Public Administration Research and Theory* 19 (2009): 917–46.
9. This discussion is based on Imran Rasul et al., "Management, Organizational Performance, and Task Clarity: Evidence from Ghana's Civil Service," *Journal of Public Administration Research and Theory* 31, no. 2 (2021): 259–277. For a broader methodological discussion, see Imran Rasul et al., "Government Analytics Using Data on Task and Project Completion," in *The Government Analytics Handbook: Leveraging Data to Strengthen Public Administration*, ed. Daniel Rogger and Christian Schuster (World Bank, 2023), 365–83.
10. Rasul et al., "Management, Organizational Performance, and Task Clarity," 266.
11. Rasul et al., "Management, Organizational Performance, and Task Clarity," 260, 266.

12. This and other sections draw in part on material from: Martin J. Williams, "From Institutions to Organizations: Management and Informality in Ghana's Bureaucracies," Working paper (London School of Economics and Political Science, September 9, 2015); and Martin J. Williams, "There Is More Than One 'Public Sector Way': The Diversity of Management Practices in Ghana's Government," Policy brief (November 2013).

13. The Office of the Head of Civil Service and Public Services Commission in Ghana are heavily involved in almost all human resources decisions pertaining to pay, promotion, hiring, and firing, including the definition of the staff appraisal process. Most of the organizations I interviewed were part of the civil service, while others were part of the public service but not civil service. For all intents and purposes the staff appraisal process was formally identical within the civil service and public service, although, in general, the public service organizations have a slightly higher degree of autonomy in making personnel decisions than the civil service organizations.

14. Justice N. Bawole et al., "Performance Appraisal or Praising Performance The Culture of Rhetoric in Performance Management in Ghana Civil Service," *International Journal of Public Administration* 36, no. 13 (2013): 953.

15. Frank L. Kwaku Ohemeng et al., "Performance Appraisal and Its Use for Individual and Organizational Improvement in the Civil Service of Ghana: The Case of Much Ado About Nothing?" *Public Administration and Development* 35 (2015): 179.

16. Within organizational economics, for example, see: Robert Gibbons and Rebecca Henderson, "Relational Contracts and Organizational Capabilities," *Organization Science* 23, no. 5 (2012): 1350–64; James N. Baron and David M. Kreps, "Employment as an Economic and Social Relationship," in *The Handbook of Organizational Economics*, ed. Robert Gibbons and John Roberts (Princeton University Press, 2013), 315–341.

17. See, for example, Douglass C. North, *Institutions, Institutional Change and Economic Performance* (Cambridge University Press, 1990); Peter Evans and James Rauch, "Bureaucracy and Growth: A Cross-National Analysis of the Effects of 'Weberian' State Structures on Economic Growth," *American Sociological Review* 64, no. 5 (1999): 748–65; Mushtaq H. Khan, "Political Settlements and the Governance of Growth-Enhancing Institutions" (Mimeo, 2010); Timothy Besley and Torsten Persson, *Pillars of Prosperity: The Political Economics of Development Clusters* (Princeton University Press, 2011); Daron Acemoglu and James A. Robinson, *Why Nations Fail: The Origins of Power, Prosperity, and Poverty* (Crown, 2012).

18. See, among many others, Nicholas Bloom and John Van Reenen, "Measuring and Explaining Management Practices Across Firms and Countries," *Quarterly Journal of Economics* 122 (2007): 1351–1408; Nicholas Bloom et al., "The Organization of Firms Across Countries," *Quarterly Journal of Economics* 127, no. 4 (2012): 1663–1705.

19. Following Bloom and Van Reenen, "Measuring and Explaining Management," these included: asking about de facto rather than de jure practices; scoring by the interviewer against an absolute scale with qualitative benchmarks rather than a relative, Likert-style scale; and beginning asking about each process with open, nonleading questions followed by probing follow-ups and requests for examples. See Williams, "From Institutions to Organizations," for additional details of data and methodology.

20. Practice-level scores were normalized first and averaged to compute organizational management scores, which were then renormalized for presentational purposes.

21. As Rasul et al., "Management, Organizational Performance, and Task Clarity," 265, describes, we matched the tasks listed in our reports to data to a subsample of tasks that had been audited by consultants commissioned by OHCS for another purpose. We were able to corroborate 94 percent of the reported completion levels from the reports we used, and the rare discrepancies were minor, suggesting that the data on task completion in the organizational self-reports was largely accurate.

22. Rasul et al., "Management, Organizational Performance, and Task Clarity," 265.

23. Imran Rasul and Daniel Rogger, "Management of Bureaucrats and Public Service Delivery: Evidence from the Nigerian Civil Service," *Economic Journal* 128, no. 608 (2018): 413–46.

24. Francis Owusu, "Differences in the Performance of Public Organisations in Ghana: Implications for Public-Sector Reform Policy," *Development Policy Review* 24, no. 6 (2006): 693–705.

25. Erin McDonnell, "Patchwork Leviathan: How Pockets of Bureaucratic Governance Flourish Within Institutionally Diverse Developing States," *American Sociological Review* 82, no. 3 (2017): 476–510; Erin McDonnell, *Patchwork Leviathan: Pockets of Bureaucratic Effectiveness in Developing States* (Princeton University Press, 2020).

26. See, for example, Merilee Grindle, "Divergent Cultures? When Public Organizations Perform Well in Developing Countries," *World Development* 25 (1997): 481–95; Judith Tendler, *Good Government in the Tropics* (Johns Hopkins University Press, 1997); David Leonard, "'Pockets' of Effective Agencies in Weak Governance States: Where Are They Likely and Why Does It Matter?" *Public Administration and Development* 30 (2010): 91–101; Michael Roll, ed., *The Politics of Public Sector Performance: Pockets of Effectiveness in Developing Countries* (Routledge, 2013).

27. McDonnell, *Patchwork Leviathan*, 20–21.

28. Daniel Gingerich, "Governance Indicators and the Level of Analysis Problem: Empirical Findings from South America," *British Journal of Political Science* 43, no. 3 (2013), 505–40; Katherine Bersch et al., "State Capacity, Bureaucratic Politicization, and Corruption in the Brazilian State," *Governance* 30, no. 1 (2016): 105–24.

29. Michael Carlos Best et al., "Individuals and Organizations as Sources of State Effectiveness," *American Economic Review* 113, no. 8 (2023): 2121–67.

30. Patricia W. Ingraham et al., *Government Performance: Why Management Matters* (Johns Hopkins University Press, 2003).

31. See, for example, Bloom and Van Reenen, "Measuring and Explaining Management"; Gibbons and Henderson, "Relational Contracts and Organizational Capabilities"; Chad Syverson, "What Determines Productivity?" *Journal of Economic Literature* 49, no. 2 (2011): 326–65.

3. WHAT DOES REFORM LOOK LIKE?
MAPPING REFORM EFFORTS OVER TIME

1. World Bank, *Report and Recommendation of the President of the International Development Association to the Executive Directors on a Proposed Credit in the Amount Equivalent to US$200 Million to the Republic of Zambia for a Privatization and Industrial Reform Adjustment Credit* (report P-5786-ZA, June 3, 1992), 6.

2. World Bank, *Implementation Completion Report—Zambia—Economic and Social Adjustment Credit (Credit 2577-ZA)* (report 15837, June 28, 1996), 3. The PSRP also included a component on decentralization, which is beyond the scope of this book.

3. Interview, ZAM11.

4. Interview, Ndashe Yumba.

5. Interview, Moses Kondowe.

6. World Bank, *Implementation Completion Report (Ida-33290 Ppfi-Q1440 Ppfi-Q1441) on a Credit in the Amount of Sdr 20.4 Million (US$28 Million Equivalent) to the Republic of Zambia for a Public Service Capacity Building Project in Support of the First Phase of the Public Service Capacity Building Program* (Report 34450, December 28, 2005), 9.

7. World Bank, *Implementation Completion Report (Ida-33290 Ppfi-Q1440 Ppfi-Q1441*, 9.

8. Mike Stevens and Stefanie Teggemann, "Comparative Experience with Public Service Reform in Ghana, Tanzania, and Zambia," in *Building State Capacity in Africa: New Approaches, Emerging Lessons*, ed. Brian Levy and Sahr Kpundeh, 43–86 (World Bank Institute, 2004), 72.

9. Interview, Moses Kondowe.
10. Theodore R. Valentine, *A Medium-Term Strategy for Enhancing Pay and Conditions of Service in the Zambian Public Service* (Crown Consultants International, 2002), 92.
11. University of Zambia, *Report on The Public Service Reform Programme (PSRP) and the Public Service Capacity Building Programme (PSCAP) Impact* Assessment, April 15, 2005, quoted in Universalia, *Assessment of the Current Performance Management System Final Report* (Legend Consulting Services and Universalia, 2008), 3.
12. Universalia, *Assessment of the Current Performance Management System*, 25.
13. Universalia, *Assessment of the Current Performance Management System*, 27.
14. Interview, John Kasanga.
15. Valentine, *A Medium-Term Strategy*, 88.
16. Universalia, *Assessment of the Current Performance Management System*, 29.
17. Interview, GHA7.
18. I am grateful to Leonardo Arriola for suggesting that I include this figure.
19. The reform content tables in the appendix distinguish among reform episodes in a more aggregated way than the reform timelines, in order to avoid "double-counting" overlapping or linked efforts to introduce a particular type of reform. The figures for how many times countries tried to introduce different types of reforms are therefore not commensurable with the total number of reform efforts listed earlier in the chapter, which correspond to the number of discrete entries on the reform timelines.
20. Interview, William Kartey; Interview, GHA7; Joseph R. A. Ayee, "Civil Service Reform in Ghana: A Case Study of Contemporary Reform Problems in Africa," *African Association of Political Science*, 6, no. 1 (2001), 1–41.
21. Government of Ghana, "Civil Service Performance Improvement Programme: The Way Forward" (pamphlet, n.d); Ayee, "Civil Service Reform in Ghana"; Stephen Adei and Yaw Boachie-Danquah, "The Civil Service Performance Improvement Programme (CSPIP) in Ghana: Lessons of Experience" (paper presented at the 24th AAPAM Annual Roundtable Conference on the African Public Service in the 21st Century—New Initiatives in Performance Management, November 25–29, 2002); Interview, Nana Agyekum-Dwamena; Interview, William Kartey; Interview, GHA7. That said, some rank-and-file officers reported seeing little impact from these activities on their day-to-day work (Interview, GHA12), and Adei and Boachie-Danquah, "The Civil Service Performance Improvement Programme," are strongly critical of CSPIP.
22. Interview, GHA7.
23. National Institutional Renewal Programme, *Annual Report for 1997* (NIRP Secretariat, Office of the President, Accra, 1997); National Institutional Renewal Programme, *Annual Report for 1998* (NIRP Secretariat, Office of the President, Accra, 1998).
24. Interview, William Kartey.
25. Stevens and Teggemann, "Comparative Experience with Public Service Reform," 70.
26. Interview, Nana Agyekum-Dwamena.
27. Interview, GHA7.
28. Interview, Moses Kondowe.
29. World Bank, *Implementation Completion Report (Ida-33290 Ppfi-Q1440 Ppfi-Q1441)*, 9.
30. Interview, GHA2.
31. Interview, Kwame Adorbor.
32. See, among many others: Christopher Pollitt and Geert Bouckaert, *Public Management Reform: A Comparative Analysis* (Oxford University Press, 2004); John Halligan, *Reforming Public Management and Governance: Impact and Lessons from Anglophone Countries* (Edward Elgar, 2020).
33. Charles Polidano, "Why Civil Service Reforms Fail," *Public Management Review* 3, no. 3 (2001): 346.
34. Mai Hassan, *Regime Threats and State Solutions: Bureaucratic Loyalty and Embeddedness in Kenya* (Cambridge University Press, 2020); Sylvester Odhiambo Obong'o, "Political Influence,

Appointments and Public Sector Management Reform In Kenya, 1963–2014" (PhD diss., University of Newcastle, Australia, 2015).

35. Daniel Appiah and Abdul-Gafaru Abdulai, "Competitive Clientelism and the Politics of Core Public Sector Reform in Ghana," ESID Working Paper 82 (March 2017); Frank L. Kwaku Ohemeng and Felix K. Anebo, "The Politics of Administrative Reforms in Ghana: Perspectives from Path Dependency and Punctuated Equilibrium Theories," *International Journal of Public Administration* 35, no. 3 (2012): 161–76.

36. République du Sénégal, "Rapport national sur la gouvernance au Senegal," Secretariat General de la Presidence de la République, Delegation a la Reforme de l'Etat et a l'Assistance Technique, Programme National de Bonne Gouvernance, 2011, 64; République du Sénégal, "Schema Directeur de Modernisation de l'Administration Publique (SDMAP) 2015–2022," (presentation, Bureau Organisation et Méthodes, Presidence de la République, Secretariat Général. n.d.), 10.

37. Reform start and end dates were coded as per the timelines in the appendix. Reform start or end dates that occur in the same year as an election are coded as zero. Since data is not always available on the exact month of start/end, some of the reforms coded as zero may have started before/ended after the election and thus would be assigned to different year bins if full data were available. Reforms that extended past 2019 were not assigned an end date, and reforms that started before the start of the democratic era in each country were excluded. In general, start dates for each reform are clear and easy to code, while coding end dates sometimes involved a judgment about when a reform ceased being active since many reforms are never formally terminated or repealed but rather cease being de facto relevant. In particular, some reforms (such as the passing of laws) by definition occur at single points in time and then remain in force indefinitely unless amended or repealed. On the timeline, such reforms are generally coded as lasting one year both for clarity and because the timeline represents reforms that are active at each point in time *as active reforms*, not necessarily which policies are in force at different points in time. Although assigning an end year to such reforms is an imperfect approach, the alternatives of excluding them altogether or coding them as active indefinitely would be more misleading. In any case, these challenges serve to reinforce the more important point that the boundaries of reforms are often blurry and ambiguous. I coded dates of elections as the years in which presidential elections actually took place in each country, including by-elections and delayed elections.

38. One might expect that government reforms may be more likely to conform to electoral cycles than donor-driven reforms, but excluding the thirty-one donor reforms identified later in this chapter does not change these general patterns.

39. Nicholas van de Walle, *African Economies and the Politics of Permanent Crisis* (Cambridge University Press, 2001).

40. Matt Andrews, *The Limits of Institutional Reform in Development: Changing Rules for Realistic Solutions* (Cambridge University Press, 2013), 215.

41. Rosina Foli and Frank L. K. Ohemeng, "The Role and Impact of International Bureaucrats in Policymaking in Africa," in *Routledge Handbook of Public Policy in Africa*, ed. Gedion Onyango (Routledge, 2021), 117–27.

42. Mark T. Buntaine et al., "Aiming at the Wrong Targets: The Domestic Consequences of International Efforts to Build Institutions," *International Studies Quarterly* 61 (2017): 471–88.

43. Tunji Olaopa. *The Nigerian Civil Service of the Future: A Prospective Analysis* (Bookcraft, 2014), 92.

44. See, for example: John Boli and George M. Thomas, eds., *Constructing World Culture: International Nongovernmental Organizations Since 1875* (Stanford University Press, 1999); Ngaire Woods, *The Globalizers: The IMF, the World Bank, and Their Borrowers* (Cornell University Press, 2014); Liam Swiss, *The Globalization of Foreign Aid: Developing Consensus* (Routledge, 2018).

45. There is some variation across countries and time in the extent to which donors were involved in reform efforts, which largely follows the expected pattern of donors being more involved during periods of fiscal stress and in countries with relatively less own-source revenue.

46. Interview, Nana Agyekum-Dwamena; Interview, GHA7.

47. Interview, ZAM11.

48. Interview, KEN2; Interview, Gemma Mbaya; Sylvester Odhiambo Obong'o, "Political Influence"; Chweya Ludeki, "Democratization and Civil Service Reform in Kenya" (PhD diss., Queen's University, Kingston, Ontario, Canada, 2003).

49. Interview, Kithinji Kiragu.

50. Interview, KEN6.

51. Interview, GHA4.

52. Folashadé Soulé-Kohndou, "Bureaucratic Agency and Power Asymmetry in Benin-China Relations," in *New Directions in Africa-China Studies*, ed. Chris Alden and Daniel Large (Routledge, 2018) 189–204.

53. Lindsay Whitfield, ed., *The Politics of Aid: African Strategies for Dealing with Donors* (Oxford University Press, 2009).

54. Obong'o, "Political Influence." Obong'o locates the cause of the failure of both these eras of reforms in the resistance of Kenyan politicians to reforms that would have diluted their patronage powers.

55. Interview, GHA15.

56. Interview, SA5.

57. Robert Dodoo, "Performance Standards and Measuring Performance in Ghana," *Public Administration and Development* 17 (1997): 115–21.

58. Margaret Kobia and Nura Mohammed, "The Kenyan Experience with Performance Contracting" (African Association for Public Administration and Management 28th Annual Roundtable Conference, Arusha, Tanzania, December 4–8, 2006.

59. Geraldine Joslyn Fraser-Moleketi, "Public Service Reform In South Africa: An Overview Of Selected Case Studies From 1994–2004" (MA thesis, University of Pretoria, South Africa, 2006).

60. Interview, KEN6; Innovations for Successful Societies, "Building A Culture Of Results Institutionalizing Rapid Results Initiatives In Kenya, 2005–2009," 2012; Abraham Rugo Muriu, "Performance Management in Kenya's Public Service: A Study on Performance Information Use" (PhD diss., University of Potsdam, Potsdam, Germany, 2017).

61. Interview, Ismail Akhalwaya.

62. Interview, John Kasanga; Interview, ZAM7; Interview, Moses Kondowe.

63. Innovations for Successful Societies, "Interview of Robertson Nii Akwei Allotey by Ashley McCants," Interview C-2, August 20, 2008.

4. THE "WHAT" OF REFORM

1. See, for example, Antoinette Weibel et al., "Pay for Performance in the Public Sector—Benefits and (Hidden) Costs," *Journal of Public Administration Research and Theory* 20, no. 2 (2010): 387–412; Zahid Hasnain et al., "The Promise of Performance Pay? Reasons for Caution in Policy Prescriptions in the Core Civil Service," *World Bank Research Observer* 29 (2014): 235–64; Frederico Finan et al., "The Personnel Economics of the Developing State," in *Handbook of Economic Field Experiments*, ed. Abhijit V. Banerjee and Esther Duflo (Elsevier, 2017), 467–514.

2. Author's calculations from table 6.6 in Organisation for Economic Cooperation and Development (OECD), *Government at a Glance 2019* (OECD, 2019) 123. For this purpose, I count a country as having an individual-level performance-linked incentive policy if it is recorded as having at least one of the following in place for its senior managers: existence of a performance-management regime for senior managers; performance related pay; performance agreement with the minister; performance agreement with the administrative head of the civil service; promotion for good performance; dismissal for bad performance. Comparable figures for rank-and-file officers were not available for 2019.

3. Universalia, *Assessment of the Current Performance Management System Final Report* (Legend Consulting Services and Universalia, 2008), 25–28.

4. J. J. Rawlings, "New Year Broadcast to the Nation," *Daily Graphic*, January 2, 1991, quoted in Joseph R. A. Ayee, "Civil Service Reform in Ghana: A Case Study of Contemporary Reform Problems in Africa," *African Association of Political Science* 6, no. 1 (2001): 18.

5. Interview, ZAM21.

6. Interview, Gemma Mbaya.

7. Office of the Head of Civil Service, *Towards an Effective Performance Appraisal System in the Civil Service* (report, Dr. S. A. Nkrumah, OHCS Archives, n.d).

8. Office of the Head of Civil Service, *Introduction of Merit/Performance Award System in the Civil Service*, circular ref. no. PNDC/SCR/A.08/15 (OHCS Archives, 1991).

9. Office of the Head of Civil Service, "Minutes of Meeting of Steering Committee on CSRP Held at the Conference Room of the Government Secretarial School Accra, on Wednesday, 17th November, 1993," 1993.

10. Theodore R. Valentine, *A Medium-Term Strategy for Enhancing Pay and Conditions of Service in the Zambian Public Service* (Crown Consultants International, 2002), 92.

11. See, for example, Interview, GHA9; Interview, GHA17; Interview, ZAM17; Interview, ZAM21; Interview, ZAM26.

12. Office of the Head of Civil Service, "Minutes of Meeting of Steering Committee on CSRP."

13. Office of the Head of Civil Service, *Merit/Performance Award Scheme in the Civil Service*," circular ref. no. OHCS/GEN/BC98/231/01 (OHCS Archives, 1995).

14. Government of Ghana, "National Public Sector Reform Strategy 2018–2023," Office of the Senior Minister, 2017.

15. As the appendix discusses, there is disagreement among sources about how many years this actually was delivered for, with one source reporting two years and others reporting around six years.

16. Interview, SA6.

17. Interview, GHA7; Public Services Commission Ghana, "Performance Management Policy for the Public Services of Ghana,"n.d.

18. Interview, ZAM22.

19. Office of the Head of Civil Service, *Introduction of Merit/Performance Award System*.

20. Interview, Sylvester Obong'o.

21. Universalia, "Assessment of the Current Performance Management System," 31.

22. Danny Sing, "Human Resource Challenges Confronting the Senior Management Service of the South African Public Service," *Public Personnel Management* 41, no. 2 (2012): 383–84.

23. Interview, ZAM22.

24. Interview, Felix Mushabati; Interview, ZAM11.

25. Interview, Roland Msiska.

26. Interview, SA5.

27. Interview, KEN6.

28. Abraham Rugo Muriu, "Performance Management in Kenya's Public Service: A Study on Performance Information Use" (PhD diss., University of Potsdam, Potsdam, Germany, 2017), 70.

29. Interview, Sean Phillips.

30. Interview, Chandiwira Nyirenda.

31. Interview, Joe Abah.

32. Interview, GHA13.

33. Interview, SA1.

34. Several sources cited unions' resistance to high-powered performance incentives, noting that unions feared that such systems could be subject to political manipulation (e.g. interview, Kodjo Mensah-Abrampa).

35. Interview, SA5.

36. Interview, GHA7.
37. Interview, SA5.
38. Interview, Moses Kondowe. Interview, SA1 also noted similar tensions in South Africa: "One of our big [battles] was about who's the employer of the DG [director-general]. Constitutionally the President appoints DGs, but their performance management is done mostly by Ministers. So there were some issues about 'if you don't appoint me you can't fire me.'"
39. Interview, SA6.
40. Interview, Sylvester Obong'o.
41. Universalia, "Assessment of the Current Performance Management System," 27.
42. Interview, Ismail Akhalwaya.
43. Allan Schick, "Why Most Developing Countries Should Not Try New Zealand's Reforms," *World Bank Research Observer* 13, no. 1 (1998): 123–31.
44. Office of the Head of Civil Service, "Minutes of Meeting of Steering Committee on CSRP," 7.
45. Republic of South Africa, *Report of the Presidential Review Commission on the Reform and Transformation of the Public Service in South Africa* (1998).
46. Interview, Roland Msiska.
47. Interview, Ian Ball.
48. Ian Ball, "Reinventing Government: Lessons Learned from the New Zealand Treasury," *Government Accountants Journal* 43, no. 3 (1994).
49. Interview, Ian Ball.
50. Ian Ball, "Presentation to the NZSA Public Sector Convention," November 1992.
51. Allan Schick, *The Spirit Of Reform: Managing the New Zealand State Sector in a Time of Change* (report prepared for the State Services Commission and The Treasury, New Zealand, August 1996), 74.
52. Ball, "Reinventing Government."
53. Schick, *The Spirit Of Reform.*
54. Interview, Ian Ball. Interestingly, one interviewee commented that the nontransparent confidential appraisal system that existed in Kenya prior to the CSRP reforms actually allowed for more differentiation in performance ratings—"good performers were actually noted, and good performers were actually promoted"—while also noting that nontransparent systems were also at risk of politically driven unfairness (interview, Sylvester Obong'o).
55. Interview, Ian Ball.
56. Schick, *The Spirit Of Reform,* 49.
57. In addition to works already cited, see (among many others): Graham Scott et al., "Reform of the Core Public Sector: New Zealand Experience," *Governance* 3, no. 2 (1990): 138–67; Jonathan Boston, "Assessing the Performance of Departmental Chief Executives: Perspectives from New Zealand," *Public Administration* 70 (1992): 405–28; Enid Wistrich, "Restructuring Government New Zealand Style," *Public Administration* 70 (1992): 119–35.
58. Government Accountability Office (GAO), "Federal Workforce: Distribution of Performance Ratings Across the Federal Government, 2013," response to Ron Johnson, May 9 2016, GAO-16-520R Federal Employee Performance Ratings.
59. Alessandro Spano and Patrizio Monfardini, "Performance-Related Payments in Local Governments: Do They Improve Performance or Only Increase Salary?" *International Journal of Public Administration* 41, no. 4 (2018): 327.
60. Organisation for Economic Cooperation and Development (OECD), *Performance-Related Pay Policies for Government Employees* (OECD, 2005), 11, 13–14.
61. OECD, "Performance-Related Pay Policies," 65.
62. Beryl Radin, *Challenging the Performance Movement* (Georgetown University Press, 2006); Donald P. Moynihan, *The Dynamics of Performance Management: Constructing Information and Reform* (Georgetown University Press, 2008).

63.   Christian Schuster et al., "The Global Survey of Public Servants: Evidence from 1,300,000 Public Servants in 1,300 Government Institutions in 23 Countries," *Public Administration Review* 83, no. 4 (2023): 982–93.

64.   Interview, SA1.

65.   Interview, Ismail Akhalwaya.

66.   Matt Andrews, *The Limits of Institutional Reform in Development: Changing Rules for Realistic Solutions* (Cambridge University Press, 2013).

67.   Kate Bridges and Michael Woolcock, "How (Not) to Fix Problems That Matter: Assessing and Responding to Malawi's History of Institutional Reform," World Bank Policy Research Working Paper 8289 (2017), 15.

68.   Jeffrey Braithwaite, "Changing How We Think About Healthcare Improvement," *British Medical Journal* 361 (1998): 2.

69.   C.f. Weibel et al., "Pay for Performance in the Public Sector"; Hasnain et al., "The Promise of Performance Pay?"; Finan et al., "The Personnel Economics of the Developing State."

70.   See, for example, Tessa Bold et al., "Experimental Evidence on Scaling Up Education Reforms in Kenya," *Journal of Public Economics* 168 (2018): 1–20.

71.   Tunji Olaopa, *The Nigerian Civil Servicve of the Future: A Prospective Analysis* (Bookcraft, 2014, 94).

72.   Interview, Joe Abah.

73.   Interview, Joe Abah.

5. THE "HOW" OF REFORM

1.   Kurt Lewin, *Field Theory in Social Science* (Harper and Row, 1951). The use of the term *episodic* to describe Lewinian models of change is drawn from the seminal review by Karl E. Weick and Robert E. Quinn, "Organizational Change and Development," *Annual Review of Psychology* 50 (1999): 361–86.

2.   World Bank, *ICR Review—Public Service Capacity Building Project (PSCAP)* (Independent Evaluation Group Report ICRR12372, 2006). In the end, PSCAP was cancelled after phase 1 fell short of its objectives.

3.   Government of Ghana, "Civil Service Performance Improvement Programme: The Way Forward" (pamphlet, n.d.), 4, 6, 9.

4.   Interview, Roland Msiska.

5.   Daniel Kahneman and Amos Tversky, "Intuitive Prediction: Biases and Corrective Procedures," *TIMS Studies in Management Science* 12 (1979): 313–27.

6.   Interview, Anand Rajaram.

7.   Gael Raballand et al., "How Civil Servants and Bank Staff Incentives and Behaviors Explain Outcomes of World Bank Public Sector Projects? Lessons from World Bank Completion Reports from 2000" (draft, 2016), quoted in Kate Bridges and Michael Woolcock, "How (Not) to Fix Problems That Matter: Assessing and Responding to Malawi's History of Institutional Reform," World Bank Policy Research Working Paper 8289 (2017), 21.

8.   Bent Flyvbjerg, "Policy and Planning for Large-Infrastructure Projects: Problems, Causes, Cures," *Environment and Planning B: Planning and Design* 34 (2007): 578.

9.   Flyvbjerg, "Policy and Planning," 584.

10.   Stefan Sveningsson and Nadja Sorgarde, *Managing Change in Organizations: How, What, and Why?* (SAGE Publications, 2019), 3.

11.   Interview, Nana Agyekum-Dwamena.

12.   Interview, Nana Agyekum-Dwamena.

13. Interview, Anand Rajaram.

14. Lavagnon Ika, "Project Management for Development in Africa: Why Projects Are Failing and What Can Be Done About It," *Project Management Journal* 43, no. 4 (2011): 27–41; Matt Andrews, *The Limits of Institutional Reform in Development: Changing Rules for Realistic Solutions* (Cambridge University Press, 2013); Matt Andrews et al., *Building State Capability: Evidence, Analysis, Action* (Oxford University Press, 2017); Mark T. Buntaine et al., "Aiming at the Wrong Targets: The Domestic Consequences of International Efforts to Build Institutions," *International Studies Quarterly* 61 (2017): 471–88; Kate Bridges and Michael Woolcock, "How (Not) to Fix Problems That Matter: Assessing and Responding to Malawi's History of Institutional Reform," World Bank Policy Research Working Paper 8289 (2017).

15. Anand Rajaram et al., "Public Sector Reform—Changing Behavior with Cars and Computers?" World Bank Blogs, February 16 2010, https://blogs.worldbank.org/africacan/public-sector-reform -changing-behavior-with-cars-and-computers.

16. Interview, Sean Phillips.

17. Interview, SA1.

18. Interview, GHA13.

19. Interview, GHA13.

20. Interview, Nana Agyekum-Dwamena.

21. World Bank, *Implementation Completion And Results Report (IDA-51040) On Three Credits In The Amount Of SDF 51.5 Million (US$ 80 Million Equivalent) To The Republic Of Zambia For Poverty Reduction Support Credits (PRSC) I, II And III* (report ICR2761, June 24 2013), 16.

22. Interview, ZAM14.

23. Interview, GHA7.

24. Interview, NIG1.

25. Interview, Sean Phillips.

26. Interview, ZAM5.

27. Herman Aguinis, *Performance Management*, 3rd edition (Pearson, 2013), quoted in Sabina Schnell et al., "Performance Management in the Public Administration: Seven Success Factors" (World Bank Equitable Growth, Finance, and Institutions Insight, 2021), 8.

28. E.g., Interview, GHA18; Interview, GHA21; Interview, GHA22; Interview, GHA30; Interview, GHA31.

29. Abraham Rugo Muriu, "Performance Management in Kenya's Public Service: A Study on Performance Information Use" (PhD diss., University of Potsdam, Potsdam, Germany, 2017); Frank L. Kwaku Ohemeng, "Institutionalizing the Performance Management System in Public Organizations in Ghana," *Public Performance & Management Review* 34, no. 4 (2011): 467–88.

30. Robert Dodoo, "Performance Standards and Measuring Performance in Ghana," *Public Administration and Development* 17 (1997): 115–21; Stephen Adei and Yaw Boachie-Danquah, "The Civil Service Performance Improvement Programme (CSPIP) in Ghana: Lessons of Experience" (paper presented at the 24th AAPAM Annual Roundtable Conference on the African Public Service in the 21st Century-New Initiatives in Performance Management, November 25–29, 2002); Joseph R. A. Ayee, "Civil Service Reform in Ghana: A Case Study of Contemporary Reform Problems in Africa," *African Association of Political Science*, 6, no. 1 (2001): 1–41; The top-down vs. bottom-up language and tension in public sector reform and development is also explored by numerous other authors, such as: Joseph R. A. Ayee, *Reforming the African Public Sector: Retrospect and Prospects* (CODESRIA Green Book, 2008); Willy McCourt, "Models of Public Service Reform: A Problem-Solving Approach," World Bank Policy Research Working Paper 6428 (2013); Frank L. Kwaku Ohemeng and Joseph R. A. Ayee, "The 'New Approach' to Public Sector Reforms in Ghana: A Case of Politics as Usual or a Genuine Attempt at Reform?" *Development Policy Review* 34, no. 2 (2016): 277–300. However, some authors use this language to refer to the tension between

government-led versus civil society- and voter-led instigation of change. In this book, I use these terms only to refer to the locus of change efforts and leadership within the bureaucracy.

31. Andrews, *The Limits of Institutional Reform in Development*.

32. Interview, NIG1.

33. Interview, Joe Abah.

34. Interview, NIG3; Interview, Nnenna Akajemeli.

35. Interview, Joe Abah.

36. Interview, NIG1.

37. Interview, Roland Msiska.

38. Interview, anonymous.

39. Interview, GHA13.

40. Interview, Tunji Olaopa.

41. Rogerio F. Pinto, "Projectizing the Governance Approach to Civil Service Reform: An Institutional Environment Assessment for Preparing a Sectoral Adjustment Loan in the Gambia," World Bank Discussion Paper 252 (1994).

42. Peter D. Toon, "Projectitis? Supporting Health Reform," *British Medical Journal* 331 (2005); Harald Schutzeichel, "Projectitis Is Curable," *Sun-Connect-News*, 2014, https://www.sun-connect-news.org/articles/business/details/projectitis-is-curable; Larisa Owen, "Projectitis vs. Systems Change: The Infusion of the Broader System Instead of Staying Inside the Silo of the Project," *PA Times Online* February 18, 2020, https://patimes.org/projectitis-vs-systems-change-the-infusion-of-the-broader-system-instead-of-staying-inside-the-silo-of-the-project/.

43. Arvi Kuura, "25 Years of Projectification Research," *PM World Journal* 9, no. 8 (2020): 2, referring to R. Müller, *Project Governance* (Routledge, 2009). See also P. D. Turnbull, "Effective Investment in Information Infrastructures," *Information and Software Technology* 33, no. 3 (1991): 191–99.

44. Charlotte Pickles and James Sweetland, "Breaking Down the Barriers: Why Whitehall Is so Hard to Reform," Reform, August 2023, 9.

6. MECHANISMS OF SUCCESS

1. Interview, GHA32.

2. Interview, ZAM27.

3. Interview, GHA10.

4. Universalia, *Assessment of the Current Performance Management System Final Report*, (Legend Consulting Services and Universalia, 2008), 5.

5. Interview, SA1.

6. Interview, Sylvester Obong'o.

7. Interview, SA1; interview, Sean Phillips.

8. Interview, SA5.

9. Interview, SA5.

10. Interview, NIG1; interview, Joe Abah; interview, NIG3; interview, Nnenna Akajemeli.

11. République du Sénégal, "Programme Nationale de Bonne Gouvernance," April 2002; Serigne Ahmadou Gaye, "La construction de l'administration du Senegal: entre realites societales et genie de modernisation?" Mimeo, 2020; interview, Souleymane Nasser Niane.

12. Innovations for Successful Societies, "Building A Culture Of Results Institutionalizing Rapid Results Initiatives In Kenya, 2005–2009," 2012; interview, Gemma Mbaya; interview, Sylvester Obong'o; interview KEN6.

13. Interview, Sean Phillips.

14. Republic of South Africa, "White Paper on Public Service Delivery," Government Gazette Notice 1459 of 1997, vol. 388, no. 18340, (October 1, 1997), 12–13.

15. Mashwahle Diphofa, "Towards Intensifying the Batho Pele Campaign," *Service Delivery Review: A Learning Journal for Public Managers* 1, no. 1 (2002): 35.

16. Interview, Ismail Akhalwaya.

17. Geraldine Joslyn Fraser-Moleketi, "Public Service Reform In South Africa: An Overview Of Selected Case Studies From 1994–2004" (MA thesis, University of Pretoria, South Africa, 2006), 71.

18. Public Service Commission, *Report on the Assessment of the Effectiveness of the Batho Pele Policy in Public Service Delivery* (June 2012).

19. Interview, Kithinji Kiragu; Interview KEN6.

20. Interview, Tunji Olaopa.

21. Interview, Sean Phillips.

22. Donald P. Moynihan, *The Dynamics of Performance Management: Constructing Information and Reform* (Georgetown University Press, 2008).

23. Sabina Schnell et al., "Performance Management in the Public Administration: Seven Success Factors" (World Bank Equitable Growth, Finance, and Institutions Insight, 2021), 21.

7. REFORM AS PROCESS: THEORY

1. James N. Baron and David M. Kreps, "Employment as an Economic and Social Relationship," in *The Handbook of Organizational Economics*, ed. Robert Gibbons and John Roberts (Princeton University Press, 2013), 321.

2. Robert Gibbons and Rebecca Henderson, "Relational Contracts and Organizational Capabilities," *Organization Science* 23, no. 5 (2012): 1350–64.

3. C.f. Marc Esteve and Christian Schuster, *Motivating Public Employees* (Cambridge Elements, 2017); James Perry, *Managing Organizations to Sustain Passion for Public Service* (Cambridge University Press, 2020); Dan Honig, *Mission Driven Bureaucrats: Empowering People to Help Government Do Better* (Oxford University Press, 2024).

4. Among others, see: Armen A. Alchian and Harold Demsetz, "Production, Information Costs, and Economic Organization," *American Economic Review* 62, no. 5 (1972): 777–95; Jack H. Knott, "Comparing Public and Private Management: Cooperative Effort and Principal-Agent Relationships," *Journal of Public Administration Research and Theory* 3, no. 1 (1993): 93–119; Gary Miller and Andrew B. Whitford, "The Principal's Moral Hazard: Constraints on the Use of Incentives in Hierarchy," *Journal of Public Administration Research and Theory* 17, no. 2 (2007): 213–33.

5. Sean Nicholson et al., "Measuring the Effects of Work Loss on Productivity With Team Production," *Health Economics* 15 (2006): 115–16.

6. For generality, I do not make strong assumptions about the production function through which individual tasks are aggregated into team-produced outputs. All that is necessary for the team-production aspect of this theory to be relevant is that performance across workers is not completely substitutable, such that poor performance from worker 1 can't be fully made up for by extra effort from worker 2, and so on. An extreme version of team-production would be an "O-ring" production function (Michael Kremer, "The O-Ring Theory of Economic Development," *Quarterly Journal of Economics* 108, no. 3 [1993]: 551–75) such that the quality of the output is determined by the minimum performance of contributing workers.

7. Baron and Kreps, "Employment as an Economic and Social Relationship"; Robert Gibbons and Rebecca Henderson, "What Do Managers Do?" in *The Handbook of Organizational Economics*, ed. Robert Gibbons and John Roberts (Princeton University Press, 2013), 680–731.

8. Robert Axelrod, *The Evolution of Cooperation* (Basic Books, 1984).

9. c.f. Sylvain Chassang, "Building Routines: Learning, Cooperation, and the Dynamics of Incomplete Relational Contracts," *American Economic Review* 100, no. 1 (2010): 448–65; Robert Gibbons et al., "What Situation Is This? Shared Frames and Collective Performance" (mimeo, June 2020).

10. Michael Lipsky, "Toward a Theory of Street-Level Bureaucracy," IRP Discussion Papers no. 48–69, Madison, WI (1969); Jeffrey L. Pressman, and Aaron Wildavsky, *Implementation* (University of California Press, 1974).

11. Yamini Aiyar et al., *Rewriting the Grammar of the Education System: Delhi's Education Reform (A Tale of Creative Resistance and Creative Disruption)* (Research on Improving Systems of Education [RISE], 2021), 3.

12. Richard F. Elmore, "Backward Mapping: Implementation Research and Policy Decisions," *Political Science Quarterly* 94, no. 4 (1979): 601–16.

13. See for example: Andrew M. Pettigrew, "Longitudinal Field Research on Change: Theory and Practice," *Organization Science* 1, no. 3 (1990): 267–92; Wanda J. Orlikowski, "Improvising Organizational Transformation Over Time: A Situated Change Perspective," *Information Systems Research* 7, no. 1 (1996): 63–92; Martha S. Feldman, "Organizational Routines as a Source of Continuous Change," *Organization Science* 11, no. 6 (2000): 611–29; Haridimos Tsoukas and Robert Chia, "On Organizational Becoming: Rethinking Organizational Change," *Organization Science* 13, no. 5 (2002): 567–82; Leni Wild et al., *Doing Development Differently: Who We Are, What We're Doing and What We're Learning* (Overseas Development Institute, 2016); Matt Andrews et al., *Building State Capability: Evidence, Analysis, Action* (Oxford University Press, 2017).

14. David Kreps, "Corporate Culture and Economic Theory," in *Perspectives on Positive Political Economy*, ed. James Alt and Kenneth Shepsle (Cambridge University Press, 1990), 90–143; Sylvain Chassang, "Building Routines: Learning, Cooperation, and the Dynamics of Incomplete Relational Contracts," *American Economic Review* 100, no. 1 (2010): 448–65; Gibbons and Henderson, "Relational Contracts and Organizational Capabilities"; Gibbons et al., "What Situation Is This?"

15. Peter Madsen et al., "Mitigating Hazards Through Continuing Design: The Birth and Evolution of a Pediatric Intensive Care Unit," *Organization Science* 17, no. 2 (2006): 239.

16. Quoted in Robert Gibbons, "Visible Hands: Governance of Value Creation—Within Firms and Beyond," *American Economic Review Papers and Proceedings* 110, no. 5 (2020): 175.

17. This use of the phrase is slightly different than Feldman's reference to organizational routines as "ongoing accomplishments" (in Feldman, "Organizational Routines," 613; quoted in Tsoukas and Chia, "On Organizational Becoming," 572), though in a similar spirit.

18. As very rough and suggestive evidence of the divergence between the (each enormous) literature on continuous improvement and on continuous/process-focused approaches to studying organizational change/process, the phrase "continuous improvement" appears only once across four classic articles on models of organizational change (Orlikowski, "Improvising Organizational Transformation"; Tsoukas and Chia, "On Organizational Becoming"; Karl E. Weick and Robert E. Quinn, "Organizational Change and Development," *Annual Review of Psychology* 50 (1999): 361–86; Andrew H. Van de Ven and Marshall Scott Poole, "Alternative Approaches for Studying Organizational Change," *Organization Studies* 26, no. 9 (2005): 1377–1404.

19. Nadia Bhuiyan and Amit Baghel, "An Overview of Continuous Improvement: From the Past to the Present," *Management Decision* 43, no. 5 (2005): 761.

20. Donald M. Berwick, "Continuous Improvement as an Ideal in Health Care," *New England Journal of Medicine* 320, no. 1 (1989): 54, summarizing M. Imai, *Kaizen: The Key to Japanese Competitive Success* (Random House, 1986).

21. c.f. Berwick, "Continuous Improvement"; Braithwaite, "Changing How We Think About Healthcare Improvement," *British Medical Journal* 361 (1998): 1–5; Maxwell M. Yurkofsky et al., "Research

on Continuous Improvement: Exploring the Complexities of Managing Educational Change," *Review of Research in Education* 44 (2020): 403–33; Anthony S. Bryk et al., *How a City Learned to Improve Its Schools* (Harvard University Press, 2023).

22. Bhuiyan and Baghel, "An Overview," 766.

23. Matt Andrews, *The Limits of Institutional Reform in Development: Changing Rules for Realistic Solutions* (Cambridge University Press, 2013); Matt Andrews et al., *Building State Capability: Evidence, Analysis, Action* (Oxford University Press, 2017).

24. T. Reay et al., "Legitimizing a New Role: Small Wins and Microprocesses of Change," *Academy of Management Journal* 49, no. 5 (2006): 977.

25. e.g. Edgar H. Schein, *Organizational Culture and Leadership* (Jossey-Bass, 1985); D. M. Rousseau, *Psychological Contracts in Organizations: Understanding Written and Unwritten Agreements* (Sage Publications, 1995); Luigi Guiso et al., "The Value of Corporate Culture," *Journal of Financial Economics* 117 (2015): 60–76; Elizabeth Martinez et al., "Organizational Culture and Performance," *American Economic Review Papers and Proceedings* 105, no. 5 (2015): 331–35.

26. For a review and synthesis, see Martha S. Feldman and Wanda J. Orlikowski, "Theorizing Practice and Practicing Theory," *Organization Science* 22, no. 5 (2011): 1240–53.

27. Aung Hein, "Essays on the Organizational Socialization of New Recruits in the Public Sector" (PhD diss., University of Oxford, 2023).

28. W. Warner Burke, *Organization Change: Theory and Practice*, 5th ed. (SAGE, 2018), 255. Capitalization has been changed from title case to sentence case. For related discussion, see, among others, Anne M. Khademian, "Leading Through Cultural Change," in *The Oxford Handbook of American Bureaucracy*, ed. Robert F. Durant (Oxford University Press, 2010), 303–23.

29. e.g. Orlikowski, "Improvising Organizational Transformation"; Weick and Quinn, "Organizational Change and Development"; Ben S. Kuipers et al., "The Management of Change in Public Organizations: A Literature Review," *Public Administration* 92, no. 1, (2014): 1–20 make this point in their excellent review of the public sector literature on organizational change.

30. Karl E. Weick, "Small Wins: Redefining the Scale of Social Problems," *American Psychologist* 39, no. 1 (1984): 40–49.

31. Interview, Kithinji Kiragu; Interview, KEN6.

32. I am grateful to Clare Leaver for this point.

33. Jillian Chown, "The Appealing Illusion of Frontline Employee-Driven Continuous Improvement: The Challenges of Empowering Frontline Employees to Solve Organizational Problems" (mimeo, November 2021).

34. Andrews et al., *Building State Capability*.

35. Judith Tendler. *Good Government in the Tropics* (Johns Hopkins University Press, 1997); Merilee Grindle, "Divergent Cultures? When Public Organizations Perform Well in Developing Countries," *World Development* 25 (1997): 481–95; Erin McDonnell, "Patchwork Leviathan: How Pockets of Bureaucratic Governance Flourish Within Institutionally Diverse Developing States," *American Sociological Review* 82, no. 3 (2017): 476–510; Erin McDonnell, *Patchwork Leviathan: Pockets of Bureaucratic Effectiveness in Developing States* (Princeton University Press, 2020); Akshay Mangla, *Making Bureaucracy Work: Norms, Education and Public Service Delivery in Rural India* (Cambridge University Press, 2022).

36. Charles Polidano, "Why Civil Service Reforms Fail," *Public Management Review* 3, no. 3 (2001): 345–61; Joseph R. A. Ayee, *Reforming the African Public Sector: Retrospect and Prospects* (CODESRIA Green Book, 2008); Christopher Pollitt and Geert Bouckaert, *Public Management Reform: A Comparative Analysis* (Oxford University Press, 2004); Willy McCourt, "Models of Public Service Reform: A Problem-Solving Approach," World Bank Policy Research Working Paper 6428 (2013); Ben S. Kuipers et al., "The Management of Change in Public Organizations: A Literature Review," *Public Administration* 92, no. 1 (2014): 1–20.

37. Robert Dodoo, draft speech on theme "Civil Service Reform in Africa: Past Experience and Future Trends," for panel discussion on "The Core Elements of Civil Service Reform: An Assessment of Relevance and Impact," prepared for African Association for Public Administration and Management (AAPAM) 17th Roundtable Conference, Egypt, March 2–5, 1996, OHCS archives.

38. McCourt, "Models of Public Service Reform"; Katherine Bersch, *When Democracies Deliver: Governance Reform in Latin America* (Cambridge University Press, 2019).

39. Andrews et al., *Building State Capability*.

40. Hugh Heclo, *Modern Social Politics in Britain and Sweden* (Yale University Press, 1974); Charles E. Lindblom, "The Science of 'Muddling Through,'" *Public Administration Review* 19, no. 2 (1959): 79–88.

41. Leni Wild et al., *Doing Development Differently: Who We Are, What We're Doing and What We're Learning*" (Overseas Development Institute, 2016); World Bank, "GovEnable: Locally Co-Created Solutions to Government Service Delivery Challenges," accessed April 19, 2024, https://shorturl.at /TSZh3.

42. Imran Rasul and Daniel Rogger, "Management of Bureaucrats and Public Service Delivery: Evidence from the Nigerian Civil Service," *Economic Journal* 128, no. 608 (2018): 413–46; Imran Rasul et al., "Management, Organizational Performance, and Task Clarity: Evidence from Ghana's Civil Service," *Journal of Public Administration Research and Theory* 31, no. 2 (2021): 259–77; Oriana Bandiera et al., "The Allocation Of Authority In Organizations: A Field Experiment With Bureaucrats," *Quarterly Journal of Economics* (2021), 2195–2242.

43. Organisation for Economic Cooperation and Development (OECD), *Public Employment and Management 2021: The Future Of The Public Service* (OECD, 2021).

44. McDonnell, "Patchwork Leviathan"; McDonnell, *Patchwork Leviathan*.

45. c.f. Bernard M. Bass, *Leadership and Performance Beyond Expectations* (Free Press, 1985); Ulrich Thy Jensen et al., "Conceptualizing and Measuring Transformational and Transactional Leadership," *Administration and Society* 51, no. 1 (2019): 3–33.

46. For an education-focused review, see Alma Harris et al., "System Leaders and System Leadership: Exploring the Contemporary Evidence Base," *School Leadership & Management* 41, nos. 4–5 (2021), 387–408. For a health-focused review, see Lucy Gilson and Irene Akua Agyepong, "Strengthening Health System Leadership for Better Governance: What Does It Take?" *Health Policy and Planning* 33 (2018): iii–ii4.

47. Thubelihle Mathole et al., "Leadership and the Functioning of Maternal Health Services in Two Rural District Hospitals in South Africa," *Health Policy and Planning* 33 (2018): ii5.

48. For excellent reviews, see Elinor Ostrom, "Beyond Markets and States: Polycentric Governance of Complex Economic Systems," *American Economic Review* 100 (2010), 641–72; Andreas Thiel et al., eds., *Governing Complexity: Analyzing and Applying Polycentricity* (Cambridge University Press, 2019). Much of this work focuses on scenarios where these decisionmakers are formally independent; this can sometimes be the case within bureaucratic systems, although de facto and partial independence of power bases and decision authorities tends to be more common.

49. For a review, see Zahra Mansoor and Martin J. Williams, "Systems Approaches to Public Service Delivery: Methods and Frameworks," *Journal of Public Policy* 44, no. 2 (2024): 258–83.

50. Tunji Olaopa, *Managing Complex Reforms: A Public Sector Respective* (Bookcraft, 2011). Quote is from Andrews et al., *Building State Capability*, 1.

51. Douglas C. Engelbart, "Toward High-Performance Organizations: A Strategic Role for Groupware," in *Proceedings of the GroupWare '92 Conference* (Morgan Kaufmann Publishers, 1992), 77–100; Jennifer Lin Russell et al., "A Framework for the Initiation of Networked Improvement Communities," *Teachers College Record* 119 (2017): 1–36.

8. REFORM AS PROCESS IN GHANA, 2014–2019

1. Parts of this chapter draw on a longer teaching case I coauthored with Sarah McAra, which is available for free online and can be used in classes, executive education, trainings, meetings, and workshops to animate group discussion of these issues. The main case and epilogue can be downloaded at: https://www.thecasecentre.org/products/view?id=189062. Instructors can request the teaching note through the same website (all free of charge). A Portuguese translation is also available at: https://www.thecasecentre.org/products/view?id=189065.

2. Given the nature of this chapter, I shared a complete draft with Agyekum-Dwamena to ensure that my analysis of his approach resonated with his own thinking and perspective on what he tried to do. At his request, minor changes of emphasis and corrections were made, though the core analysis of the chapter remains mine.

3. Interview, Nana Agyekum-Dwamena.

4. Interview, Nana Agyekum-Dwamena.

5. Personal communication, Nana Agyekum-Dwamena.

6. Interview, Nana Agyekum-Dwamena.

7. Various in Martin J. Williams and Sarah McAra, "Civil Service Reform in Ghana," Blavatnik School of Government Teaching Case, 2022.

8. Personal communication, Nana Agyekum-Dwamena.

9. Francis Owusu, "Differences in the Performance of Public Organisations in Ghana: Implications for Public-Sector Reform Policy," *Development Policy Review* 24, no. 6 (2006): 693–705; Martin J. Williams, "From Institutions to Organizations: Management and Informality in Ghana's Bureaucracies," Working paper, London School of Economics and Political Science, (September 9, 2015); Erin McDonnell, "Patchwork Leviathan: How Pockets of Bureaucratic Governance Flourish Within Institutionally Diverse Developing States," *American Sociological Review* 82, no. 3 (2017): 476–510.

10. Rachel Sigman, "Which Jobs for Which Boys? Party Financing, Patronage and State Capacity in African Democracies" (PhD diss., Maxwell School Syracuse University, 2015), 147.

11. Interview, Nana Agyekum-Dwamena.

12. Various in Williams and McAra, "Civil Service Reform in Ghana.

13. Interview, Nana-Agyekum-Dwamena.

14. Interview, Nana-Agyekum-Dwamena.

15. Interview, Nana-Agyekum-Dwamena.

16. Ghana News Agency, "The Civil Service Endorses Punctuality Campaign," GhanaWeb, October 4, 2018, https://www.ghanaweb.com/GhanaHomePage/NewsArchive/The-Civil-Service-endorses-Punctuality-Campaign-690024.

17. Nana Agyekum-Dwamena, interview with case writers, April 7, 2022.

18. Blavatnik School of Government "Public Sector Deep Dive: Professionalism for Performance: Innovative Public Management," Presentation by Nana Agyekum-Dwamena, Challenges of Government Conference, June 20, 2017, 1 hour, 11 min., 31 sec., YouTube video, https://www.youtube.com/watch?v=txAnw8YA-Ns.

19. Interview, Nana Agyekum-Dwamena.

20. Interview, Nana-Agyekum-Dwamena.

21. Interview, Nana Agyekum-Dwamena.

22. Interview, Nana Agyekum-Dwamena.

23. Interview, Nana Agyekum-Dwamena.

24. Interview and personal communication, Nana Agyekum-Dwamena.

25. Interview and personal communication, Nana Agyekum-Dwamena.

26. Interview, Nana Agyekum-Dwamena.
27. Interview, Nana Agyekum-Dwamena.
28. Personal communication, Nana Agyekum-Dwamena.
29. Interview and personal communication, Nana Agyekum-Dwamena.
30. Interview, Nana Agyekum-Dwamena.
31. Interview, Nana Agyekum-Dwamena.
32. Interview, Nana Agyekum-Dwamena.
33. Personal communication, Nana Agyekum-Dwamena.
34. Ernest Zume, "PSRRP Implementation: The Journey so Far," *Modern Ghana*, May 16, 2022, https://www.modernghana.com/news/1158400/psrrp-implementation-the-journey-so.html; Freedom Radio, "COVID-19 Pandemic: Civil Service Goes Digital," August 9, 2021, accessed June 2022, https://freedomradiogh.com/covid-19-pandemic-civil-service-goes-digital/; interview, Nana Agyekum-Dwamena.
35. Interview, Nana Agyekum-Dwamena.
36. Interview, GHA15; personal communication, Nana Agyekum-Dwamena.
37. Interview, Nana Agyekum-Dwamena.
38. Interview, GHA15.
39. Interview, GHA20; interview, GHA29.
40. Interview, Dora Dei-Tumi; interview GHA7.
41. E.g., interview, GHA23; interview, GHA28; interview GHA32.
42. Interview, GHA14; interview, GHA17; interview, GHA31.
43. Interview, GHA9.
44. Interview, GHA10.
45. Interview, GHA19.
46. Interview, GHA15.
47. Interview, GHA11.
48. Interview, GHA15; interview, GHA17; interview, GHA22; interview, GHA29; interview, GHA30.
49. Interview, William Kartey.
50. Interview, GHA13.
51. Interview, GHA22.
52. Interview, GHA28.
53. Interview, GHA9.
54. Interview, GHA26.
55. Interview, GHA7.
56. Interview, GHA17.
57. Interview, GHA7.
58. Interview, GHA26.
59. E.g., interview, GHA9; interview, GHA11, interview, GHA29; interview, GHA31; interview, GHA32.
60. Interview, GHA18.
61. Interview, GHA29.
62. Interview, GHA21; interview, GHA22; interview, GHA24.
63. Imran Rasul et al., "How Do Management Practices in Government Change Over Time? Evidence from Ghana" (Policy brief for International Growth Centre and Economic Development and Institutions research initiative, 2019).
64. This figure is based on comparing the averages of individual-level management indices across approximately three thousand interviewees per survey wave. Comparing organization-level average management indices yields a larger estimated increase (0.17 standard deviations) but is less statistically significant due to the smaller sample size.

65. All quotes in paragraph from interview, GHA13.

66. Interview, Dora Dei-Tumi.

67. Interview, Dora Dei-Tumi.

68. Interview, Dora Dei-Tumi.

69. Interview, Dora Dei-Tumi; interview, William Kartey; interview GHA7; interview GHA29.

70. Among many studies, see for example, Martin J. Williams and Liah Yecalo-Tecle, "Innovation, Voice, and Hierarchy in the Civil Service: Evidence from Ghana's Civil Service," *Governance* 33, no. 4 (2020): 789–807; James Perry, *Managing Organizations to Sustain Passion for Public Service* (Cambridge University Press, 2020); Dan Honig, *Mission Driven Bureaucrats: Empowering People to Help Government Do Better* (Oxford University Press, 2024).

71. Interview, Nana Agyekum-Dwamena.

72. Interview, Nana Agyekum-Dwamena.

73. Personal communication, Nana Agyekum-Dwamena.

74. Interview and personal communication, Nana Agyekum-Dwamena. This quote should be read as Agyekum-Dwamena's account of the meeting. Due to the nature of the conversations, I have not attempted to independently verify them.

75. Interview, Nana Agyekum-Dwamena.

76. Interview, GHA7.

77. Interview, GHA27.

78. Interview, Nana Agyekum-Dwamena.

9. A PRAGMATIC APPROACH TO REFORM

1. Abhijit Banerjee et al., "Decision Theoretic Approaches to Experiment Design and External Validity," in *Handbook of Economic Field Experiments*, ed. A. V. Banerjee and E. Duflo (Elsevier, 2017), 141–74.

2. For related discussions on how task type might affect management and reform strategies, see: Lant Pritchett and Michael Woolcock, "Solutions When the Solution Is the Problem: Arraying the Disarray in Development," *World Development* 32, no. 2 (2004): 191–12; Matt Andrews et al., *Building State Capability: Evidence, Analysis, Action* (Oxford University Press, 2017).

3. c.f., Steven Levitsky and Maria Victoria Murrillo, "Variation in Institutional Strength," *Annual Review of Political Science* 12 (2009): 115–33; Robert Gibbons and Woody Powell, "Why Are Organizations So Full of Rules That Are Not Followed or Enforced?" Presentation to Economic History Association, October 29, 2021.

4. I am grateful to Jurgen Blum for helpful prompting and discussions on this point.

5. For an especially thoughtful and balanced discussion on this issue in the context of post-conflict settings, see Jurgen Rene Blum et al., *Building Public Services in Postconflict Countries: A Comparative Analysis of Reform Trajectories in Afghanistan, Liberia, Sierra Leone, South Sudan, and Timor-Leste* (World Bank, 2019).

6. Dana Qarout, "The Accountability Paradox: Delivery Units in Jordan's Education Sector 2010–2019," DeliverEd Initiative Working Paper (November 2022).

7. Among many others, see for example: Tim Kelsall and David Booth, "Developmental Patrimonialism? Questioning the Orthodoxy on Political Governance and Economic Progress in Africa," Africa Power and Politics Programme Working Paper 9 (2010); Mushtaq H. Khan, "Political Settlements and the Governance of Growth-Enhancing Institutions" (mimeo, 2010); Brian Levy, *Working with the Grain: Integrating Governance and Growth in Development Strategies* (Oxford University Press, 2014); Daniel Appiah and Abdul-Gafaru Abdulai, "Competitive Clientelism and the Politics of Core Public Sector Reform in Ghana," ESID Working Paper 82 (March 2017); Pablo Yanguas,

"Varieties of State-Building in Africa: Elites, Ideas and the Politics of Public Sector Reform," ESID Working Paper no. 89 (August 2017).

8. Sylvester Odhiambo Obong'o, "Particularistic Exchanges and Pacts of Domination In Africa: Examining How Patronage Appointments May Have Increased Resistance to Public Sector Reforms in Kenya," *International Public Management Review* 14, no. 1, (2013): 27–46; Sylvester Odhiambo Obong'o, "Political Influence, Appointments and Public Sector Management Reform In Kenya, 1963–2014" (PhD diss., University of Newcastle, Australia, 2015); Appiah and Abdulai, "Competitive Clientelism."

APPENDIX: COUNTRY REFORM HISTORIES

1. I was fortunate to have support in compiling these reform histories from a number of excellent research assistants: Aisha Ali, Bashar Hobbi, Morgan DaCosta, Allan Kasapa, Oshmita Ray, and Liah Yecalo-Tecle.

2. These were the AidData Research Release v3.1 (AidDataCore_ResearchRelease_Level1_v3, released October 6, 2017) and Dan Honig's Project Performance Database (July 3, 2018 release). Projects with CRS/AidData purpose codes 15110 (public sector policy and administrative management) or 15111 (public finance management) were flagged as potentially fitting the definition of reform.

3. For example, "Ghana" + "civil service reform," "Nigeria" + "government performance improvement," "South Africa" + "Department of Public Service and Administration." Searches were undertaken on: Google Scholar; Oxford's SOLO search system that covers numerous databases of journal articles, media, books, and other material; and Google.

4. I conducted interviews with elite interviewees (i.e., reform designers and implementers) myself, sometimes in conjunction with a research assistant. Interviews with rank-and-file civil servants in Ghana and Zambia and one elite interviewee in Zambia were undertaken by Liah Yecalo-Tecle under my supervision. Elite interviewees were each offered a choice about whether they would prefer to be named or to be anonymous and whether their interview would be audio recorded; all rank-and-file interviews were undertaken anonymously and without recording by default. Direct quotations reported from elite interviewees are verbatim (from recording transcripts or from typed/handwritten notes where it was possible to capture certain phrases verbatim), while quotations from rank-and-file interviewees are close paraphrases. The research received ethical approval from the University of Oxford.

5. In Ghana, the ministries involved were the Ministry of Food and Agriculture, Ministry of Transport, and Ministry of Youth and Sport. Within these ministries, participants came from two divisions: Policy, Planning, Monitoring and Evaluation (PPME) and Human Resource Management (HRM). In Zambia, the ministries involved were the Ministry of Agriculture, Ministry of Transport and Communications, and Ministry of Youth, Sport and Child Development. Within these ministries, participants came from three divisions: Human Resource and Administration (HRA), Planning and Policy (P&P), and Monitoring and Evaluation (M&E).

6. Joseph R. A. Ayee, "Civil Service Reform in Ghana: A Case Study of Contemporary Reform Problems in Africa," *African Association of Political Science*, 6, no. 1 (2001): 1–41.

7. Ben Eghan, "Enhancing the Performance of the Public Service in a Developmental State: Ghana Case Study," African Association for Public Administration and Management 30th Annual Roundtable Conference, Accra, Ghana, October 6–10, 2008; interview, Ben Eghan.

8. World Bank, *"Staff Appraisal Report: Republic of Ghana Structural Adjustment Institutional Support Project,"* (World Bank, 20 March 20, 1987); Stephen Adei and Yaw Boachie-Danquah, "The Civil Service Performance Improvement Programme (CSPIP) in Ghana: Lessons of Experience," Paper paper presented at the 24th AAPAM Annual Roundtable Conference on the African Public Service in the 21st Century—New Initiatives in Performance Management, 25th–29th November 25–29, 2002.

9. Ayee, "Civil Service Reform in Ghana," 1.

10. World Bank, *Project Completion Report: Republic of Ghana Structural Adjustment Institutional Support Project (Credit 1778-GH)* (World Bank Report No. 12502, November 15, 1993), 2.

11. Office of the Head of Civil Service, *Introduction of Merit/Performance Award System in the Civil Service*, Circular Ref. No. PNDC/SCR/A.08/15 (OHCS Archives, 1991), 1.

12. United Kingdom Overseas Development Administration, "Evaluation of the Ghana Civil Service Reform Project" (ODA Evaluation Department, April 1993). Cited in International Labour Organization, "Improving the Performance of the Public Sector in LDCs: New Approaches to Human Resource Planning and Management," Interdepartmental Project on Structural Adjustment, Occasional Paper 25 (P. Bennell, 1994).

13. Office of the Head of Civil Service, "Minutes of the Special Chief Directors Meeting Held on Wednesday, 22nd March, 1995" (OHCS Archives, 1995).

14. World Bank, *Project Completion Report*.

15. Government of Ghana, "Civil Service Performance Improvement Programme: The Way Forward," (pamphlet, n.d.); Ayee, "Civil Service Reform in Ghana"; Department for International Development (DFID), *Ghana Civil Service Reform Programme* (summary report, 2004).

16. Ayee, "Civil Service Reform in Ghana."

17. J. J. Rawlings, "New Year Broadcast to the Nation," *Daily Graphic*, January 2, 1991, quoted in Ayee, "Civil Service Reform in Ghana," 18.

18. Office of the Head of Civil Service, *Towards an Effective Performance Appraisal System in the Civil Service* (Dr. S. A. Nkrumah, OHCS Archives, n.d.), 5.

19. Public Services Commission Ghana, "Performance Management Policy for the Public Services of Ghana" (n.d.)

20. Office of the Head of Civil Service, *Towards an Effective Performance Appraisal*, 5.

21. Interview, Nana Agyekum-Dwamena.

22. Office of the Head of Civil Service, *Introduction of Merit/Performance Award System*.

23. World Bank, *Project Completion Report*, 1, 7.

24. Robert Dodoo, draft speech on theme, "Civil Service Reform in Africa: Past Experience and Future Trends," for panel discussion on "The Core Elements of Civil Service Reform: An Assessment of Relevance and Impact," prepared for African Association for Public Administration and Management (AAPAM) 17th Roundtable Conference, Egypt, March 2–5, 1996, OHCS archives, 15. In this passage, Dodoo is referring both to Ghana's Civil Service Reform Programme and to similar reforms undertaken by other African countries under structural adjustment programs.

25. Government of Ghana, "Civil Service Performance Improvement Programme," 8.

26. Office of the Head of Civil Service, *Merit/Performance Award Scheme in the Civil Service*, Circular Ref. No. OHCS/GEN/BC98/231/01 (OHCS Archives, 1995); interview, Nana Agyekum-Dwamena.

27. Interview, Nana Agyekum-Dwamena; interview, GHA12; interview, GHA13.

28. Interview, GHA9.

29. Office of the Head of Civil Service, "Minutes of the Special Chief Directors Meeting."

30. Dodoo, "Civil Service Reform in Africa," 18.

31. Interview, William Kartey; interview, Nana Agyekum-Dwamena.

32. See for example: G. W. Glentworth, *Ghana Developments in Civil Service Reform and UK Support: Report on a Visit to Ghana, 1–9 June 1995*, OHCS Archives, GID.95/021 (ODA, June 1995); Office of the Head of Civil Service, "Minutes of Meeting of Steering Committee on CSRP Held at the Conference Room of the Government Secretarial School Accra, on Wednesday, 17th November, 1993," (1993). Archived OHCS correspondence indicates that the program was initially called the Public Service Performance Improvement Support Programme (PIMSUP) by the ODA's Garth Glentworth (Glentworth, *Ghana Developments in Civil Service Reform*); in his opening remarks to a 2000 workshop, Dodoo stated that the name CSPIP also came from Glentworth (Office of the Head of Civil Service, *Civil Service Performance Improvement Programme (CSPIP: 1996–2001) Second Joint CSPIP-DFID Internal Review at Sogakope 5th–8th July, 2000* [OHCS Archives, 2000], 1).

33. Interview, Nana Agyekum-Dwamena.

34. Office of the Head of Civil Service, "Letter OHCS/SCR/AD100/201/01," (Office of the Head of Civil Service Archives, October 20, 1994).

35. Office of the Head of Civil Service, "Minutes of Meeting of Steering Committee."

36. Interview, Nana Agyekum-Dwamena.

37. Interview, William Kartey; interview, GHA7; Robert Dodoo, "Performance Standards and Measuring Performance in Ghana," *Public Administration and Development* 17 (1997): 115–121.

38. Government of Ghana (n.d.).

39. Dodoo, "Performance Standards"; Ayee, "Civil Service Reform in Ghana"; United Nations Economic Commission for Africa, *Innovations and Best Practices in Public Sector Reforms: The Case of Civil Service in Ghana, Kenya, Nigeria and South Africa*" (report, December 2010); interview, Nana Agyekum-Dwamena.

40. Government of Ghana, "Civil Service Performance Improvement Programme"; Ayee, "Civil Service Reform in Ghana"; Adei and Boachie-Danquah, "Civil Service Performance Improvement Programme"; interview, Nana Agyekum-Dwamena; interview, William Kartey.

41. Interview, GHA7.

42. Interview, Nana Agyekum-Dwamena.

43. Interview, GHA12.

44. Office of the Head of Civil Service, *Towards an Effective Performance Appraisal*; United Nations Economic Commission for Africa, *Innovations and Best Practices*.

45. Interview, William Kartey; Interview, Nana Agyekum-Dwamena. Interestingly, both interviewees reported that Ghana's local governments were more successful at CSPIP implementation than national level ministries and departments. Their hypotheses for this included greater political enthusiasm at local level because of more direct service delivery impacts as well as district assemblies being more creative in coming up with strategies that made use of existing resources rather than requiring new ones.

46. Office of the Head of Civil Service, *Civil Service Performance Improvement Programme*.

47. Interview, Nana Agyekum-Dwamena; interview, GHA32.

48. Public Services Commission, "Performance Management Policy."

49. Office of Head of Civil Service, *Merit/Performance Award Scheme*.

50. Interview, Nana Agyekum-Dwamena.

51. Office of the Head of Civil Service, *Civil Service Performance Improvement Programme*; interview, William Kartey; interview, Nana Agyekum-Dwamena

52. Frank L. Kwaku Ohemeng and Felix K. Anebo, "The Politics of Administrative Reforms in Ghana: Perspectives from Path Dependency and Punctuated Equilibrium Theories," *International Journal of Public Administration* 35, no. 3 (2012): 161–76.

53. Samiatu Bogobiri Seidu, "Institutionalizing Reforms in the Public Sector: A Comparative Study of Public Sector Reform Agencies in Ghana and Nigeria" (master's thesis, Erasmus University, Rotterdam, 2010).

54. Interview, GHA4.

55. Ministry of Public Sector Reform, "Work Programme to Coordinate the Implementation of Public Sector Reforms: Reference Document" (Ministry of Public Sector Reform, OHCS Archives, January 2006).

56. Ministry of Public Sector Reform, "Work Programme to Coordinate"; interview, William Kartey; interview GHA7; interview, Nana Agyekum-Dwamena.

57. Interview, Kwame Adorbor.

58. Interview, GHA12.

59. Interview, Kodjo Mensah-Abrampa.

60. Elizabeth Annan-Prah and Frank L. Kwaku Ohemeng, "Improving Productivity Through Performance Management in Public Sector Organizations in Ghana—Is Change Management the Answer?" Paper prepared for XVII annual meeting of the International Research Society for Public Management (IRSPM), University of Birmingham, UK, March 30–April 1, 2015.

61. Seth Oppong et al., "Implementation of Single Spine Pay Policy in Public Sector of Ghana: Analysis and Recommendations from Organizational Development Perspective," *Poslovna Izvrsnost Zagreb* IX, no. 2 (2015): 83–100; Innovations for Successful Societies, "Interview of Robertson Nii Akwei Allotey by Ashley McCants," interview C-2, August 20, 2008.

62. Interview, Kwame Adorbor.

63. Oppong et al., "Implementation of Single Spine Pay Policy."

64. Interview, Kwame Adorbor; interview, Kodjo Mensah-Abrampa; Oppong et al., "Implementation of Single Spine Pay Policy"; Innovations for Successful Societies, "Interview of Robertson Nii Akwei Allotey."

65. Interview, Kodjo Mensah-Abrampa.

66. Interview, GHA4.

67. Annan-Prah and Ohemeng, "Improving Productivity."

68. Interview, Ben Eghan.

69. Interview, Ben Eghan.

70. Interview, William Kartey; interview, GHA7.

71. Frank L. Kwaku Ohemeng and Joseph R. A. Ayee, "The 'New Approach' to Public Sector Reforms in Ghana: A Case of Politics as Usual or a Genuine Attempt at Reform?" *Development Policy Review* 34, no. 2 (2016): 277–300.

72. Commonwealth, *Key Principles of Public Sector Reforms Case Studies and Frameworks* (Commonwealth Secretariat, December 2016).

73. Frank L. Kwaku Ohemeng et al., "Performance Appraisal and Its Use for Individual and Organizational Improvement in the Civil Service of Ghana: The Case of Much Ado About Nothing?" *Public Administration and Development* 35 (2015): 179; Justice N. Bawole et al., "Performance Appraisal or Praising Performance The Culture of Rhetoric in Performance Management in Ghana Civil Service," *International Journal of Public Administration* 36, no. 13 (2013): 953; Martin J. Williams, "From Institutions to Organizations: Management and Informality in Ghana's Bureaucracies," working paper, London School of Economics and Political Science (September 9, 2015).

74. Interview, GHA10; interview, GHA11; interview, GHA32.

75. Interview, GHA11.

76. Interview, GHA10.

77. e.g., interview, GHA17.

78. Interview, GHA7.

79. Interview, Dora Dei-Tumi.

80. Public Services Commission, "Performance Management Policy," 3.

81. Interview, William Kartey; interview, Nana Agyekum-Dwamena; interview, GHA7; interview, GHA13; interview GHA32.

82. Interview, GHA13.

83. Interview, GHA9.

84. Interview, GHA10.

85. Interview, GHA7.

86. Interview, GHA32.

87. Interview, Ben Eghan; interview GHA7.

88. Ghana News Agency, "Gov't Explains Performance Contract with Ministers," Ghana Business News, June 25, 2013, https://www.ghanabusinessnews.com/2013/06/25/govt-explains-performance-contract-with-ministers/.

89. Peace FM, "Mahama's Appraisal of Ministers Is Deceitful—NPP," Ghana Web, 2013, https://mobile.ghanaweb.com/GhanaHomePage/business/Mahama-s-appraisal-of-ministers-is-deceitful-NPP-295630.

90. Interview, Samuel Abu-Bonsrah.

91. Interview, Kodjo Mensah-Abrampa.

92. Interview, Kodjo Mensah-Abrampa.

93. Interview, Samuel Abu-Bonsrah.

94. Interview, Kodjo Mensah-Abrampa.

95. World Bank, *Public Sector Reform for Results Project (P164665): Implementation Status and Results Report* (February 14, 2019).

96. Interview, Kodjo Mensah-Abrampa.

97. Government of Ghana, "National Public Sector Reform Strategy 2018–2023" (Office of the Senior Minister, 2017).

98. Frank L. Kwaku Ohemeng and Augustina Akonnor, "The New Public Sector Reform Strategy in Ghana: Creating a New Path for a Better Public Service?" *Public Organization Review* 23 (2022): 839–55.

99. Given the scope of this book, I focus my attention on reforms from 1992 onward, but Sylvester Odhiambo Obong'o, "Political Influence, Appointments and Public Sector Management Reform In Kenya, 1963–2014" (PhD diss., University of Newcastle, Australia, 2015) discusses at length the reform thinking and commissions of the 1960s and 1970s that prefigured these reforms, and one interviewee traced the roots of the 1992/1993 central government reforms to district-level reforms beginning in 1983 (interview, Gemma Mbaya).

100. Chweya Ludeki, "Democratization and Civil Service Reform in Kenya" (PhD diss., Queen's University, Kingston, Ontario, Canada, 2003), 139.

101. Obong'o, "Political Influence, Appointments and Public Sector."

102. Ludeki, "Democratization and Civil Service Reform in Kenya."

103. Interview, KEN6.

104. Kempe Ronald Hope Sr., "Managing the Public Sector in Kenya: Reform and Transformation for Improved Performance," *Journal of Public Administration and Governance*, 2, no. 4 (2012): 128–43; Ludeki, "Democratization and Civil Service Reform in Kenya"; Obong'o, "Political Influence, Appointments and Public Sector"; United Nations Economic Commission for Africa, *Innovations and Best Practices*.

105. Interview, KEN6; Abraham Rugo Muriu, "Performance Management in Kenya's Public Service: A Study on Performance Information Use" (PhD diss., University of Potsdam, Potsdam, Germany, 2017).

106. Ludeki, "Democratization and Civil Service Reform in Kenya."

107. Stephen Mworsho Lorete, "The Kenya Civil Service Reform Programme: Analysis of the Design and Implementation of Retrenchment Policy" (master's thesis, Institute of Social Studies of Erasmus University Rotterdam, The Hague, Netherlands, 2002); Ludeki, "Democratization and Civil Service Reform in Kenya."

108. Ludeki, "Democratization and Civil Service Reform in Kenya."

109. Figures calculated from (respectively): Lorete, "The Kenya Civil Service Reform Programme," 43; Kithinji Kiragu, "Civil Service Reform in Southern & Eastern Africa, Lessons of Experience," report on Proceedings of a Consultative Workshop held at Arusha, Tanzania, March 4–8, 1998, 19; and Ludeki, "Democratization and Civil Service Reform in Kenya," 180. It is unclear where this discrepancy arises from. These figures do not include additional nominal reductions in staff strength due to the elimination of ghost workers and abolishing of vacant posts.

110. Ludeki, "Democratization and Civil Service Reform in Kenya," 167.

111. Lorete, "The Kenya Civil Service Reform Programme," 38.

112. World Bank, *Implementation Completion Report (IDA-26710) on a Credit in the Amount of SDRs 17.2 Million to the Government of the Republic of Kenya for an Institutional Development and Civil Service Reform Project*, report No. 21363 (March 29, 2001); Lorete, "The Kenya Civil Service Reform Programme"; Ludeki, "Democratization and Civil Service Reform in Kenya"; interview, KEN6.

113. Lorete, "The Kenya Civil Service Reform Programme."

114. Interview, KEN6.
115. World Bank, *Implementation Completion Report (IDA-26710)*, 7–8, 19.
116. Ludeki, "Democratization and Civil Service Reform in Kenya."
117. Lorete, "The Kenya Civil Service Reform Programme," 46–47.
118. Ludeki, "Democratization and Civil Service Reform in Kenya"; Obong'o, "Political Influence, Appointments and Public Sector."
119. Interview, KEN6; Lorete, "The Kenya Civil Service Reform Programme."
120. Ludeki, "Democratization and Civil Service Reform in Kenya."
121. Interview, Sylvester Obong'o.
122. Interview, Gemma Mbaya.
123. Obong'o, "Political Influence, Appointments and Public Sector."
124. Interview, Gemma Mbaya.
125. Interview, KEN2.
126. Interview, KEN2; interview, Gemma Mbaya.
127. Interview, Kithinji Kiragu.
128. Interview, Kithinji Kiragu.
129. Interview, KEN6.
130. Interview, KEN6.
131. Government of Kenya, *Economic Recovery Strategy for Wealth and Employment Creation 2003–2007* (Ministry of Planning and National Development, 2003), 12.
132. Interview, Kithinji Kiragu.
133. Interview, KEN6.
134. Interview, KEN6; Innovations for Successful Societies, "Building A Culture Of Results: Institution-alizing Rapid Results Initiatives In Kenya, 2005–2009" (2012); Muriu, "Performance Management in Kenya's Public Service." Some official documents refer to the program as "Results for Kenyans" while others refer to "Results for Kenya"; I use "Results for Kenya" throughout for consistency.
135. Interview, Gemma Mbaya.
136. Interview, KEN6.
137. Innovations for Successful Societies, "Interview of Stanley Murage by Rushda Majeed," (Interview ZP3, July 12, 2012), 1.
138. Interview, KEN2.
139. Performance contracts were rolled out to ministries, departments, and agencies (MDAs); I refer simply to "ministries" or "institutions" here for brevity and convenience.
140. Sylvester Odhiambo Obong'o, "Implementation of Performance Contracting in Kenya," *International Public Management Review* 10, no. 2 (2009): 66–84.
141. Interview, KEN2; interview KEN6.
142. Obong'o, "Implementation of Performance Contracting in Kenya"; Margaret Kobia and Nura Mohammed, "The Kenyan Experience with Performance Contracting," African Association for Public Administration and Management 28th Annual Roundtable Conference, Arusha, Tanzania, December 4–8, 2006; Interview, KEN6. As these sources note, the first use of performance con-tracts in Kenya actually dates to the early 1990s when they were used with a handful of state-owned enterprises for a short period. Following their revival in 2003, they were also rolled out to numerous state-owned enterprises and local governments. These institutions are beyond the scope of this book, so here, I focus exclusively on their use in central government ministries.
143. Obong'o, "Implementation of Performance Contracting in Kenya."
144. Obong'o, "Implementation of Performance Contracting in Kenya," 78.
145. Department for International Development (DFID), "Project Completion Review: Results for Kenya Public Sector Reform Programme (PSR)" (2012).
146. Interview, KEN2.

147. Interview, KEN6.

148. Interview, KEN2; interview, KEN6.

149. Obong'o, "Implementation of Performance Contracting in Kenya." The "thousands" figure refers to staff from the whole public sector (state-owned enterprises, central government institutions, and local governments), not just the central civil service.

150. Obong'o, "Implementation of Performance Contracting in Kenya"; interview, KEN2.

151. Interview, Sylvester Obong'o; interview, KEN6. Muriu ("Performance Management in Kenya's Public Service," 80) reports that "most respondents at the ministry studied indicated how in 2006, they each got a 13th salary (bonus) after their ministry was ranked first in the evaluation of the implementation of the performance contracts of the 2005/2006 financial year. However, this rewarding practice seems to have ended after only two years of implementation."

152. Interview, KEN2; interview, Kithinji Kiragu; interview, KEN6; Muriu, "Performance Management in Kenya's Public Service."

153. Interview, KEN2; Interview, KEN6.

154. Interview, Sylvester Obong'o.

155. Interview, Kithinji Kiragu.

156. Interview, KEN6.

157. Muriu, "Performance Management in Kenya's Public Service," 70.

158. Roselyn W. Gakure et al., "Role of Performance Contracting in Enhancing Effectiveness of Performance in the Civil Service in Kenya, State Department of Infrastructure," *IOSR Journal of Business and Management* 14, no. 6 (2013): 78–79.

159. Innovations for Successful Societies, "Building A Culture Of Results."

160. Innovations for Successful Societies, "Building A Culture Of Results"; interview, KEN6. The RRI secretariat was initially based in the Ministry of Planning and National Development during its pilot phase before shifting to PSRDS.

161. Interview, Sylvester Obong'o.

162. Innovations for Successful Societies, "Building A Culture Of Results."

163. Interview, Sylvester Obong'o.

164. Interview, KEN6.

165. Interview, Sylvester Obong'o; World Bank, *Implementation Completion And Results Report (Ida41460-Trust Fund No.: Tf57287,Tf56158) On A Credit In The Amount Of Sdr 17.3 Million (Us$ 25.12 Million Equivalent) To The Government Of Kenya For An Institutional Reform & Capacity Building Project*, Report No ICR2129 (March 29 2012); Innovations for Successful Societies, "Building A Culture Of Results."

166. Interview, Sylvester Obong'o; Innovations for Successful Societies, "Building A Culture Of Results."

167. Interview, Sylvester Obong'o.

168. Interview, Gemma Mbaya.

169. Innovations for Successful Societies, "Building A Culture Of Results."

170. World Bank, *Implementation Completion And Results Report (Ida41460)*, 55.

171. Department for International Development (DFID), "Project Completion Review," 7.

172. Department for International Development (DFID), "Project Completion Review:"; interview, KEN6.

173. Interview, Kithinji Kiragu.

174. Africa Development Professional Group, *End Phase Evaluation of the Results for Kenya Programme* (unpublished, 2011), cited in United Nations Development Program (UNDP), *From Reform to Transformation: UNDP's Support to Public Sector Reforms in Kenya. Lessons Learnt for Devolution* (Joseph L. M. Mugore, Mugore Associates, June 2015), 11.

175. Government of Kenya, *Sector Plan for Public Sector Reforms 2013–2017* (Ministry of Transport and Infrastructure, 2013), 2–3.

176. Department for International Development (DFID), "Project Completion Review," 14.

177. Innovations for Successful Societies, "Building A Culture Of Results."

178. Interview, Sylvester Obong'o; interview KEN6.

179. Muriu, "Performance Management in Kenya's Public Service," 69.

180. Interview, Sylvester Obong'o; interview, KEN6; Innovations for Successful Societies, "Building A Culture Of Results"; Muriu, "Performance Management in Kenya's Public Service."

181. Interview, Kithinji Kiragu; interview, Gemma Mbaya; interview, Sylvester Obong'o.

182. Department for International Development (DFID), "Project Completion Review"; World Bank, *Implementation Completion And Results Report (Ida41460)*.

183. Muriu, "Performance Management in Kenya's Public Service," 80–82.

184. World Bank, *Implementation Completion And Results Report (Ida41460)*, 54.

185. Interview, Sylvester Obong'o.

186. Author's calculations from data in Obong'o, "Political Influence, Appointments and Public Sector," 253–57.

187. World Bank, *Implementation Completion And Results Report (Ida41460)*, 54.

188. Department for International Development (DFID), "Project Completion Review," 5.

189. World Bank, *Implementation Completion And Results Report (Ida41460)*, 53–54; interview, Gemma Mbaya.

190. Salome C. R. Korir et al., "Performance Management and Public Service Delivery in Kenya," *European Journal of Research and Reflection in Management Sciences* 3, no. 4 (2015): 42–54.

191. United Nations Development Program (UNDP), *End of Programme Evaluation: Public Sector Reforms Programme, Phase II* (PWC, May 2013).

192. Department for International Development (DFID), *An Evaluation of DFID-Funded Technical Cooperation for Economic Management in Sub-Saharan Africa* (evaluation report, vol. 2, EV667, 2006), 80; Government of Kenya, *Investment Programme For The Economic Recovery Strategy For Wealth And Employment Creation, 2003–2007* (March 12 2004, revised), 63–64.

193. Department for International Development (DFID), "Project Completion Review"; interview, KEN6.

194. Muriu, "Performance Management in Kenya's Public Service."

195. World Bank, *Implementation Completion And Results Report (Ida41460)*; Department for International Development (DFID), "Project Completion Review"; United Nations Development Program (UNDP), *End of Programme Evaluation*.

196. Interview, KEN6.

197. Hope, "Managing the Public Sector in Kenya."

198. World Bank, *Implementation Completion And Results Report (Ida41460)*, 54; Department for International Development, "Project Completion Review," 5.

199. United Nations Development Program (UNDP), *End of Programme Evaluation*.

200. United Nations Development Program (UNDP), *Project Closure Report: 00045420-Public Sector Reforms* (2013); Government of Kenya, *Sector Plan for Public Sector Reforms 2013–2017*, 3; interview, Gemma Mbaya.

201. Interview, Kithinji Kiragu.

202. Interview, Gemma Mbaya; interview KEN6; Rachel Sohn Firestone et al., *Citizen Service Centers in Kenya: The Role of Huduma Centers in Advancing Citizen-Centered Service Delivery in a Context of Devolution and Digitization* (World Bank, Citizen Service Centers: Pathways Toward Improved Public Service Delivery, 2017).

203. Muriu, "Performance Management in Kenya's Public Service," 92; interview, Gemma Mbaya.

204. Firestone et al., *Citizen Service Centers in Kenya*.

205. Firestone et al., *Citizen Service Centers in Kenya*; interview, Kithinji Kiragu.

206. Firestone et al., *Citizen Service Centers in Kenya*. This source also reports that rewards are associated with these rankings, but it is unclear what these constitute or how they are given.

207. Firestone et al., *Citizen Service Centers in Kenya*.

208. Interview, Gemma Mbaya.

209. Government of Kenya, *Sector Plan for Public Sector Reforms 2013–2017*.

210. Firestone et al., *Citizen Service Centers in Kenya*.

211. Alfred Ong'era and Beverly Musili, *Public Sector Reforms In Kenya: Challenges And Opportunities* (Kenya Institute for Public Policy Research and Analysis WP/29/2019, 2019); interview, Sylvester Obong'o. These devolution-driven reforms fall outside the scope of this book.

212. Muriu, "Performance Management in Kenya's Public Service."

213. Muriu, "Performance Management in Kenya's Public Service," 69.

214. Government of Kenya, *Sector Plan for Public Sector Reforms 2013–2017*; Government of Kenya, *Public Service Transformation Framework* (Presidency, Ministry of Public Service, Youth and Gender Affairs, 2017).

215. Interview, Mahmud Yayale Ahmed; interview, Tunji Olaopa; Haruna Dantaro Dlakwa, "Salient Features of the 1988 Civil Service Reforms in Nigeria," *Public Administration and Development* 12 (1992): 297–311.

216. Alex Sekwat, "Civil Service Reform in Post-Independence Nigeria: Issues and Challenges," *Public Administration Quarterly* 25, no. 2 (2002): 498–517.

217. Interview, Mahmud Yayale Ahmed; Dlakwa, "Salient Features."

218. Interview, Tunji Olaopa.

219. Cornelius Ofobuisi Okorie and Sunday O. Onwe, "Appraisal of Civil Service Reforms in Nigeria and Options for Stability," *Public Policy and Administration Research* 6, no. 9 (2016): 15–24; Solomon Adebayo Adedire, "Reinventing Nigerian Civil Service for Effective Service Delivery in the 21st Century," *Fountain Journal of Management and Social Sciences* 4, no. 1 (2014): 104–19.

220. Okorie and Onwe, "Appraisal of Civil Service Reforms."

221. Caleb Imuetinyan Ogbegie, "The Need for a Civil Service Reform in Nigeria" (master's thesis, University of Vaasa, 2008), 46–47; Sekwat, "Civil Service Reform."

222. Cornelius Ofobuisi Okorie and Stella Odo, "A Survey of Public Service Reforms in Nigeria: 1999–2013," *International Journal of Humanities and Social Science* 4, no. 10 (2014): 267–75.

223. Interview, Tunji Olaopa.

224. Interview, Mahmud Yayale Ahmed.

225. Joseph Okwesili Nkwede, "Public Sector Restructuring and Governance in Nigeria: Perspectives, Processes and Challenges," *Journal of Business and Management* 2, no. 3 (2013): 32–44.

226. Interview, Mahmud Yayale Ahmed; interview, Tunji Olaopa.

227. Interview, Tunji Olaopa.

228. Interview, Mahmud Yayale Ahmed; interview, Tunji Olaopa.

229. Interview, Mahmud Yayale Ahmed; interview, Tunji Olaopa.

230. Interview NIG1; iInterview, Nnenna Akajemeli; Interviewinterview, Mahmud Yayale Ahmed.

231. Interview, Tunji Olaopa.

232. Interview, Mahmud Yayale Ahmed; interview, Tunji Olaopa. The public service reform strategy was subsequently integrated into the broader national economic empowerment development strategy (NEEDS) national development plan as its public administration component; I therefore do not include NEEDS as a distinct reform effort on its own in the timeline even though it was under the NEEDS banner that many people encountered these reforms.

233. Interview, Mahmud Yayale Ahmed.

234. Interview, Tunji Olaopa; Okorie and Odo, "A Survey of Public Service Reforms."

235. Okorie and Odo, "A Survey of Public Service Reforms"; Office of the Secretary to the Government of the Federation, *Public Service Reforms in Nigeria: 1999–2014, A Comprehensive Review* (April 2015); interview, Joe Abah; interview, Mahmud Yayale Ahmed.

236. Office of the Secretary to the Government of the Federation, *Public Service Reforms*.

237. Office of the Secretary to the Government of the Federation, *Public Service Reforms*, 28.

238. Interview, Tunji Olaopa.

239. Interview, Tunji Olaopa.

240. Interview, NIG1; interview, Nnenna Akajemeli.

241. SERVICOM, "Delivering Service in Nigeria: A Roadmap" (2004).

242. Office of the Secretary to the Government of the Federation, *Public Service Reforms*; Okorie and Odo, "A Survey of Public Service Reforms."

243. Interview, NIG1; Okorie and Odo, "A Survey of Public Service Reforms."

244. Office of the Secretary to the Government of the Federation, *Public Service Reforms*.

245. Florence O. Ogunrin and Andrew E.O. Erhijakpor, "SERVICOM Policy Intervention: Improving Service Quality in Nigerian Public Sector," *Global Journal of Social Sciences* 8, no. 1 (2009): 51–60.

246. Interview, Joe Abah.

247. Interview, NIG1.

248. Interview, Nnenna Akajemeli.

249. Interview, NIG1.

250. Office of the Secretary to the Government of the Federation, *Public Service Reforms*, 155.

251. SERVICOM, "Delivering Service in Nigeria"; Interview, Nnenna Akajemeli.

252. Office of the Secretary to the Government of the Federation, *Public Service Reforms*.

253. Interview, Joe Abah.

254. Interview, Joe Abah.

255. Interview, NIG1.

256. Interview, NIG3

257. Interview, Joe Abah.

258. Interview, Joe Abah.

259. Okorie and Odo, "A Survey of Public Service Reforms"; John Olushola Magbadelo, "Reforming Nigeria's Federal Civil Service," *India Quarterly* 72, no. 1 (2016): 78, 80.

260. Interview, Tunji Olaopa.

261. Interview, Tunji Olaopa.

262. Federal Republic of Nigeria, "National Strategy for Public Service Reform" (July 2017).

263. Federal Republic of Nigeria, "National Strategy for Public Service Reform," 27.

264. Office of the Secretary to the Government of the Federation, *Public Service Reforms*.

265. Office of the Secretary to the Government of the Federation, *Public Service Reforms*; interview, Mahmud Yayale Ahmed.

266. John Olushola Magbadelo, "The Problematics of Service Delivery in Nigeria," (*Annals of Social Sciences and Management Studies* 5, no. 3, (2020),): 0053–0059.

267. Lawal Bello Dogarawa, "A New Model for Performance Measurement in the Nigerian Public Service," *International Journal of Business and Management* 6, no. 12 (2011): 212–21; interview, Joe Abah.

268. Interview, Tunji Olaopa.

269. Office of the Secretary to the Government of the Federation, *Public Service Reforms*, 33; Folasade Yemi-Esan, "FG Replaces APER with PMS to Assess Civil Servants' Performance," This Day, November 17, 2020, https://www.thisdaylive.com/index.php/2020/11/17/fg-replaces-aper-with-pms-to-assess-civil-servants-performance/.

270. Interview, Tunji Olaopa; interview, Joe Abah; interview, NIG6.

271. Amina M. B. Shamaki, "An Effective Performance Management System For The Federal Public Service," presentation, Office of the Head of the Civil Service, accessed August 22, 2022, https://studylib.net/doc/9713525/final-an-effective-performance-management-system.

272. Interview, Joe Abah.

273. Interview, Joe Abah.

274. Interview, Joe Abah.

275. Interview, Joe Abah.

276. Okorie and Odo, "A Survey of Public Service Reforms." The committee also had a mandate to examine issues related to personnel management. Its chief recommendation on this was the

2009 reform of tenure policy for permanent secretaries discussed earlier, which was subsequently reversed in 2015.

277. Okorie and Odo, "A Survey of Public Service Reforms"; Office of the Secretary to the Government of the Federation, *Public Service Reforms*; interview, Dozie Okpalaobieri.

278. Interview, Dozie Okpalaobieri.

279. Federal Republic of Nigeria, "White Paper on the Report of the Presidential Committee on Restructuring and Rationalization of Federal Government Parastatals, Commissions and Agencies" (March 2014); interview, Dozie Okpalaobieri.

280. Interview, Joe Abah.

281. Interview, NIG1.

282. Interview, Nnenna Akajemeli.

283. Interview, NIG1; Interviewinterview, Nnenna Akajemeli; Office of the Secretary to the Government of the Federation, *"Public Service Reforms."*

284. Office of the Secretary to the Government of the Federation, *"Public Service Reforms,"* 156.

285. Office of the Secretary to the Government of the Federation, *Public Service Reforms*, 156.

286. Interview, NIG1; Otive Igbuzor, "An Overview Of Service Delivery Initiative: 12 Years After," paper presented at the National Policy Dialogue on Strategies for Improving Service Delivery in Government Parastatals, Agencies and Commissions in Nigeria, State House, Abuja, March 27, 2017, https://thewillnews.com/opinion-an-overview-of-service-delivery-initiative-12-years-after/.

287. Interview, NIG1.

288. Okey Marcellus Ikeanyibe, "New Public Management and Administrative Reforms in Nigeria," *International Journal of Public Administration* 39, no. 7 (2015): 563–76.

289. Federal Republic of Nigeria, "National Strategy for Public Service Reform," 14.

290. Federal Republic of Nigeria, "National Strategy for Public Service Reform."

291. Federal Republic of Nigeria, "National Strategy for Public Service Reform," 149.

292. République du Sénégal, "Bureau Organisation et Méthodes: Evolution institutionnelle," accessed September 14, 2022, https://www.bom.gouv.sn/?q=node/9; Aminatou Ahne, "Quand l'Etat perd son cerveau," *Enquête+*, June 10, 2015, https://www.enqueteplus.com/content/bom-absence-de-statut-recrutement-sans-épreuves-écrites . . .-quand-l'état-perd-son-cerveau; Mamadou Ndiaye and Babacar Aw, "The M&E System in Senegal," in *African Monitoring and Evaluation Systems: Exploratory Case Studies* (University of the Witwatersrand, Johannesburg, 2012); République du Sénégal, *Etude Diagnostique Du Service Public: Tome 1: Analyse de Synthese des Reformes Publiques* (Ministère De La Fonction Publique, De La Rationalisation Des Effectifs Et Du Renouveau Du Service Public, EXA-Consulting, May 18, 2016).

293. International Labour Organization, "Improving the Performance"; République du Sénégal, *Etude Diagnostique Du Service Public*; interview, Souleymane Nasser Niane. All translations from French in this section are the author's. The original French is included in some endnotes for cases in which the English translation is ambiguous or loses some of the meaning of the original text.

294. Interview, Souleymane Nasser Niane. « Moins d'état, et mieux d'état ».

295. International Labour Organization, "Improving the Performance."

296. Interview, Souleymane Nasser Niane; International Labour Organization, "Improving the Performance"; Abdoul Aziz Tall, "L'ajustement dans le secteur public: et la gestion des ressources humaines: Le cas du Senegal," S.A.P. 4.33/W.P. 87, International Labor Organization, 1995.

297. Interview, Souleymane Nasser Niane.

298. Interview, Souleymane Nasser Niane; Tall, "L'ajustement dans le secteur public."

299. Tall, "L'ajustement dans le secteur public."

300. Tall, "L'ajustement dans le secteur public."

301. Interview, Souleymane Nasser Niane.

302. Tall, "L'ajustement dans le secteur public"; interview, Souleymane Nasser Niane.

303. World Bank, *Rapport d'evaluation Retrospective—Senegal - Quatrieme Credit d'Ajustement Structurel—Credit 2090 SE - Credit d'Ajustement du Secteur Financier—Credit 2077 SE—May 3, 1995* (WB IBRD/IDA/AFR 44001I, P002338, May 3, 1995).

304. Tall, "L'ajustement dans le secteur public."

305. International Labour Organization, "Improving the Performance."

306. World Bank, *Rapport d'evaluation Retrospective*, 23.

307. Tall, "L'ajustement dans le secteur public"; interview, Souleymane Nasser Niane.

308. Tall, "L'ajustement dans le secteur public," 46.

309. Tall, "L'ajustement dans le secteur public,", 42. « accessoire ».

310. International Labour Organization, "Improving the Performance," 26.

311. Tall, "L'ajustement dans le secteur public," 46.

312. Tall, "L'ajustement dans le secteur public.".

313. World Bank, *Rapport d'evaluation Retrospective*, 24.

314. Tall, "L'ajustement dans le secteur public," 20.

315. Interview, Souleymane Nasser Niane.

316. World Bank, *Rapport d'evaluation Retrospective*, 23–24.

317. République du Sénégal, *Etude Diagnostique Du Service Public*, 90.

318. World Bank, *Rapport d'evaluation Retrospective*, 25.

319. Interview, Souleymane Nasser Niane.

320. Tall, "L'ajustement dans le secteur public,", 27.

321. Tall, "L'ajustement dans le secteur public," 27.

322. République du Sénégal, "Programme Nationale de Bonne Gouvernance" (April 2002), 15; Serigne Ahmadou Gaye, "La construction de l'administration du Senegal: Entre realites societales et genie de modernisation?" (mimeo, 2020), 18.

323. Ahne, "Quand l'Etat perd son cerveau"; interview, Ibrahima Ndiaye.

324. International Monetary Fund (IMF), "Senegal—Enhanced Structural Adjustment Facility Policy Framework Paper, 1998–2000," accessed June 21, 2021, https://www.imf.org/external/np/pfp/senegal/seng-01.htm.

325. International Monetary Fund (IMF), "Enhanced Structural Adjustment Facility Economic and Financial Policy Framework Paper (1999–2001)," accessed September 14, 2022, https://www.imf.org/external/np/pfp/1999/senegal/.

326. Gaye, "La construction de l'administration du Senegal," 16.

327. Interview, Souleymane Nasser Niane.

328. République du Sénégal, "Programme Nationale de Bonne Gouvernance," 15.

329. Interview, Souleymane Nasser Niane.

330. Gaye, "La construction de l'administration du Senegal," 18.

331. Interview, Souleymane Nasser Niane.

332. Interview, Souleymane Nasser Niane.

333. Interview, Souleymane Nasser Niane.

334. Interview, SEN3.

335. Interview, Ibrahima Ndiaye.

336. République du Sénégal, "Programme Nationale de Bonne Gouvernance," 27–28.

337. Interview, Souleymane Nasser Niane.

338. Interview, Souleymane Nasser Niane.

339. République du Sénégal, "Programme Nationale de Bonne Gouvernance," 16.

340. Interview, SEN3.

341. Interview, Ibrahima Ndiaye; République du Sénégal, *Rapport national sur la gouvernance au Senegal* (Secretariat General de la Presidence de la République, Delegation a la Reforme de l'Etat et a l'Assistance Technique, Programme National de Bonne Gouvernance, 2011).

342. République du Sénégal, "Programme Nationale de Bonne Gouvernance," 18.

343. CODESRIA, "État De La Gouvernance En Afrique De L'ouest : Sénégal." Project de Suivi de la Gouvernance en Afrique de l'Ouest, Mamadou Dansokho, Babacar Gueye, and Mbathio Samb, 2011, 12.

344. République du Sénégal, *Etude Diagnostique Du Service Public*, 91.

345. CODESRIA, "État De La Gouvernance En Afrique De L'ouest," 12.

346. République du Sénégal, "Programme Nationale de Bonne Gouvernance," 7.

347. République du Sénégal, "Programme Nationale de Bonne Gouvernance"; Interview, Ibrahima Ndiaye.

348. République du Sénégal, "Programme Nationale de Bonne Gouvernance," 54.

349. Interview, Ibrahima Ndiaye.

350. République du Sénégal, "Programme Nationale de Bonne Gouvernance," 55.

351. République du Sénégal, "Programme Nationale de Bonne Gouvernance," 55, 66.

352. République du Sénégal, "Programme Nationale de Bonne Gouvernance," 71. « gestion de proximité des ressources humaines ».

353. République du Sénégal, *Rapport national sur la gouvernance au Senegal*.

354. Interview, Ibrahima Ndiaye.

355. Interview, Ibrahima Ndiaye.

356. United Nations Development Programme (UNDP), "Projet de Renforcement des Capacités de Bonne Gouvernance (PRECABG)" (n.d.), 3.

357. Interview, Abdoul Wahab Ba.

358. Interview, SEN3; interview, Abdoul Wahab Ba.

359. République du Sénégal, *Rapport national sur la gouvernance au Senegal*, 69.

360. Interview, SEN3.

361. Interview, Ibrahima Ndiaye.

362. Interview, Ibrahima Ndiaye.

363. Gaye, "La construction de l'administration du Senegal," 18–19.

364. République du Sénégal, *Rapport national sur la gouvernance au Senegal*, 65.

365. Interview, Abdoul Wahab Ba.

366. Interview, Abdoul Wahab Ba; interview, Souleymane Nasser Niane.

367. Interview, Abdoul Wahab Ba.

368. Interview, Abdoul Wahab Ba.

369. République du Sénégal, *Rapport national sur la gouvernance au Senegal*, 64; République du Sénégal, "Schema Directeur de Modernisation de l'Administration Publique (SDMAP) 2015–2022," Presentation, Bureau Organisation et Méthodes, Presidence de la République, Secretariat Général, n.d., 10.

370. République du Sénégal, *Rapport national sur la gouvernance au Senegal*; République du Sénégal, "Schema Directeur de Modernisation de l'Administration Publique." The SDRE/SDMAP are perhaps most different from preceding reforms in their emphasis on deconcentration and decentralization, although these are beyond the scope of this book.

371. Interview, Abdoul Wahab Ba.

372. République du Sénégal. "Bureau Organisation et Méthodes"; interview, Ibrahima Ndiaye.

373. République du Sénégal, "DECRET n° 2010–1812 en date du 31 décembre 2010," Journal Officiel N. 6577 du Samedi March 19, 2011.

374. Interview, SEN3.

375. Interview, Ibrahima Ndiaye.

376. République du Sénégal, "Arrêté ministériel n° 8625 en date du 23 mai 2017 fixant les modalités d'organisation et de fonctionnement du Comité de modernisation de l'Administration publique," Journal Officiel du Sénégal, 2017. « à favoriser l'appropriation par les acteurs de la culture d'innovation et l'efficacité des actions de modernisation au sein des ministères.»

377. Interview, Ibrahima Ndiaye.

378. Interview, Ibrahima Ndiaye.

379. Geraldine Joslyn Fraser-Moleketi, "Public Service Reform in South Africa: An Overview of Selected Case Studies From 1994–2004" (master's thesis, University of Pretoria, South Africa, 2006), 18.

380. Ministry for the Public Service and Administration, "White Paper on the Transformation of the Public Service," notice 1227 of 1995 (November 15, 1995), 8.

381. Republic of South Africa, *Report of the Presidential Review Commission on the Reform and Transformation of the Public Service in South Africa* (1998).

382. Robert Cameron, "Public Service Reform in South Africa: From Apartheid to New Public Management," in *The International Handbook of Public Administration and Governance*, ed. Andrew Massey and Karen Johnston (Edward Elgar Press, 2015), 135–57; interview, SA1; interview, SA5.

383. Republic of South Africa, "White Paper on Human Resource Management of the Public Service" (n.d.), 27.

384. Cameron, "Public Service Reform in South Africa."

385. Nyana Faith Rakate, "Transformation In The South African Public Service: The Case Of Service Delivery in the Department of Health" (master's thesis, University of Pretoria, South Africa, 2006), 12. See also Ministry for the Public Service and Administration, "White Paper on the Transformation of the Public Service."

386. Paseka Ncholo et al., "Reforming the Public Service in South Africa: A Policy Framework," *Public Administration and Development* 20, no. 2 (2000), 87–102; Fraser-Moleketi, "Public Service Reform in South Africa"; Jerry O. Kuye, "Public Sector Reforms: The Case for South Africa—1994–2005," *Journal of Public Administration* 41, no. 2.2 (2006), 290–309; Rakate, "Transformation In The South African Public Service"; Zwelakhe Tshandu and Samuel Kariuki, "Public Administration and Service Delivery Reforms: A Post-1994 South African Case," *South African Journal of International Affairs* 17, no. 2 (2010): 189–208.

387. Cameron, "Public Service Reform in South Africa," 141.

388. Ministry for the Public Service and Administration, "White Paper on the Transformation of the Public Service," 5. The white paper distinguishes this short-term transformation from administrative reform more generally, which it presumes will be ongoing.

389. Department of Public Service and Administration (DPSA), "White Paper: Affirmative Action in the Public Service," March, general notice 564 of 1998, *Government Gazette* 394, no. 18800 (April 23, 1998): 19.

390. Department of Public Service and Administration (DPSA), "White Paper."

391. Fraser-Moleketi, "Public Service Reform in South Africa"; Ncholo et al., "Reforming the Public Service in South Africa"; Kuye, "Public Sector Reforms"; interview, SA1.

392. Sergio Fernandez, *Representative Bureaucracy and Performance: Public Service Transformation in South Africa* (Palgrave MacMillan, 2020).

393. Fraser-Moleketi, "Public Service Reform in South Africa," 87.

394. Cameron, "Public Service Reform in South Africa,", 144–45.

395. Cameron, "Public Service Reform in South Africa," 144–145.

396. Interview, Ruan Kitshoff.

397. Cameron, "Public Service Reform in South Africa."

398. Interview, Ruan Kitshoff.

399. Republic of South Africa, "White Paper on Public Service Delivery," *Government Gazette* 388, no. 18340, notice 1459 of 1997 (October 1, 1997): 12–13.

400. Republic of South Africa, "White Paper on Public Service Delivery," 11.

401. Mashwahle Diphofa, "Towards Intensifying the Batho Pele Campaign," *Service Delivery Review* 1, no. 1 (2002): 35.

402. Fraser-Moleketi, "Public Service Reform in South Africa."

403. Public Service Commission, *Report on the Assessment of the Effectiveness of the Batho Pele Policy in Public Service Delivery* (June 2012), 7–8.

404. Interview, SA1; interview, Ruan Kitshoff.
405. Centre for Public Service Innovation, "Ten Years of Unearthing Innovation: CPSI Showcasing and Rewarding Public Sector Innovative Solutions" (n.d.); Centre for Public Service Innovation, "CPSI Entrenching Innovation in the Public Sector: Selected Case Studies" (n.d.).
406. Fraser-Moleketi, "Public Service Reform in South Africa," 70–71.
407. Interview, Ruan Kitshoff.
408. Interview, Ruan Kitshoff.
409. Department of Public Service and Administration (DPSA), "Batho Pele Handbook" (n.d.).
410. Department of Public Service and Administration (DPSA), "Batho Pele Handbook," 11.
411. Fraser-Moleketi, "Public Service Reform in South Africa."
412. Fraser-Moleketi, "Public Service Reform in South Africa," 71.
413. e.g. BusinessTech, "Home Affairs Considers Banning Staff Mobile Phones," January 14, 2019, https://businesstech.co.za/news/technology/293412/home-affairs-considers-banning-staff-mobile-phones/; Patricia de Lille, "Paying Suppliers on Time Keeps Economy Growing," City Press, August 22, 2019, https://www.news24.com/citypress/business/patricia-de-lille-paying-suppliers-on-time-keeps-economy-growing-20190822.
414. Department of Public Service and Administration (DPSA), *Report on the Implementation of the Batho Pele Programmes in the Public Service, July 2018* (2018).
415. Interview, Ismail Akhalwaya; interview, Ruan Kitshoff; Public Service Commission, *Report on the Assessment.*
416. Public Service Commission, *"Report on the Assessment* of the Effectiveness of the Batho Pele Policy in Public Service Delivery."
417. Public Service Commission, *Report on the Assessment.*
418. Interview, SA1.
419. Interview, SA1.
420. Interview, Ismail Akhalwaya.
421. Interview, SA5.
422. Public Service Commission, *Report on the Assessment.*
423. Interview, Ismail Akhalwaya.
424. Interview, SA5.
425. Interview, Ruan Kitshoff.
426. Interview, SA5.
427. Interview, Sean Phillips.
428. Interview, SA1.
429. Interview, Ismail Akhalwaya.
430. Department of Performance Monitoring and Evaluation (DPME), "Management Performance Assessment Tool (MPAT) User's Guide" (n.d.).
431. Precious Tirivanhu et al., "Advancing Evidence-Based Practice for Improved Public Sector Performance: Lessons from the Implementation of the Management Performance Assessment Tool in South Africa," *Journal of Public Administration* 52, no. 4 (2017): 681–704.
432. Interview, SA5.
433. Department of Performance Monitoring and Evaluation (DPME), "Management Performance Assessment Tool," 4.
434. Department of Performance Monitoring and Evaluation (DPME), "DPME Practice Note No. 4.1.1: Process for Implementing Management Performance Assessment Tool (MPAT) in National Departments" (November 1, 2011, updated), 2.
435. Tirivanhu et al., "Advancing Evidence-Based Practice," 698.
436. Interview, SA1.
437. Interview, Ismail Akhalwaya.

438. Department of Performance Monitoring and Evaluation (DPME), "MPAT 2012 to 2015: Lessons and Support to the Public Service" (n.d.), 16.

439. Fraser-Moleketi, "Public Service Reform in South Africa," 72.

440. Dieketseng Gail Maphela, "Implementation of the Management Performance Assessment Tool (MPAT)" (master's thesis, University of the Witwatersrand, Johannesburg, South Africa, 2015).

441. Interview, Sean Phillips.

442. Interview, SA1; interview, Ismail Akhalwaya; Aisha Ali, "Introducing Context-Based Reforms: Comparative Case Studies on Management Performance Assessment Tool in South Africa and Uganda" (MA diss., University of Witwatersrand, April 2019).

443. Interview, SA1.

444. Interview, SA1.

445. Ali, "Introducing Context-Based Reforms," 64.

446. Interview, SA5.

447. Interview, Ismail Akhalwaya.

448. Management Performance Assessment Tool, "MPAT 1.3: Good Practice Cases" (n.d.); Department of Performance Monitoring and Evaluation (DPME), "MPAT 2012 to 2015."

449. Interview, Sean Phillips.

450. Department of Performance Monitoring and Evaluation (DPME), "MPAT 2012 to 2015," 10–11.

451. Interview, SA1.

452. Interview, Ismail Akhalwaya.

453. Interview, Sean Phillips.

454. Interview, SA6.

455. Interview, SA6.

456. Interview, SA1.

457. Interview, SA6.

458. Interview, SA1.

459. Ali, "Introducing Context-Based Reforms," 62.

460. Interview, SA1.

461. Interview, Ismail Akhalwaya.

462. Interview, SA5.

463. In 2019, the DPME announced a "new MPAT," but the design details and implementation of this were not defined within the temporal scope of this book (Republic of South Africa, "Deputy Minister Thembi Siweya/ Planning and Monitoring Dept Budget Vote 2019/20," DPME Budget Vote Address by Thembi Siweya, Old Assembly of the Parliament of the Republic of South Africa, Cape Town, 2019). One anonymous official with knowledge of the process remarked that this new tool would "try to move away from scoring and focus on just improving, we don't want this to be part of accountability frameworks or nothing."

464. Interview, Ismail Akhalwaya.

465. Interview, Ismail Akhalwaya.

466. Danny Sing, "Human Resource Challenges Confronting the Senior Management Service of the South African Public Service," *Public Personnel Management* 41, no. 2 (2012).

467. Interview, SA1.

468. For more discussion on state capture and related debates, see (among many others): Ivor Chipkin and Mark Swilling, eds., *Shadow State: The Politics of State Capture* (Wits University Press, 2018); *Representative Bureaucracy and Performance.*

469. Interview, SA6.

470. Cameron, "Public Service Reform in South Africa."

471. Jonathan Friedman, "Sticking to the Numbers: Performance Monitoring in South Africa, 2009–2011" (Innovations for Successful Societies, 2011), 2–3.

472. Sing, "Human Resource Challenges,Confronting the Senior Management Service of the South African Public Service," 384.

473. Sing, "Human Resource Challenges," 383–84.

474. Interview, SA1.

475. Interview, SA5.

476. Interview, SA5.

477. Interview, SA6.

478. Interview, SA5.

479. Interview, SA5; Interview, Ruan Kitshoff.

480. Interview, SA5.

481. Interview, Sean Phillips.

482. Interview, SA1.

483. Interview, Sean Phillips.

484. Interview, Ruan Kitshoff.

485. Interview, SA5, Interview SA6.

486. Interview, SA5.

487. Interview, SA6.

488. Interview, SA1.

489. Interview, Ruan Kitshoff.

490. Interview, SA1.

491. Interview, SA1.

492. Interview, SA1.

493. Interview, SA1.

494. Interview, SA1.

495. Interview, Ruan Kitshoff.

496. Interview, SA5.

497. Interview, Sean Phillips.

498. Jacob Zuma, "Address by President Jacob Zuma at the Launch of Operation Phakisa Big Fast Results Implementation Methodology, Inkosi Albert Luthuli International Convention Centre, Durban," July 19, 2014; Kathrin A. Plangemann, "Strengthening Performance Monitoring and Evaluation," in *Making It Happen: Selected Case Studies of Institutional Reforms in South Africa*, ed. Asad Alam et al. (World Bank Group, 2016), 71–89; Gabi Khumalo, "Building the Ideal Clinic," *Service Delivery Review* 10, no. 3 (2015): 49–51.

499. Interview, SA1.

500. Interview, SA1.

501. Brighton Litula, "An Evaluation of Public Service Reform Programme [PSRP] Being Implemented in Zambia's Public Service," Copperbelt University, School of Business, Department of Postgraduate Studies, MBA Class 2000/2001, 2001, 5; interview, Ngosa Chisupa.

502. Interview, Chandiwira Nyirenda; interview, Jacob Mwanza.

503. World Bank, *Report and Recommendation of the President of the International Development Association to the Executive Directors on a Proposed Credit in the Amount Equivalent to US$200 Million to the Republic of Zambia for a Privatization and Industrial Reform Adjustment Credit*, Report P-5786-ZA (June 3, 1992).

504. Litula, "Evaluation of Public Service"; interview, ZAM11; interview, Ndashe Yumba.

505. Clever Madimutsa, "Implications of Public Sector Reform for Public Sector Unions in Zambia: A Case Study of the Civil Servants and Allied Workers Union of Zambia in Lusaka District" (PhD diss., School of Government, University of Western Cape, 2016).

506. World Bank, *Report and Recommendation*, 6.

507. Theodore R. Valentine, *A Medium-Term Strategy for Enhancing Pay and Conditions of Service in the Zambian Public Service* (Crown Consultants International, 2002), xiii.

508. World Bank, *Implementation Completion Report—Zambia—Economic and Social Adjustment Credit (Credit 2577-ZA)*, report 15837 (June 28, 1996), 3.

509. World Bank, *Report and Recommendation*, 3; Valentine, *Medium-Term Strategy*, 17.

510. World Bank, *Report and Recommendation*, 3.

511. Mike Stevens and Stefanie Teggemann, "Comparative Experience with Public Service Reform in Ghana, Tanzania, and Zambia," in *Building State Capacity in Africa: New Approaches, Emerging Lessons*, ed. Brian Levy and Sahr Kpundeh, 43–86 (World Bank Institute, 2004), 58.

512. Valentine, *Medium-Term Strategy*, 17; Stevens and Teggemann, "Comparative Experience," 82.

513. Litula, "Evaluation of Public Service," 57.

514. Stevens and Teggemann, "Comparative Experience," 58; World Bank, *Implementation Completion Report—Zambia*, 7.

515. Valentine, *"A Medium-Term Strategy."*

516. Interview, ZAM11.

517. Interview, Chandiwira Nyirenda.

518. Interview, Jacob Mwanza.

519. Interview, Jacob Mwanza.

520. Interview, Jacob Mwanza.

521. Interview, Moses Kondowe.

522. Stevens and Teggemann, "Comparative Experience," 52.

523. Interview, Leonard Hikaumba.

524. Interview, Roland Msiska.

525. Interview, Moses Kondowe.

526. Interview, Moses Kondowe.

527. Interview, Moses Kondowe; interview, ZAM11; interview, Ngosa Chisupa; interview, Jacob Mwanza.

528. Interview, ZAM11.

529. Interview, Ngosa Chisupa.

530. Interview, Moses Kondowe.

531. Interview, Ndashe Yumba.

532. Interview, Ndashe Yumba.

533. Interview, Ndashe Yumba.

534. Interview, Moses Kondowe; interview, Leonard Hikaumba.

535. Madimutsa, "Implications of Public Sector Reform"; interview, Leonard Hikaumba.

536. Interview, ZAM21.

537. Kiragu, "Civil Service Reform in Southern & Eastern Africa"; interview, Chandiwira Nyirenda; interview, Leonard Hikaumba.

538. Litula, "Evaluation of Public Service," 57.

539. Universalia, *Assessment of the Current Performance Management System Final Report* (Legend Consulting Services Ltd and Universalia, 2008), 5.

540. University of Zambia, *The Public Service Reform Programme (PSRP) and the Public Service capacity Building Programme (PSCAP) Impact Assessment* (April 15, 2005), quoted in Universalia, *Assessment of the Current Performance.*

541. Interview, ZAM11.

542. Litula, "Evaluation of Public Service," 67, 73.

543. The PSRP did not formally cease in 1999 and stayed in existence as an umbrella for subsequent reforms. However, I refer to PSRP in the narrow sense commonly used in Zambia under which PSRP refers only to the pre-PSCAP reforms in the 1990s.

544. World Bank, *Implementation Completion Report (Ida-33290 Ppfi-Q1440 Ppfi-Q1441) on a Credit in the Amount of Sdr 20.4 Million (Us$28 Million Equivalent) to the Republic of Zambia for a Public Service Capacity Building Project in Support of the First Phase of the Public Service Capacity Building Program*," Report 34450 (December 28, 2005), 14.

545. Interview, ZAM11.

546. Interview, John Kasanga.

547. Interview, Moses Kondowe.

548. World Bank, *Implementation Completion Report (Ida-33290 Ppfi-Q1440 Ppfi-Q1441)*; interview, Moses Kondowe.

549. Interview, Moses Kondowe; interview, ZAM15.

550. Stevens and Teggemann, "Comparative Experience."

551. World Bank, *Implementation Completion Report (Ida-33290 Ppfi-Q1440 Ppfi-Q1441)*, 9.

552. World Bank, *Implementation Completion Report (Ida-33290 Ppfi-Q1440 Ppfi-Q1441)*, 9.

553. Interview, ZAM15.

554. Stevens and Teggemann, "Comparative Experience," 72.

555. Universalia, *Assessment of the Current Performance*, 5.

556. Interview, Moses Kondowe.

557. World Bank, *ICR Review—Public Service Capacity Building Project (PSCAP)*, (Independent Evaluation Group Report ICRR12372, 2006), 4.

558. World Bank, *Project Appraisal Document on a Proposed Credit in the Amount of SDR 20.4 Million (US$28 Million Equivalent) to the Republic of Zambia for a Public Service Capacity Building Project in Support of the First Phase of the Public Service Capacity Building Program*, (February 22, 2000); Annie Chitentu Malambo, "Retirement and the Zambia Public Service Reform Programme in the Ministry of Agriculture and Cooperatives 1993–2003" (Master's thesis, University of Zambia, 2013); interview, John Kasanga.

559. World Bank, *Implementation Completion Report (Ida-33290 Ppfi-Q1440 Ppfi-Q1441)*.

560. Interview, Moses Kondowe.

561. Valentine, *Medium-Term Strategy*, 92.

562. University of Zambia, *The Public Service Reform Programme (PSRP)*; Universalia, *Assessment of the Current Performance*.

563. University of Zambia, *The Public Service Reform Programme (PSRP)*, 3.

564. Universalia, *Assessment of the Current Performance*, 25.

565. Universalia, *"Assessment of the Current Performance* Management System", 26.

566. Universalia, *"Assessment of the Current Performance* Management System", 26.

567. Universalia, *"Assessment of the Current Performance* Management System", 27.

568. Universalia, *Assessment of the Current Performance*, 26, 27, 31.

569. Interview, Chandiwira Nyirenda.

570. Universalia, *Assessment of the Current Performance*, 27.

571. Interview, Chandiwira Nyirenda.

572. Universalia, *Assessment of the Current Performance*, 28.

573. Universalia, *Assessment of the Current Performance*, 27–28.

574. Universalia, *Assessment of the Current Performance*, 27.

575. Interview, Roland Msiska; Valentine, *Medium-Term Strategy*.

576. Interview, ZAM11.

577. World Bank, *Implementation Completion Report (Ida-33290 Ppfi-Q1440 Ppfi-Q1441)*, 6; interview, Roland Msiska.

578. Interview, Roland Msiska.

579. Interview, John Kasanga.

580. Interview, ZAM11.

581. Valentine, *Medium-Term Strategy*, 88.

582. Universalia, *Assessment of the Current Performance*, 29.

583. World Bank, *Implementation Status & Results—Zambia—Public Sector Management Program Support Project (P082452)*, Report ISR6541 (2012).

584. World Bank, *Implementation Status & Results*, 2.

585. World Bank, *Implementation Completion Report (Ida-33290 Ppfi-Q1440 Ppfi-Q1441)*; interview, ZAM11. PSMP also had two major components that were out of the scope of this book, related to decentralization and public financial management.

586. Interview, ZAM14.

587. World Bank, *Implementation Completion and Results Report (IDA-51040) on Three Credits in the Amount of SDF 51.5 Million (US$ 80 Million Equivalent) to the Republic of Zambia for Poverty Reduction Support Credits (PRSC) I, II And III*, report ICR2761 (June 24 2013), 16.

588. Interview, ZAM20, for instance, speaks of a service charter being adopted in one ministry in 2015/2016.

589. World Bank, *Implementation Completion And Results Report (IDA-51040)*, 16.

590. Interview, ZAM24.

591. Interview, ZAM20.

592. Interview, ZAM26.

593. Interview, ZAM20.

594. Interview, ZAM20.

595. Interview, ZAM14.

596. World Bank, *Implementation Completion And Results Report (IDA-51040)*.

597. Valentine, *Medium-Term Strategy*; World Bank, *Implementation Completion Report (Ida-33290 Ppfi-Q1440 Ppfi-Q1441)*, 6.

598. World Bank, *Implementation Status & Results*, 7.

599. World Bank, *Implementation Status & Results*, 7.

600. Interview, ZAM11; World Bank, *Implementation Status & Results*.

601. Interview, Ndashe Yumba.

602. Interview, Roland Msiska; interview ZAM11; interview ZAM15.

603. World Bank, *Implementation Completion Report (Ida-33290 Ppfi-Q1440 Ppfi-Q1441)*, 6.

604. Interview, ZAM5; interview ZAM15; interview, Felix Mushubati.

605. Interview, Roland Msiska.

606. Interview, ZAM15.

607. Interview, Roland Msiska.

608. Interview, Felix Mushubati; Interview, Roland Msiska.

609. Interview, ZAM5.

610. Interview, Roland Msiska.

611. Interview, Roland Msiska.

612. Interview, Felix Mushubati.

613. Interview, Oliver Saasa.

614. Interview, Felix Mushubati.

615. Interview, ZAM15.

616. Interview, ZAM5.

617. Interview, Felix Mushubati.

618. Interview, ZAM20.

619. Interview, ZAM23, Interview, ZAM27.

620. Interview, Oliver Saasa.

621. Interview, Oliver Saasa.

622. Republic of Zambia, "Strategy for the Public Service Transformation Programme for Improved Service Delivery 2013–2018," (Public Service Management Secretariat, Management Development Division, 2012).

623. e.g. Interview, Roland Msiska; interview, Felix Mushubati; interview ZAM14; interview, Leonard Hikaumba.
624. Interview, ZAM17.
625. Interview, ZAM24.
626. e.g. Interview, ZAM17, interview, ZAM21, interview, ZAM26.
627. Interview, Felix Mushubati; interview, ZAM14.
628. Interview, ZAM17.
629. Interview, ZAM14.
630. Interview, ZAM14.
631. Interview, ZAM27.
632. Interview, ZAM18.
633. Interview, ZAM26.
634. Interview, ZAM18.
635. Interview, ZAM11, interview, ZAM14.
636. Interview, Roland Msiska; interview, Felix Mushubati.
637. Lusaka Times, "Performance Based Contracts Extended to Directors-Msiska," March 24, 2017, https://www.lusakatimes.com/2017/03/24/performance-based-contract-system-extended-directors-msiska/; interview, Felix Mushubati.
638. Interview, ZAM14.
639. Interview, Roland Msiska.
640. Interview, Roland Msiska; interview, Felix Mushubati; interview, ZAM11.
641. Interview, ZAM2.
642. Interview, Roland Msiska.
643. Interview, ZAM14.
644. Interview, ZAM14.
645. Interview, Roland Msiska.
646. Interview, Moses Kondowe.
647. Interview, Felix Mushubati.
648. Interview, ZAM14.
649. Interview, ZAM11.
650. Interview, ZAM22.
651. Interview, ZAM20.
652. Interview, ZAM11.
653. Interview, Roland Msiska.
654. Interview, ZAM14.
655. Interview, ZAM11.
656. Interview, ZAM2.
657. Department for International Development (DFID), "Annual Review—Summary Sheet—Public Sector Performance (PSP) Programme," 2019, vi; interview ZAM2.
658. Interview, Roland Msiska.
659. Interview, Roland Msiska.

Bibliography

Acemoglu, Daron, and James A Robinson. *Why Nations Fail: The Origins of Power, Prosperity, and Poverty.* Crown, 2012.

Adamolekun, Ladipo, ed. *Public Administration in Africa: Main Issues And Selected Country Studies.* Westview Press, 1999.

Adedire, Solomon Adebayo. "Reinventing Nigerian Civil Service for Effective Service Delivery in the 21st Century." *Fountain Journal of Management and Social Sciences* 4, no. 1 (2014): 104–19.

Adei, Stephen, and Yaw Boachie-Danquah. "The Civil Service Performance Improvement Programme (CSPIP) in Ghana: Lessons of Experience." Paper presented at the 24th AAPAM Annual Roundtable Conference on the African Public Service in the 21st Century—New Initiatives in Performance Management, November 25–29, 2002.

Africa Development Professional Group. *End Phase Evaluation of the Results for Kenya Programme.* Unpublished, 2011.

Agyekum-Dwamena, Nana. "Public sector deep dive: Professionalism for performance: Innovative public management," Presentation at Challenges of Government Conference, 20 June 2017, https://www.youtube.com/watch?v=txAnw8YA-Ns, accessed June 2022.Aguinis, Herman. *Performance Management.* 3rd ed. Pearson, 2013.

Ahne, Aminatou. "Quand l'Etat perd son cerveau." *Enquête+*, June 10, 2015. https://www.enqueteplus.com/content/bom-absence-de-statut-recrutement-sans-épreuves-écrites ...-quand-l'état-perd-son-cerveau.

Aiyar, Yamini, Vincy Davis, Gokulnath Govindan, and Taanya Kapoor. *Rewriting the Grammar of the Education System: Delhi's Education Reform (A Tale of Creative Resistance and Creative Disruption).* Research on Improving Systems of Education (RISE), 2021.

Alchian, Armen A., and Harold Demsetz. "Production, Information Costs, and Economic Organization." *American Economic Review* 62, no. 5 (1972): 777–95.

Ali, Aisha. "Introducing Context-Based Reforms: Comparative Case Studies on Management Performance Assessment Tool in South Africa and Uganda." MA Diss., University of Witwatersrand, April 2019.

Andrews, Matt. *The Limits of Institutional Reform in Development: Changing Rules for Realistic Solutions.* Cambridge University Press, 2013.

Andrews, Matt, Lant Pritchett, and Michael Woolcock. *Building State Capability: Evidence, Analysis, Action.* Oxford University Press, 2017.

Ang, Yuen Yuen. *How China Escaped the Poverty Trap.* Cornell University Press, 2017.

Annan-Prah, Elizabeth, and Frank L. Kwaku Ohemeng. "Improving Productivity Through Performance Management in Public Sector Organizations in Ghana—Is Change Management the Answer?" Paper prepared for XVII annual meeting of the International Research Society for Public Management (IRSPM), University of Birmingham, UK, March 30–April 1, 2015.

Appiah, Daniel, and Abdul-Gafaru Abdulai. "Competitive Clientelism and the Politics of Core Public Sector Reform in Ghana." ESID Working Paper 82. March 2017.

Axelrod, Robert. *The Evolution of Cooperation.* Basic Books, 1984.

Ayee, Joseph R. A. "Civil Service Reform in Ghana: A Case Study of Contemporary Reform Problems in Africa." *African Association of Political Science,* 6, no. 1 (2001): 1–41.

Ayee, Joseph R. A. *Reforming the African Public Sector: Retrospect and Prospects.* CODESRIA Green Book, 2008.

Baker, George P. "Incentive Contracts and Performance Measurement." *Journal of Political Economy* 100, no. 3 (1992): 598–614.

Baker, George, Robert Gibbons, and Kevin J. Murphy. "Relational Contracts and the Theory of the Firm." *Quarterly Journal of Economics* 117, no. 1 (2002): 39–84.

Ball, Ian. "Presentation to the NZSA Public Sector Convention." November 1992.

Ball, Ian. "Reinventing Government: Lessons Learned from the New Zealand Treasury." *Government Accountants Journal* 43, no. 3 (1994).

Bandiera, Oriana, Michael Carlos Best, Adnan Qadir Khan, and Andrea Prat. "The Allocation Of Authority In Organizations: A Field Experiment With Bureaucrats." *Quarterly Journal of Economics* (2021): 2195–2242.

Banerjee, Abhijit, Sylvain Chassang, and Erik Snowberg. "Decision Theoretic Approaches to Experiment Design and External Validity." In *Handbook of Economic Field Experiments,* ed A. V. Banerjee and E. Duflo, 141–74. Elsevier, 2017.

Baron, James N., and David M. Kreps. "Employment as an Economic and Social Relationship." In *The Handbook of Organizational Economics,* ed. Robert Gibbons and John Roberts, 315–41. Princeton University Press, 2013.

Basheka, Benon C., and Lukamba-Muhiya Tshombe. *New Public Management in Africa: Emerging Issues and Lessons.* Routledge, 2017.

Bass, Bernard M. *Leadership and Performance Beyond Expectations.* Free Press, 1985.

Bawole, Justice N., Farhad Hossain, Kwame Ameyaw Domfeh, Hamza Zakaria Bukari, and Francis Sanyare. "Performance Appraisal or Praising Performance The Culture of Rhetoric in Performance Management in Ghana Civil Service." *International Journal of Public Administration* 36, no. 13 (2013): 953–62.

Bersch, Katherine. *When Democracies Deliver: Governance Reform in Latin America.* Cambridge University Press, 2019.

Bersch, Katherine, Sérgio Praça, and Matthew M. Taylor. "State Capacity, Bureaucratic Politicization, and Corruption in the Brazilian State." *Governance* 30, no. 1 (2016): 105–24.

Berwick, Donald M. "Continuous Improvement as an Ideal in Health Care." *New England Journal of Medicine* 320, no. 1 (1989): 53–56.

Besley, Timothy, Robin Burgess, Adnan Khan, and Guo Xu. "Bureaucracy and Development." *Annual Review of Economics* 14 (2022): 397–424.

Besley, Timothy, and Torsten Persson. *Pillars of Prosperity: The Political Economics of Development Clusters.* Princeton University Press, 2011.

Best, Michael Carlos, Jonas Hjort, and David Szakonyi. "Individuals and Organizations as Sources of State Effectiveness." *American Economic Review* 113, no. 8 (2023): 2121–67.

Bevan, Gwyn, and Christopher Hood. "What's Measured Is What Matters: Targets and Gaming in the English Health Care System." *Public Administration* 84, no. 3 (2006): 517–38.

Bhuiyan, Nadia, and Amit Baghel. "An Overview of Continuous Improvement: From the Past to the Present." *Management Decision* 43, no. 5 (2005): 761–71.

Bloom, Nicholas, Raffaella Sadun, and John Van Reenen. "The Organization of Firms Across Countries." *Quarterly Journal of Economics* 127, no. 4 (2012): 1663–1705.

Bloom, Nicholas, and John Van Reenen. "Measuring and Explaining Management Practices Across Firms and Countries." *Quarterly Journal of Economics* 122 (2007): 1351–1408.

Blum, Jurgen Rene, Marcos Ferreiro-Rodriguez, and Vivek Srivastava. *Building Public Services in Postconflict Countries: A Comparative Analysis of Reform Trajectories in Afghanistan, Liberia, Sierra Leone, South Sudan, and Timor-Leste.* World Bank, 2019.

Bold, Tessa, Mwangi Kimenyi, Germano Mwabu, Alice Ng'ang'a, and Justin Sandefur. "Experimental Evidence on Scaling Up Education Reforms in Kenya." *Journal of Public Economics* 168 (2018): 1–20.

Boli, John, and George M. Thomas, eds. *Constructing World Culture: International Nongovernmental Organizations Since 1875.* Stanford University Press, 1999.

Boston, Jonathan. "Assessing the Performance of Departmental Chief Executives: Perspectives from New Zealand." *Public Administration* 70 (1992): 405–28.

Boston, Jonathan. "The Challenge of Evaluating Systemic Change: The Case of Public Management Reform." *International Public Management Journal* 3 (2000): 23–46.

Braithwaite, Jeffrey. "Changing How We Think About Healthcare Improvement." *British Medical Journal* 361 (1998): 1–5.

Bridges, Kate, and Michael Woolcock. "How (Not) to Fix Problems That Matter: Assessing and Responding to Malawi's History of Institutional Reform." World Bank Policy Research Working Paper 8289. 2017.

Bryk, Anthony S., Sharon Greenberg, Albert Bertani, Penny Sebring, Steven E. Tozer, and Timothy Knowles. *How a City Learned to Improve Its Schools.* Harvard University Press, 2023.

Buntaine, Mark T., Bradley C. Parks, and Benjamin P. Buch. "Aiming at the Wrong Targets: The Domestic Consequences of International Efforts to Build Institutions." *International Studies Quarterly* 61 (2017): 471–88.

Burke, W. Warner. *Organization Change: Theory and Practice.* 5th ed. SAGE, 2018.

BusinessTech. "Home Affairs Considers Banning Staff Mobile Phones." January 14, 2019. https://businesstech.co.za/news/technology/293412/home-affairs-considers-banning-staff-mobile-phones/.

Cameron, Robert. "Public Service Reform in South Africa: From Apartheid to New Public Management." In *The International Handbook of Public Administration and Governance*, ed. Andrew Massey and Karen Johnston, 135–57. Edward Elgar Press, 2015.

Centre for Public Service Innovation. "CPSI Entrenching Innovation in the Public Sector: Selected Case Studies." N.d.

Centre for Public Service Innovation. "Ten Years of Unearthing Innovation: CPSI Showcasing and Rewarding Public Sector Innovative Solutions." N.d.

Chassang, Sylvain. "Building Routines: Learning, Cooperation, and the Dynamics of Incomplete Relational Contracts." *American Economic Review* 100, no. 1 (2010): 448–65.

Chipkin, Ivor, and Mark Swilling, eds. *Shadow State: The Politics of State Capture.* Wits University Press, 2018.

Chown, Jillian. "The Appealing Illusion of Frontline Employee-Driven Continuous Improvement: The Challenges of Empowering Frontline Employees to Solve Organizational Problems." Mimeo, November 2021.

Chun, Young Han, and Hal G. Rainey. "Goal Ambiguity and Organizational Performance in U.S. Federal Agencies." *Journal of Public Administration Research and Theory* 15 (2005): 529–57.

CODESRIA. "État De La Gouvernance En Afrique De L'ouest : Sénégal." Project de Suivi de la Gouvernance en Afrique de l'Ouest. Mamadou Dansokho, Babacar Gueye, and Mbathio Samb. 2011.

Commonwealth. *Key Principles of Public Sector Reforms Case Studies and Frameworks.* Commonwealth Secretariat, December 2016.

de Lille, Patricia. "Paying Suppliers on Time Keeps Economy Growing." City Press, August 22, 2019. https://www.news24.com/citypress/business/patricia-de-lille-paying-suppliers-on-time-keeps-economy-growing-20190822.

Department for International Development (DFID). "Annual Review—Summary Sheet—Public Sector Performance (PSP) Programme." 2019.

Department for International Development (DFID). *An Evaluation of DFID-Funded Technical Cooperation for Economic Management in Sub-Saharan Africa.* Evaluation Report, vol. 2, EV667, 2006.

Department for International Development (DFID). *Ghana Civil Service Reform Programme.* Summary report, 2004.

Department for International Development (DFID). "Project Completion Review: Results for Kenya Public Sector Reform Programme (PSR)." 2012.

Department of Performance Monitoring and Evaluation (DPME). "DPME Practice Note No. 4.1.1: Process for Implementing Management Performance Assessment Tool (MPAT) in National Departments)." November 1, 2011, updated.

Department of Performance Monitoring and Evaluation (DPME). "Management Performance Assessment Tool (MPAT) User's Guide." N.d.

Department of Performance Monitoring and Evaluation (DPME). "MPAT 2012 to 2015: Lessons and Support to the Public Service." N.d.

Department of Public Service and Administration (DPSA). "Batho Pele Handbook." N.d.

Department of Public Service and Administration (DPSA). *Report on the Implementation of the Batho Pele Programmes in the Public Service, July 2018.* 2018.

Department of Public Service and Administration (DPSA). "White Paper: Affirmative Action in the Public Service." March, General Notice 564 of 1998, *Government Gazette* 394, no. 18800 (April 23, 1998).

Diphofa, Mashwahle. "Towards Intensifying the Batho Pele Campaign." *Service Delivery Review: A Learning Journal for Public Managers* 1, no. 1 (2002): 35–37.

Dixit, Avinash. "Incentives and Organizations in the Public Sector: An Interpretative Review." *Journal of Human Resources* 37, no. 4 (2002): 696–727.

Dlakwa, Haruna Dantaro. "Salient Features of the 1988 Civil Service Reforms in Nigeria." *Public Administration and Development* 12 (1992): 297–311.

Dodoo, Robert. Draft speech on the theme "Civil Service Reform in Africa: Past Experience and Future Trends," panel discussion on "The Core Elements of Civil Service Reform: An Assessment of Relevance and Impact," prepared for African Association for Public Administration and Management (AAPAM) 17th Roundtable Conference, Egypt, March 2–5, 1996. OHCS archives.

Dodoo, Robert. "Performance Standards and Measuring Performance in Ghana." *Public Administration and Development* 17 (1997): 115–21.

Dogarawa, Lawal Bello. "A New Model for Performance Measurement in the Nigerian Public Service." *International Journal of Business and Management* 6, no. 12 (2011): 212–21.

Eghan, Ben. "Enhancing the Performance of the Public Service in a Developmental State: Ghana Case Study." African Association for Public Administration and Management 30th Annual Roundtable Conference, Accra, Ghana, October 6–10, 2008.

Elmore, Richard F. "Backward Mapping: Implementation Research and Policy Decisions." *Political Science Quarterly* 94, no. 4 (1979): 601–16.

Engelbart, Douglas C. "Toward High-Performance Organizations: A Strategic Role for Groupware." In *Proceedings of the GroupWare '92 Conference,* 77–100. Morgan Kaufmann Publishers, 1992.

Esteve, Marc, and Christian Schuster. *Motivating Public Employees.* Cambridge Elements, 2017.

Evans, Peter and James Rauch. "Bureaucracy and Growth: A Cross-National Analysis of the Effects of 'Weberian' State Structures on Economic Growth." *American Sociological Review* 64, no. 5 (1999): 748–65.

Federal Republic of Nigeria. "National Strategy for Public Service Reform." July 2017.

Federal Republic of Nigeria. "White Paper on the Report of the Presidential Committee on Restructuring and Rationalization of Federal Government Parastatals, Commissions and Agencies." March 2014.

Feldman, Martha S. "Organizational Routines as a Source of Continuous Change." *Organization Science* 11, no. 6 (2000): 611–29.

Feldman, Martha S., and Wanda J. Orlikowski. "Theorizing Practice and Practicing Theory." *Organization Science* 22, no. 5 (2011): 1240–53.

Fernandez, Sergio. *Representative Bureaucracy and Performance: Public Service Transformation in South Africa*. Palgrave MacMillan, 2020.

Finan, Frederico, Benjamin A. Olken, and Rohini Pande. "The Personnel Economics of the Developing State." In *Handbook of Economic Field Experiments*, ed. Abhijit V. Banerjee and Esther Duflo, 467–514. Elsevier, 2017.

Firestone, Rachel Sohn, Berenike Schott, Kimberly Johns, and Saki Kumagai. *Citizen Service Centers in Kenya: The Role of Huduma Centers in Advancing Citizen-Centered Service Delivery in a Context of Devolution and Digitization*. World Bank, Citizen Service Centers: Pathways Toward Improved Public Service Delivery, 2017.

Flyvbjerg, Bent. "Policy and Planning for Large-Infrastructure Projects: Problems, Causes, Cures." *Environment and Planning B: Planning and Design* 34 (2007): 578–97.

Foli, Rosina, and Frank L. K. Ohemeng. "The Role and Impact of International Bureaucrats in Policymaking in Africa." In *Routledge Handbook of Public Policy in Africa*, ed. Gedion Onyango, 117–27. Routledge, 2021.

Fornasari, Margherita, Imran Rasul, Daniel Rogger, and Martin J. Williams. "Ideas Generation in Hierarchical Bureaucracies: Evidence from a Field Experiment and Qualitative Data." Working paper, June 2025.

Fraser-Moleketi, Geraldine Joslyn. "Public Service Reform In South Africa: An Overview Of Selected Case Studies From 1994–2004." MA thesis, University of Pretoria, South Africa, 2006.

Freedom Radio. "COVID-19 Pandemic: Civil Service Goes Digital," August 9, 2021, accessed June 2022, https://freedomradiogh.com/covid-19-pandemic-civil-service-goes-digital/.

Friedman, Jonathan. "Sticking to the Numbers: Performance Monitoring in South Africa, 2009–2011)." Innovations for Successful Societies, 2011.

Gakure, Roselyn W., Stephen Macharia Muriu, and George Orwa. "Role of Performance Contracting in Enhancing Effectiveness of Performance in the Civil Service in Kenya, State Department of Infrastructure." *IOSR Journal of Business and Management* 14, no. 6 (2013): 73–82.

Gaye, Serigne Ahmadou. "La construction de l'administration du Senegal: Entre realites societales et genie de modernisation?" Mimeo, 2020.

Ghana News Agency. "The Civil Service Endorses Punctuality Campaign." GhanaWeb, October 4, 2018. https://www.ghanaweb.com/GhanaHomePage/NewsArchive/The-Civil-Service-endorses-Punctuality-Campaign-690024.

Ghana News Agency. "Gov't Explains Performance Contract with Ministers." Ghana Business News, June 25, 2013. https://www.ghanabusinessnews.com/2013/06/25/govt-explains-performance-contract-with-ministers/.

Gibbons, Robert. "Visible Hands: Governance of Value Creation—Within Firms and Beyond." *American Economic Review Papers and Proceedings* 110, no. 5 (2020): 172–76.

Gibbons, Robert, and Rebecca Henderson. "Relational Contracts and Organizational Capabilities." *Organization Science* 23, no. 5 (2012): 1350–64.

Gibbons, Robert, and Rebecca Henderson. "What Do Managers Do?" In *The Handbook of Organizational Economics*, ed. Robert Gibbons and John Roberts, 680–731. Princeton University Press, 2013.

Gibbons, Robert, Marco LiCalzi, and Massimo Warglien. "What Situation Is This? Shared Frames and Collective Performance." Mimeo, June 2020.

Gibbons, Robert, and Woody Powell. "Why Are Organizations So Full of Rules That Are Not Followed or Enforced?" Presentation to Economic History Association, October 29, 2021.

Gilson, Lucy, and Irene Akua Agyepong. "Strengthening Health System Leadership for Better Governance: What Does It Take?" *Health Policy and Planning* 33 (2018): iii–ii4.

Gingerich, Daniel. "Governance Indicators and the Level of Analysis Problem: Empirical Findings from South America." *British Journal of Political Science* 43, no. 3 (2013): 505–40.

Glentworth, G. W. *Ghana Developments in Civil Service Reform and UK Support: Report on a Visit to Ghana, 1–9 June 1995*. OHCS Archives. GID.95/021. ODA, June 1995.

Goertz, Gary, and James Mahoney. *A Tale of Two Cultures: Qualitative and Quantitative Research in the Social Sciences*. Princeton University Press, 2012.

Government Accountability Office (GAO). "Federal Workforce: Distribution of Performance Ratings Across the Federal Government, 2013." Response to Ron Johnson, May 9 2016, GAO-16-520R Federal Employee Performance Ratings.

Government of Ghana. "Civil Service Performance Improvement Programme: The Way Forward." Pamphlet, n.d.

Government of Ghana. "National Public Sector Reform Strategy 2018–2023." Office of the Senior Minister, 2017.

Government of Kenya. *Economic Recovery Strategy for Wealth and Employment Creation 2003–2007*. Ministry of Planning and National Development, 2003.

Government of Kenya. *Investment Programme for the Economic Recovery Strategy for Wealth and Employment Creation, 2003–2007*. March 12, 2004, revised.

Government of Kenya. *Public Service Transformation Framework*. The Presidency, Ministry of Public Service, Youth and Gender Affairs, 2017.

Government of Kenya. *Sector Plan for Public Sector Reforms 2013–2017*. Ministry of Transport and Infrastructure, 2013.

Grindle, Merilee. "Divergent Cultures? When Public Organizations Perform Well in Developing Countries." *World Development* 25 (1997): 481–95.

Guiso, Luigi, Paola Sapienza, and Luigi Zingales. "The Value of Corporate Culture." *Journal of Financial Economics* 117 (2015): 60–76.

Halligan, John. *Reforming Public Management and Governance: Impact and Lessons from Anglophone Countries*. Edward Elgar, 2020.

Harris, Alma, Michelle Jones, Nashwa Hashim. "System Leaders and System Leadership: Exploring the Contemporary Evidence Base." *School Leadership & Management*, 41, no. 4–5 (2021): 387–408.

Hasnain, Zahid, Nick Manning, and Jan Henryk Pierskalla. "The Promise of Performance Pay? Reasons for Caution in Policy Prescriptions in the Core Civil Service." *World Bank Research Observer* 29 (2014): 235–64.

Hassan, Mai. *Regime Threats and State Solutions: Bureaucratic Loyalty and Embeddedness in Kenya*. Cambridge University Press, 2020.

Hassan, Mai, and Ahmed Kodouda. "Dismantling Old—or Forging New—Clientelistic Ties? Sudan's Civil Service Reform After Uprising." Mimeo, 2022.

Heclo, Hugh. *Modern Social Politics in Britain and Sweden*. Yale University Press, 1974.

Hein, Aung. "Essays on the Organizational Socialization of New Recruits in the Public Sector." PhD diss., University of Oxford, 2023.

Herbst, Jeffrey. *States and Power in Africa: Comparative Lessons in Authority and Control*. Princeton University Press, 2000.

Hickey, Sam, and Naomi Hossain, eds. *The Politics of Education in Developing Countries: From Schooling to Learning*. Oxford University Press, 2019.

Honig, Dan. *Mission Driven Bureaucrats: Empowering People to Help Government Do Better*. Oxford University Press, 2024.

Honig, Dan. *Navigation by Judgment: Why and When Top-Down Management of Foreign Aid Doesn't Work*. Oxford University Press, 2018.

Hope, Kempe Ronald Sr. "Managing the Public Sector in Kenya: Reform and Transformation for Improved Performance." *Journal of Public Administration and Governance*, 2, no. 4 (2012): 128–43.

Igbuzor, Otive. "An Overview Of Service Delivery Initiative: 12 Years After." Paper presented at the National Policy Dialogue on Strategies for Improving Service Delivery in Government Parasatals,

Agencies and Commissions In Nigeria, State House, Abuja, March 27, 2017. https://thewillnews.com /opinion-an-overview-of-service-delivery-initiative-12-years-after/.

Ika, Lavagnon. "Project Management for Development in Africa: Why Projects Are Failing and What Can Be Done About It." *Project Management Journal* 43, no. 4 (2011): 27–41.

Ikeanyibe, Okey Marcellus. "New Public Management and Administrative Reforms in Nigeria." *International Journal of Public Administration* 39, no. 7 (2015): 563–76.

Imai, M. *Kaizen: The Key to Japanese Competitive Success.* Random House, 1986.

Ingraham, Patricia W., Philip G. Joyce, and Amy Kneedler Donahue. *Government Performance: Why Management Matters.* Johns Hopkins University Press, 2003.

Innovations for Successful Societies. "Building A Culture Of Results: Institutionalizing Rapid Results Initiatives In Kenya, 2005–2009." 2012.

Innovations for Successful Societies. "Interview of Robertson Nii Akwei Allotey by Ashley McCants," Interview C-2, August 20, 2008.

Innovations for Successful Societies. "Interview of Stanley Murage by Rushda Majeed," interview ZP3, July 12, 2012.

International Labour Organization. "Improving the Performance of the Public Sector in LDCs: New Approaches to Human Resource Planning and Management." Interdepartmental Project on Structural Adjustment, Occasional Paper 25. P. Bennell. Geneva, 1994.

International Monetary Fund (IMF). "Enhanced Structural Adjustment Facility Economic and Financial Policy Framework Paper (1999–2001)." Accessed September 14, 2022. https://www.imf.org/external /np/pfp/1999/senegal/.

International Monetary Fund (IMF). "Senegal—Enhanced Structural Adjustment Facility Policy Framework Paper, 1998–2000." Accessed June 21, 2021. https://www.imf.org/external/np/pfp/senegal/seng -01.htm.

Jensen, Ulrich Thy, Lotte Bøgh Andersen, Louise Ladegaard Bro, Anne Bøllingtoft, Tine Louise Mundbjerg Eriksen, Ann-Louise Holten et al. "Conceptualizing and Measuring Transformational and Transactional Leadership." *Administration and Society* 51, no. 1 (2019): 3–33.

Kahneman, Daniel, and Amos Tversky. "Intuitive Prediction: Biases and Corrective Procedures." *TIMS Studies in Management Science* 12 (1979): 313–27.

Kaufmann, Herbert. *The Forest Ranger: A Study in Administrative Behavior.* Johns Hopkins University Press, 1960.

Kelman, Steven, and John N. Friedman. "Performance Improvement and Performance Dysfunction: An Empirical Examination of Distortionary Impacts of the Emergency Room Wait-Time Target in the English National Health Service." *Journal of Public Administration Research and Theory* 19 (2009): 917–46.

Kelsall, Tim, and David Booth. "Developmental Patrimonialism? Questioning the Orthodoxy on Political Governance and Economic Progress in Africa." Africa Power and Politics Programme Working Paper 9, 2010.

Khademian, Anne M. "Leading Through Cultural Change." In *The Oxford Handbook of American Bureaucracy,* ed. Robert F. Durant, 303–23. Oxford University Press, 2010.

Khan, Muhammad Yasir. "Mission Motivation and Public Sector Performance: Experimental Evidence from Pakistan." Mimeo, September 14, 2023.

Khan, Mushtaq H. "Political Settlements and the Governance of Growth-Enhancing Institutions." Mimeo, 2010.

Khumalo, Gabi. "Building the Ideal Clinic." *Service Delivery Review* 10, no. 3 (2015): 49–51.

Kiragu, Kithinji. *Civil Service Reform in Southern & Eastern Africa, Lessons of Experience.* Report on Proceedings of a Consultative Workshop held at Arusha, Tanzania. March 4–8, 1998.

Knott, Jack H. "Comparing Public and Private Management: Cooperative Effort and Principal-Agent Relationships." *Journal of Public Administration Research and Theory* 3, no. 1 (1993): 93–119.

Kobia, Margaret, and Nura Mohammed. "The Kenyan Experience with Performance Contracting." African Association for Public Administration and Management 28th Annual Roundtable Conference, Arusha, Tanzania, December 4–8, 2006.

Korir, Salome C. R., Jacob Rotich, and Joseph Bengat. "Performance Management and Public Service Delivery in Kenya." *European Journal of Research and Reflection in Management Sciences*, 3, no. 4 (2015): 42–54.

Kremer, Michael. "The O-Ring Theory of Economic Development." *Quarterly Journal of Economics* 108, no. 3 (1993): 551–75.

Kreps, David. "Corporate Culture and Economic Theory." In *Perspectives on Positive Political Economy*, ed. James Alt and Kenneth Shepsle, 90–143. Cambridge University Press, 1990.

Kuipers, Ben S., Malcolm Higgs, Walter Kickert, Lars Tummers, Jolien Grandia, and Joris van der Voet. "The Management of Change in Public Organizations: A Literature Review." *Public Administration* 92, no. 1 (2014): 1–20.

Kuura, Arvi. "25 Years of Projectification Research." *PM World Journal* 9, no. 8 (2020).

Kuye, Jerry O. "Public Sector Reforms: The Case for South Africa—1994–2005." *Journal of Public Administration* 41, no. 2.2 (2006): 290–309.

Leonard, David. " 'Pockets' of Effective Agencies in Weak Governance States: Where Are They Likely and Why Does It Matter?" *Public Administration and Development* 30 (2010): 91–101.

Levitsky, Steven, and Maria Victoria Murrillo. "Variation in Institutional Strength." *Annual Review of Political Science* 12 (2009): 115–33.

Levy, Brian. *Working with the Grain: Integrating Governance and Growth in Development Strategies*. Oxford University Press, 2014.

Levy, Brian, and Sahr Kpundeh, eds. *Building State Capacity in Africa: New Approaches, Emerging Lessons*. World Bank Institute, 2004.

Lewin, Kurt. *Field Theory in Social Science*. Harper and Row, 1951.

Lindblom, Charles E. "The Science of 'Muddling Through.' " *Public Administration Review* 19, no. 2 (1959): 79–88.

Lipsky, Michael. "Toward a Theory of Street-Level Bureaucracy." IRP Discussion Papers No. 48–69, Madison, WI, 1969.

Litula, Brighton. "An Evaluation of Public Service Reform Programme [PSRP] Being Implemented in Zambia's Public Service" Copperbelt University, School of Business, Department of Postgraduate Studies, MBA Class 2000/2001, 2001.

Lorete, Stephen Mworsho. "The Kenya Civil Service Reform Programme: Analysis of the Design and Implementation of Retrenchment Policy." Master's thesis, Institute of Social Studies of Erasmus University Rotterdam, The Hague, Netherlands, 2002.

Ludeki, Chweya. "Democratization and Civil Service Reform in Kenya." PhD diss., Queen's University, Kingston, Ontario, Canada, 2003.

Lusaka Times. "Performance Based Contracts Extended to Directors-Msiska." March 24, 2017. https://www.lusakatimes.com/2017/03/24/performance-based-contract-system-extended-directors-msiska/.

Madimutsa, Clever. "Implications of Public Sector Reform for Public Sector Unions in Zambia: A Case Study of the Civil Servants and Allied Workers Union of Zambia in Lusaka District." PhD diss., School of Government, University of Western Cape, 2016.

Madsen, Peter, Vinit Desai, Karlene Roberts, and Daniel Wong. "Mitigating Hazards Through Continuing Design: The Birth and Evolution of a Pediatric Intensive Care Unit." *Organization Science* 17, no. 2 (2006): 239–48.

Magbadelo, John Olushola. "The Problematics of Service Delivery in Nigeria." *Annals of Social Sciences and Management Studies* 5, no. 3 (2020): 0053–0059.

Magbadelo, John Olushola. "Reforming Nigeria's Federal Civil Service." *India Quarterly* 72, no. 1 (2016): 78–80.

Malambo, Annie Chitentu. "Retirement and the Zambia Public Service Reform Programme in the Ministry of Agriculture and Cooperatives 1993–2003." Master's thesis, University of Zambia, 2013.

Management Performance Assessment Tool. "MPAT 1.3: Good Practice Cases." N.d.

Mangla, Akshay. *Making Bureaucracy Work: Norms, Education and Public Service Delivery in Rural India.* Cambridge University Press, 2022.

Mansoor, Zahra, and Martin J. Williams. "Systems Approaches to Public Service Delivery: Methods and Frameworks." *Journal of Public Policy* 44, no. 2 (2024): 258–83.

Maphela, Dieketseng Gail. "Implementation of the Management Performance Assessment Tool (MPAT)." Master's thesis, University of the Witwatersrand, Johannesburg, South Africa, 2015.

Martinez, Elizabeth, Nancy Beaulieu, Robert Gibbons, Peter Provonost, and Thomas Wang. "Organizational Culture and Performance." *American Economic Review Papers and Proceedings* 105, no. 5 (2015): 331–35.

Mathole, Thubelihle, Martha Lembani, D. Jackson, Christina Zarowsky, Leon A. Bijlmàkers, and David Sanders. "Leadership and the Functioning of Maternal Health Services in Two Rural District Hospitals in South Africa." *Health Policy and Planning* 33 (2018): ii5–ii15.

McCourt, Willy. "Models of Public Service Reform: A Problem-Solving Approach." World Bank Policy Research Working Paper 6428. 2013.

McDonnell, Erin. "Patchwork Leviathan: How Pockets of Bureaucratic Governance Flourish Within Institutionally Diverse Developing States." *American Sociological Review* 82, no. 3 (2017): 476–510.

McDonnell, Erin. *Patchwork Leviathan: Pockets of Bureaucratic Effectiveness in Developing States.* Princeton University Press, 2020.

Mergel, Ines, Sukumar Ganapati, and Andrew B. Whitford. "Agile: A New Way of Governing." *Public Administration Review* 18, no. 1 (2020): 161–65.

Miller, Gary, and Andrew B. Whitford. "The Principal's Moral Hazard: Constraints on the Use of Incentives in Hierarchy." *Journal of Public Administration Research and Theory* 17, no. 2 (2007): 213–33.

Ministry for the Public Service and Administration. "White Paper on the Transformation of the Public Service." Notice 1227 of 1995. November 15, 1995.

Ministry of Public Sector Reform. "Work Programme to Coordinate the Implementation of Public Sector Reforms: Reference Document." Ministry of Public Sector Reform, January 2006. OHCS Archives.

Moynihan, Donald P. *The Dynamics of Performance Management: Constructing Information and Reform.* Georgetown University Press, 2008.

Müller, R. *Project Governance.* Routledge, 2009.

Muralidharan, Karthik. *Accelerating India's Development: A State-Led Roadmap for Effective Governance.* Penguin, 2024.

Muriu, Abraham Rugo. "Performance Management in Kenya's Public Service: A Study on Performance Information Use." PhD diss., University of Potsdam, Potsdam, Germany, 2017.

Mutahaba, Gelase, ed. "Human Resource Management in African Public Sector: Current State and Future Direction." African Public Sector Human Resource Managers' Network, 2013.

National Institutional Renewal Programme. *Annual Report for 1997.* NIRP Secretariat, Office of the President, Accra, 1997.

National Institutional Renewal Programme. *Annual Report for 1998.* NIRP Secretariat, Office of the President, Accra, 1998.

Ncholo, Paseka, Robert Cameron, and Chris Tapscott. "Reforming the Public Service in South Africa: A Policy Framework." *Public Administration and Development* 20, no. 2 (2000): 87–102.

Ndiaye, Mamadou, and Babacar Aw. "The M&E System in Senegal." In *African Monitoring and Evaluation Systems: Exploratory Case Studies.* University of the Witwatersrand, Johannesburg, 2012.

Nicholson, Sean, Mark V. Pauly, Daniel Polsky, Claire Sharda, Helena Szrek, and Marc L. Berger. "Measuring the Effects of Work Loss on Productivity With Team Production." *Health Economics* 15 (2006): 111–23.

Nkwede, Joseph Okwesili. "Public Sector Restructuring and Governance in Nigeria: Perspectives, Processes and Challenges." *Journal of Business and Management* 2, no. 3 (2013): 32–44.

North, Douglass C. *Institutions, Institutional Change and Economic Performance*. Cambridge University Press, 1990.

Obong'o, Sylvester Odhiambo. "Implementation of Performance Contracting in Kenya." *International Public Management Review* 10, no. 2 (2009): 66–84.

Obong'o, Sylvester Odhiambo. "Particularistic Exchanges and Pacts of Domination in Africa: Examining How Patronage Appointments May Have Increased Resistance to Public Sector Reforms in Kenya." *International Public Management Review* 14, no. 1 (2013): 27–46.

Obong'o, Sylvester Odhiambo. "Political Influence, Appointments and Public Sector Management Reform In Kenya, 1963–2014." PhD diss., University of Newcastle, Australia, 2015.

Office of the Head of Civil Service. *Towards an Effective Performance Appraisal System in the Civil Service*. Report, Dr. S. A. Nkrumah, OHCS Archives, n.d.

Office of the Head of Civil Service. *Civil Service Performance Improvement Programme (CSPIP: 1996–2001) Second Joint CSPIP-DFID Internal Review at Sogakope 5th-8th July, 2000*. OHCS Archives. 2000.

Office of the Head of Civil Service. *Introduction of Merit/Performance Award System in the Civil Service*. Circular Ref. No. PNDC/SCR/A.08/15, OHCS Archives, 1991.

Office of the Head of Civil Service. "Letter OHCS/SCR/AD100/201/01." Office of the Head of Civil Service Archives, October 20, 1994.

Office of the Head of Civil Service. *Merit/Performance Award Scheme in the Civil Service*. Circular Ref. No. OHCS/GEN/BC98/231/01. OHCS Archives, 1995.

Office of the Head of Civil Service. "Minutes of Meeting of Steering Committee on CSRP Held at the Conference Room of the Government Secretarial School Accra, on Wednesday, 17th November, 1993." 1993.

Office of the Head of Civil Service. "Minutes of the Special Chief Directors Meeting Held on Wednesday, 22nd March, 1995." OHCS Archives. 1995.

Office of the Secretary to the Government of the Federation. *Public Service Reforms in Nigeria: 1999–2014, A Comprehensive Review*. April 2015.

Ogbegie, Caleb Imuetinyan. "The Need for a Civil Service Reform in Nigeria." Master's thesis, University of Vaasa, 2008.

Ogunrin, Florence O., and Andrew E.O. Erhijakpor. "SERVICOM Policy Intervention: Improving Service Quality in Nigerian Public Sector," *Global Journal of Social Sciences* 8, no. 1 (2009): 51–60.

Ohemeng, Frank L. Kwaku. "Institutionalizing the Performance Management System in Public Organizations in Ghana." *Public Performance & Management Review* 34, no. 4 (2011): 467–88.

Ohemeng, Frank L. Kwaku, and Augustina Akonnor. "The New Public Sector Reform Strategy in Ghana: Creating a New Path for a Better Public Service?" *Public Organization Review* 23 (2022): 839–55.

Ohemeng, Frank L. Kwaku, and Felix K. Anebo. "The Politics of Administrative Reforms in Ghana: Perspectives from Path Dependency and Punctuated Equilibrium Theories." *International Journal of Public Administration* 35, no. 3 (2012): 161–76.

Ohemeng, Frank L. Kwaku, and Joseph R. A. Ayee. "The 'New Approach' to Public Sector Reforms in Ghana: A Case of Politics as Usual or a Genuine Attempt at Reform?" *Development Policy Review* 34, no. 2 (2016): 277–300.

Ohemeng, Frank L. Kwaku, Hamza B. Zakari, and Augustina Adusah-Karikari. "Performance Appraisal and Its Use for Individual and Organizational Improvement in the Civil Service of Ghana: The Case of Much Ado About Nothing?" *Public Administration and Development* 35 (2015): 179–91.

Okorie, Cornelius Ofobuisi, and Stella Odo. "A Survey of Public Service Reforms in Nigeria: 1999–2013." *International Journal of Humanities and Social Science* 4, no.10 (2014): 267–75.

Okorie, Cornelius Ofobuisi, and Sunday O. Onwe. "Appraisal of Civil Service Reforms in Nigeria and Options for Stability." *Public Policy and Administration Research* 6, no. 9 (2016): 15–24.

Olaopa, Tunji. *Managing Complex Reforms: A Public Sector Respective*. Bookcraft, 2011.

Olaopa, Tunji. *The Nigerian Civil Service of the Future: A Prospective Analysis*. Bookcraft, 2014.

Ong'era, Alfred, and Beverly Musili. *Public Sector Reforms In Kenya: Challenges And Opportunities.* Kenya Institute for Public Policy Research and Analysis WP/29/2019, 2019.

Oppong, Seth, Erica Dickson, and Maxwell Asumeng. "Implementation of Single Spine Pay Policy in Public Sector of Ghana: Analysis and Recommendations from Organizational Development Perspective." *Poslovna Izvrsnost Zagreb* IX, no. 2 (2015): 83–100.

Organisation for Economic Cooperation and Development (OECD). *Government at a Glance 2019.* OECD, 2019.

Organisation for Economic Cooperation and Development (OECD). *Performance-Related Pay Policies for Government Employees.* OECD, 2005.

Organisation for Economic Cooperation and Development (OECD). *Public Employment and Management 2021: The Future Of The Public Service.* OECD, 2021.

Orlikowski, Wanda J. "Improvising Organizational Transformation over Time: A Situated Change Perspective." *Information Systems Research* 7, no. 1 (1996): 63–92.

Ostrom, Elinor. "Beyond Markets and States: Polycentric Governance of Complex Economic Systems." *American Economic Review* 100 (2010): 641–72.

Owen, Larisa. "Projectitis vs. Systems Change: The Infusion of the Broader System Instead of Staying Inside the Silo of the Project." *PA Times Online,* February 18, 2020, https://patimes.org/projectitis-vs-systems-change-the-infusion-of-the-broader-system-instead-of-staying-inside-the-silo-of-the-project/.

Owusu, Francis. "Differences in the Performance of Public Organisations in Ghana: Implications for Public-Sector Reform Policy." *Development Policy Review* 24, no. 6 (2006): 693–705.

Peace FM. "Mahama's Appraisal of Ministers Is Deceitful—NPP." Ghana Web, 2013. https://mobile.ghanaweb.com/GhanaHomePage/business/Mahama-s-appraisal-of-ministers-is-deceitful-NPP-295630.

Pepinsky, Thomas, Jan Pierskalla, and Audrey Sacks. "Bureaucracy and Service Delivery." *Annual Review of Political Science* 20 (2017): 249–268.

Perry, James. *Managing Organizations to Sustain Passion for Public Service.* Cambridge University Press, 2020.

Pettigrew, Andrew M. "Longitudinal Field Research on Change: Theory and Practice." *Organization Science* 1, no. 3 (1990): 267–92.

Pickles, Charlotte, and James Sweetland. "Breaking Down the Barriers: Why Whitehall Is so Hard to Reform." Reform, August 2023.

Pinto, Rogerio F. "Projectizing the Governance Approach to Civil Service Reform: An Institutional Environment Assessment for Preparing a Sectoral Adjustment Loan in the Gambia." World Bank Discussion Paper 252, 1994.

Plangemann, Kathrin A. "Strengthening Performance Monitoring and Evaluation." In *Making It Happen: Selected Case Studies of Institutional Reforms in South Africa,* ed. Asad Alam, Renosi Mokate, and Kathrin A. Plangemann, 71–89. World Bank Group, 2016.

Polidano, Charles. "Why Civil Service Reforms Fail." *Public Management Review* 3, no. 3 (2001): 345–61.

Pollitt, Christopher, and Geert Bouckaert. *Public Management Reform: A Comparative Analysis.* Oxford University Press, 2004.

Prendergast, Canice. "The Limits of Bureaucratic Efficiency." *Journal of Political Economy* 111, no. 5 (2003): 929–58.

Pressman, Jeffrey L., and Aaron Wildavsky. *Implementation.* University of California Press, 1974.

Pritchett, Lant, and Michael Woolcock. "Solutions When the Solution Is the Problem: Arraying the Disarray in Development." *World Development* 32, no. 2 (2004): 191–212.

Public Service Commission. *Report on the Assessment of the Effectiveness of the Batho Pele Policy in Public Service Delivery.* June 2012.

Public Services Commission. "Performance Management Policy for the Public Services of Ghana," n.d.

Qarout, Dana. "The Accountability Paradox: Delivery Units in Jordan's Education Sector 2010–2019." DeliverEd Initiative Working Paper, November 2022.

Raballand, Gael, Thomas Roundell, and Michel Mallberg. "How Civil Servants and Bank Staff Incentives and Behaviors Explain Outcomes of World Bank Public Sector Projects? Lessons from World Bank Completion Reports from 2000." Draft, 2016.

Radin, Beryl. *Challenging the Performance Movement*. Georgetown University Press, 2006.

Rajaram, Anand, Patricia Palale and Gael Raballand. "Public Sector Reform—Changing Behavior with Cars and Computers?" *World Bank Blogs*, February 16 2010. https://blogs.worldbank.org/africacan /public-sector-reform-changing-behavior-with-cars-and-computers.

Rakate, Nyana Faith. "Transformation in the South African Public Service: The Case of Service Delivery in the Department of Health." Master's thesis, University of Pretoria, South Africa, 2006.

Rasul, Imran, and Daniel Rogger. "Management of Bureaucrats and Public Service Delivery: Evidence from the Nigerian Civil Service." *Economic Journal* 128, no. 608 (2018): 413–46.

Rasul, Imran, Daniel Rogger, and Martin J. Williams. "How Do Management Practices in Government Change Over Time? Evidence from Ghana." Policy brief for International Growth Centre and Economic Development and Institutions research initiative, 2019.

Rasul, Imran, Daniel Rogger, and Martin J. Williams. "Management, Organizational Performance, and Task Clarity: Evidence from Ghana's Civil Service." *Journal of Public Administration Research and Theory* 31, no. 2 (2021): 259–77.

Rasul, Imran, Daniel Rogger, Martin J. Williams, and Eleanor F. Woodhouse. "Government Analytics Using Data on Task and Project Completion." In *The Government Analytics Handbook: Leveraging Data to Strengthen Public Administration*, ed. Daniel Rogger and Christian Schuster, 365–83. World Bank, 2023.

Reay, Trish, Karen Golden-Biddle, and Kathy Germann. "Legitimizing a New Role: Small Wins and Microprocesses of Change." *Academy of Management Journal* 49, no. 5 (2006): 977–98.

Republic of South Africa. "Deputy Minister Thembi Siweya/ Planning and Monitoring Dept Budget Vote 2019/20." DPME Budget Vote Address by Thembi Siweya, Old Assembly of the Parliament of the Republic of South Africa, Cape Town, 2019.

Republic of South Africa. *Report of the Presidential Review Commission on the Reform and Transformation of the Public Service in South Africa*. 1998.

Republic of South Africa. "White Paper on Human Resource Management of the Public Service." N.d.

Republic of South Africa. "White Paper on Public Service Delivery." *Government Gazette* Notice 1459 of 1997, vol. 388, no. 18340, October 1, 1997.

Republic of Zambia. "Strategy for the Public Service Transformation Programme for Improved Service Delivery 2013–2018." Public Service Management Secretariat, Management Development Division, 2012.

République du Sénégal. "Arrêté ministériel n° 8625 en date du 23 mai 2017 fixant les modalités d'organisation et de fonctionnement du Comité de modernisation de l'Administration publique." Journal Officiel du Sénégal, 2017.

République du Sénégal. "Bureau Organisation et Méthodes: Evolution institutionnelle." Accessed September 14, 2022. https://www.bom.gouv.sn/?q=node/9.

République du Sénégal. "DECRET n° 2010–1812 en date du 31 décembre 2010." Journal Officiel N. 6577 du Samedi. March 19, 2011.

République du Sénégal. *Etude Diagnostique Du Service Public: Tome 1: Analyse de Synthese des Reformes Publiques*. Ministère De La Fonction Publique, De La Rationalisation Des Effectifs Et Du Renouveau Du Service Public. EXA-Consulting, May 18, 2016.

République du Sénégal. "Programme Nationale de Bonne Gouvernance." April 2002.

République du Sénégal. *Rapport national sur la gouvernance au Senegal*. Secretariat General de la Presidence de la République, Delegation a la Reforme de l'Etat et a l'Assistance Technique, Programme National de Bonne Gouvernance, 2011.

République du Sénégal. "Schema Directeur de Modernisation de l'Administration Publique (SDMAP) 2015–2022." Presentation, Bureau Organisation et Méthodes, Presidence de la République, Secretariat Général, n.d.

Roll, Michael, ed. *The Politics of Public Sector Performance: Pockets of Effectiveness in Developing Countries*. Routledge, 2013.

Rousseau, D. M. *Psychological Contracts in Organizations: Understanding Written and Unwritten Agreements*. Sage Publications, 1995.

Russell, Jennifer Lin, Anthony S. Bryk, Jonathan Dolle, Louis M. Gomez, Paul G. Lemahieu, and Alicia Grunow. "A Framework for the Initiation of Networked Improvement Communities." *Teachers College Record* 119 (2017): 1–36.

Schein, Edgar H. *Organizational Culture and Leadership*. Jossey-Bass, 1985.

Schick, Allen. *The Spirit Of Reform: Managing the New Zealand State Sector in a Time of Change*. Report prepared for the State Services Commission and the Treasury, New Zealand, August 1996.

Schick, Allan. "Why Most Developing Countries Should Not Try New Zealand's Reforms." *World Bank Research Observer* 13, no. 1 (1998): 123–31.

Schnell, Sabina, Dimitrie Miheş, Anita Sobjak, and Wouter van Acker. "Performance Management in the Public Administration: Seven Success Factors." World Bank Equitable Growth, Finance, and Institutions Insight, 2021.

Schuster, Christian, Kim Sass Mikkelsen, Daniel Rogger, Francis Fukuyama, Zahid Hasnain, Dinsha Mistree et al., "The Global Survey of Public Servants: Evidence from 1,300,000 Public Servants in 1,300 Government Institutions in 23 Countries." *Public Administration Review* 83, no. 4 (2023): 982–93.

Schutzeichel, Harald. "Projectitis Is Curable." *Sun-Connect-News*, 2014, https://www.sun-connect-news .org/articles/business/details/projectitis-is-curable/.

Scott, Graham, Peter Bushnell, and Nikitin Sallee. "Reform of the Core Public Sector: New Zealand Experience." *Governance* 3, no. 2 (1990): 138–67.

Seidu, Samiatu Bogobiri. "Institutionalizing Reforms in the Public Sector: A Comparative Study of Public Sector Reform Agencies in Ghana and Nigeria." Master's thesis, Erasmus University, Rotterdam, 2010.

Sekwat, Alex. "Civil Service Reform in Post-Independence Nigeria: Issues and Challenges." *Public Administration Quarterly* 25, no. 2 (2002): 498–517.

SERVICOM. "Delivering Service in Nigeria: A Roadmap." 2004.

Shamaki, Amina M. B. "An Effective Performance Management System For The Federal Public Service." Presentation, Office of the Head of the Civil Service, accessed August 22, 2022. https://studylib.net /doc/9713525/final-an-effective-performance-management-system.

Sigman, Rachel. "Which Jobs for Which Boys? Party Financing, Patronage and State Capacity in African Democracies." PhD diss., Maxwell School Syracuse University, 2015.

Sing, Danny. "Human Resource Challenges Confronting the Senior Management Service of the South African Public Service." *Public Personnel Management* 41, no. 2 (2012): 379–88.

Soulé-Kohndou, Folashadé. "Bureaucratic Agency and Power Asymmetry in Benin-China Relations." In *New Directions in Africa-China Studies*, ed. Chris Alden and Daniel Large, 189–204. Routledge, 2018.

Spano, Alessandro, and Patrizio Monfardini. "Performance-Related Payments in Local Governments: Do They Improve Performance or Only Increase Salary?" *International Journal of Public Administration* 41, no. 4 (2018): 321–34.

Srivastava, Vivek, and Marco Larizza. "Working with the Grain for Reforming the Public Service: A Live Example from Sierra Leone." *International Review of Administrative Sciences* 79, no. 3 (2013): 458–85.

Stevens, Mike, and Stefanie Teggemann. "Comparative Experience with Public Service Reform in Ghana, Tanzania, and Zambia." In *Building State Capacity in Africa: New Approaches, Emerging Lessons*, ed. Brian Levy and Sahr Kpundeh, 43–86. World Bank Institute, 2004.

Sveningsson, Stefan, and Nadja Sorgarde. *Managing Change in Organizations: How, What, and Why?* SAGE Publications, 2019.

Swiss, Liam. *The Globalization of Foreign Aid: Developing Consensus*. Routledge, 2018.

Syverson, Chad. "What Determines Productivity?" *Journal of Economic Literature* 49, no. 2 (2011): 326–65.

Talbot, Colin. *Theories of Performance: Organizational and Service Improvement in the Public Domain.* Oxford University Press, 2010.

Tall, Abdoul Aziz. "L'ajustement dans le secteur public: et la gestion des ressources humaines: Le cas du Senegal." S.A.P. 4.33/W.P. 87, International Labor Organization, 1995.

Tendler, Judith. *Good Government in the Tropics.* Johns Hopkins University Press, 1997.

Thiel, Andreas, William A. Blomquist, and Dustin E. Garrick, eds. *Governing Complexity: Analyzing and Applying Polycentricity.* Cambridge University Press, 2019.

Tirivanhu, Precious, Wole Olaleye and Angela Bester. "Advancing Evidence-Based Practice for Improved Public Sector Performance: Lessons From the Implementation of the Management Performance Assessment Tool in South Africa." *Journal of Public Administration* 52, no. 4 (2017): 681–704.

Toon, Peter D. "Projectitis? Supporting Health Reform." *British Medical Journal* 331 (2005).

Tshandu, Zwelakhe, and Samuel Kariuki. "Public Administration and Service Delivery Reforms: A Post-1994 South African Case." *South African Journal of International Affairs* 17, no. 2 (2010): 189–208.

Tsoukas, Haridimos, and Robert Chia. "On Organizational Becoming: Rethinking Organizational Change." *Organization Science* 13, no. 5 (2002): 567–82.

Turnbull, P. D. "Effective Investment in Information Infrastructures." *Information and Software Technology* 33, no. 3 (1991): 191–99.

United Kingdom Overseas Development Administration. "Evaluation of the Ghana Civil Service Reform Project." ODA Evaluation Department, April 1993.

United Nations Development Program (UNDP). *End of Programme Evaluation: Public Sector Reforms Programme, Phase II.* PWC, May 2013.

United Nations Development Program (UNDP). *From Reform to Transformation: UNDP's Support to Public Sector Reforms in Kenya. Lessons Learnt for Devolution.* Joseph L. M. Mugore, Mugore Associates, June 2015.

United Nations Development Program (UNDP). *Project Closure Report: 00045420-Public Sector Reforms.* 2013.

United Nations Development Programme (UNDP). "Projet de Renforcement des Capacités de Bonne Gouvernance (PRECABG)." N.D.

United Nations Economic Commission for Africa. *Innovations and Best Practices in Public Sector Reforms: The Case of Civil Service in Ghana, Kenya, Nigeria and South Africa.* Report, December 2010.

Universalia. *Assessment of the Current Performance Management System Final Report.* Legend Consulting Services and Universalia, 2008.

University of Zambia. *The Public Service Reform Programme (PSRP) and the Public Service Capacity Building Programme (PSCAP) Impact Assessment, April 15, 2005,* in Universalia, *Assessment of the Current Performance Management System Final Report.* Legend Consulting Services and Universalia, 2008.

Valentine, Theodore R. *A Medium-Term Strategy for Enhancing Pay and Conditions of Service in the Zambian Public Service.* Crown Consultants International, 2002.

Van de Ven, Andrew H., and Marshall Scott Poole. "Alternative Approaches for Studying Organizational Change." *Organization Studies* 26, no. 9 (2005): 1377–1404.

van de Walle, Nicholas. *African Economies and the Politics of Permanent Crisis.* Cambridge University Press, 2001.

Weibel, Antoinette, Katja Rost, and Margit Osterloh. "Pay for Performance in the Public Sector—Benefits and (Hidden) Costs." *Journal of Public Administration Research and Theory* 20, no. 2 (2010): 387–412.

Weick, Karl E. "Small Wins: Redefining the Scale of Social Problems." *American Psychologist* 39, no. 1 (1984): 40–49.

Weick, Karl E., and Robert E. Quinn. "Organizational Change and Development." *Annual Review of Psychology* 50 (1999): 361–86.

Whitfield, Lindsay, ed. *The Politics of Aid: African Strategies for Dealing with Donors.* Oxford University Press, 2009.

Wild, Leni, Matt Andrews, Jamie Pett, and Helen Dempster. *Doing Development Differently: Who We Are, What We're Doing and What We're Learning.* Overseas Development Institute, 2016.

Wilfahrt, Martha. *Precolonial Legacies in Postcolonial Politics Representation and Redistribution in Decentralized West Africa.* Cambridge University Press, 2021.

Williams, Martin J. "From Institutions to Organizations: Management and Informality in Ghana's Bureaucracies." Working paper, London School of Economics and Political Science, September 9, 2015.

Williams, Martin J. "There Is More Than One 'Public Sector Way': The Diversity of Management Practices in Ghana's Government." Policy brief, November 2013.

Williams, Martin J., and Sarah McAra. "Civil Service Reform in Ghana." Blavatnik School of Government Teaching Case, 2022.

Williams, Martin J., and Liah Yecalo-Tecle. "Innovation, Voice, and Hierarchy in the Civil Service: Evidence from Ghana's Civil Service." *Governance* 33, no. 4 (2020): 789–807.

Williamson, Oliver. *The Economic Institutions of Capitalism.* Free Press, 1985.

Wilson, James Q. *Bureaucracy.* Basic Books, 1989.

Wistrich, Enid. "Restructuring Government New Zealand Style." *Public Administration* 70 (1992): 119–35.

Woods, Ngaire. *The Globalizers: The IMF, the World Bank, and Their Borrowers.* Cornell University Press, 2014.

World Bank. "GovEnable: Locally Co-Created Solutions to Government Service Delivery Challenges." Accessed April 19, 2024, https://shorturl.at/TSZh3.

World Bank. *ICR Review—Public Service Capacity Building Project (PSCAP).* Independent Evaluation Group Report ICRR12372. 2006.

World Bank. *Implementation Completion and Results Report (Ida41460-Trust Fund No.:Tf57287,Tf56158) on a Credit in the amount of Sdr 17.3 Million (Us$ 25.12 Million Equivalent) to the Government Of Kenya for an Institutional Reform & Capacity Building Project.* Report No ICR2129. March 29 2012.

World Bank. *Implementation Completion and Results Report (IDA-51040) on Three Credits in the Amount of SDF 51.5 Million (US$ 80 Million Equivalent) to the Republic of Zambia for Poverty Reduction Support Credits (PRSC) I, II And III.* Report ICR2761, June 24, 2013.

World Bank. *Implementation Completion Report (IDA-26710) on a Credit in the Amount of SDRs 17.2 Million to the Government of the Republic of Kenya for an Institutional Development and Civil Service Reform Project.* Report No. 21363, March 29 2001.

World Bank. *Implementation Completion Report (Ida-33290 Ppfi-Q1440 Ppfi-Q1441) on a Credit in the amount of Sdr 20.4 Million (Us$28 Million Equivalent) to the Republic of Zambia for a Public Service Capacity Building Project in Support of the First Phase of the Public Service Capacity Building Program.* Report 34450, December 28, 2005.

World Bank. *Implementation Completion Report—Zambia—Economic and Social Adjustment Credit (Credit 2577-ZA).* Report 15837, June 28, 1996.

World Bank. *Implementation Status & Results—Zambia—Public Sector Management Program Support Project (P082452).* Report ISR6541, 2012.

World Bank. *Project Appraisal Document on a Proposed Credit in the Amount of SDR 20.4 Million (US$28 Million Equivalent) to the Republic of Zambia for a Public Service Capacity Building Project in Support of the First Phase of the Public Service Capacity Building Program.* February 22, 2000.

World Bank. *Project Completion Report: Republic of Ghana Structural Adjustment Institutional Support Project (Credit 1778-GH).* World Bank Report No. 12502, November 15, 1993.

World Bank. *Public Sector Reform for Results Project (P164665): Implementation Status and Results Report.* February 14, 2019.

World Bank. *Rapport d'evaluation Retrospective—Senegal—Quatrieme Credit d'Ajustement Structurel—Credit 2090 SE—Credit d'Ajustement du Secteur Financier—Credit 2077 SE—May 3, 1995.* WB IBRD/IDA/AFR 44001I, P002338, May 3, 1995.

World Bank. *Report and Recommendation of the President of the International Development Association to the Executive Directors on a Proposed Credit in the Amount Equivalent to US$200 Million to the Republic of Zambia for a Privatization and Industrial Reform Adjustment Credit.* Report P-5786-ZA, June 3, 1992.

World Bank. *Staff Appraisal Report: Republic of Ghana Structural Adjustment Institutional Support Project.* March 20, 1987.

Yanguas, Pablo. "Varieties of State-Building in Africa: Elites, Ideas and the Politics of Public Sector Reform." ESID Working Paper No. 89, August 2017.

Yemi-Esan, Folasade. "FG Replaces APER with PMS to Assess Civil Servants' Performance." This Day, November 17, 2020. https://www.thisdaylive.com/index.php/2020/11/17/fg-replaces-aper-with-pms-to-assess-civil-servants-performance/.

Yurkofsky, Maxwell M., Amelia J. Peterson, Jal D. Mehta, Rebecca Horwitz-Willis, and Kim. M. Frumin. "Research on Continuous Improvement: Exploring the Complexities of Managing Educational Change." *Review of Research in Education* 44 (2020): 403–33.

Zuma, Jacob. "Address by President Jacob Zuma at the Launch of Operation Phakisa Big Fast Results Implementation Methodology, Inkosi Albert Luthuli International Convention Centre, Durban." July 19, 2014.

Zume, Ernest. "PSRRP Implementation: The Journey so Far." *Modern Ghana*, May 16, 2022, accessed June 20200, https://www.modernghana.com/news/1158400/psrrp-implementation-the-journey-so.html.

Index

Sai, E. A., 220

SAIS. *See* Structural Adjustment Institutional Support

salaries, 99, 223–24; allowances and, 300–301; performance influencing, 46; reforms to, 57

salary scale, decompress, 57

Sall, Macky, 266

sanctions, 27

Schéma Directeur de la Réforme de l'Etat. See State Reform Master Plan

Schéma Directeur de Modernisation de l'Administration Publique. See Public Administration Modernization Master Plan

Schick, Allen, 94, 96–97

Schuster, Christian, 151

scope, of empirical analysis, 11–12

SCR. *See* Steering Committee on Reform

SDMAP. *See* Public Administration Modernization Master Plan

SDRE. *See* State Reform Master Plan

sector ministries, line directorates engaging with, 183

Sector Plan for Public Sector Reforms, 243

sector-specific reform programs, ministers developing, 224

Senegal, 256, 257–62; CASFPA of, 261–62; civil service reforms in, *260, 264*; CMAP of, 267; content in, *59*; data sources from, *14*; DMP of, 263; DREAT of, 263; individual-level performance-linked incentive policies in, 80; Interministerial Steering Committee for the Integrated Public Sector Reform Program of, 263; MFP of, 257; MMET of, 261–62; NEPAD of, 263; PNBG of, 262–63, 265; SDMAP of, 266, 340n370; SDRE of, 266, 340n70; timeline of reform efforts in, *52*

senior civil service leadership, 91

senior leadership, 192–93, 204–5

senior management service, 53

Senior Management Service conferences, in South Africa, 132

senior managers, individual-level performance-linked incentive policy for, 315n2

service charters, 299

service charter system, OHCS reinvigorating, 190

service delivery, 132, 255, 269, 271; ministers and, 57, 304; redundancies impacting, 290; SERVICOM focusing on, 249; systemic reforms improving, 57

service-delivery-focused reforms, 57, 101

"Service Delivery in Nigeria" (diagnostic study), 247

service delivery organizations, in Nigeria, 55–56

Service Delivery Review (journal), 277

SERVICOM (Nigeria), 55–58, 116, 119–21, 137, 247–48, 250; DFID funding, 251, 255; participatory service delivery evaluations conducted by, 132; service delivery focused on by, 249

SERVICOM Help Desk (radio program), 121

Sigman, Rachel, 177

Single Spine Pay Policy (Ghana), 99, 177, 223–24

Skweyiya, Zola, 134

small wins, 163

S.M.A.R.T. *See* specific, measurable, achievable, relevant, and time-bound (S.M.A.R.T.) targets

social science, 8

social science research, reforms in, 7

social systems, as polycentric, 169–70

Sörgärde, Nadja, 110

Soulé-Kohndou, Folashadé, 70

South Africa, 116, 317n38; civil service reforms in, *267, 270, 282*; content in, *59*; data sources from, *14*; Department of Home Affairs of, 134, 274–75; DPME of, 276–79, 286, 343n463; DPSA of, 134, 268, 271–72, 275; funding in, 114; individual-level performance-linked incentive policies in, 80; integration-oriented reforms in, 269; MPAT of, 73, 100, 133, 137, 276–81; PCS of, 268, 272, 274–75; People First of, 133–35, 137, 269, 271–76; performance bonuses in, 93; Performance Management and Development System of, 83; PMDS of, 83, 86, 281, 283–87; Presidential Review Commission report by, 94; Senior Management Service conferences in, 132; timeline of reform efforts in, *52*

specific, measurable, achievable, relevant, and time-bound (S.M.A.R.T.) targets, 84, 131

staff appraisals, 31–33, 46, 78, 217–18, 226; behavior not changed by, 19; implementation of, 79

staffing, 47

stakeholder consultations, under CSPIP, 184

start dates, of reforms, 314n37

state capacity, geographical determinants of, 308n6

State Modernization Committee (*Comité de modernisation de l'État*), 261

State Reform Master Plan (*Schéma Directeur de la Réforme de l'Etat*) (SDRE) (Senegal), 266, 340n70

GPSR Authorized Representative: Easy Access System Europe, Mustamäe tee
50, 10621 Tallinn, Estonia, gpsr.requests@easproject.com

www.ingramcontent.com/pod-product-compliance
Lightning Source LLC
Chambersburg PA
CBHW021845020426
42334CB00013B/195